Readings in Mergers and Acquisitions

Readings in Mergers
and Acquisitions

Edited by
Patrick A. Gaughan

BLACKWELL
Finance

First published 1994

Blackwell Publishers
238 Main Street
Cambridge, Massachusetts 02142
USA

108 Cowley Road
Oxford OX4 1JF
UK

Library of Congress Cataloging-in-Publication Data

Readings in mergers and acquisitions / edited by Patrick A. Gaughan.
    p.   cm.
  Includes index.
  ISBN 1-55786-408-X (hard: acid-free paper). – ISBN 1-55786-409-8
(pbk.: acid-free paper)
    1. Consolidation and merger of corporations – United States.
I. Gaughan, Patrick A.
HD2746.55.U5R43   1994
338.8'3'0973 – dc20

                                94-6135
                                  CIP

British Library Cataloguing in Publication Data

A CIP catalogue record for this book is available from the British Library.

Typeset in 11 on 13 pt Garamond
by Best-set Typesetter Ltd., Hong Kong
Printed in Great Britain by Hartnolls Ltd., Bodmin

This book is printed on acid-free paper

Contents

Contents

Figures

Tables

Contributors

Edward I. Altman is Professor of Finance at the Leonard N. Stern School of Business, New York University, New York, New York.

Paul Asquith is Associate Professor in the School of Management, MIT, Cambridge, Massachusetts.

Marshall E. Blume is Professor of the Finance Department and Director of the Financial Research Center, Wharton School, University of Pennsylvania, Philadelphia, Pennsylvania.

James A. Brickley is Professor at the William E. Simon Graduate School of Business Administration, University of Rochester, Rochester, New York.

Harry DeAngelo is Professor of Finance and Business Economics in the School of Business Administration, University of California, Los Angeles, California.

Linda DeAngelo is Professor of Finance and Business Economics in the School of Business Administration, University of California, Los Angeles, California.

Patrick Gaughan is Associate Professor of Economics and Finance at Fairleigh Dickinson University, Rutherford, New Jersey. He is also president of Economatrix Research Associates, an economic and financial consulting firm.

Gregg A. Jarrell is Professor of Economics and Finance and Director of the Bradley Policy Research Center, University of Rochester, Rochester, New York.

Michael C. Jensen is Professor of Business Administration, Harvard Business School, Cambridge, Massachusetts.

Donald B. Keim is Assistant Professor of the Finance Department, Wharton School, University of Pennsylvania, Philadelphia, Pennsylvania.

Robert Kleiman is Associate Professor of Finance, School of Business, Babson College, Wellesley, Massachusetts.

Ken Lehn is Professor of Business Administration and Director of the Center for Research on Contracts and the Structure of Enterprises, University of Pittsburgh, Pittsburgh, Pennsylvania.

Mark Mitchell is Assistant Professor of Finance, Graduate School of Business, University of Chicago, Chicago, Illinois.

David Mullins is a Partner in Long Term Capital Management, L.P., Greenwich, Connecticut.

Jeffry M. Netter is Associate Professor of Banking and Finance, Terry College of Business, University of Georgia, Athens, Georgia.

Tim C. Opler is Assistant Professor, Edwin L. Cox School of Business, Southern Methodist University, Dallas, Texas.

Sandeep Patel teaches at Texas Christian University.

Annette Poulsen is Associate Professor of Banking and Finance, Terry College of Business, University of Georgia, Athens, Georgia.

John Pound is Assistant Professor at the John F. Kennedy School of Government, Harvard University, Cambridge, Massachusetts.

Richard Roll is Professor at the Anderson Graduate School of Management and AllState Chair in Finance and Insurance, University of California, Los Angeles, California.

Katherine Schipper is Professor of Accounting and Director, Graduate School of Business, University of Chicago, Chicago, Illinois.

Abbie Smith is Professor at the Graduate School of Business, University of Chicago, Chicago, Illinois.

J. Fred Weston is Professor Emeritus of Money and Financial Markets, Anderson Graduate School of Management, University of California, Los Angeles, California.

Barrie A. Wigmore is a Partner at Goldman Sachs, New York, New York.

Eric D. Wolff is a Ph.D. Candidate in Accounting, School of Management, MIT, Cambridge, Massachusetts.

1

Introduction: The Fourth Merger Wave and Beyond

Patrick A. Gaughan

The 1980s featured the last in a series of four merger waves that have occurred in modern US economic history. The wave was characterized by many interesting features. These included the hostile takeovers of large, established corporations, junk bond financed takeovers and leveraged buyouts. Many of these takeovers were fueled by the newly established original issue junk bond market. The growth of this market, in turn, was facilitated by the increased availability of debt financing through investment banks such as Drexel Burnham Lambert and its leading financier, Michael Milken. Access to debt financing through the junk bond market, as well as through other sources, enabled firms to pursue various leveraged takeovers such as leveraged buyouts.

This article provides an overview of the United States history of takeovers through a discussion of the four merger waves. After establishing what the historical experience with mergers has been in the economy, the fourth merger wave is examined. Some of the more notable features of this wave are highlighted. These include the increased incidence of hostile takeovers, and the installation of various antitakeover defenses by corporations and their resulting shareholder wealth effects. Other notable trends, such as the use of leverage to finance takeovers, are also discussed. The fourth merger wave is then contrasted to the early takeover experience in the 1990s. The mergers that took place in the 1990s proved to be in sharp contrast to those of the 1980s. The contrasting characteristics included the use of equity as opposed to debt, as well as a preference for friendly, strategically motivated deals instead of hostile financially motivated deals.

Historical Overview of US Merger Waves

Prior to the 1980s, there were three periods of more intense merger activity in the United States. The first merger wave started in approximately 1897 and ended in

1904. The wave began during the economic recovery from the Depression of 1893. It featured mainly horizontal mergers that often resulted in monopolies or near monopolistic industry structures. Large corporations, such as DuPont, American Tobacco, US Steel and International Harvester were formed in this wave. Ironically, the horizontal combinations that occurred during this wave took place in spite of the passage of the Sherman Antitrust Act of 1890. This law was designed to prevent anti-competitive monopolies. However, the Justice Department, which was charged with the responsibility of enforcing the Act, lacked the resources and the mindset to vigorously enforce this law. This drawback was partially remedied by the passage of the Clayton Act of 1914 and the formation of the Federal Trade Commission in that same year.

The development of the infrastructure within the economy created conditions that allowed this first merger wave to prosper. Specifically, the development of a transportation system through the growth of railroads allowed regional firms to compete in national markets. This intensified competition and allowed companies to expand beyond their regional borders. Better communications and increasingly specialized management helped firms pursue expansion. Their growth was financed by increasingly aggressive investment bankers, such as J. P. Morgan of Morgan Bank and Jacob Schiff of Kuhn Loeb & Co. These bankers organized voting trusts to facilitate the recapitalizations of many failing businesses. The investment bankers helped organize these failing enterprises into a smaller number of larger and more profitable firms.

The first wave came to an end in 1904 when the economy turned down again. The pace of takeovers remained low until 1916, when the second takeover wave began. Approximately 70 percent of the mergers in the second wave were horizontal combinations with the remainder being mostly vertical transactions. Once again, the horizontal deals were not impeded by the strong antitrust laws that were in effect or even the newly formed Federal Trade Commission which, along with the Justice Department, was charged with the enforcement of such laws. The primary reason for the relaxed antitrust enforcement during this wave was the desire of the government to foster cooperation among businesses to help with the war effort.

Just as in the first wave, investment bankers played an aggressive role in providing the necessary capital to finance the second merger wave deals. Indeed, capital within the investment banking industry was concentrated in the hands of a relatively small number of bankers who were more willing to lend to industries that were more concentrated and had less competition. The companies that expanded through acquisitions during this wave were able to take advantage of economies of scale and other productivity advantages that come from greater size.

The second wave came to an abrupt end in 1929 with the start of the Great Depression and the collapse of the Stock Market in October, 1929. With the exception of a small increase in the 1940s, the number of mergers and acquisitions remained at a low level until the late 1960s, when the third takeover wave began. This wave, which is known as the conglomerate era, began in approximately 1965 and ended in 1969. It followed a period of intense antitrust enforcement in the 1950s and 1960s, using the newly enacted Celler–Kefauver Act along with the other antitrust laws. During this period, even vertical combinations were challenged. This left expansion minded firms with no alternative but to expand into dissimilar lines of business. Such companies included conglomerates like ITT, Gulf & Western, LTV, Litton Industries, Textron and Teledyne. The conglomerates took advantage of various market inefficiencies while playing the "P/E Game" and engaging in other accounting manipulations which allowed the firms to demonstrate rising accounting earnings without necessarily having a commensurate increase in shares outstanding.[1] Some of these accounting manipulations became more difficult to pursue after the Tax Reform Act of 1969. This law, combined with a downturn in the stock market, helped bring about the end to the conglomerate era in 1969.

While the 1970s did not have a sufficient number of mergers to constitute a merger wave, it did feature a number of path-breaking deals that set the stage for the type of hostile transactions that took place in the fourth merger wave. The principal trend-setting deal was the 1973 Inco–ESB merger, which was the first hostile takeover by a major reputable company. This deal was followed by two other trend-setting hostile takeovers in 1975 – the takeover of Otis Elevator by United Technologies and the takeover of Garlock by Colt Industries. Together they paved the way for the marked increase in the number of large hostile takeovers that were about to take place in the next decade.

The Fourth Merger Wave (1984–9)

Figures 1.1 and 1.2 show that while the number of mergers increased only 0.39 percent between 1983 and 1984, the dollar value of mergers increased at a dramatic 67 percent rate. The dollar volume of mergers had actually been increasing since 1982. While the exact starting date can be a matter of debate, 1984 is probably a reasonable choice. The dollar volume of mergers reached a peak in 1988. The following year also showed a high dollar volume of mergers. However, in 1990, the dollar amount of merger offers fell to approximately one half of the prior year's level. This, in turn, was followed by another decline in 1991. This trend was reversed in 1992, when there was a significant increase in the number of large mergers.

A number of reasons have been put forward to explain why the fourth merger wave began. The US economy rebounded in 1983 from a severe recession that occurred in the years 1982–3. The economy then entered the longest recovery in post-war US economic history. This recovery continued until 1990, when the economy entered a mild recession in mid-1990 which lasted for approximately eight months. However, the stock-market crash of 1987 and the related collapse of the junk bond market and failure of Drexel Burnham Lambert, combined to bring about the end of the fourth merger wave in 1989.

The fourth merger wave featured many unique characteristics which separated it from previous waves. These characteristics include the use of aggressive takeover tactics, leveraged buyouts and junk bond financing. Table 1.1 reveals that the majority of the deals in the fourth wave were not hostile. However, the large scale hostile battles

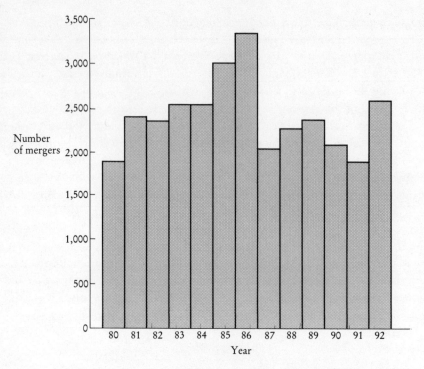

Figure 1.1 Net merger and acquisition announcements, 1980–92
Source: Mergerstat Review

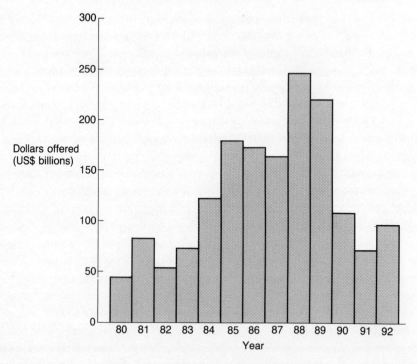

Figure 1.2 Total amount offered in mergers
Source: Mergerstat Review

Table 1.1 M&A transactions: total versus hostile (majority or remaining stake acquisitions)

| Announcement date | Volume totals – announcement date volumes | | | | |
	Value ($mil)	# of Deals	Value ($mil)	# of Deals	Chg. %
1986	319,112.0	3,390	62,542.4	65	1.92%
1987	320,001.8	3,282	67,628.1	73	2.22%
1988	558,026.3	4,161	126,961.0	85	2.04%
1989	422,466.5	5,634	44,552.1	44	0.78%
1990	226,571.8	5,696	12,951.1	18	0.32%
1991	167,079.1	5,208	4,020.3	9	0.17%
1992	149,502.4	5,322	1,843.8	8	0.15%
1993	180,955.4	4,438	1,880.6	32	0.72%

Source: Securities Data Corp.

that took place in the fourth wave were one of the principal unique characteristics which differentiate this wave from those that preceded it. The discussion that follows highlights some of the more notable characteristics of the fourth wave.

Takeover Tactics

The aggressive and defensive tactics of hostile takeovers became increasingly sophisticated during the fourth merger wave. Investment bankers and legal advisors reached their limits of creativity in their pursuit of clients' takeover aspirations. With the development of each new takeover tactic, new defensive strategies evolved to adapt to the tactic. The takeover weapon of choice in the 1980s was the tender offer. This is an offer made directly to the target's shareholders at a premium above the pre-announcement price. The method of pursuing a legal tender offer was codified in the Williams Act of 1968. Rather than limit takeovers, however, this law provided a path which hostile bidders could follow to conduct a "legal tender offer". This Act was later amended to render less effective certain types of tender offers, such as two-tiered offers that were "front-end loaded" with superior compensation for a control position and inferior compensation to the minority "back-end" shareholders. In spite of these legal developments, hostile bidders took advantage of their access to the newly developed junk bond market, to acquire large amounts of debt financing to pursue the megadeals that characterized the fourth wave. Many of these deals were initiated by comparatively smaller bidders. Bidders, such as Boone Pickens of Mesa Petroleum, were able to frighten previously impervious targets, such as the Gulf Corporation and Phillips Petroleum. This was accomplished by the use of a *Highly Confident Letter*, which is a statement by an investment banker indicating that it is highly confident that it can raise the necessary capital through sources such as the junk bond market.

For a period of time the development of takeover defenses lagged behind the aggressive tactics employed by raiders. Soon, however, a myriad of defensive strategies came to be deployed in the path of hostile bidders. These included both preventive and active measures. Preventive measures are those defenses that can be put in place in advance of a takeover bid so as to make the bid unprofitable or difficult to complete. These included a variety of corporate charter amendments, such as supermajority provisions, staggered terms of the board of directors and fair price provisions.[2] Other more drastic defenses included dual capitalizations and changes in the state of incorporation. However, perhaps the most effective preventive measure was the poison pill defense. Poison pills are warrants authorized by the potential target corporation which will allow target shareholders to purchase $100 worth of shares in combined bidder/target for US$50. This defense was initially found to be legal in November, 1985, for poison pills issued by the Household International Corporation. However, in 1988 the use of poison pills was found in both Delaware and New York to be legally improper when it was used in a discriminatory manner to favor one bid over another.

The ability of a target corporation to defend itself can be enhanced by other active defenses that it may deploy in the midst of a takeover battle. The array of these defenses used to prominently include greenmail and standstill agreements. However, the use of greenmail, which is the payment of a premium to certain shareholders in exchange for their shares and an agreement not to take over the target, was rendered less effective by changes in tax laws. Other more drastic active defenses include physical restructuring of the company as well as financial restructuring, which included alterations of the capital structure of the target. One of the more dramatic forms of defensive financial restructuring is the recapitalization plan. Companies faced with a hostile bid, such as Interco in 1988, which found itself in a takeover battle with the Rales Brothers, borrowed to finance an alternative offer to shareholders. In such a financial package, the company may offer shareholders a cash payout in the form of a large dividend as well as other compensation, such as a bond or other equity. If shareholders accept the company's own offer, it is left with highly leveraged capital structure. Interco is a prime example of a company that could not withstand the heavy pressure of the leverage brought on by debt assumed as a result of the recapitalization. The company was forced to file for bankruptcy under Chapter 11 of the Bankruptcy Code following a default on its debt obligations.

Shareholder Wealth Effects

The impact of takeovers, and the various aggressive and defensive tactics employed by participants, on shareholder wealth was a constant topic of debate among policy makers and academic researchers during the 1980s. The evidence that target shareholders unequivocally benefited from takeovers is strong. The average shareholder's premium was approximately 30%.[3] Mergerstat Review shows that the average premium above market price during the period 1983–92 ranged between 35.1% and 42.0%.[4] It is noteworthy that the lowest average premium occurred in 1991. The rate of return to target shareholders was similar in going-private transactions where premiums averaged 27% in a study done by DeAngelo, DeAngelo and Rice.[5] However, data from the fourth merger wave, as opposed to this study's earlier time period, shows similar returns to target shareholders as were apparent in regular mergers.

The shareholder wealth effects for acquiring firm shareholders presents a more ambiguous picture. The results of various studies seem to indicate that the gains range from close to zero to negative.[6] The poor response by the market to announcements of takeovers by bidding firms seems to indicate that market is not optimistic that the target will bring gains to the bidder that will offset the costs of the acquisition. For example, Jarrell and Poulsen pointed out that bidder returns in the 1980s were lower than in the prior decade.[7] This seems to imply that the competitive effects brought on by increased volume of bidders participating in the fourth merger wave served to bid up target prices and to reduce bidder gains. In sum, the fourth takeover wave was good for target shareholders but failed to yield clear benefits to acquiring firm shareholders.

Another area where shareholder returns are a controversial issue is in the impact that takeover defenses have on shareholder wealth. This is a particularly controversial area, since the use of some of these defenses, such as litigation, greenmail and poison pills, do not require shareholder approval. Other defenses, however, such as anti-takeover charter amendments, may require shareholder approval. Given the traditional inactive role that most shareholders play, as opposed to a more interested management, it is difficult to successfully oppose management proposals to install preventive antitakeover defenses. Brickley, Lease and Smith showed that 96 percent of their sample of 288 management-sponsored antitakeover defenses were approved.[8] The results of the abundant research studies on the shareholder wealth effects of antitakeover defenses is somewhat mixed. Jarrell and Poulsen have showed that non-fair price amendments have a statistically significant negative 2.95 percent effect on stock prices while fair price amendments failed to show a significant impact on shareholder wealth.[9]

Role of Leverage in the Takeovers of the 1980s

Many of the takeovers of the 1980s featured the aggressive use of debt. The term Leveraged Buyouts (LBOs) became an integral part of the vocabulary in the financial community. A typical LBO is a transaction financed primarily with debt, in which a public company becomes a private firm. There is usually a small equity component in the financing package which may include many layers of debt each with different rates and maturities. Some investment companies, such as Kohlberg, Kravis and Roberts (KKR), specialized in leveraged buyouts. The LBO craze reached a peak in 1988 when KKR took RJR Nabisco private for $24.8 billion. The post-1980 picture of leveraged buyouts is a mixed one. Some deals, such as Safeway Stores and RJR Nabisco, have fared well even in the presence of a recession during 1990–1. Several other LBOs, such as Seamans Furniture and Hillsborough Holdings, ended up in bankruptcy court. It is clear that increased leverage by itself does not doom a deal to failure. Rather, the lessons of the 1980s tell us that some deals involving companies with stable cash flows and unused debt capacity, and which operate in non-cyclical industries, can be good LBO candidates. Other deals that involve companies with volatile cash flows in cyclical industries may not be able to withstand the pressures that a temporary downturn may bring.

The goal of an LBO is to take advantage of unused debt capacity combined with anticipated cost economies to allow the buyers to eventually retire much of the LBO and possibly issue new equity after several years. Companies, such as Gibson Greeting Cards, went private only to go public once again in what is known as a "Reverse LBO". The deals have attracted much criticism from those who believe that the dealmakers did little to take advantage of a temporary lull in the market for the firm's stock. Supporters, however, contend that they purchased the stock at a premium from willing sellers and subsequently reorganized the company, thus creating value that buyers of the new shares recognize.

The leveraged buyouts of the 1980s also featured a conflict between equityholders and bondholders. Bondholders saw the market value of their bonds collapse as their ratings fell from high quality to low quality in response to the increased leverage brought on by the LBO. They contended that stockholders realized their LBO premiums by expropriating value from their debt investments. Unfortunately, the courts failed to agree with bondholders when they filed suit. The market responded with new covenants in bond indenture contracts that provide protection to buyers of new bonds in the form of put options as well as other protective provisions.

A variation on the leveraged buyout process, a management buyout, presented still more conflicts. In a management buyout, the management of a company or a division makes an offer to buy the entity. The potential for conflict of interest arises because managers are supposed to be fiduciaries for shareholders and maximizing the return on shareholder investment. However, in a management buyout, managers are the buyer as well as the agents of the seller. This conflict was brought to the fore in the landmark leveraged buyout of RJR Nabisco when a management group led by Ross Johnson made an initial offer that proved to be significantly below the ultimate buyout price of $22.8 billion that was paid by Kohlberg Kravis and Roberts.

Still another problem associated with the leveraged buyouts of the fourth merger wave, as well as other highly leveraged transactions (HLTs), was the pressure that such debt placed upon Corporate America. While some have argued that such pressure can be efficiency enhancing, the real test of such deals came during the recession that followed the end of the fourth merger wave. The decline in aggregate demand that occurs in an economic downturn tends to lower revenues while the increased leverage increases the fixed obligations that companies must meet. Many companies that pursued leveraged buyouts were unable to survive in the recessed economic climate of the early 1990s and were forced to seek protection under Chapter 11 of the Bankruptcy Code. While the number of LBO dealmaking firms declined dramatically at the end of the fourth merger wave, the number of workout and bankruptcy specialists rose. It is ironic to note that some of the same dealmakers in the LBO field became dealmakers in the bankruptcy.

Junk Bond Market

Contrary to what is sometimes heralded in the media, the junk bond market existed for decades prior to the start of the fourth takeover wave. Those junk bonds were referred to as "Fallen Angels". The ranks of these fallen angels swelled during the aftermath of the Great Depression. These bonds differed from the junk bonds that were issued during the 1980s in that the fallen angels were high quality bonds when they were first issued. Bonds were investments purchased by conservative investors who sought regular income and low risk. In 1977, however, this market changed when Lehman Brothers offered the first original issue, high-yield/low-rating bonds. Drexel Burnham Lambert, along with its pioneering financier Michael Milken, quickly took advantage of a demand that they saw in the market to sell bonds with the potential for a higher yield. They were supported in their efforts by certain academic studies that purported to show that these bonds had a default rate that was not that different from their higher quality counterparts.[10] Other studies appeared to indicate that junk bonds were not as volatile as anticipated but did pay a significantly higher return than investment grade bonds.[11] The favorable research results enhanced the aggressive selling tactics of securities dealers which successfully appealed to such normally conservative institutional investors as pension funds, insurance companies and thrift institutions. However, the ability of junk bond dealers to market junk bonds was even more influenced by the fact that Drexel Burnham Lambert became an aggressive market-maker for the junk bond market. This afforded these bonds a new degree of liquidity that enabled them to favorably compete with other investment vehicles.

As shown in figure 1.3, the junk bond market collapsed in 1990. Its fall was as sudden as its rise in the mid-1980s. The first step in the collapse was the Stock Market Crash of 1987. This led investors to flee to higher quality investments. Perhaps the greatest blow to the market, however, was the indictment and eventual conviction of its founder and leading proponent Michael Milken. Wary bankers tightened the lines of short-term liquidity to Drexel. The liquidity crisis brought about a quick end to the once fifth largest investment bank in the United States. Without an active market-maker, the junk bond market floundered for a couple of years. Ironically, junk bond investors who did not sell their holdings actually realized good returns on their high yield investments.

The junk bond market revised substantially in 1992 and 1993. Figure 1.3 shows that total high yield proceeds reached an all time high through the third quarter of 1993. This rebound clearly indicates that the high yield bond market has a permanent place in modern corporate finance. Figures 1.4 and 1.5 show, however, that the high yield bond market grew in 1992 and 1993 through more traditional financing activities and not as a result of financing for mergers and acquisitions or leveraged buyouts. The high yield financing for mergers and acquisitions continued to fall through 1993, while high yield financing for leveraged buyouts collapsed in 1990 and remained at insignificant levels thereafter.

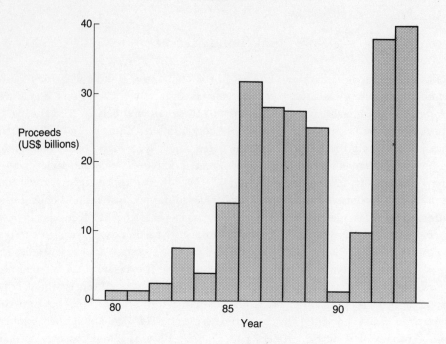

Figure 1.3 Total high yield issues, 1980–93
Source: Securities Data Corp.

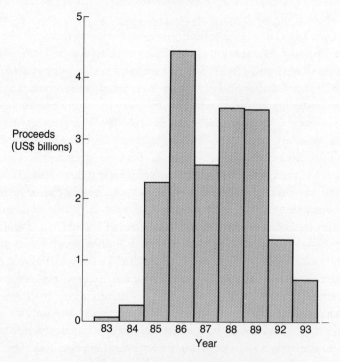

Figure 1.4 High yield proceeds for mergers
Source: Securities Data Corp.

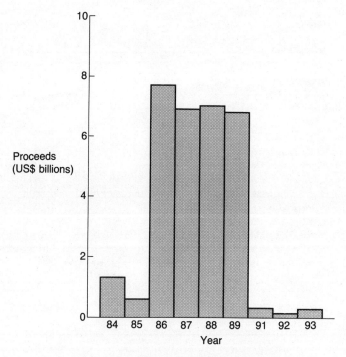

Figure 1.5   High yield proceeds for LBOs
Source: Securities Data Corp.

Beyond the Fourth Merger Wave

Following the fourth merger wave, many US companies were left with highly lever-aged balance sheets. The decline in economic demand caused by the 1990–1 recession and the weak recovery that followed caused many companies to take steps to reduce their leverage. Some companies sought to issue equity to replace the debt that they had assumed. Others who were interested in expanding through a merger or acquisition were reluctant to assume more debt to do so. This is why many of the early 1990 deals were equity financed transactions. Instead of borrowing, corporate bidders in the 1990s used their own equity as the currency to finance acquisitions. This was facili-tated by the robust growth of the stock-market. As of the third quarter of 1993, the Dow Jones Industrial Average had reached the 3,600 level. While this made the stock of potential targets more expensive, it also increased the ability of bidders to pay higher prices.

The revitalization of the merger and acquisitions business that took place in 1993 was underscored by the fact that through the first three quarters of that year there were already ten announced deals with a value of 2 billion dollars or more (see table 1.2). Two of the largest of these were the $12.6 billion merger between AT&T and McCaw Cellular and the $12 billion Bell Atlantic/TCI merger. This was followed by the $10 billion tender offer by Viacom for Paramount Communications. Other large acquisitions included $6 billion purchase of Medco Containment Services by Merck & Co.

Table 1.2 Ten largest announced mergers and acquisitions of 1993 (as of December 31, 1993)

Buyer/Seller	Value (millions)
Bell Atlantic Corp./Tele-Communications Inc.	16,000.0
AT&T/McCaw Cellular	12,600.0
QVC Network/Paramount	9,900.0
KeyCorp./Society Corp.	7,800.0
Merck & Co./Medco Containment Services	6,000.0
Columbia Healthcare Corp./HCA Hospital Corp.	5,700.0
Costco Wholesale Corp./Price Company Inc.	4,600.0
Primerica Corp./Travelers Corp.	4,200.0
Tele-Communications Inc./Liberty Media Corp.	3,800.0
British Telecommunications PLC/MCI Communications	3,400.0

Source: Mergerstat Review (Viacom eventually purchased QVC in 1994)

Even when faced with the competitive pressures of a bidding contest, companies looked to bring in equity partners rather than resort to financing through debt. Such was the case in the Viacom–Paramount–QVC merger contest. Viacom, when faced with a rival $9.5 billion bid by the cable company, QVC Network, sought out equity partners such as Blockbuster Video and Nynex. The use of equity instead of debt lowered the riskiness of the deals. However, the use of equity was not without clear costs to stockholders. Shareholders of the bidding corporations would see their share of ownership decline as more shares were issued. If the target corporation does not generate returns that more than offset the equity dilution costs, the rate of return on equity would decline. The potential dilution effects could be quite significant. For example, AT&T's total equity increased 15 percent as a result of its acquisition of McCaw Cellular. The number of Viacom shares outstanding were projected to increase by more than 100 percent if its offer was accepted, while QVC's shares would more than triple.

The megadeal offers of 1993 underscore the fact that mergers, even large-scale megadeals, have a permanent place in the world of corporate finance. While the method of financing may have changed, the desire of companies to engage in major expansions through acquisitions, as opposed to internal expansion, remains strong. These deals were not the inspiration of deal making investment bankers seeking large fees. Rather, they mainly were conceived internally as part of an overall expansion strategy. The bidders were not looking to exploit short-term gains from the sale of undervalued assets. Instead, they were seeking to pursue certain strategic goals. For example, AT&T bought McCaw, the largest cellular company, to return to the local telephone business it had been forced to leave with divestiture. It also sought to purchase a company that would enable it to instantly enter the closely related cellular business and hopefully realize synergistic gains. Merck, one the world's largest drug manufacturers, acquired Medco, one of the largest wholesale drug distributors, in an effort to realize scale and scope economies and obtain a competitive edge within the pharmaceutical industry. While there are still risks for bidding shareholders in the form of a lower rate of return on their investment, the risk of bankruptcy from such equity financed transactions was considerably less than with debt financed deals.

While the clear majority of mergers that occurred in the 1990s were friendly, equity financed, strategically motivated transactions, there were some prominent exceptions to the friendly tone that was set by such mergers. For example, while sensing less than enthusiastic support by takeover target Paramount Communications, QVC Network initiated a two-tiered $9.5 billion tender offer for the company. Viacom responded with its own tender offer that was valued at $9.9 billion. As of the date of this writing, neither firm had been declared the winner in this contest. However, the battle between QVC and Viacom was reminiscent of the large-scale hostile takeover battles that were commonplace in the 1980s. This transaction served as a reminder that large-scale hostile takeovers have not disappeared.

Conclusion

The fourth merger wave was a fascinating period in US economic history. Large corporations changed hands in unprecedented numbers. The capital structure of many corporations changed dramatically as companies used debt to finance acquisitions or to pursue defensive antitakeover strategies. A whole new market, the original issue high yield bond market, was born. While its aggressive market-marker Drexel Burnham Lambert did not survive the tumultuous period, the high yield bond market remains still viable as another source of financing for corporations. Many of the inefficient corporations whose management failed to provide shareholders a reasonable return continue to be sold or broken into more efficient subunits. While companies have developed new protections against hostile takeovers, management must still take the threat of hostile takeover more seriously after the fourth merger wave. In doing so, the fourth merger wave may have served the purpose of helping to keep management honest in the future. If this proves to be the case, increased shareholder values in the 1990s may be the result. Regardless of the existence of such beneficial effects of takeovers, the revival of takeovers that occurred in 1993 serves as notice that the field of mergers and acquisitions is alive and well.

Notes

1   Patrick A. Gaughan, 1991, *Mergers and Acquisitions*, Harper Collins, 20–7.
2   Ibid., 154–79.
3   Gregg Jarrell, James Brickley, and Jeffry M. Netter, 1988, The Market for Corporate Control: The Empirical Evidence Since 1980, *Journal of Economic Perspectives*, Winter,   49–68. (See chapter 17 below.)
4   *Mergerstat Review*, 1992, Merrill Lynch Business Services, 84.

5   Harry DeAngelo, Linda DeAngelo, and Eugene Rice, 1984, Going Private: Minority Freezeouts and Shareholder Wealth, *Journal of Law and Economics*, 27, 367–402.

6   Gregg A. Jarrell and Annette B. Poulsen, 1989, The Returns to Acquiring Firms in Tender Offers: Evidence From Three Decades, *Financial Management*, 18 (3), Autumn, 12–19. (See chapter 16 below.)

7   Ibid.

8   James Brickley, Ronald Lease, and Clifford Smith, 1988, Ownership Structure and the Voting on Antitakeover Amendments, *Journal of Financial Economics*, 20 (1/2), January/March, 267–92.

9   Gregg A. Jarrell and Annette B. Poulsen, 1987, Shark Repellents and Stock Prices: The Effects of Antitakeover Amendments Since 1980, *Journal of Financial Economics*, 19 (1), September, 127–68.

10 Edward I. Altman and Scott A. Namacher, 1985, The Default Rate Experience on High Yield Corporate Debt, Morgan Stanley & Co.

11 Marshall E. Blume and Donald E. Keim, 1989, Risk and Return Characteristics of Lower Grade Bonds: 1977–1987, Rodney L. White Center for Financial Research, The Wharton School of the University of Pennsylvania, Philadelphia, August.

2

Takeovers: Their Causes and Consequences

Michael C. Jensen

Economic analysis and evidence indicate that the market for corporate control is benefiting shareholders, society, and the corporate form of organization. The value of transactions in this market ran at a record rate of about $180 billion per year in 1985 and 1986, 47 percent above the 1984 record of $122 billion. The gains to shareholders from these transactions have been huge. The gains to selling firm shareholders from mergers and acquisition activity in the ten-year period 1977–86 total $346 billion (in 1986 dollars).[1] The gains to buying firm shareholders are harder to estimate, and no one to my knowledge has done so as yet, but my guess is that they will add at least another $50 billion to the total. These gains, to put them in perspective, equal 51 percent of the total cash dividends (valued in 1986 dollars) paid to investors by the entire corporate sector in the past decade.[2]

These corporate control transactions and the restructurings that often accompany them are frequently wrenching events in the lives of those linked to the involved organizations: the managers, employees, suppliers, customers and residents of surrounding communities. Restructurings usually involve major organizational change (such as shifts in corporate strategy) to meet new competition or market conditions, increased use of debt, and a flurry of recontracting with managers, employees, suppliers and customers. This activity sometimes results in expansion of resources devoted to certain areas and at other times in contractions involving plant closings, layoffs of top-level and middle managers, staff and production workers, and reduced compensation.

Those threatened by the changes that restructuring brings about argue that corporate restructuring is damaging the American economy, damaging the morale and productivity of organizations, and pressuring executives to manage for the short-term. Further, they hold that the value restructuring creates does not come from increased efficiency and productivity; instead, the gains come from lower tax payments, broken

contracts with managers, employees and others, and mistakes in valuation by inefficient capital markets. Since the benefits are illusory and the costs are real, they argue,
takeover activity should be restricted.

The controversy has been accompanied by strong pressure on regulators and legislatures to enact restrictions that would curb activity in the market for corporate
control. Dozens of congressional bills in the last several years have proposed new
restrictions on takeovers, but none have passed as of this writing. The Business
Roundtable, composed of the chief executive officers of the 200 largest corporations in
the country, has pushed hard for restrictive legislation. Within the past several years
the legislatures of New York, New Jersey, Maryland, Pennsylvania, Connecticut,
Illinois, Kentucky, Michigan, Ohio, Indiana and Minnesota have passed antitakeover
laws. The Federal Reserve Board implemented new restrictions in early 1987 on the
use of debt in certain takeovers.

In all the controversy over takeover activity, it is often forgotten that only 40 (an
all-time record) out of the 3,300 takeover transactions in 1986 were hostile tender
offers. There were 110 voluntary or negotiated tender offers (unopposed by management) and the remaining 3,100-plus deals were also voluntary transactions agreed to
by management, although this simple classification is misleading since many of the
voluntary transactions would not occur absent the threat of hostile takeover. A major
reason for the current outcry is that in recent years mere size alone has disappeared as
an effective takeover deterrent, and the managers of many of our largest and least
efficient corporations now find their jobs threatened by disciplinary forces in the
capital markets.

Economists have accumulated considerable evidence and knowledge on the effects
of the takeover market. Most of the earlier work is well summarized elsewhere (Jensen
and Ruback, 1983; Jensen, 1984). Here, I focus on current aspects of the controversy.
In brief, the previous work tells us the following:

1   Takeovers benefit shareholders of target companies. Premiums in hostile offers
    historically exceed 30 percent on average, and in recent times have averaged about
    50 percent.
2   Acquiring-firm shareholders on average earn about 4 percent in hostile takeovers
    and roughly zero in mergers, although these returns seem to have declined from
    past levels.
3   Takeovers do not waste credit or resources. Instead, they generate substantial
    gains: historically, 8 percent of the total value of both companies. Those value
    gains represent gains to economic efficiency, not redistribution between various
    parties.
4   Actions by managers that eliminate or prevent offers or mergers are most suspect
    as harmful to shareholders.
5   Golden parachutes for top-level managers do not, on average, harm shareholders.
6   The activities of takeover specialists (such as Icahn, Posner, Steinberg, and
    Pickens) benefit shareholders on average.

7   Merger and acquisition activity has not increased industrial concentration. Indeed, over 1,200 divestitures valued at $59.9 billion occurred in 1986, also a record level (Grimm, 1986).

8   Takeover gains do not come from the creation of monopoly power.

The market for corporate control is creating large benefits for shareholders and for the economy as a whole by loosening control over vast amounts of resources and enabling them to move more quickly to their highest-valued use. This is a healthy market in operation, on both the takeover side and the divestiture side, and it is playing an important role in helping the American economy adjust to major changes in competition and regulation of the past decade.

The Market for Corporate Control

The market for corporate control is best viewed as a major component of the managerial labor market. It is the arena in which alternative management teams compete for the rights to manage corporate resources (Jensen and Ruback, 1983). Understanding this point is crucial to understanding much of the rhetoric about the effects of hostile takeovers.

Managers often have trouble abandoning strategies they have spent years devising and implementing, even when those strategies no longer contribute to the organization's survival. Such changes can require abandonment of major projects, relocation of facilities, changes in managerial assignments, and closure or sale of facilities or divisions. Takeovers generally occur because changing technology or market conditions require a major restructuring of corporate assets, and it is easier for new top-level managers with a fresh view of the business and no ties with current employees or communities to make such changes. Moreover, normal organizational resistance to change is commonly significantly lower early in the reign of new top-level managers. For example, the premium Carl Icahn was able to offer for TWA and his victory over Texas Air for the acquisition of TWA were made possible in part by the willingness of TWA unions to negotiate favorable contract concessions with Icahn – concessions that TWA management was unable to win prior to the takeover conflict. On the other hand, lack of detailed knowledge about the firm poses risks for new managers and increases the likelihood of mistakes.

A variety of political and economic conditions in the 1980s have created a climate where economic efficiency requires a major restructuring of corporate assets. These factors include the relaxation of restrictions on mergers imposed by the antitrust laws, withdrawal of resources from industries that are growing more slowly or that must shrink, deregulation in the financial services, oil and gas, transportation, and broadcasting markets, and improvements in takeover technology, including a larger supply of increasingly sophisticated legal and financial advisers, and improvements in financing technology such as the strip financing commonly used in leveraged buyouts and the original issuance of high-yield non-investment-grade bonds.

Each of these factors has contributed to the increase in total takeover and reorganization activity. Moreover, the first three factors (antitrust relaxation, exit, and deregulation) are generally consistent with data showing the intensity of takeover activity by industry. For example, the value of merger and acquisition transactions by industry in the period of 1981–4 given in table 2.1 indicates that acquisition activity was highest in oil and gas, followed by banking and finance, insurance, food processing, and mining and minerals. For comparison purposes, the last column of the table presents data on industry size measured as a fraction of the total value of all firms. All but two of the industries, retail and transportation, represent a larger fraction of total takeover activity than their representation in the economy as a whole, indicating that the takeover market is concentrated in particular industries, not spread evenly throughout the corporate sector.

Many sectors of the US economy have been experiencing slowing growth and, in some cases, even retrenchment. This phenomenon has many causes, including substantially increased foreign competition. This slow growth has increased takeover activity because takeovers play an important role in facilitating exit from an industry or activity. Major changes in energy markets, for example, have required a radical restructuring and retrenchment in that industry and takeovers have played an important role in accomplishing these changes; oil and gas rank first in takeover activity, with twice their proportionate share of total activity. Managers who are slow to recognize that many old practices and strategies are no longer viable are finding that takeovers are doing the job for them. Exit is cheaper to accomplish through merger and the orderly liquidation of marginal assets of the combined firms than by disorderly, expensive bankruptcy in an industry saddled with overcapacity. The end of the competitive struggle in such an industry often comes in the bankruptcy courts, with the unnecessary destruction of valuable parts of organizations that could be used productively by others.

Similarly, deregulation of the financial services market is consistent with the number 2 rank of banking/finance and the number 3 rank of insurance in table 2.1. Deregulation has also been important in the transportation and broadcasting industries. Mining and minerals have been subject to many of the same forces impinging on the energy industry, including the changes in the value of the dollar.

The development of innovative financing vehicles, such as high-yield non-investment-grade bonds (junk bonds), has removed size as a significant impediment to competition in the market for corporate control. A 1987 update by the Investor Responsibility Research Center of an earlier SEC study finds that the investment grade and high-yield debt issues combined were associated with 9.8 percent of all tender offer financing from January 1981 through September 1986. Even though not yet widely used in takeovers, these new financing techniques have had important effects because they permit small firms to obtain resources for acquisition of much larger firms by issuing claims on the value of the venture (that is, the target firm's assets) just as in any other corporate investment activity.

Table 2.1 Intensity of industry takeover activity as measured by the value of merger and acquisition transactions in the period 1981–4 (as a percent of total takeover transactions for which valuation data are publicly reported) compared to industry size (as measured by the fraction of overall corporate market value)

Industry classification of seller	Percent of total takeover activity[a]	Percent of total corporate market value[b]
Oil and gas	26.3%	13.5%
Banking and finance	8.8	6.4
Insurance	5.9	2.9
Food processing	4.6	4.4
Mining and minerals	4.4	1.5
Conglomerate	4.4	3.2
Retail	3.6	5.2
Transportation	2.4	2.7
Leisure and entertainment	2.3	0.9
Broadcasting	2.3	0.7
Other	39.4	58.5

[a] Grimm, 1984, p. 41.
[b] As of 12/31/84. Total value is measured as the sum of the market value of common equity for 4,305 companies, including 1,501 companies on the NYSE, 724 companies on the ASE plus 2,080 companies in the over-the-counter market.
Source: The Media General Financial Weekly, December 31, 1984, p. 17

Managerial myopia vs. market myopia

It has been argued that far from pushing managers to undertake needed structural changes, growing institutional equity holdings and the fear of takeover cause managers to behave myopically and therefore to sacrifice long-term benefits to increase short-term profits. The arguments tend to confuse two separate issues: (1) whether managers are shortsighted and make decisions that undervalue future cash flows while overvaluing current cash flows (myopic managers); and (2) whether security markets are shortsighted and undervalue future cash flows while overvaluing near-term cash flows (myopic markets).

There is little formal evidence on the myopic managers issue, but I believe this phenomenon does occur. Sometimes it occurs when managers hold little stock in their companies and are compensated in ways that motivate them to take actions to increase accounting earnings rather than the value of the firm. It also occurs when managers make mistakes because they do not understand the forces that determine stock values.

There is much evidence inconsistent with the myopic markets view and no evidence that indicates it is true.

First, the mere fact that price-earnings ratios differ widely among securities indicates the market is valuing something other than current earnings. For example, it values growth as well. Indeed, the essence of a growth stock is one that has large investment projects yielding few short-term cash flows but high future earnings and cash flows. The continuing marketability of new issues for start-up companies with little record of current earnings, the Genentechs of the world, is also inconsistent with the notion that the market does not value future earnings.

Second, McConnell and Muscarella (1985) provide evidence that (except in the oil industry) stock prices respond positively to announcements of increased investment expenditures and negatively to reduced expenditures. Their evidence is also inconsistent with the notion that the equity market is myopic, since it indicates the market values spending current resources on projects which promise returns in the future.

Third, the vast evidence on efficient markets indicating that current stock prices appropriately incorporate all currently available public information is also inconsistent with the myopic markets hypothesis. Although the evidence is not literally 100 percent in support of the efficient market hypothesis, no proposition in any of the sciences is better documented.[3]

The large positive stock price reactions to announced restructurings in the oil industry are inconsistent with the notion that the market values only short-term earnings, because the restructurings involve large write-offs that reduce accounting earnings in the year. ARCO's stock price, for example, increased by 30 percent when it announced its major restructuring in 1985. The market responded positively even though ARCO simultaneously announced a $1.2 billion write-off.

Fourth, recent versions of the myopic markets hypothesis emphasize increases in the amount of institutional holdings and the pressures they face to generate high returns on a quarter-to-quarter basis. It is argued that these pressures on institutions are a major cause of pressures on corporations to generate high current earnings on a quarter-to-quarter basis. The institutional pressures are said to lead to increased takeovers of firms (because institutions are not loyal shareholders) and to decreased research and development expenditures. It is hypothesized that because R&D expenditures reduce current earnings, firms making them are therefore more likely to be taken over, and that reductions in R&D are leading to a fundamental weakening of the corporate sector of the economy.

A study of 324 firms by the Office of the Chief Economist of the SEC (April 1985) finds substantial evidence that is inconsistent with this version of the myopic markets argument. The evidence indicates the following: increased institutional stock holdings are not associated with increased takeovers of firms; increased institutional holdings are not associated with decreases in research and development expenditures; firms with high R&D expenditures are not more vulnerable to takeovers; stock prices respond positively to announcements of such increases in R&D expenditures.

Moreover, total spending on R&D is increasing concurrent with the wave of merger and acquisition activity. Total spending on R&D in 1984, a year of record acquisition activity, increased by 14 percent according to *Business Week*'s annual survey. This represented "the biggest gain since R&D spending began a steady climb in the late 1970s." All industries in the survey increased R&D spending with the exception of steel. In addition, R&D spending increased from 2 percent of sales, where it had been for five years, to 2.9 percent. In 1985 and 1986, two more record years for acquisition activity, R&D also set new records. R&D spending increased by 10 percent (to 3.1 percent of sales) in 1985, and in 1986, R&D spending again increased by 10 percent to $51 billion (to 3.5 percent of sales), in a year when total sales decreased by 1 percent.[4]

Bronwyn Hall (1987), in a detailed study of all US manufacturing firms in the years 1976–85, finds in approximately 600 acquisitions that firms which are acquired do not have higher R&D expenditures (measured by the ratio of R&D to sales) than firms in the same industry which are not acquired. Also, she finds that "firms involved in mergers showed no difference in their pre- and post-merger R&D performance over those not so involved."

I know of no evidence that supports that argument that takeovers reduce R&D expenditures, even though this is a prominent argument among many of those who favor restrictions on takeovers.

A simple alternative hypothesis explains the current facts, including the criticisms of managers, quite well. Instead of supposing that the myopic market is punishing managers for their foresightedness and for being right, suppose some managers are simply mistaken – that is, their strategies are wrong – and that the financial markets are telling them they are wrong. If they don't change, their stock prices will remain low. If the managers are indeed wrong, it is desirable for the stockholders and for the economy to remove them to make way for a change in strategy and more efficient use of the resources.

The internal control mechanisms of corporations, operating through the board of directors, should encourage reluctant managers to restructure. But when the internal processes for change in large corporations are too slow, costly, and clumsy to bring about the required restructuring or change in managers efficiently, the capital markets, through the market for corporate control, are doing so. The takeover market serves as an important source of protection for investors in these situations. Other management teams that recognize an opportunity to reorganize or redeploy an organization's assets and thereby create new value can bid for the control rights in the takeover market. To be successful, such bids must be at a premium over current market value. This gives investors an opportunity to realize part of the gains from reorganization and redeployment of the assets.

Free Cash Flow Theory

More than a dozen separate forces drive takeover activity, including such factors as deregulation, synergies, economies of scale and scope, taxes, the level of managerial competence, and increasing globalization of US markets (Roll, 1987). One major cause of takeover activity, the agency costs associated with conflicts between managers and shareholders over the payout of free cash flow, has received relatively little attention. Yet it has played an important role in acquisitions over the last decade.[5]

Managers are the agents of shareholders, and because both parties are self-interested, there are serious conflicts between them over the choice of the best corporate strategy. Agency costs are the total costs that arise in such arrangements. They consist of the costs of monitoring and bonding managerial behavior (such as the costs of producing audited financial statements and devising and implementing compensation plans that reward managers for actions that increase investors' wealth) and the efficiency losses that are incurred because the conflicts of interest can never be resolved perfectly. When these costs are large, the threat or actuality of takeovers can reduce them.

Free cash flow is cash flow in excess of that required to fund all of a firm's projects that have positive net present values when discounted at the relevant cost of capital. Such free cash flow must be paid out to shareholders if the firm is to be efficient and to maximize value for shareholders.

However, payment of cash to shareholders reduces the resources controlled by managers, thereby reducing the power of managers and potentially subjecting them to the monitoring by capital markets that occurs when a firm must obtain new capital. Further, managers have incentives to expand their firms beyond the size that maximizes shareholder wealth.[6] Growth increases managers' power by increasing the resources under their control, and changes in management compensation are positively related to growth.[7] Moreover, the tendency of firms to reward middle managers through promotion rather than year-to-year bonuses also creates an organizational bias toward growth to supply the new positions that such promotion-based reward systems require (Baker, 1986).

Conflicts of interest between shareholders and managers over payout policies are especially severe when the organization generates substantial free cash flow. The problem is how to motivate managers to disgorge the cash rather than invest it at below the cost of capital or waste it through organizational inefficiencies.

The theory developed here offers a seeming paradox. Increases in financial flexibility that give managers control over free cash flow may actually cause the value of the firm to decline. This result occurs because it is difficult to assure that managers will use their discretion over resources to further the interests of shareholders.

The theory explains: (1) how debt for stock exchanges reduces the organizational inefficiencies fostered by substantial free cash flow; (2) how debt can substitute for dividends; (3) why "diversification" programs are more likely to be associated with losses than are expansion programs in the same line of business; (4) why mergers within an industry and liquidation-motivated takeovers will generally create larger gains than cross-industry mergers; (5) why the factors stimulating takeovers in such diverse businesses as broadcasting, tobacco, cable systems, and oil are essentially identical; and (6) why bidders and some targets tend to show abnormally good performance prior to takeover.

The Role of Debt in Motivating Organizational Efficiency

The agency costs of debt have been widely discussed (Jensen and Meckling, 1976; Smith and Warner, 1979), but, with the exception of Grossman and Hart (1980), the benefits of debt in motivating managers and their organizations to be efficient have largely been ignored.

Debt creation, *without retention of the proceeds of the issue*, enables managers effectively to bond their promise to pay out future cash flows. Thus, debt can be an effective substitute for dividends, something not generally recognized in the corporate finance literature.[8] Debt reduces the agency cost of free cash flow by reducing the cash flow available for spending at the discretion of managers. By issuing debt in exchange for stock, managers bond their promise to pay out future cash flows in a way that simple dividend increases do not. In doing so, they give shareholder-recipients of the debt the right to take the firm into bankruptcy court if they do not keep their promise to make the interest and principal payments.

Of course, managers can also promise to pay out future cash flows by announcing a "permanent" increase in the dividend.[9] But because there is no contractual obligation to make the promised dividend payments, such promises are weak.[10] The fact that capital markets punish dividend cuts with large stock price reductions (Charest, 1978; Aharony and Swary, 1980) can be interpreted as an equilibrium market response to the agency costs of free cash flow.

Issuing large amounts of debt to buy back stock sets up organizational incentives to motivate managers to pay out free cash flow. In addition, the exchange of debt for stock helps managers overcome the normal organizational resistance to retrenchment that the payout of free cash flow often requires. The threat of failure to make debt-service payments serves as a strong motivating force to make such organizations more efficient.

Increased leverage also has costs. As leverage increases, the usual agency costs of debt, including bankruptcy costs, rise. The incentives to take on projects that reduce total firm value but benefit shareholders through a transfer of wealth from bondholders is one source of these costs. These costs put a limit on the desirable level of debt. The optimal debt/equity ratio is the point at which firm value is maximized, the point where the marginal costs of debt just offset the marginal benefits.

The debt created in a hostile takeover (or takeover defense) of a firm suffering severe agency costs of free cash flow need not be permanent. Indeed, sometimes "overleveraging" such a firm is desirable. In these situations, levering the firm so highly that it cannot continue to exist in its old form creates the crisis to motivate cuts in expansion programs and the sale of those divisions that are more valuable outside the firm. The proceeds are used to reduce debt to a more normal or permanent level. This process results in a reexamination of an organization's strategy and structure. When it is successful, a much leaner, more efficient, and competitive organization results.

This control hypothesis does not imply that debt issues will always have positive control effects. For example, these control effects will not be as important for rapidly growing organizations with large and highly profitable investment projects but no free cash flow. Such organizations will have to go regularly to the financial markets to obtain capital. At these times the markets have an opportunity to evaluate the company, its management, and its proposed projects. Investment bankers and analysts play an important role in this monitoring, and the market's assessment is made evident by the price investors pay for the financial claims.

The control function of debt is more important in organizations that generate large cash flows but have low growth prospects, and it is even more important in organizations that must shrink. In these organizations the pressure to waste cash flows by investing them in uneconomic projects is most serious.

Leveraged buyouts and free cash flow theory

Many of the benefits in going-private and leveraged buyout transactions seem to be due to the control function of debt. These transactions are creating a new organizational form that competes successfully with the open corporate form because of advantages in controlling the agency costs of free cash flow. In 1985, going-private and LBO transactions totaled $37.4 billion and represented 32 percent of the value of all public acquisitions. In 1986, the total value increased to $44.3 billion representing 39 percent of all public acquisitions (Baker, 1986; Grimm, 1986). Average premiums paid for publicly held firms have exceeded 50 percent.

Desirable leveraged buyout candidates are frequently firms or divisions of larger firms that have stable business histories, low growth prospects and high potential for generating cash flows; that is, situations where agency costs of free cash flows are likely to be high.

Leveraged buyouts are frequently financed with high debt; 10:1 ratios of debt to equity are not uncommon, and they average 5.25:1 (Schipper and Smith, 1986; Kaplan, 1987; DeAngelo and DeAngelo, 1986). Moreover, the use of "strip financing" and the allocation of equity in the deals reveal a sensitivity to incentives, conflicts of interest, and bankruptcy costs. Strip financing, the practice in which risky nonequity securities are held in approximately equal proportions, limits the conflict of interest among such securityholders and therefore limits bankruptcy costs. Top managers and the sponsoring venture capitalists hold disproportionate amounts of equity.

A somewhat oversimplified example illustrates the organizational effects of strip financing. Consider two firms identical in every respect except financing. Firm A is entirely financed with equity, and Firm B is highly leveraged with senior debt, subordinated debt, convertible debt, and preferred as well as common equity. Suppose Firm B securities are sold only in strips; that is, a buyer purchasing a certain percent of any security must purchase the same percent of all securities, and the securities are "stapled" together so they cannot be separated later. Security holders of both firms have identical unlevered claims on the cash flow distribution, but organizationally the two firms are very different. If Firm B managers withhold dividends to invest in value-reducing projects or if they are incompetent, stripholders have recourse to remedial powers not available to the equityholders of Firm A. Each Firm B security specifies the rights its holder has in the event of default on its dividend or coupon payment – for example, the right to take the firm into bankruptcy or to have board representation. As each security above equity goes into default, the stripholder receives new rights to intercede in the organization. As a result, it is quicker and less expensive to replace managers in Firm B.

Moreover, because every securityholder in the highly levered Firm B has the same claim on the firm, there are no conflicts between senior and junior claimants over reorganization of the claims in the event of default; to the stripholders it is a matter of moving funds from one pocket to another. Thus, Firm B will not go into bankruptcy; a required reorganization can be accomplished voluntarily, quickly, and with less expense and disruption than through bankruptcy proceedings.

Securities commonly subject to strip practices are often called "mezzanine" financing and include securities with priority superior to common stock yet subordinate to senior debt. This arrangement seems to be sensible, because several factors ignored in our simplified example imply that strictly proportional holdings of all securities is not desirable. For example, IRS restrictions deny tax deductibility of debt interest in such situations and bank holdings of equity are restricted by regulation. Riskless senior debt need not be in the strip because there are no conflicts with other claimants in the event of reorganization when there is no probability of default on its payments.

Furthermore, it is advantageous to have top level managers and venture capitalists who promote the transactions hold a larger share of the equity. Top level managers on average receive over 30 percent of the equity, and venture capitalists and the funds they represent generally retain the major share of the remainder (Schipper and Smith, 1986; Kaplan, 1987). The venture capitalists control the board of directors (in fact, they often *are* the board) and monitor managers directly. Large equity claims by managers and venture capitalists give them a strong interest in making the venture successful because their equity interests are subordinate to other claims.

Leveraged buyouts increased dramatically in the last decade from $1.2 billion in 1979, when W.T. Grimm began collecting the data, to $44.3 billion in 1986. Less than a handful of these management buyouts have ended in bankruptcy, although more have gone through private reorganizations. A thorough test of this organizational form requires the passage of time and recessions.

Some have asserted that managers engaging in a buyout of their firm are insulating themselves from monitoring. The opposite is true in the typical leveraged buyout because the venture capitalist is generally the largest stockholder and controls the board of directors. The venture capitalist therefore has both greater ability and greater incentive to monitor managers than do directors with little or no equity who represent diffuse shareholders in the typical public corporation.

Applying Free Cash Flow Theory to Takeovers

Free cash flow theory is consistent with a wide range of previously unexplained data. Here I sketch some empirical predictions of the free cash flow theory for takeovers and mergers and some of the facts that lend it credence.

The oil industry

The importance of takeovers and the relevance of free cash flow theory in motivating change and efficiency are particularly clear in the oil industry. Radical changes in the energy market from 1973 to the late 1970s meant that a major restructuring of the petroleum industry had to occur. The optimal level of refining and distribution capacity and crude reserves fell over this period; as of the late 1970s, the industry was plagued with excess capacity, although this was not generally recognized at the time. Reserves are reduced by reducing the level of exploration and development, and it pays to concentrate these reductions in high-cost areas such as the United States.

Substantial reductions in exploration and development and in refining and distribution capacity meant that some firms had to leave the industry. This is especially true because holding reserves is subject to economies of scale, while exploration and development are subject to diseconomies of scale.

At the same time price increases generated large cash flows, creating a particularly puzzling period in the oil industry because at the same time that change in the environment required a reduction of capacity, cash flows and profits were high; 1984 cash flows of the ten largest oil companies were $48.5 billion, 28 percent of the total cash flows of the top 200 firms in *Dun's Business Month* (July, 1985) survey. This condition, in which high profits coincided with the necessity to shrink the industry, is somewhat unusual. It was caused by an increase in the average productivity of resources in the industry while the marginal productivity decreased.[11] However, management did not pay out the excess resources to shareholders. Instead, the industry continued to spend heavily on exploration and development even though the returns on these expenditures were below the cost of capital.

Paradoxically, the profitability of oil exploration and drilling activity can decrease even though the price of oil increases, if the value of reserves in the ground falls. This decrease can occur when the price increase is associated with reductions in consumption that make marketing newly discovered oil difficult. In the late 1970s the increased holding costs associated with higher real interest rates, reductions in expected future oil price increases, increased exploration and development costs, and contrived reductions in current supply (and thus larger future potential supply) combined to make many current exploration and development projects uneconomic. The industry, however, continued to spend heavily on such projects.

The waste associated with excessive exploration and development expenditures explains why buying oil on Wall Street was considerably cheaper than obtaining it by drilling holes in the ground, even after adjustment for differential taxes and regulations on prices of old oil. Wall Street was not undervaluing the oil; it was valuing it correctly, but it was also correctly valuing the wasted expenditures on exploration and development that oil companies were making. When these managerially imposed "taxes" on the reserves were taken into account in stock prices, the net price of oil on Wall Street was low. This low price provided incentives for firms to obtain reserves by purchasing other oil companies and reducing expenditures on non-cost-effective exploration. In this way the capital markets provided incentives for firms to make adjustments that were not effectively motivated by competition in the product markets.

The fact that oil industry managers tried to invest funds outside the industry is also evidence that they could not find enough profitable projects within the industry to use the huge inflow of resources efficiently. Unfortunately these efforts failed. The diversification programs involved purchases of companies in retailing (Marcor by Mobil), manufacturing (Reliance Electric by Exxon), office equipment (Vydec by Exxon), and mining (Kennecott by Sohio, Anaconda Minerals by ARCO, Cyprus Mines by Amoco). These acquisitions turned out to be among the least successful of the last decade, partly because of bad luck (like the collapse of the minerals industry) and partly because of a lack of managerial expertise outside the oil industry. In sum, the stage was set for retrenchment in the oil industry in the early 1980s. Yet the product and capital markets could not force management to change its strategy because the industry's high internal cash flows insulated them from these pressures.

Ultimately the capital markets, through the takeover market, forced managers to respond to the new market conditions. T. Boone Pickens of Mesa Petroleum perceived early that the industry had to be restructured. Partly as a result of Mesa's efforts, firms in the industry were led to merge, and in the merging process they paid out large amounts of capital to shareholders, reduced excess expenditures on exploration and development, and reduced excess capacity in refining and distribution. The result has been large gains in efficiency. Total gains to shareholders in the Gulf/Chevron, Getty/Texaco and Du Pont/Conoco mergers, for example, were over $17 billion. Much more is possible. Jacobs (1986) estimates total potential gains of approximately $200 billion from eliminating the inefficiencies in 98 petroleum firms as of December 1984.

Recent events indicate that actual takeover is not necessary to induce the required adjustments; the Phillips, Unocal and Arco restructurings all involve large stock repurchases with debt and cash, increases in dividend payments, and reductions in exploration and development. They generated increases of 20 percent to 35 percent in market value, totaling $6.6 billion.

Other industries in theory and practice

Acquisitions are one way managers spend cash instead of paying it out to shareholders. Free cash flow theory implies that managers of firms with unused borrowing power and large free cash flows are more likely to undertake low-benefit or even value-destroying mergers. Diversification programs generally fit this category, and the theory predicts that they will generate lower total gains. Thus, some acquisitions are a solution to the agency problem of free cash flow while others, such as diversification programs, are symptoms of those problems.

The major benefit of diversification mergers may be that they involve less waste of resources than if the funds had been invested internally in unprofitable projects. Acquisitions made with cash or securities other than stock involve payout of resources to shareholders of the target company, and this can create net benefits even if the merger creates operating inefficiencies. To illustrate, consider an acquiring firm with substantial free cash flow that the market expects will be invested in low-return projects with a negative net present value of $100 million. If this firm uses up its free cash flow (and thereby prevents its waste) by acquiring another firm that generates zero synergies, the combined market value of the two firms will rise by $100 million. The market value increases because the acquisition eliminates the expenditures on internal investments with negative market value of $100 million.

Because the bidding firms are using funds that would otherwise have been spent on low or negative-return projects, the opportunity cost of the funds is lower than their cost of capital. As a result, they will tend to overpay for the acquisition and thereby transfer some, if not all, of the gains to the target firm's shareholders. In extreme cases they may pay so much that the bidding firm's share price falls, in effect giving the target shareholders more than 100 percent of the gains. These predictions are consistent with the evidence that shareholders of target companies reap most of the gains from a takeover.

Low-return mergers are more likely to occur in industries with large cash flows whose economics dictate retrenchment. Horizontal mergers (where cash or debt is the form of payment) within declining industries will tend to create value because they facilitate exit – the cash or debt payments to shareholders of the target firm cause resources to leave the industry directly. When Socal acquired Gulf in 1984 for $13.2 billion in cash, the oil industry shrank by $13.2 billion as soon as the checks were mailed. Mergers outside the declining industry are more likely to have low or even negative returns because managers are likely to know less about managing such firms. Oil fits this description, and so does tobacco. Tobacco firms face declining demand as a result of changing smoking habits but generate large free cash flow and have been involved in major diversifying acquisitions, as in the $5.6 billion purchase of General Foods by Philip Morris. The theory predicts that these acquisitions in nonrelated industries are more likely to reduce productivity, although the positive total gains to buyers and sellers indicate these negative productivity effects are outweighed by the reductions in waste from internal expansion.

Forest products is another industry with excess capacity and acquisition activity, including the acquisition of St. Regis by Champion International and Crown Zellerbach by Sir James Goldsmith. Horizontal mergers for cash or debt in such an industry generate gains by encouraging exit of resources (through payout) and by substituting existing capacity for investment in new facilities by firms that are short of capacity. Food industry mergers also appear to reflect the expenditure of free cash flow. The industry apparently generates large cash flows with few growth opportunities. It is, therefore, a good candidate for leveraged buy-outs, and these are now occurring; the $6.3 billion Beatrice LBO was, up to 1988, the largest ever.

The broadcasting industry generates rents in the form of large cash flows on its licenses and also fits the theory. Regulation limits the overall supply of licenses and the number owned by a single entity. Thus, profitable internal investments are limited, and the industry's free cash flow has been spent on organizational inefficiencies and diversification programs, making these firms takeover targets. The CBS debt-for-stock exchange and restructuring as a defense against the hostile bid by Turner fits the theory, and so does the $3.5 billion purchase of American Broadcasting Company by Capital Cities Communications. Complete cable systems also create agency problems from free cash flows in the form of rents on their franchises and quasi rents on their installed capital and are likely to generate free cash flow problems. Drug companies with large cash flows from previous successful discoveries and few potential future prospects are also candidates for large agency costs of free cash flow.

Free cash flow theory predicts that many acquirers will tend to perform exceptionally well prior to acquisition. Empirical evidence from studies of both stock prices and accounting data indicates exceptionally good performance for acquirers prior to acquisition (Magenheim and Mueller, 1985; Bradley and Jarrell, 1985). This exceptional stock price performance is often associated with increased free cash flow, which is then used for acquisition programs as observed in the oil industry. Targets will be of two kinds: firms with poor management that have done poorly before the merger, and firms that have done exceptionally well and have large free cash flow that they refuse to pay out to shareholders. Both kinds of targets seem to exist.[12]

The theory predicts that takeovers financed with cash and debt will create larger benefits than those accomplished through exchange of stock. Stock acquisitions do nothing to take up the organizations' financial slack and are therefore unlikely to motivate managers to use resources more efficiently. The recent evidence on takeover premiums is consistent with this prediction.[13]

In the best study to date of the determinants of takeover, Palepu (1986) finds strong evidence consistent with the free cash flow theory of mergers. He studied a sample of 163 firms acquired in the period 1971–9 and a random sample of 256 firms that were not acquired. Both samples were in mining and manufacturing and were listed on either the New York or American stock exchange. He finds that firms with a mismatch between growth and resources are more likely to be taken over. These are firms with high growth (measured by average sales growth), low liquidity (measured by the ratio of liquid assets to total assets) and high leverage, and firms with low growth, high liquidity, and low leverage. He also finds that poor prior performance (measured by the net of market returns in the four years before the acquisition) is significantly related to the probability of takeover and, interestingly, that accounting measures of past performance such as return on equity are unrelated to the probability of takeover.

Free cash flow is only one of the many factors that go into a takeover decision. But the evidence indicates that it is an important factor and provides a useful perspective on the conflict.

Controversial Issues from an Agency Perspective

High-yield, non-investment grade bonds: "junk" bonds

The past several years have witnessed a major innovation in the financial markets – the establishment of active markets in high-yield bonds. These bonds, rated below investment grade by the bond-rating agencies, are frequently referred to as junk bonds, a disparaging term that bears no relation to their pedigree. High-yield bonds are best viewed as commercial loans that can be resold in secondary markets. They are further evidence of the securitization that has converted formerly illiquid financial claims such as mortgages into marketable claims. Total publicly held high-yield bonds have risen from $7 billion in 1970 to $125 billion in 1986, or 23 percent of the total corporate bond market (Taggart, 1986; Drexel Burnham Lambert, 1987). By traditional standards they are more risky than investment-grade bonds and therefore carry interest rates 3 to 5 percentage points higher than the yields on government bonds of comparable maturity. In an early study, Blume and Keim (1984) find that the default rates on these bonds have been low and the realized returns have been disproportionately higher than their risk.

High-yield bonds have been attacked by those who wish to inhibit their use, particularly in the financing of takeover bids. However, companies commonly raise funds to finance ventures by selling claims to be paid from the proceeds of the venture; this is the essence of debt or stock issues used to finance new ventures. High-yield bonds used in takeovers work similarly. The bonds provide a claim on the proceeds of the venture, using the assets and cash flows of the target plus the equity contributed by the acquirer as collateral. Similarly, individuals purchase homes using the home plus their down payment as collateral for the mortgage. The structure of this contract offers nothing inherently unusual.

Some might argue that the risk of high-yield bonds used in takeover attempts is "too high." But high-yield bonds are less risky by definition than common stock claims on the same venture, since the claims of common stockholders are subordinate to those of the holders of high-yield bonds. Would these same critics argue that the stock claims are too risky and thus should be barred? The risk argument makes logical sense only as an argument that transactions costs associated with bankruptcy or recontracting are too high in these ventures or that the bonds are priced too high and that investors who purchase them will not earn returns high enough to compensate for the risk they are incurring. This overpricing argument makes little sense because there is vast evidence that investors are capable of pricing risks in all sorts of other markets.

In January 1986 the Federal Reserve Board issued a new interpretation of the margin rules that restricts the use of debt in takeovers to 50 percent or less of the purchase price. The rule has had little effect on takeovers because bidders otherwise subject to the constraint have instead used high-yield preferred stock rated below investment grade which is converted to debt after completion of the acquisition or bridge loans. This rule was apparently motivated by the belief that the use of corporate debt has become abnormally and dangerously high and was threatening the economy. This assessment is not consistent with the facts. Table 2.2 presents measures of debt use by nonfinancial corporations in the United States. The debt–equity ratio is measured relative to three bases: market value of equity, estimated current asset value of equity, and accounting book value of equity measured at historical cost.

Although debt-equity ratios were higher in 1985 than in 1961, they were not at record levels. The book value debt-equity ratio reached a high of 81.4 percent in 1984 but declined to 78 percent in 1985. Debt–equity ratios measured on a historical cost

Table 2.2 Debt-to-equity ratios: non-financial corporations

Year	Book value	Current value	Market value
1961	57.1%	41.1%	38.5%
1962	58.2	42.5	45.6
1963	59.6	44.5	41.7
1964	59.9	45.4	39.8
1965	61.1	46.5	40.0
1966	62.7	47.4	48.4
1967	64.7	48.7	41.3
1968	67.2	50.5	40.2
1969	68.1	50.3	50.3
1970	70.5	50.7	54.7
1971	70.4	50.7	50.0
1972	70.2	50.3	48.1
1973	70.9	48.9	67.7
1974	70.2	43.9	105.2
1975	66.7	41.6	79.5
1976	65.6	41.1	74.2
1977	67.7	41.4	87.6
1978	69.1	41.1	94.8
1979	69.9	39.9	88.7
1980	68.3	37.8	70.0
1981	71.0	38.3	82.7
1982	74.3	40.0	77.7
1983	73.0	40.6	69.2
1984	81.4	46.1	80.5
1985	78.0	46.5	60.8

Source: Federal Reserve Board (1986)

basis are relatively high because of the previous decade of inflation. Maintenance of the same inflation-adjusted debt ratios in time of inflation implies that the book value ratio must rise because the current value of assets in the denominator of the inflation-adjusted ratio is rising. The current value ratio, which takes account of inflation, fell from 50.7 percent in 1970 to 46.5 percent in 1985. The market-value ratio rose from 54.7 percent in 1970 to 80.5 percent in 1984 and plummeted to 60.8 percent in 1985. The 1985 market-value ratio was 45 percentage points below its 1974 peak of 105.2 percent. Thus, the Federal Reserve System's own data are inconsistent with the reasons given for its restrictions on the use of debt.

High-yield bonds were first used in a takeover bid in 1984 and were involved in relatively few bids in total. In 1984, only about 12 percent of the $14.3 billion of new high-yield debt was associated with mergers and acquisitions. In 1985, 26 percent of the $14.7 billion of new high-yield debt was used in acquisitions.[14] According to *Mergers & Acquisitions*, 1986 acquisition-related high-yield debt still represents less than one of every 12 dollars in acquisition value. Nevertheless, high-yield bonds are an important innovation in the takeover field because they help eliminate size as a deterrent to takeover. They have been particularly influential in helping to bring about reorganizations in the oil industry.

Historical default rates on high-yield bonds have been low, but many of the bonds are so new that the experience could prove to be different in the next downturn. Various opponents (including executives who desire protection from the takeover market and members of the financial community, such as commercial banks and insurance companies, who want to restrict competition from this new financing vehicle) have backed regulations and legislation to restrict the issuance of high-yield bonds, to penalize their tax status, and to restrict their holding by thrifts, which can now buy them as substitutes for the issuance of nonmarketable commercial loans. These proposals are premature, to say the least.

Severance contracts: "golden parachutes"

The increasing sophistication of takeover experts and the availability of high-yield bond financing for profitable takeover ventures means that the largest of the Fortune 500 companies are now potentially subject to takeover; mere size is no longer an effective defense. This susceptibility to takeover has created a new contracting environment for top-level managers. Roughly 50 percent of the top level managers of target firms are gone within three years of acquisition – either hostile or voluntary. Many managers are legitimately anxious, and it will take time for the system to work out an appropriate set of practices and contracts reflecting the risks and rewards of the new environment.

Unfortunately, a major component of the solution to the conflict of interest between shareholders and managers has been vastly misunderstood. I am referring to severance contracts that compensate managers for the loss of their jobs in the event of a change in control. These have been popularly labeled "golden parachutes."

These control-related contracts are beneficial when correctly implemented, because they help reduce the conflict of interest between shareholders and managers at times of takeover and therefore make it more likely that the productive gains stemming from changes in control will be realized. The evidence indicates that stock prices of firms that adopt severance-related compensation contracts for managers on average rise about 3 percent when adoption of the contracts is announced (Lambert and Larcker, 1985). There is no easy way to tell what proportion of the effect is due to the market interpreting the announcement as a signal that a takeover bid is more likely and what proportion is due to the reduction in conflict between managers and shareholders.

At times of takeover, shareholders are implicitly asking the top-level managers of their firm to negotiate a deal for them that frequently involves the imposition of large personal costs on the managers and their families. These involve moving costs, the loss of position, power and prestige, and even the loss of their jobs. Shareholders are asking the very people who are most likely to have invested considerable time and energy (in some cases a life's work) in building a successful organization to negotiate its sale and the possible redirection of its resources.

It is important to confront these conflicts and to structure contracts with managers to reduce them. It would make no sense to hire a realtor to sell your house and then penalize him for doing so. Yet that is the implication of many of the emotional reactions to control-related severance contracts. The restrictions and tax penalties imposed on these severance payments by the Deficit Reduction Act of 1984 are unwise interferences in the contracting freedoms of shareholders and managers and should be eliminated.

Golden parachutes can be used to restrict takeovers and to entrench managers at the expense of shareholders. The key to deciding whether a contract is well-designed is whether it helps solve the conflict-of-interest problem between shareholders and managers. Solving this problem requires extending control-related severance contracts beyond the chief executive to those members of the top-level management team who must play an important role in negotiating and implementing any transfer of control. Contracts that award severance contracts to substantial numbers of managers beyond this group are unlikely to be in the shareholders' interest. Beneficial Corp. awarded such contracts to over 200 of its managers (Morrison, 1982). These are likely to be difficult to justify as in the shareholders' interests.

Severance-related compensation contracts are particularly important in situations where it is optimal for managers to invest in organization-specific human capital; that is, in skills and knowledge that have little or no value in other organizations. Managers will not so invest where the likelihood is high that their investment will be eliminated by an unexpected transfer of control and the loss of their jobs. In such situations, the firm will have to pay for all costs associated with the creation of such organization-specific human capital, and it will be more costly for the firm to attract and retain highly talented managers when they have better opportunities elsewhere. In addition, contracts that award excessive severance compensation to the appropriate group of managers will tend to motivate managers to sell the firm at too low a price.

No simple rules can be specified that will easily prevent the misuse of golden parachutes because the appropriate solution will depend on many factors that are specific to each situation (like the amount of stock held by the managers and the optimal amount of investment in organization-specific human capital). In general, contracts that award inappropriately high payments to an excessively large group will reduce efficiency and harm shareholders by raising the cost of acquisition and by transferring wealth from shareholders to managers. The generally appropriate solution is to make the control-related severance contracts pay off in a way that is tied to the premium earned by the stockholders. Stock options or restricted stock appreciation rights that pay off only in the event of a change in control are two options that have some of the appropriate properties. In general, policies that encourage increased stock ownership by managers and the board of directors will provide incentives that will tend to reduce the conflicts of interests with managers.

Targeted repurchases: "greenmail"

Most proposals to restrict or prohibit targeted repurchases (transactions pejoratively labeled "greenmail") are nothing more than antitakeover proposals in disguise. Greenmail is actually a targeted repurchase, an offer by management to repurchase the shares of a subset of shareholders at a premium, an offer not made to other shareholders. Greenmail is an appellation that suggests blackmail; yet the only effective threat possessed by a greenmailer is the right to offer to purchase stock from shareholders at a substantial premium. The "damage" to shareholders caused by this action is difficult to find. Those who propose to "protect" shareholders by paying greenmail hide this fact behind emotional language designed to mislead. But management can easily prohibit greenmail without legislation: it need only announce a policy that prohibits the board or management from making such payments.

The ease with which managers can prevent targeted repurchases makes it clear that the problem lies with managers who use such payments to protect themselves from competition in the market for corporate control. Three careful studies of these transactions indicate that, when measured from the initial toehold purchase to the final repurchase of the shares, the stock price of target firms rises (Holderness and Sheehan, 1985; Mikkelson and Ruback 1985, 1986). Therefore, shareholders are benefited, not harmed, by the whole sequence of events. However, when greenmail is used to buy off an acquirer who has made an offer for the firm, shareholders are harmed by the loss of the takeover premium. There is some indication that the stock price increases represent the expectation of future takeover premiums in firms in which the targeted repurchase was not sufficient to prevent ultimate takeover of the firm (see Mikkelson and Ruback, 1986). If so, then, as in the final defeat of tender offers found by Bradley, Desai and Kim (1983), all premiums are lost to shareholders in firms for which the repurchase and associated standstill agreements successfully lock up the firm, preventing any voluntary reorganization.

Problems in the Delaware court: "poison pills"

Delaware courts have created over the years a highly productive fabric of corporate law that has benefited the nation. The court is having difficulty, however, sorting out the complex issues it faces in the takeover area. The result has been a confusing set of decisions that, in contrast to much of the court's previous history, appears to make little economic sense.[15]

One key case involved a unilateral decision from the board of directors of Household International to change the nature of the contractual relationship with Household's shareholders in a fundamental way. Effectively, the board restricted the alienability of the common stock by prohibiting shareholders from selling their shares, without permission of the board, into a control transaction leading to merger at a premium over market value lower than about $6 billion. Since Household had a market value of about $2 billion at the time, this step prevented its shareholders from accepting any premium less than 200 percent – more than four times the average takeover premium of 50 percent common in recent times. This decision is difficult to justify as in the shareholders' interests, but the Delaware Supreme Court upheld in November 1985 the right of the board to take such action.

The Delaware court's model of the corporation is founded in the business judgment rule – the legal doctrine that holds that unless explicit evidence of fraud or self-dealing exists the board of directors is presumed to be acting in the interests of the shareholders. In particular, the board is presumed to act altruistically and never out of incentives to preserve the interests of managers or their own positions as board members.

The altruistic model of the board that is the implicit foundation of the business judgment rule is obviously incorrect as a description of human behavior. But in spite of its falsity, the altruistic model has been sufficiently robust to yield good law for a wide range of cases for many years. Alternative agency models of the

Good institutional detail on US Market

rights to hire, fire, and set the compensation of the agent (Fama and Jensen, 1985). If the principal were to delegate the control rights to the agent, the agent could not be fired and would have the right to set his own compensation. In this circumstance the agent would become the effective owner of the decision rights (although he probably could not alienate them) and could be expected to use them in his own interests.

If the business judgment rule is applied to conflicts over control rights between principals and agents, the courts are effectively giving the agent the right to change the control rights unilaterally. In the long run, this interpretation of the contract will destroy the possibility of such cooperative arrangements, because it will leave principals with few effective rights.

The courts have applied the business judgment rule to conflicts between management and shareholders over the issuance of poison pill preferred stock, poison pill rights, and discriminatory targeted repurchases, and have given managers and boards the rights to use these devices.[17] Poison pill securities change fundamental aspects of the corporate rules that govern the relationship between shareholders, managers, and the board of directors when a control-related event occurs. They are called "poison pills" because they alter the company to make it indigestible to an acquirer. In doing so, the courts are essentially giving the agents (managers and the board) the right to change unilaterally critical control aspects of the contract, in particular, the right to prevent the firing of the agents.

The Delaware court decision upholding the decision of the board of Household International has unleashed a flood of poison pill adoptions by American corporations. Ryngaert (forthcoming) and Malatesta and Walkling (forthcoming) study the effects of over 300 of these plans adopted primarily in the period since the *Household* and *Unocal* decisions. They find statistically significant negative stock price effects on the announcement of the adoption of the plans; they find also that the plans tend to be implemented in firms in which managers own relatively little of their firm's stock. Malatesta and Walkling also find that firms adopting such plans are significantly less profitable than other firms in their industries in the year prior to adoption.

The court has erred in allowing the Household board, under the business judgment rule, to make the fundamental change in the structure of the organization implied by the rights issue without vote of its shareholders. Several other poison pill cases have been heard by the courts with similar outcomes, but one New Jersey and two New York courts have recently ruled against poison pills that substantially interfere with the voting rights of large-block shareholders.[18] An Illinois district court recently voided a poison pill (affirmed by the Seventh Circuit Court of Appeals) and two weeks later approved a new pill issued by the same company.[19]

The problem with these special securities and the provision they contain is not with their appropriateness (some might well be desirable), but with the manner in which they are being adopted; that is, without approval by shareholders. Boards of directors show little inclination to refer such issues to shareholders.

The continued application of the business judgment rule to conflicts over control has far-reaching consequences. If the current trend continues, this process will erode the limits to judicial interference in the management of corporations historically provided by the business judgment rule and severely cripple the corporation in the competition for survival. Indeed, the protection afforded managers by the business judgment rule is already eroding.[20] The court seems to be imposing a higher standard on corporations that adopt a poison pill. This erosion of the business judgment rule appears to be motivated by the court's understanding that the pill gives management and the board great power. So the court is brought into the business of second-guessing managers' business decisions. The court currently seems to be inclined to give this scrutiny only to control transactions.

I believe that this erosion of the business judgment rule will be checked because the court will recognize the problems with its current approach. The easiest solution to the problem is for the court to deny protection under the business judgment rule to managerial decisions on control issues unless those decisions have been ratified by shareholder vote.[21]

SEC 13d disclosure rules and the creation of externalities

It has become popular to argue there is too much takeover activity. Yet the opposite is most likely true because of free-riding problems caused by the current regulations that require disclosure of holdings and intentions of the purchaser in SEC 13d reports.[22] These reports must be filed within 10 days of acquisition of 5 percent or more of a company's shares and must disclose the number of shares owned, the identity of the owner, and the purpose of the acquisition. Current rules allow the acquiring firm to buy as many additional shares as it can in the 10-day window between the time the 5 percent filing barrier is reached and the time of filing. This rule allows buyers to acquire shares that average 13.9 percent of the target firm.[23]

Since market prices adjust to the expected value of the takeover bid immediately after the 13d announcement, most of the acquirer's profits are made almost entirely on the difference between the price paid for the shares purchased prior to the filing of the 13d and their value after the acquisition. This drives a wedge, however, between the private benefits earned by the acquirer and the total social benefits of the acquisition; the acquirer pays 100 percent of the acquisition costs and, on average, captures less than 14 percent of the benefits. The remaining benefits go to the other shareholders. The activities of Mesa Petroleum, for example, have yielded benefits to the shareholders of companies involved in its transactions that exceed $13 billion. Mesa itself has paid hundreds of millions of dollars in financing, legal, and investment banking fees and borne all the risks of loss. Yet it has earned only about $750 million on these transactions.

Consider an acquisition that promises total expected gains of $100 million. If the acquirer expects to capture only $14 million of this amount if the bid is successful, the bid will occur only if the legal, investment banking, and other costs (including the required risk premium) are less than $14 million. All such acquisitions that are expected to cost more than this will not be made, and shareholders and society are thus denied the benefits of those reorganizations. If the costs, for example, are expected to be $15 million, the bid will not occur and the $85 million benefit will not be realized.

The solution to this problem is to abolish the SEC 13d reporting requirement or to increase significantly the trigger point from the current 5 percent level. Unfortunately, current proposals in Congress to reduce the 10-day window to one or two days and to reduce the trigger point to 1 percent or 2 percent are moves in exactly the wrong direction. It is clear why antitakeover forces want such restrictive legislation. But the effect of this proposal is equivalent to that of an anti-patent law which requires public disclosure of all inventions and denies the inventor all but a one or two percent property right in the proceeds of his or her invention. Shareholders will clearly be harmed by such regulation.

Conclusion

Although economic analysis and the evidence indicate that the market for corporate control is benefiting shareholders, society, and the corporation as an organizational form, it is also making life more uncomfortable for top level executives. This discomfort is creating strong pressures at both the state and federal levels for restrictions that will seriously cripple the working of this market. In 1985, 1986 and 1987 there were dozens of bills in the congressional hopper proposing various restrictions on the market for corporate control. Others proposed major new restrictions on share ownership and financial instruments. Within the past several years the legislatures of numerous states have passed antitakeover laws and the Supreme Court has recently upheld the Indiana law that prohibits someone who purchases 20 percent or more of a firm's shares without permission of the board of directors from voting those shares unless such approval is granted by a majority vote of disinterested shareholders. The New York state law bars the purchaser of even 100 percent of a firm's shares from doing anything with the assets for five years unless permission of the incumbent board is obtained.

This political activity is another example of special interests using the democratic political system to change the rules of the game to benefit themselves at the expense of society as a whole. In this case, the special interests are top level corporate managers and other groups who stand to lose from competition in the market for corporate control. If these special interests are successful, the results will be a reduction in efficiency and a significant weakening of the corporation as an organizational form.

Notes

This research is supported by the Division of Research, Harvard Business School, and the Managerial Economics Research Center, University of Rochester. I am grateful for the research assistance of Michael Stevenson and the helpful comments of Sidney Davidson, Harry DeAngelo, Jay Light, Robert Kaplan, Nancy Macmillan, David Mullins, Susan Rose-Ackerman, Richard Ruback, Carl Shapiro, Timothy Taylor, Wolf Weinhold, Toni Wolcott, and, especially, Armen Alchian. The analysis here draws heavily on that in Jensen (1986).

1   Estimated from data in Grimm (1986). Grimm provides total dollar values for all M&A deals for which there are publicly announced prices amounting to $500,000 or 10 percent of the firm in which at least one of the firms was a US company. Grimm also counts in its numerical totals deals with no publicly announced prices that it believes satisfy this criteria. I assumed that the deals with no announced prices were on average equal to 20 percent of the size of the announced transactions. (The symbol "$" refers to US dollars throughout, unless otherwise specified.)

2   Total dividend payments by the corporate sector, unadjusted for inflation, are given in Weston (1986, p. 649). I extended these estimates to 1986.

3   For an introduction to the literature and empirical evidence on the theory of efficient markets, see Elton and Gruber (1984), chapter 15, p. 375ff. and the 167 studies referenced in the bibliography. For some anomalous evidence on market efficiency see Jensen (1978), Shiller (1981). Merton (1985) provides an excellent discussion of the current state of the efficient market hypothesis.

4   The "R&D Scoreboard" is an annual survey covering companies that account for 95 percent of total private-sector R&D expenditures. The three years referenced here can be found under "R&D Scoreboard" (1985, 1986, 1987) in the reference list. In 1984 the survey covered 820 companies; in 1985, it covered 844 companies; in 1986, it covered 859 companies.

5   This discussion is based on Jensen (1986).

6   Gordon Donaldson (1984), in a detailed study of twelve large Fortune 500 firms, concludes that managers of these firms were not driven by maximization of the value of the

firm, but rather by the maximization of "corporate wealth." He defines corporate wealth (p. 3, emphasis in original) as "*the aggregate purchasing power available to management for strategic purposes during any given planning period* . . . this wealth consists of the stocks and flows of cash and cash equivalents (primarily credit) that management can use at its discretion to implement decisions involving the control of goods and services." He continues (p. 22), "In practical terms it is cash, credit, and other corporate purchasing power by which management commands goods and services."

7 Where growth is measured by increases in sales (Murphy, 1985). This positive relation-ship between compensation and sales growth need not imply, although it is consistent with, causality.

8 Literally, principal and interest payments are substitutes for dividends. Dividends and debt are not perfect substitutes, however, because interest is tax-deductible at the corporate level and dividends are not.

9 Rozeff (1982) and Easterbrook (1984a) argue that regular dividend payments can be effective in reducing agency costs with managers by assuring that managers are forced more frequently to subject themselves and their policies to the discipline of the capital markets when they acquire capital.

10 Interestingly, Graham and Dodd (1951, chapters 32, 34, and 36) place great importance on the dividend payout in their famous valuation formula $V = M(D + .33E)$. V is value, M is the earnings multiplier when the dividend payout rate is a "normal two-thirds of earnings," D is the expected dividend, and E is expected earnings. In their formula, dividends are valued at three times the rate of retained earnings – a proposition that has puzzled many students of modern finance (at least of my vintage). The agency cost of free cash flow that leads to over-retention and waste of shareholder resources is consistent with the deep suspicion with which Graham and Dodd viewed the lack of payout. Their discussion (chapter 34) reflects a belief in the tenuous nature of the future benefits of such retention. Although they do not couch the issues in terms of the conflict between managers and shareholders, the free cash flow theory explicated here implies that their beliefs, sometimes characterized as a conviction that "a bird in the hand is worth two in the bush," were perhaps well founded.

11 More detailed analysis of this point is available in Jensen (1987).

12 Asquith (1983) finds evidence of below-normal stock price performance for 302 target firms in the 400 days before 20 days prior to the takeover bid. Mandelker (1974) finds negative abnormal performance for target firms in the period from 40 months before until 9 months before the outcome of the merger bid is known. Langtieg (1978) reports significant negative returns in the period from 72 months before until 19 months before the outcome date, but positive abnormal returns in the 19 months preceding the merger date.

13 See Wansley, Lane and Yang (1987) who find higher returns to targets and to bidders in cash transactions, and Wansley and Fayez (1986).

14 Source: Drexel Burnham Lambert, private correspondence.

15 See, for example, *Moran* v. *Household Intl., Inc.*, 490 A.2d 1059 (Del. Ch. 1985) aff'd 500 A.2d 1346 (Del. 1985) (upholding poison pill rights issue), *Smith* v. *Van Gorkom*, 488 A.2d 858, (holding board liable for damages in sale of firm at substantial premium over market price), *Unocal* v. *Mesa*, 493 A.2d 946, 954 (Del. 1985) (allowing discriminatory targeted repurchase that confiscates wealth of largest shareholder), *Revlon Inc.* v. *MacAndrews & Forbes Holdings Inc.* 506 A.2d 173, (Del. 1986) (invalidation of Revlon's lockup sale of a prime division to Forstmann Little at a below-market price).

16   Easterbrook (1984b) and Jensen and Smith (1985) provide summaries of much of the
     work in the area.
17   *Moran* v. *Household Intl.*, and *Unocal* v. *Mesa*. Full citations provided in note 15.
18   *Ministar Acquiring Corp.* v. *AMF Inc.*, 621 Fed Sup 1252. Dis NY, 1985 *Unilever Acquisi-
     tion Corp.* v. *Richardson-Vicks, Inc.*, 618 Fed Supp 407. So Dist. NY 1985, *Asarco Inc.* v.
     M.R.H. Holmes a Court, 611 Fed Sup 468. Dist. Ct. of NJ, 1985, and *Dynamics Corp. of
     America* v. *CTS Corporation*.
19   *Dynamics Corp. of America* v. *CTS Corp.*, *et al.* US District Court, Northern District of
     Illinois, Eastern Division, No. 86 C 1624, (April 17, 1986), affirmed Seventh Circuit
     Court of Appeals Nos. 86-1601, 86-1608, and *Dynamics Corp. of America* v. *CTS Corp.*,
     et al. (May 3, 1986).
20   See *Revlon Inc.* v. *MacAndrews & Forbes Holdings Inc.*, 506 A.2nd 173, 180 (Del. 1986), in
     which the court seems to be reviewing very detailed aspects of the board's decision leading
     to the invalidation of Revlon's lockup sale of a prime division to Forstmann Little at a
     below-market price. The Court of Appeals for the Second Circuit in *Hanson Trust* v. *SCM
     Corp.*, (Nos. 85-7951, 85-7953, 2d Cir. Jan. 6, 1986) (written opinion filed Jan. 6, 1986),
     enjoined lockups given by SCM defending itself from takeover by Hanson Trust. See also
     Herzel, Colling, and Carlson (1986) for detailed analysis of these cases and lockups in
     general.
21   See Koleman (1985) and Investor Responsibility Research Center (1985).
22   Grossman and Hart (1980) present an extensive discussion of the free-riding problem in
     corporate takeovers.
23   Mikkelson and Ruback (1985) show that average holdings for 397 initial 13d filings in
     1928–80 is 20.9 percent. However, 120 of these 13ds (with average holdings of 37
     percent) were filed simultaneously with announcement of a takeover. Eliminating these
     yields estimated average holdings for non-takeover filings of 13.9 percent.

References

Aharony, Joseph, and Itzhak Swary, 1980, Quarterly Dividend and Earnings Announcements
     and Stockholder's Returns: An Empirical Analysis, *Journal of Finance* 35, 1–12.
Asquith, Paul R., 1983, Merger Bids, Uncertainty, and Stockholders Returns, *Journal of
     Financial Economics* 11, 51–83.
Asquith, Paul R., Robert F. Bruner, and David Mullins, 1987, Merger Returns and the Form
     of Financing, unpublished working paper, Harvard Business School, June.
Baker, George, 1986, Compensation and Hierarchies, Harvard Business School, January.
Blume, Marshall E. and Donald B. Keim, 1984, Risk and Return Characteristics of Lower-
     Grade Bonds, The Wharton School of Finance, December.
Bradley, Michael, Anand Desai, and E. Han Kim, 1983, The Rationale Behind Interfirm
     Tender Offers: Information or Synergy? *Journal of Financial Economics* 11, April, 183–206.
Bradley, Michael, and Gregg Jarrell, 1985, Evidence on Gains from Mergers and Takeovers,
     presented at the Conference on Takeovers and Contests for Corporate Control, Columbia
     University, November.
Bruner, Robert F., 1985, The Use of Excess Cash and Debt Capacity as a Motive for Merger,
     Colgate Darden Graduate School of Business, December.
——, 1985, Cash Flow: The Top 200, *Dun's Business Month*, July, 44–50.

Charest, Guy, 1978, Dividend Information, Stock Returns, and Market Efficiency – II, *Journal of Financial Economics* 6, 297–330.

DeAngelo, Harry and Linda DeAngelo, 1986, Management Buyouts of Publicly Traded Corporations, In Copeland, Thomas E., ed., *Modern Finance and Industrial Economics: Papers in Honor of J. Fred Weston.* Oxford, England: Basil Blackwell.

Donaldson, Gordon, 1984, *Managing Corporate Wealth.* New York: Praeger.

Drexel Burnham Lambert, 1987, The Case for High Yield Bonds, company report, 4–5.

Easterbrook, F. H., 1984a, Two Agency-Cost Explanations of Dividends, *American Economic Review* 74, 650–9.

Easterbrook, F. H., 1984b, Managers' Discretion and Investors' Welfare: Theories and Evidence, *Delaware Journal of Corporate Law* 9, no. 3, 540–71.

Elton, E. and M. Gruber, 1984, *Modern Portfolio Theory and Investment Analysis.* New York: Wiley.

Fama, Eugene F. and Michael C. Jensen, 1985, Organizational Forms and Investment Decisions, *Journal of Law and Economics* 14, 101–19.

Federal Reserve Board, 1986, Balance Sheets, Flow of Funds. Washington, D.C.: GPO, October.

Graham, Benjamin and David L. Dodd, 1951, *Security Analysis: Principles and Technique.* New York: McGraw-Hill.

Grimm, W. T., 1984, 1985, 1986, *Mergerstat Review.* Annual editions.

Grossman, S. and Oliver Hart, 1980, Takeover Bids, the Free-Rider Problem, and the Theory of the Corporation, *Bell Journal of Economics*, Spring, 42–64.

Hall, Bronwyn, 1987, The Effect of Takeover Activity on Corporate Research and Development, presented at NBER Conference on the Effects of Mergers & Acquisitions, February.

Herzel, Leo, Dale E. Colling, and James B. Carlson, 1986, Misunderstanding Lockups, *Securities Regulation*, September, 150–80.

Holderness, Clifford G. and Dennis P. Sheehan, 1985, Raiders or Saviors? The Evidence of Six Controversial Investors, *Journal of Financial Economics* 14, December, 555–79.

Investor Responsibility Research Center, Inc., 1985, Voting by Institutional Investors on Corporate Governance Questions, Proxy Season, Corporate Governance Service, 19–25.

Jacobs, E. Allen, 1986, The Agency Cost of Corporate Control: The Petroleum Industry, Massachusetts Institute of Technology, March.

Jensen, Michael C., ed., 1978, Symposium on Some Anomalous Evidence on Market Efficiency, *Journal of Financial Economics* 6, June/September, 95–101.

Jensen, Michael C., 1984, Takeovers: Folklore and Science, *Harvard Business Review*, Nov.–Dec., 109–21.

Jensen, Michael C., 1986, Agency Costs of Free Cash Flow, Corporate Finance and Takeovers, *American Economic Review* 76, May, 323–9.

Jensen, Michael C., 1986, The Takeover Controversy: Analysis and Evidence. In Coffee, John, Louis Lowenstein, and Susan Rose-Ackerman, eds., *Takeovers and Contests for Corporate Control.* New York: Oxford University Press, 1987. Also published in slightly abridged form in the *Midland Corporate Finance Journal*, Summer.

Jensen, Michael C. and William H. Meckling, 1976, Theory of the Firm: Managerial Behavior, Agency Costs and Ownership Structure, *Journal of Financial Economics* 3, 305–60.

Jensen, Michael C. and R. Ruback, 1983, The Market for Corporate Control: The Scientific Evidence, *Journal of Financial Economics* 11, April, 5–50.

Jensen, Michael C. and Clifford Smith, Jr., 1985, Stockholder, Manager, and Creditor Interests: Applications of Agency Theory. In Altman, Edward I., and Marti G. Subrahmanyam, eds., *Recent Advances in Corporate Finance*. Homewood, Illinois: Irwin, pp. 93–131.

Kaplan, Steven, 1987, Management Buyouts: Efficiency Gains or Value Transfers, manuscript, Harvard Business School, November.

Koleman, Joe, 1985, The Proxy Pressure on Pension Fund Managers, *Institutional Investor*, July, 145–7.

Lambert, R. and D. Larcker, 1985, Golden Parachutes, Executive Decision-Making, and Shareholder Wealth, *Journal of Accounting and Economics 7*, April, 179–204.

Langtieg, T. C., 1978, An Application of a Three-Factor Performance Index to Measure Stockholder Gains from Merger, *Journal of Financial Economics* 6, December, 365–84.

Magenheim, Ellen B. and Dennis Mueller, 1985, On Measuring the Effect of Acquisitions on Acquiring Firm Shareholders, or, Are Acquiring Firm Shareholders Better Off After an Acquisition Than They Were Before? Presented at the Conference on Takeovers and Contests for Corporate Control, Columbia University, November.

Malatesta, Paul H. and Ralph A. Walkling, The Impact of Poison Pill Securities on Stockholder Wealth, *Journal of Financial Economics*, forthcoming.

Mandelker, Gershon, 1974, Risk and Return: The Case of Merging Firms, *Journal of Financial Economics* 1, December, 303–36.

McConnell, J. and C. Muscarella, 1985, Corporate Capital Expenditure Decisions and the Market Value of the Firm, *Journal of Financial Economics*, September, 399–422.

——, 1987, *Mergers and Acquisitions* 21, May–June, 16.

Merton, Robert C., 1985, On the Current State of the Stock Market Rationality Hypothesis, Working Paper No. 1717-85, Sloan School of Management, MIT, October.

Mikkelson, Wayne H. and Richard S. Ruback, 1985, An Empirical Analysis of the Interfirm Equity Investment Process, *Journal of Financial Economics* 14, December, 523–53.

Mikkelson, Wayne H. and Richard S. Ruback, 1986, Targeted Repurchases and Common Stock Returns, manuscript, June.

Morrison, Ann, 1982, Those Executive Bailout Deals, *Fortune*, December 13, 82–7.

Murphy, Kevin J., 1985, Corporate Performance and Managerial Remuneration: An Empirical Analysis, *Journal of Accounting and Economics* 7, April, 11–42.

Palepu, Krishna G., 1986, Predicting Takeover Targets: A Methodological and Empirical Analysis, *Journal of Accounting and Economics* 8, 3–35.

——, 1986, R&D Scoreboard: Now, R&D is Corporate America's Answer to Japan Inc., *Business Week*, June 23.

——, 1985, R&D Scoreboard: Reagan & Foreign Rivalry Light a Fire Under Spending, *Business Week*, July 8, 86–7.

——, 1987, R&D Scoreboard: Research Spending is Building Up to a Letdown, *Business Week*, June 23, 139–40.

Roll, Richard, 1987, Empirical Evidence on Takeover Activity and Shareholder Wealth. In Coffee, John, Louis Lowenstein, and Susan Rose-Ackerman, eds., *Takeovers and Contests for Corporate Control*, New York: Oxford University Press.

Rozeff, M., 1982, Growth, Beta and Agency Costs as Determinants of Dividend Payout Ratios, *Journal of Financial Research* 5, 249–59.

Ryngaert, Michael, The Effect of Poison Pill Securities on Shareholder Wealth, *Journal of Financial Economics*, forthcoming.

Schipper, Katherine, and Abbie Smith, 1986, Corporate Income Tax Effects of Management Buyouts, unpublished manuscript, University of Chicago, July.

Shiller, Robert J., 1981, Do Stock Prices Move Too Much to be Justified By Subsequent Changes in Dividends? *American Economic Review*, 421–36.

Smith, Clifford W., Jr. and Jerold B. Warner, 1979, On Financial Contracting: An Analysis of Bond Covenants, *Journal of Financial Economics* 7, 117–61.

Taggart, Robert A., 1986, The Growth of the "Junk" Bond Market and Its Role in Financing Takeovers, manuscript, Boston University, September.

Wansley, James W. and A. Fayez, 1986, Determinants of Return to Security Holders from Mergers, manuscript, Louisiana State University.

Wansley, James W., William R. Lane, and Ho C. Yang, 1983, Abnormal Returns to Acquired Firms by Type of Acquisition and Method of Payment, *Financial Management* Autumn 12, no. 3, 16–22.

Wansley, James W., William R. Lane, and Ho C. Yang, 1987, Gains to Acquiring Firms in Cash and Securities Transactions, *Financial Review*.

Weston, J. Fred. and Thomas E. Copeland, 1986, *Managerial Finance*. Chicago: Dryden Press, p. 649.

3

The Hubris Hypothesis of Corporate Takeovers

Richard Roll

Finally, knowledge of the source of takeover gains still eludes us. [Jensen and Ruback 1983. p. 47]

I   Introduction

Despite many excellent research papers, we still do not fully understand the motives behind mergers and tender offers or whether they bring an increase in aggregate market value. In their comprehensive review article (from which the above quote is taken), Jensen and Ruback (1983) summarize the empirical work presented in over 40 papers. There are many important details in these papers, but Jensen and Ruback interpret them to show overall "that corporate takeovers generate positive gains, that target firm shareholders benefit, and that bidding firm shareholders do not lose" (p. 47).

My purpose here is to suggest a different and less conclusive interpretation of the empirical results. This interpretation may not turn out to be valid, but I hope to show that it has enough plausibility to be at least considered in further investigations. It will be argued here that takeover gains may have been overestimated if they exist at all. If there really are no aggregate gains associated with takeovers, or if they are small, it is not hard to understand why their sources are "elusive."

The mechanism by which takeover attempts are initiated and consummated suggests that at least part of the large price increases observed in target firm shares might represent a simple transfer from the bidding firm, that is, that the observed takeover premium (tender offer or merger price less preannouncement market price of the target firm) overstates the increase in economic value of the corporate combination. To see why this could be the case, let us follow the steps undertaken in a takeover.

First, the bidding firm identifies a potential target firm.

Second, a "valuation" of the equity of the target is undertaken. In some cases this may include nonpublic information. The valuation definitely would include, of course, any estimated economies due to synergy and any assessments of weak management etc. that might have caused a discount in the target's current market price.

Third, the "value" is compared to the current market price. If value is below price, the bid is abandoned. If value exceeds price, a bid is made and becomes part of the public record. The bid would not generally be the previously determined "value" since it should include provision for rival bids, for future bargaining with the target, and for valuation errors *inter alia*.

The key element in this series of events is the valuation of an asset (the stock) that already has an observable market price. The preexistence of an active market in the identical item being valued distinguishes takeover attempts from other types of bids, such as for oildrilling rights and paintings. These other assets trade infrequently and no two of them are identical. This means that the seller must make his own independent valuation. There is a symmetry between the bidder and the seller in the necessity for valuation.

In takeover attempts, the target firm shareholder may still conduct a valuation, but it has a lower bound, the current market price. The bidder knows for certain that the shareholder will not sell below that; thus when the valuation turns out to be below the market price, no offer is made.

Consider what might happen if there are no potential synergies or other sources of takeover gains but when, nevertheless, some bidding firms believe that such gains exist. The valuation itself can then be considered a random variable whose mean is the target firm's current market price. When the random variable exceeds its mean, an offer is made; otherwise there is no offer. Offers are observed only when the valuation is too high; outcomes in the left tail of the distribution of valuations are never observed. The takeover premium in such a case is simply a random error, a mistake made by the bidding firm. Most important, the observed error is always in the same direction. Corresponding errors in the opposite direction are made in the valuation process, but they do not enter our empirical samples because they are not made public.

If there were no value at all in takeovers, why would firms make bids in the first place? They should realize that any bid above the market price represents an error. This latter logic is alluring because market prices do seem to reflect rational behavior. But we must keep in mind that prices are averages. There is no evidence to indicate that every individual behaves as if he were the rational economic human being whose behavior seems revealed by the behavior of market prices. We may argue that markets behave as if they were populated by rational beings. But a market actually populated by rational beings is observationally equivalent to a market characterized by grossly irrational individual behavior that cancels out in the aggregate, leaving the trace of the only systematic behavioral component, the small thread of rationality that all individuals have in common. Indeed, one possible definition of irrational or aberrant behavior is independence across individuals (and thus disappearance from view under aggregation).

Psychologists are constantly bombarding economists with empirical evidence that individuals do not always make rational decisions under uncertainty. For example, see Oskamp (1965), Tversky and Kanhneman (1981), and Kahneman, Slovic, and Tversky (1982). Among psychologists, economists have a reputation for arrogance mainly because this evidence is ignored; but psychologists seem not to appreciate that economists disregard the evidence on individual decision making because it usually has little predictive content for market behavior. Corporate takeovers are, I believe, one area of research in which this usually valid reaction of economists should be abandoned; takeovers reflect individual decisions.

There is little reason to expect that a particular individual bidder will refrain from bidding because he has learned from his own past errors. Although some firms engage in many acquisitions, the average individual bidder/manager has the opportunity to make only a few takeover offers during his career. He may convince himself that the valuation is right and that the market does not reflect the full economic value of the combined firm. For this reason, the hypothesis being offered in this paper to explain the takeover phenomenon can be termed the "hubris hypothesis." If there actually are no aggregate gains in takeover, the phenomenon depends on the overbearing presumption of bidders that their valuations are correct.

Even if gains do exist for some corporate combinations, at least part of the average observed takeover premium could still be caused by valuation error and hubris. The left tail of the distribution of valuations is truncated by the current market price. To the extent that there are errors in valuation, fewer negative errors will be observed other than positive errors. When gains exist, a smaller fraction of the distribution will be truncated than when there are no gains at all. Nonetheless, truncation will occur in every situation in which the gain is small enough to allow the distribution of valuations to have positive probability below the market price.

Rational bidders will realize that valuations are subject to error and that negative errors are truncated in repeated bids. They will take this into account when making a bid. Takeover attempts are thus analogous to the auctions discussed in bidding theory wherein the competing bidders make public offers. In the takeover situation, the initial bidder is the market, and the initial public offer is the current price. The second bidder is the acquiring firm who, conscious of the "winner's curse," biases his bid downward from his estimate of value. In fact, he frequently abandons the auction altogether, allowing the first bidder to win.

In a standard auction, we would observe all cases, including those in which the initial bid was victorious. Theory predicts that the winning bid is an accurate assessment of value. In takeovers, however, if the initial bid (by the market) wins the auction, we throw away the observation. If all bidders accounted properly for the "winner's curse," there would be no particular bias associated with discarding bids won by the market; but if bidders are infected by hubris, the standard bidding theory conclusion would not be valid. Empirical evidence from repeated sealed bid auctions (Capan, Clapp, and Campbell 1971; and Dougherty and Lohrenz 1976), indicates that bidders do not fully incorporate the winner's curse. Unless there is something curative about the public nature of corporate takeover auctions, we should at least consider the possibility that the same phenomenon exists in them.

The hubris hypothesis is consistent with strong-form market efficiency. Financial markets are assumed to be efficient in that asset prices reflect all information about individual firms. Product and labor markets are assumed efficient in the sense that (*a*) no industrial reorganization can bring gains in an aggregate output at the same cost or reductions in aggregate costs with the same output, and (*b*) management talent is employed in its best alternative use.

Most other explanations of the takeover phenomenon rely on strong-form market inefficiency of at least a temporary duration. Either financial markets are ignorant of relevant information possessed by bidding firms, or product markets are inefficiently organized so that potential synergies, monopolies, or tax savings are being ineffectively exploited (at least temporarily), or labor markets are inefficient because gains could be obtained by replacement of inferior managers. Although perfect strong-form efficiency is unlikely, the concept should serve as a frictionless ideal, the benchmark of comparison by which other degrees of efficiency are measured. This is, I claim, the proper role for the hubris hypothesis of takeovers; it is the null against which other hypotheses of corporate takeovers should be compared.

Section II presents the principal empirical predictions of the hubris hypothesis and discusses supportive and disconfirming empirical results. Section III concludes the paper by summarizing the results and by discussing various objections to the hypothesis.

II   Evidence For and Against the Hubris Hypothesis

If there are absolutely no gains available to corporate takeovers, the hubris hypothesis implies that the average increase in the target firm's market value should then be more than offset by the average decrease in the value of the bidding firm. Takeover expenses would constitute the aggregate net loss. The market price of a target firm should increase when a previously unanticipated bid is announced, and it should decline to the original level or below if the first bid is unsuccessful and if no further bids are received.

Implications for the market price reaction of a bidding firm are somewhat less clear. If we could be sure that (*a*) the bid was unanticipated and (*b*) the bid conveys no information about the bidder other than that it is seeking a combination with a particular target, then the hubris hypothesis would predict the following market price movements in bidding firms:

1)   a price decline on announcement of a bid;
2)   a price increase on abandoning a bid or on losing a bid; and
3)   a price decline on actually winning a bid.

It has been pointed out by several authors, most forcefully by Schipper and Thompson (1983), that condition *a* above is by no means assured in all cases. Bids are not always surprises. As Jensen and Ruback (1983, pp. 18–20) observe, this alone complicates the measurement of bidder firm returns.

The possibility that a bid conveys information about the bidding firm's own operations, that is, violation of condition *b*, is an equally serious problem (cf. Jensen and Ruback 1983, p. 19 and n.14). For example, the market might well interpret a bid as signaling that the bidding firm's immediate past or expected future cash flows are higher than previously estimated, that this has actually prompted the bid, and that, although the takeover itself has a negative value, the combination of takeover and new information is on balance positive.

Similarly, abandoning a previous bid could convey negative information about the bidding firm's ability to pay for the proposed acquisition, perhaps because of negative events in its own operations. Losing a bid to rivals could signal limited resources. These problems of contaminating information make it difficult to interpret bidding firm price movements and to interpret the combined price movements of bidder and target.

A.   *The evidence about target firms*

Let us first examine, therefore, the more straightforward implications of the hubris hypothesis for target firms. Bradley, Desai, and Kim (1983*b*) present results for target firms in tender offers that are consistent with the implications. Target firms display increases in value on the announcement of a tender offer, and they fall back to about the original level if no combination occurs then or later.

A similar pattern is observed in Asquith's (1983) sample of target firms in unsuccessful mergers. These firms were targets in one or more merger bids that were later abandoned and for whom no additional merger bids occurred during the year after the last original bid was withdrawn. The original merger bid announcement was accompanied by a 7.0% average increase in target firm value that appears to be almost entirely reversed within 60 days (fig. 1, p. 62). By the date when the last bid is abandoned, the target's price decline amounts to 8.1% (table 9, p. 81), slightly more than offsetting the original increase.

The result may be partially compromised by the following problem. The "outcome date" of an unsuccessful bid is the withdrawal date of the final offer following which no additional bid is received for 1 year. Thus as of the outcome date the market could not have known for certain that other bids would not arrive. However, if the market had known that no other bids would arrive, the price decline would likely have been ever larger, so perhaps this partial use of hindsight was not material. In summary, target firm share behavior, as presented in Bradley et al. (1983*b*) for tender offers and in Asquith (1983) for mergers, is consistent with the hubris hypothesis.

B.   *The evidence about total gains*

The central prediction of the hubris hypothesis is that the total combined takeover gain to target and bidding firm shareholders is nonpositive. None of the evidence using returns can unambiguously test this prediction for the simple reason that average returns of individual firms do not measure average dollar gains, especially in the typical takeover situation in which the bidding firm is much larger (cf. Jensen and Ruback 1983, p. 22). In some cases, the observed price increase in the target would correspond to such a trivial loss to the bidder that the loss is bound to be hidden in the bid/ask spread and in the noise of daily return volatility.

In an attempt to circumvent the problem that returns cannot measure takeover gains when bidder and target have different sizes, Asquith, Bruner, and Mullins (1983) take the unique approach of regressing the bidder announcement period return on the relative size of target to bidder. They reason that, if acquisitions benefit bidder firms, large acquisitions should show up as having larger return effects on bidder firm returns. They do find this positive relation for bidding firms. The same relation is not significant for target firms, although, as usual, target firms have much larger average returns. The positive relation for bidding firms is consistent with more than one explanation. It is consistent with the bidding firm losing on average, but losing less the larger the target. Perhaps a more accurate valuation is conducted when the stakes are large and this results in a smaller percentage loss to the bidder. Perhaps large targets are less closely held so that the takeover premium can be smaller relative to the preoffer price and still convince shareholders to deliver their shares. Perhaps bidders for larger targets have fewer rivals and can thus get away with a bidder-perceived "bargain."

The absence of any relation for target firms is puzzling under every hypothesis unless the entire gain accrues to the target firm shareholders (and Asquith et al. [1983] interpret their results to indicate that takeover gains are shared). If synergy is the source of gains, for example, target shareholder's returns would increase with the relative size of its bidder-partner.

Several studies have attempted to measure aggregate dollar gains directly. Halpern (1973) finds average market adjusted gains of US$27.35 million in a sample of mergers between New York Stock Exchange listed firms (p. 569); the gain was calculated over a period 7 months prior to the first public announcement of the merger through the merger consummation month. The standard error of this average gain, assuming cross-sectional independence, was $19.7 ($173.2/$\sqrt{77}$ [see table 3, p. 569]). In 53 cases out of 77, there was a dollar gain.

Bradley, Desai, and Kim (1982) present dollar returns for a sample of 162 successful tender offers from 20 days before the announcement until 5 days after completion. The average combined dollar increase in value of bidder plus target was $17 million, but this was not statistically significant. The $17 million gain was divided between a $34 million average gain by targets and a $17 million average loss to bidders. The authors note that the equally weighted average rate of return to bidders is positive, though the dollar change is a loss; they argue that this can be explained by skewness in the distribution of dollar changes.

In a revision of their 1982 paper, Bradley, Desai, and Kim (1983*a*) present slightly different results. The sample is expanded from 162 and 183 tender offer events, although the underlying data base appears to be the same (698 tender offers from

October 1958 to December 1980). The only stated difference in the selection of samples is that the earlier paper excludes offers that are not "control oriented" (cf. Bradley et al. 1982, p. 13; and Bradley et al. 1983*a*, pp. 35–6). This sample change resulted in an average gain to targets of $28.1 million and to bidders to +$5.8 million (table 9). The authors say, however, that "the distributional properties of our dollar gain measures preclude any meaningful inferences about their significance" (p. 58).

Malatesta (1983) examines the combined change in target and bidder firms before, during, and after a merger. Jensen and Ruback summarize Malatesta's results as follows: "Malatesta examines a matched sample of targets and their bidders in 30 successful mergers and finds a significant average increase of $32.4 million ($t = 2.07$) in their combined equity value in the month before and the month of outcome announcement. . . . This evidence indicates that changes in corporate control increase the combined market value" (1983, p. 22).

Malatesta (1983) himself does not reach so definite a conclusion. In fact, his overall interpretation of the evidence is that "the immediate impact of merger *per se* is positive and highly significant for acquired firms but *larger in absolute value and negative* for acquiring firms" (p. 155; emphasis added). Jensen and Ruback were referring to smaller samples of matching pairs. Even for this sample, Malatesta says, the results "provide *weak* evidence that successful resolution of these mergers had a positive impact on combined shareholder wealth" (p. 170; emphasis added). In 2 months culminating in board approval of the merger, the combined gain was positive, but "over the entire interval −60 to 0 [months], the cumulative dollar return is a trivial 0.29 million dollars" (p. 171). Of course, this could be due to selection bias; bidding or acquired firms or both may tend to be involved in mergers after a period of poor performance. According to Asquith's (1983) results, however, this is true only for targets. The opposite is true for bidders; they tend to display superior performance prior to the merger bid announcement. During the culminating merger months, the acquiring firms' gains in Malatesta's sample were not statistically significant (although the acquired firms' were).

Malatesta's month zero is when the board announced merger approval, not when the merger proposal first reached the public. Even if the merger *per se* has no aggregate value, the price reaction on approval could be positive because it signals that court battles, further bids to overcome rivals, and other costly events associated with hostile mergers will not take place in this case, although their possibility was signaled originally by the merger proposal. Malatesta does not present evidence about the dollar reactions of the combined firm on the first announcement of the merger proposal.

Firth (1980) presents the results of a study of takeovers in the United Kingdom. In his sample, target firms gain, and bidding firms lose, both statistically significantly. The average total change in market value of the two firms in a successful combination, from a month prior to the takeover bid through the month of acceptance of the offer, is £ − 36.6 million. No *t*-statistic is given for this number, but we can obtain a rough measure of significance by using the fact that 224 of 434 cases displayed aggregate losses. If these cases were independent, the *t*-statistic that the true proportion of losing takeovers is greater than 50% is about 0.67.

The relative division of losses was examined by Firth (1980) in an ingenious calculation that strongly suggests the presence of bidding errors. The premium paid to the target firm (in £) as a fraction of the size of the bidding firm was cross-sectionally related to the percentage loss in the bidding firm's shares around the takeover period. The regression coefficient was -0.89 ($t = -5.94$). Firth concludes (p. 254), "This supports the view that the stock market expects zero benefits from a takeover, that the gains to the acquired firm represent an 'over-payment' and that the acquiring company's shareholders suffer corresponding losses."

Using dollar-based matched pairs of firms, Varaiya (1985) finds that the aggregate abnormal dollar gain of targets is $189.4 million while the average abnormal dollar loss of bidders is $128.7 million for 121 days around the takeover announcement. The aggregate gain of $60.7 ($189.4 $-$ 128.7) is not statistically significant, on the basis of a parametric test, though a nonparametric test does indicate significance. Varaiya also reports a cross-sectional regression that indicates that, the larger the target's dollar gain, the larger the bidder's dollar loss. The regression coefficient was -0.81 ($t = -2.81$).

To summarize, the evidence about total gains in takeovers must be judged inconclusive. Results based on returns are unreliable. Malatesta's dollar-based results show a small aggregate gain in the months just around merger approval in a small matched sample and an aggregate loss in a larger unmatched sample. The interpretation of Malatesta's results is rendered difficult by the possibility of losses or gains in prior months, after announcement of a merger possibility but before final approval is a certainty. Dollar-based results presented by Bradley et al. (1982, 1983*a*) show a small and insignificant aggregate gain. Firth's (1980) British results show an insignificant aggregate loss. Both Firth (1980) and Varaiya (1985) present persuasive evidence for the existence of overbidding. But, on balance, the existence of either gains or losses to the combined firms involved in corporate combinations remains in doubt.

This mixed and insignificant evidence is made even less conclusive (if that is possible) by potential measurement biases. There is a potential upward bias in the measured price reaction of bidding firms (and thus of the aggregate) caused by contaminating information. There is a potential downward bias due to prior anticipation of the takeover event, as explained by Schipper and Thompson (1983), and another potential downward bias in some studies due to an improper computation of abnormal returns (Chung and Weston 1985). These biases will be discussed in detail next, in connection with the empirical findings for bidding firms.

C. *Evidence about bidding firms: the announcement effect*

The hubris hypothesis predicts a decrease in the value of the bidding firm. As pointed out previously, this decrease may not be completely reflected in a market price decline because of contaminating information in a bid, because the bid has been (partly) anticipated, or simply because the economic loss is too small to be reliably reflected in prices.

The data contain several interesting patterns. Asquith (1983) finds that bidding firm shares show "no consistent pattern" around the announcement date, but, "in summary, bidding firms appear to have small but insignificant positive excess returns at the press day" (p. 66). Some of Asquith's other results are understandable under the hubris hypothesis. Before the first merger bid, for instance, firms who become successful bidders have much larger price increases than firms whose bids are unsuccessful. One would expect a higher level of hubris and thus more aggressive pursuit of a target in firms that had experienced recent good times.

Asquith's results are in conflict with those of Dodd (1980), who finds statistically significant negative returns at the bid announcement. Jensen and Ruback (1983) noted the difference in results, and they asked Dodd to check his data and computer program, which they report (Jensen and Ruback 1983, p. 17, n.12) he did without finding an error.[1]

Negative bidder returns were also found by Eger (1983) in her study of pure exchange (noncash) mergers. Bidding firm stock prices declined, on average by about 4%, from 5 days prior to merger bid announcement to 10 days afterward (Eger 1983, table 4, p. 563). The decline was statistically significant. Eger suggests that the difference between her results and Asquith's (1983) might be attributable to a difference between mergers involving cash and pure stock exchange mergers; and she notes that tender offers, which often involve cash, seem to display more positive bidder stock price reactions (see below).

In his study of United Kingdom takeovers, Firth (1980) reports statistically significant negative bidding firm returns in the month of the takeover announcement. Eighty percent of the bidders had negative abnormal returns during that month, and the t-statistic for the average return was about -5.0 (cf. Firth 1980, table 5, p. 248).

Varaiya (1985) also finds statistically significant negative returns for bidding firms on the announcement day. He reports also that the bidder's loss is significantly larger when there are rival bidders.

A recent paper by Ruback and Mikkelson (1984) documents announcement effects of corporate purchases of another corporation's shares according to the stated purpose of the acquisition (filed on form 13-D with the Securities and Exchange Commission). The 2-day announcement effect for acquiring firms was positive and statistically significant for the 370 firms whose stated purpose was not a takeover. In contrast, for 134 acquiring firms indicating an intention to effect a takeover, the announcement effect was negative and significant (table 4, p. 17).

Studies of individual cases have been mixed. For example, Ruback (1982) argues that DuPont's large stock price decline in announcing a bid to take over Conoco could be an indication that managers (of DuPont) "had an objective function different from that of shareholder wealth maximization" (p. 24). However, he rejects this explanation because of "the magnitude of Conoco's revaluation and the lack of evidence that DuPont's management benefited from the acquisition" (p. 24). He also rejects every other explanation except inside information possessed by DuPont and not yet appreciated by the market; but even this hypothesis "cannot be confirmed since the nature of the information is unknown" (p. 25).

One interesting aspect of the DuPont/Conoco case is that DuPont's decline was more than offset by Conoco's gain; that is, the total gain was positive (although the bidding firm lost). This suggests that nonhubris factors were indeed present, bringing a total gain to the corporate combination, but that overbidding was present too, resulting in a loss to DuPont shareholders.

The other case study by Ruback (1983) finds only a small negative effect for Occidental Petroleum in its bid for Cities Service. Cities Service's stock price increased by a relatively small amount for a target firm, and the total effect was positive. Apparently, there was little significant hubris evidenced by Occidental (who offered only a small premium). An interesting sidelight was the performance of Gulf Oil, a rival bidder who withdrew. It suffered a loss far in excess of Cities Service's gain.

Schipper and Thompson (1983) find a positive price reaction around the announcement that a firm is embarking on a program of conglomerate acquisitions. Also they observe negative price reactions of such firms to antimerger regulatory events. The two findings are interpreted as at least consistent with the proposition that acquisitions are positive net present value projects for the bidding firm. However, the authors emphasize the tentative nature of their conclusion (pp. 109–11). For example, they note that the announcement of an acquisition program is sometimes accompanied by "announcements of related policy decisions, such as de-emphasis of old lines of business, changes in management, changes in capital structure or specific merger proposals" (p. 89). Even without such explicit contaminating information, announcement of the program could be interpreted as good news about the future profitability of the bidder's current assets rather than about the prospect of an undisclosed future target firm to be obtained at a bargain price.

The possibility of contaminating information is a central problem in interpreting the price movement of a bidding firm on the announcement date of an intended acquisition. Bidders are activists in the takeover situation, and their announcements may convey as much information about their own prospects as about the takeover. To mention one example of the measurement problem, mergers are usually leverage-increasing events. It is well documented from studies of other leverage-increasing events, such as exchange offers (Masulis 1980) and share repurchases (Vermaelen 1981), that positive price movements are to be expected. Thus to measure properly that part of the gain of a bidding firm in a merger that is attributable to the merger *per se* and not to an increase in leverage, we ought to deduct the price increase that would have been obtained by the same firm through independently increasing its leverage by the same amount.[2]

The measurement problem induced by the disparate sizes of target and bidder is the subject of a paper by Jarrell (1983). Jarrell argues that, when a bidder is several times larger than a target, a gain to the bidder equal in size to the gain observed in the target can be hidden in the noise of the bidder's return variability; that is, the t-statistic for the bidder's effect is likely to be much smaller than for the target's effect. Jarrell suggests solving this problem by adjusting the bidder's t-statistic upward by a factor proportional to the relative sizes of bidder and target. When he makes the adjustment in his sample, bidding firms display significantly positive price movements from 30 days prior to 10 days after the takeover announcement. The mean abnormal return prior to adjustment is 2.3%; after adjustment it is 9.2%. Similarly, the combined bidder and target returns become more statistically significant.

The problem with the Jarrell adjustment is that it can be applied to any sample in order to render a sample mean of either sign statistically significant. For example, if Firth (1980) had adjusted his bidding firm returns downward according to the relative sizes of bidder and target, he could have concluded that British takeovers had significant aggregate negative effects on shareholders. This does not imply that Jarrell's conclusions are incorrect, but we are certainly entitled to remain skeptical. Several studies have reported positive bidder gains, and several others have reported losses. Applying the Jarrell technique indiscriminately to all of them could make the gains or losses more "significant," but this would simply create more confusion since the now "significant" results would disagree across studies.

D.   *Evidence about bidding firms: resolution of doubtful success*

There is some evidence available to help isolate the reevaluation of a bidding firm's own assets induced by the bid but not caused by the proposed corporate combination itself. Asquith's (1983) sample of bidding firms in mergers is separated into successful and unsuccessful bidders, and both samples are examined prior to bid announcement, between announcement and merger outcome, and after outcome. For the successful group, merger outcome is the actual date when the target firm is delisted; this is presumably the effective date of the merger. At the original bid announcement, the market cannot know for sure whether such firms actually will consummate the merger, that is, be in the "successful" group. There is only a probability of success. Between the bid announcement and the final outcome this probability goes to 1.0 for firms in the successful group. Thus if the combination itself has value for the bidder, these bidding firms should increase in value over this interim period. They do not. On average, successful bidding firms decline in value by 0.5% over the interim period (see Asquith 1983, fig. 4, p. 71; table 9, p. 81). The decrease in value is small and statistically insignificant, but the result has economic significance because the opposite sign must be observed if the corporate combination *per se* has value. If the combination has substantial value, one might have expected to observe a statistically significant upward price movement between bid announcement and outcome, provided, of course, that the upward revision in probability of success is large enough to show up.

Firms in Asquith's successful bidder group have very large prebid returns; abnormal returns average 14.3% over a 460-day period ending 20 days before the bid announcement. They have small positive returns (0.2%) on the announcement date. The entire sequence of returns for successful bidding firms is consistent with the hubris hypothesis. In the prebid period, excellent performance endows management with both hubris and cash. A target is selected. The bid itself signals a small upward revision in the market's estimate of the bidding firm's current assets that is not completely offset by the prospect of paying too much for the target. Then there is a small downward revision in bidder firm value as it becomes more probable and then certain that the target will be acquired (at too high a price).

Eckbo (1983) reports a small and insignificant decline during the 3 days subsequent to the initial merger bid. But Eckbo's "successful" bidder is defined as one who is unchallenged on antitrust grounds; this may be a less relevant representation of actual success for our purposes here.

Eger (1983, p. 563) finds significant negative bidder firm returns averaging −3.1% in the 20 days after the original announcement of a merger that is ultimately successful. Most of this decline occurs in the first 10 days after the merger announcement. The bonds of these firms also decline slightly in price over the same period. This is consistent with a price decline in the total value of the bidding firm as it becomes more certain that the merger will succeed.

The most significant price decline between merger proposal and outcome is reported by Dodd (1980). Successful bidding firms decline in value by 7.22% from 10 days before the bid is announced until 10 days after the merger outcome, where outcome is defined as target stockholder approval of merger bid. The price decline is statistically significant. In the 20 days prior to the outcome date, successful bidder firms in Dodd's sample fall in price by about 2% (p. 124).

Evidence from papers using monthly data is more difficult to interpret, but the patterns do seem consistent with a negative price movement between merger announcement and successful outcome. For example, Langetieg's (1978, p. 377) bidding firms show a significant price decline continuing in the combined firm after the merger outcome. Similarly, Chung and Weston (1982, p. 334) report price declines between merger announcement month and merger completion in pure conglomerate mergers. However, the decline is not statistically significant.

Similar evidence is given in Malatesta (1983, table 4, p. 172). Acquiring firms in this sample have significant negative price performance in the period after the first announcement of a merger proposal. Since the data are monthly, the merger outcome date could be included somewhere in the sample period. This means that part of the puzzling post-outcome negative performance detected by Langetieg (1978) and Asquith (1983) might be included in Malatesta's table 4 results. In tables 5 and 6 Malatesta presents performance results for acquiring firms after the "first announcement of board/management approval of the merger" (p. 170). The returns are strongly negative in this period. This might not be such a puzzle if "board/management approval" still leaves open the possibility of withdrawal, for then the absolute certainty of merger (and the concomitant price drop expected under the hubris hypothesis) would occur sometime after this particular event date.

In summary, during the interim period between initial bid and successful outcome, the average price movement of successful merger bids is small, so it is not possible to draw strong implications. However, the pattern is generally consistent with the hubris hypothesis, which predicts the observed loss in value of bidding firm's shares. The loss is statistically insignificant in Asquith's sample but is significant in the samples of

Dodd (1980) and Eger (1983) and in the monthly data samples of Langetieg (1978) and Malatesta (1983).

Evidence about the interim period from tender offer studies is mixed. One study seems to be clearly inconsistent with hubris alone; Bradley's (1980) sample of 88 successful bidding firms shows a price rise after the announcement data and before the execution date. The number is not given, but the plot of the mean abnormal price index (p. 366) indicates that the gain is approximately 2%–3%.

The interim price movement of the successful acquiring firm is reported by Ruback and Mikkelson (1984) as −1.07% with a *t*-statistic of −2.34 (table 6). Their sample is not dichotomized by merger versus tender offers, however, and it probably contains some of both types of takeovers.

The results given by Kummer and Hoffmeister (1978) for a 17-firm matched sample of tender offers are more difficult to interpret because the data are monthly and, apparently because of the small size of the cross-sectional sample, the time series of prices relative to the event data appears to be more variable. Abnormal returns are positive and largest in the announcement month but are also positive in months +1 and +2. If the tender offer is revolved sometime during these 2 months, the results are basically the same as Bradley's (1980). Months +3 to +12 witness a decline of about 4%. If the success of the tender offer is not known until sometime during this period, an interpretation could be made similar to the one discussed above concerning Asquith's and Dodd's samples of successful merger bids.

An identical set of nonconclusive inferences can be drawn from the monthly data of Dodd and Ruback (1977). There appears to be a positive price movement by successful bidders just after the announcement month followed by a price decline later. The decline over the 12 months after a bid amounts to −1.32%, but it is not statistically significant.

Bradley's daily results probably represent the best available evidence against the hubris hypothesis. The detected movement is small, but, unlike the case of merger's, the bidding firm's price does increase on average in Bradley's sample. This is consistent with the proposition that tender offers increase aggregate value and that some of the increase accrues to tender offer bidders. Whether the evidence is sufficiently compelling, particularly when balanced against evidence of an opposite character, is up to further investigation to decide definitely.

One other piece of evidence from the interim period between announcement and outcome is worthy of contemplation. This is the price behavior of the first bidder's stock on the announcement of a rival bid. In their study of unsuccessful tender offers, Bradley et al. (1983*b*) report a significant price drop in the first bidder's stock. In contrast, Ruback and Mikkelson (1984) report a significant price increase (table 5); however, the latter sample consists not only of ultimately unsuccessful bidders in tender offers but of all corporate investors in other stock (including many who are not contemplating a takeover).

A price drop in the first takeover bidder's stock on the announcement of a rival bid is explainable by hubris. The rival bid may set off a bidding war that the market expects to result in a large loss for the winner. It would be extremely informative to observe the price reaction of the first bidder when it becomes evident that the rival bidder has won.

Finally, it should be noted that the price change after the resolution of a successful bid (either merger or tender offer) is almost uniformly negative (cf. Jensen and Ruback 1983, table 4, p. 21) and is relatively large in magnitude. This is a result that casts doubt on all estimates of bidding firm returns because it suggests the presence of substantial measurement problems.

III   Summary and Discussion

The purpose of this paper is to bring attention to a possible explanation of the takeover phenomenon of mergers and tender offers. This explanation, the hubris hypothesis, is very simple: decision makers in acquiring firms pay too much for their targets on average in the samples we observe. The samples, however, are not random. Potential bids are abandoned whenever the acquiring firm's valuation of the target turns up with a figure below the current market price. Bids are rendered when the valuation exceeds the price. If there really are no gains in takeovers, hubris is necessary to explain why managers do not abandon these bids also since reflection would suggest that such bids are likely to represent positive errors in valuation.

The hubris hypothesis can serve as the null hypothesis of corporate takeovers because it asserts that all markets are strong-form efficient. Financial markets are aware of all information. Product markets are efficiently organized. Labor markets are characterized by managers being employed in their best operational positions.

Hubris predicts that, around a takeover, (*a*) the combined value of the target and bidder firms should fall slightly, (*b*) the value of the bidding firm should decrease, and (*c*) the value of the target should increase. The available empirical results indicate that the measured combined value has increased in some studies and decreased in others. It has been statistically significant in none. Measured changes in the prices of bidding firms have been mixed in sign across studies and mostly of a very small order of magnitude. Several studies have reported them to be significantly negative, and other studies have reported the opposite. Target firm prices consistently display large increases, but only if the initial bid or a later bid is successful. There is no permanent increase in value for target firms that do not eventually enter a corporate combination.

The interpretation of bidding firm returns is complicated by several potential measurement problems. The bid can convey contaminating information, that is, information about the bidder rather than about the takeover itself. The bid can be partially anticipated and thus result in an announcement effect smaller in absolute value than the true economic effect. Since bidders are usually much larger than targets, the effect of the bid can be buried in the noise of the bidder's return volatility. There is weak evidence from the interim period between the announcement of a merger and the merger outcome that the merger itself results in a loss to the bidding firm's shareholders; but the interim period in tender offers shows some results that favor the opposite view. Both findings have minimal statistical reliability.

The final impression one is obliged to draw from the currently available results is that they provide no really convincing evidence against even the extreme (hubris) hypothesis that all markets are operating perfectly efficiently and that individual bidders occasionally make mistakes. Bidders may indicate by their actions a belief in the existence of takeover gains, but systematic studies have provided little to show that such beliefs are well founded.

Finally, I should mention several issues that have arisen as objections by others to the hubris idea. First, the hubris hypothesis might seem to imply that managers act consciously against shareholder interests. Several recent papers that have examined nontakeover corporate control devices have concluded that the evidence is consistent with conscious management actions against the best interests of shareholders.[3] But the hubris hypothesis does not rely on this result. It is sufficient that managers act, *de facto*, against shareholder interests by issuing bids founded on mistaken estimates of target firm value. Management intentions may be fully consistent with honorable stewardship of corporate assets, but actions need not always turn out to be right.

Second, it might seem that the hubris hypothesis implies systematic biases in market prices. One correspondent argued that stock prices would be systematically too high for reasons similar to those advanced in E. M. Miller's (1977) paper. This implication is not correct, however, for the simple reason that firms can be either targets or bidders. If bidders offer too much, their stock price will fall *ex post* while their target's price will rise. On average over all stocks, this cancels. Unless one can predict which firms will be targets and which will be bidders, there is no bias in any individual firm, and there is certainly no bias on average over all firms.

Third, an argument can be advanced that the hubris hypothesis implies an inefficiency in the market for corporate control. If all takeovers were prompted by hubris, shareholders could stop the practice by forbidding managers ever to make any bid. Since such prohibitions are not observed, hubris alone cannot explain the takeover phenomenon.

The validity of this argument depends on the size of deadweight takeover costs. If such costs are relatively small, stockholders would be indifferent to hubris-inspired bids because target firm shareholders would gain what bidding firm shareholders lose. A well-diversified shareholder would receive the aggregate gain, which is close to zero.

Fourth, and finally, a frequent objection is that hubris itself is based on a market inefficiency defined in a particular way; in the words of one writer, "It seems to me that your hypothesis does not rest on strong form efficiency, because it presumes that one set of market bidders is systematically irrational" (private correspondence). This argument contends that a market is inefficient if some market participants make systematic mistakes. Perhaps one of the long-term benefits of studying takeovers is to clarify the notion of market efficiency. Does efficiency mean that every individual behaves like the rational, maximizing ideal? Or does it mean instead that market interactions generate prices and allocations indistinguishable from those that would have been generated by rational individuals?

Notes

The earlier drafts of this paper elicited many comments. It is a pleasure to acknowledge the benefits derived from the generosity of so many colleagues. They corrected several conceptual and substantive errors in the previous draft, directed my attention to other results, and suggested other interpretations of the empirical phenomena. In general, they provided me with an invaluable tutorial on the subject of corporate takeovers. The present draft undoubtedly still contains errors and omissions, but this is due mainly to my inability to distill and convey the collective knowledge of the profession. Among those who helped were C. R. Alexander, Peter Bernstein, Thomas Copeland, Harry DeAngelo, Eugene Fama, Karen Farkas, Michael Firth, Mark Grinblatt, Gregg Jarrell, Bruce Lehmann, Paul Malatesta, Ronald Masulis, David Mayers, John McConnell, Merton Miller, Stephen Ross, Richard Ruback, Sheridan Titman, and, especially, Michael Jensen, Katherine Schipper, Walter A. Smith, Jr., and J. Fred Weston. I also benefited from the comments of the finance workshop participants at the University of Chicago, the University of Michigan, and Dartmouth College, and of the referees.

1 Recently, Chung and Weston (1985) suggested that part of the difference in results could be explained by an improper calculation of "abnormal" returns around the merger announcement. Chung and Weston point out that the premerger period generally displays statistically significant positive returns for bidding firms. If data from this period are used to estimate abnormal returns at merger announcement, the measured announcement effect will be biased downward. The reported difference between, say, Dodd (1980) and Asquith (1983) would be reduced by a recalculation by Dodd excluding the preannouncement period. However, it probably would not be entirely eliminated; the bias appears to be only a small fraction of Dodd's observed announcement effect.

2 I am grateful to Sheridan Titman for pointing out this possibility.

3 See Bradley and Wakeman (1983), Dann and DeAngelo (1983), and DeAngelo and Rice (1983). Linn and McConnell (1983) disagree with the last paper. The possibility that managers do not act in the interest of stockholders has frequently been associated with the takeover phenomenon. For example, in a recent review, Lev (1983, p. 15) concludes by saying, "I think we are justified in doubting . . . the argument that mergers are done to maximize stockholder wealth." Foster (1983) seems to share this view or at least the view that bidders make big mistakes. Larcker (1983) presents interesting results that managers in large takeovers are more likely to have short-term, accounting-based compensation contracts. He finds that, the more accounting-based the compensation, the more negative is the market price reaction to a bid. Larcker also suggests that managers who own less stock in their own company are more likely to make bids.

References

Asquith, P., 1983, Merger bids, uncertainty, and stockholder returns. *Journal of Financial Economics* 11, April, 51–83.

Asquith, P., R. F. Bruner, and D. W. Mullins, Jr., 1983, The gains to bidding firms from merger. *Journal of Financial Economics* 11, April, 121–39.

Bradley, M., 1980, Interfirm tender offers and the market for corporate control. *Journal of Business* 53, October, 345–76.

Bradley, M., A. Desai, and E. H. Kim, 1982, Specialized resources and competition in the market for corporate control. Typescript. Ann Arbor: University of Michigan, Graduate School of Business.

Bradley, M., A. Desai, and E. H. Kim, 1983*a*, Determinants of the wealth effects of corporate acquisition via tender offers: Theory and evidence. Typescript. Ann Arbor: University of Michigan, Graduate School of Business.

Bradley, M., A. Desai, and E. H. Kim, 1983*b*, The rationale behind interfirm tenders offers: Information or synergy? *Journal of Financial Economics* 11, April, 183–206.

Bradley, M. and L. Mac., Wakeman, 1983, The wealth effects of targeted share repurchases. *Journal of Financial Economics* 11, April, 301–28.

Capan, E. C., R. V. Clapp, and W. M. Campbell, 1971, Competitive bidding in high risk situations. *Journal of Petroleum Technology*, June, 641–53.

Chung, K. S. and J. F. Weston, 1982, Diversification and mergers in a strategic long-range planning framework. In M. Keenan and L. I. White (eds.), *Mergers and Acquisitions*. Lexington, Mass.: D. C. Heath.

Chung, K. S. and J. F. Weston, 1985, Model-created bias in residual analysis of mergers. Working paper. Los Angeles: University of California, Los Angeles, Graduate School of Management.

Dann, L. Y. and H. DeAngelo, 1983, Standstill agreements, privately negotiated stock repurchases, and the market for corporate control. *Journal of Financial Economics* 11, April, 275–300.

DeAngelo, H. and E. M. Rice, 1983, Antitakeover charter amendments and stockholder wealth. *Journal of Financial Economics* 11, April, 329–60.

Dodd, P., 1980, Merger proposals, managerial discretion and stockholder wealth. *Journal of Financial Economics* 8, June, 105–38.

Dodd, P. and R. Ruback, 1977, Tender offers and stockholder returns: An empirical analysis. *Journal of Financial Economics* 5, December, 351–74.

Dougherty, F. L. and J. Lohrenz, 1976, Statistical analysis of bids for Federal offshore leases. *Journal of Petroleum Technology*, November, 1377–90.

Eckbo, B. E., 1983, Horizontal mergers, collusion and stockholder wealth. *Journal of Financial Economics* 11, April, 241–73.

Eger, C. E., 1983, An empirical test of the redistribution effect in pure exchange mergers. *Journal of Financial and Quantitative Analysis* 18, December, 547–72.

Firth, M., 1980, Takeovers, shareholder returns and the theory of the firm. *Quarterly Journal of Economics*, March, 235–60.

Foster, G., 1983, Comments on M & A analysis and the role of investment bankers. *Midland Corporate Finance Journal* 1, Winter, 36–8.

Halpern, P. J., 1973, Empirical estimates of the amount and distribution of gains to companies in mergers. *Journal of Business* 46, October, 554–75.

Jarrell, G. A., 1983, Do acquirers benefit from corporate acquisition? Typescript. Chicago: University of Chicago, Center for the Study of the Economy and the State.

Jensen, M. C. and R. S. Ruback, 1983, The market for corporate control. *Journal of Financial Economics* 11, April, 5–50.

Kahneman, D., P. Slovic, and A. Tversky, 1982, *Judgment under Uncertainty: Heuristics and Biases*. New York: Cambridge University Press.

Kummer, D. R. and J. R. Hoffmeister, 1978, Valuation consequences of cash tender offers. *Journal of Finance* 33, May, 505–16.

Langetieg, T. C., 1978, An application of a three-factor performance index to measure stockholder gains from merger. *Journal of Financial Economics* 6, December, 365–83.

Larcker, D., 1983, Managerial incentives in mergers and their effect on shareholder wealth. *Midland Corporate Finance Journal* 1, Winter, 29–35.

Lev, B., 1983, Observations on the merger phenomenon and review of the evidence. *Midland Corporate Finance Journal* 1, Winter, 6–16.

Linn, S. C. and J. J. McConnell, 1983, An empirical investigation of the impact of "antitakeover" amendments on common stock prices. *Journal of Financial Economics* 11, April, 361–99.

Malatesta, P. H., 1983, The wealth effect of merger activity and the objective functions of merging firms. *Journal of Financial Economics* 11, April, 155–81.

Masulis, R. W., 1980, The effects of capital structure change on security prices: A study of exchange offers. *Journal of Financial Economics* 8, June, 139–77.

Miller, E. M., 1977, Risk, uncertainty and the divergence of opinion. *Journal of Finance* 32, September, 1151–68.

Oskamp, S., 1965, Overconfidence in case study judgments. *Journal of Consulting Psychology* 29, June, 261–5.

Ruback, R. S., 1982, The Conoco takeover and stockholder returns. *Sloan Management Review* 14, Winter, 13–33.

Ruback, R. S., 1983, The Cities Service takeover: A case study. *Journal of Finance* 38, May, 319–30.

Ruback, R. S. and W. H. Mikkelson, 1984, Corporate investments in common stock. Working paper. Cambridge: Massachusetts Institute of Technology, Sloan School of Business.

Schipper, K. and R. Thompson, 1983, Evidence on the capitalized value of merger activity for acquiring firms. *Journal of Financial Economics* 11, April, 85–119.

Tversky, A. and D. Kahneman, 1981, The framing of decisions and the psychology of choice. *Science* 211, January, 30, 453–8. Reprinted in Peter Diamond and Michael Rothschild, 1978, *Uncertainty in Economics*. New York: Academic Press.

Varaiya, N., 1985, A test of Roll's Hubris Hypothesis of corporate takeovers. Working paper. Dallas, Tex.: Southern Methodist University, School of Business.

Vermaelen, T., 1981, Common stock repurchase and marketing signalling: An empirical study. *Journal of Financial Economics* 9, June, 139–84.

4

Do Bad Bidders Become Good Targets?

Mark L. Mitchell and Kenneth Lehn

Since the publication of Adolph Berle and Gardiner Means's *The Modern Corporation and Private Property* in 1932, it has been widely recognized that the interests of management and stockholders can diverge in public corporations with diffuse equity ownership. More recent developments in the theory of corporate finance – most notably, Michael Jensen and William Meckling's formulation of "agency cost" theory in the late 1970s – have called attention to the potential loss in value of public companies caused by the separation of ownership and control.[1]

Until the 1980s, however, most finance scholars, including Jensen and Meckling, continued to assume that the agency costs of separating ownership from control in our public companies could not be very great. Even if corporate boards of directors were not very effective in performing their prescribed role as overseers of stockholder interests, most financial economists reasoned that competition from international product markets and the existence of a market for executive labor should serve to limit the natural tendency of corporate management to put its own interests ahead of stockholders'. Executive compensation plans were also assumed to reduce this potential conflict of interest. And if all of these forces failed to join managerial with stockholder interests, then a vigorous takeover market (in academic parlance, the "market for corporate control") was thought to provide the ultimate deterrent to stockholder neglect.[2]

But the events of the 1980s have suggested otherwise. For most finance scholars, the proliferation of management buyouts and leveraged acquisitions by private investors has strengthened, if not indeed confirmed, the belief that the agency costs associated with outside equity ownership are far greater than once believed. In quite recent work, moreover, Jensen has argued that corporate takeovers, besides providing the ultimate "solution," may also have been an important part of the "problem." As Jensen suggests, the potential conflict between management and stockholders is most likely to surface in mature companies that generate substantial "free cash flow" – that is, more cash than management can profitably reinvest. In such cases, stockholders are best served by managements who pay out the excess capital to investors, say, in the form of large stock repurchases. But, to the extent corporate managements are more intent on maintaining growth than increasing profitability – and, as Jensen argues, there is a natural bias toward growth in large organizations with dispersed owners – they will choose to reinvest "free cash flow" at rates well below the corporate cost of capital rather than returning it to shareholders. And this practice can cause corporate stock prices to fall well below so-called "break-up" values.

One of the most prominent ways of reinvesting cash flow, and thus perpetuating unprofitable corporate growth, is by making value-reducing acquisitions – particularly, diversifying acquisitions. In this sense, as mentioned above, corporate takeovers operate not only as a disciplining force, but may also be one of the principal managerial practices that other takeovers are designed to stop. Given this potential for destroying stockholder value through corporate acquisitions, Jensen goes on to suggest that many takeovers in the 1980s – especially hostile takeovers followed by divestitures – have been motivated by the opportunity to create value simply by reversing prior mistaken acquisitions by target companies. In short, Jensen offers a plausible rationale for what have become known as "bust-up" takeovers.[3]

In this article, we report the findings of a series of statistical tests we designed to explore the following issues: Can takeover targets be distinguished from companies that do not become targets solely by the profitability of their past acquisitions? Specifically, do target companies systematically make acquisitions that the stock-market judges more harshly than the acquisitions of companies that are not later taken over? And, more generally, does the market response to announcements of acquisitions provide a useful prediction of how such acquisitions will turn out?

An illustrative case

There is, of course, considerable anecdotal evidence to support the proposition that one of the primary motives for takeovers in the 1980s was simply to reverse mistaken acquisitions. In 1986, for example, Sir James Goldsmith made an unsuccessful takeover bid for Goodyear Tire & Rubber Co. For the right to assume control, Goldsmith offered a premium of approximately US$1.13 billion over (and roughly 30 percent of) the current (pre-offer) equity value of the company. His declared intent was to sell Goodyear's petroleum and aerospace divisions, and to concentrate the company's focus on its tire and rubber operations.

What evidence do we have that Goodyear's past acquisitions were reducing the value of the company? When Goodyear announced its first major petroleum acquisition – its 1983 purchase of Celeron Oil for approximately $800 million – its stock price fell by over 10% on the day of announcement, amounting to a loss of almost $250 million for Goodyear stockholders. And, if we consider the market reaction over a longer period – one extending from five trading days before through 40 trading days after the announcement – the decline in Goodyear's stock price was almost 24%, representing shareholder losses of close to $600 million. Viewed in this light, the 30 percent premium over current market value offered by Goldsmith in 1986 could be interpreted largely as a recouping of the losses sustained by Goodyear's shareholders three years earlier when Goodyear began its diversification into the oil industry.[4]

Although Goodyear eventually defeated Goldsmith's takeover attempt, it was forced to adopt a major restructuring program similar to the one proposed by Goldsmith. Not surprisingly, the restructuring program included the sale of a substantial part of Celeron Oil. As a consequence, even after the offer was removed, Goodyear's stock price continued to reflect at least part of the 30% premium offered by Goldsmith.

The important question for economists, then, is as follows: Is this Goodyear case representative of a broadly recurring phenomenon, or is it just an isolated instance? To answer this question, we examined the stock-market's reactions to announcements of 345 major acquisitions made by two sets of companies during the period 1982–6: 113 acquisitions by 77 acquiring companies that later themselves became targets of other takeover attempts (henceforth referred to as "targets"); and a control group of 232 acquisitions by 133 acquiring companies that were not subjected to takeover bids ("nontargets"). We also attempted to distinguish between those acquiring companies that eventually became targets of hostile bids ("hostile targets") and those that received "friendly" bids ("friendly targets").

Here is a brief overview of our findings:

- For the entire sample of acquisitions over the period 1982–6, the average stock price effect associated with the acquisition announcements was not significantly different from zero.
- In the cases of the 113 acquisitions by companies that later became targets themselves, the stock prices of the acquiring companies *declined* significantly (by over 3 percent, on average) during a 45-day period surrounding the announcements of the transactions.
- In the case of the 232 acquisitions by companies that did *not* become targets of bids (at least through June 1988), the stock prices of the acquiring companies *increased* significantly upon announcement – in fact, by roughly the same 3 percent over the 45-day period.
- Of the entire sample of acquisitions made between 1982–6, 81 (or roughly 20%) were divested by the end of 1988. Over 40% of the acquisitions by companies that eventually became targets were later divested, as compared to only 9 percent for nontargets. In the case of the targets, moreover, the announcements of acquisitions later divested were associated with an average 7 percent stock price decline during the 45-day period surrounding the announcements.
- In the 81 cases of acquisitions later divested by both target and nontarget companies, the stock prices of the acquiring companies fell significantly (by 4 percent, on average) during the 45-day period surrounding the announcements. In the case of the acquisitions not divested, the average market response was a positive 1.9 percent.

- Holding size (equity value) and the percentage of equity held by management constant, the probability of a company's becoming a target – especially a hostile target – during the period 1982–8 was inversely and significantly related to the stock price effects associated with announcements of the firm's acquisitions. That is, the more negative the market's response to an acquisition, the greater the likelihood of a subsequent takeover attempt.

In short, our results suggest that one major source of value in many corporate takeovers – especially hostile takeovers – during the 1980s was the restoration of stockholder value that had been destroyed by the targets' prior acquisition strategies. Moreover, our finding of sharply negative market responses to acquisitions later divested provides strong support for the "efficiency" of the stock-market. That is, when companies announce acquisitions, the stock-market provides a useful forecast of the probability that the acquisitions will either succeed or eventually be reversed through divestiture.

The Data

The complete sample for our study consisted of 1158 public corporations in 51 industries covered by *Value Line* at the end of 1981.[5] The sample excluded two highly regulated industries (financial services and electric utility) covered by *Value Line*, as well as all companies in industries with fewer than ten listed firms. This modified sample of *Value Line* companies ended up including 64.4% of the companies in the 1981 S&P 500 Index and 75.2% of the companies in the 1981 Fortune 500.

Each of the 1158 companies was then classified into one of four groups based upon whether the firm was a takeover target during the period January 1980 through July 1988. The four categories were as follows: (1) nontargets; (2) hostile targets; (3) friendly targets; and (4) miscellaneous companies.

As shown in table 4.1, 600 (or 51.8%) of the 1158 companies were "nontargets." Such companies neither received takeover bids, paid greenmail, filed for bankruptcy, significantly restructured, nor were subjected to large unsolicited open market purchases. The "hostile" target group consisted of 228 firms (19.7% of the total) that were targets of either successful or unsuccessful hostile tender offers, proxy contests (in which the dissenting shareholder sought control), and large unsolicited open market purchases (in which the purchaser attempted to secure control). The "friendly" target group contained 240 firms (20.7% of the sample) that were targets of both successful and unsuccessful friendly tender offers, mergers, and leveraged buyouts. The miscellaneous category contained 90 companies (7.8%) that, in the absence of a tender offer, either paid greenmail, filed for bankruptcy, were subjected to large open market purchases in which the purchaser expressed no interest in securing control, or made large targeted stock repurchases or otherwise significantly restructured.

Our next step was to examine The Dow Jones *Broadtape* for the announcements of *major* acquisitions by the 1158 firms during 1982–6. By major we meant only those

Table 4.1   Frequency of different types of control transactions during 1980–8

Nontargets (N = 600)	Numbers	Percentage
No control transaction	600	(51.8%)
Hostile Targets (N = 228)		
Successful HTO	58	(5.0%)
Unsuccessful HTO	69	(6.0%)
Unsuccessful HTO, followed by merger	51	(4.4%)
Unsuccessful HTO, followed by LBO	21	(1.8%)
Unsuccessful HTO, ending in greenmail	7	(0.6%)
Proxy fight	21	(1.8%)
Unsolicited large open market purchase	1	(0.1%)
Friendly Targets (N = 240)		
Merger or friendly tender offer	163	(14.1%)
LBO	53	(4.6%)
Unsuccessful LBO	10	(0.9%)
Unsuccessful LBO, followed by merger	14	(1.2%)
Miscellaneous (N = 90)		
Greenmail, absent a tender offer	11	(0.9%)
Large targeted repurchase (possible greenmail)	10	(0.9%)
Large open market purchases	16	(1.4%)
Bankruptcy filings or NYSE suspensions	26	(2.2%)
Significant corporate restructuring	27	(2.3%)
Total Sample	1,158	(100.0%)

HTO = Hostile tender offer
LBO = Leveraged buyout

acquisitions in which the disclosed purchase price was at least five percent of the market value of the acquiring company's common equity 20 trading days prior to the first announcement of the acquisition. Such acquisitions included acquisitions of other public companies, acquisitions of private companies, and purchases of assets, divisions, subsidiaries and stock of other companies.[6]

As shown in table 4.2, 280 (or 24%) of the 1158 sample companies made a total of 401 acquisitions that amounted to at least 5% of their equity value during the period. Of these 401 acquisitions, 232 were made by 166 companies that did not become takeover targets; 113 were made by 77 companies that did become targets; and the remaining 56 were made by 38 companies classified as miscellaneous. Of the 113 acquisitions by companies that later received bids themselves, 70 were made by 48 companies that later received hostile bids; and 43 were made by 29 companies that received friendly bids.[7]

Several modes of payment can be used in making acquisitions. For each acquisition, we collected the form of payment from *Mergers and Acquisitions* and *The Wall Street Journal*. The data indicate that purely cash offers were the predominant form of payment, accounting for 254 (63%) of the acquisitions. At least some cash was used in 354 (88%) of the acquisitions. In contrast, purely stock transactions accounted for only 45 (11%) of the acquisitions, and at least some stock was used in 103 (26%) of

Table 4.2 Summary statistics for acquisitions during 1982–6

| No. of Firms[a] | No. of Acqr. Firms[b] | No. of Acquis.[c] | Avg. and Median Rel. Size of Acquis.[d] | Form of Financing | | | | | |
				All Cash[e]	All Stock	Cash and Stock	Cash and Notes	Cash and Target Debt	Other
Total sample									
1,158	280	401	.37	254	45	49	21	18	14
	(.24)	(.35)	(.18)	(.63)	(.11)	(.12)	(.05)	(.04)	(.03)
Nontargets									
600	166	232	.36	144	27	27	12	13	9
	(.28)	(.39)	(.18)	(.62)	(.12)	(.12)	(.05)	(.06)	(.04)
All Targets									
467	77	113	.35	79	13	11	5	3	2
	(.17)	(.24)	(.17)	(.70)	(.12)	(.10)	(.04)	(.03)	(.02)
Hostile Targets									
228	48	70	.30	50	9	6	1	3	1
	(.21)	(.31)	(.18)	(.71)	(.13)	(.09)	(.01)	(.04)	(.01)
Friendly Targets									
240	29	43	.42	29	4	5	4	0	1
	(.12)	(.18)	(.15)	(.67)	(.09)	(.12)	(.09)	(.00)	(.02)
Miscellaneous									
170	38	56	.44	31	5	11	4	2	3
	(.22)	(.33)	(.22)	(.55)	(.09)	(.20)	(.07)	(.04)	(.05)

[a] The number of firms in the entire sample (1,158) is less than the number of firms (1,238) obtained by adding the firms in the four categories. This discrepancy occurs because of the inclusion of some of the firms in the target categories and the miscellaneous category (see note 9). Similarly, the number of acquiring firms in the entire sample (280) is less than the number of acquiring firms (281) obtained by adding the acquiring firms in the four categories.

[b] Numbers in parentheses indicate the proportion of firms in each category that made acquisitions.

[c] Numbers in parentheses indicate the number of acquisitions as a proportion of the number of firms in each category.

[d] Median relative sizes of acquisitions are shown in parentheses below average relative sizes.

[e] Numbers in parentheses indicate the proportion of acquisitions that made up the various forms of financing for each category.

the acquisitions. Although one study has found that the form of payment is correlated with the market's reaction to an acquisition announcement,[8] we found that the form of payment did not differ substantially among the samples of nontargets, hostile targets, and friendly targets.

The Stock-market Response

For each of the 401 acquisitions in our sample, we calculated shareholder rates of return based on stock price reactions to the announcements of the transactions. We measured the market response over five different "event windows," ranging in length from just the day of the announcement itself to the 60-day period extending from 20

days before the announcement until 40 days after. We also adjusted all such calculations to eliminate the effect of general market movements and differences in risk
among individual stocks.

The market reaction to acquiring companies

As shown in the first row of table 4.3, the average announcement-day market response
to the entire sample of 401 acquisitions was −0.21%. The market-adjusted returns
over the other four windows ranged from −0.08% [day −1, day +1] to 0.70%
[−5, +40]; and none of these returns was significantly different from zero. Like most
prior "event" studies of mergers and acquisitions, these results suggest that, on
average, acquiring companies earn normal rates of return on their investments – a
finding consistent with a competitive market for corporate control.

But, as shown in the second and third rows of table 4.3, the market response to
announcements of acquisitions made by companies that later became targets differed
significantly from the response to acquisition announcements by nontarget companies.
The average announcement-day return associated with 113 acquisitions made by all
target companies was −0.78%; and, as the event window widened, the negative
response became progressively more pronounced, reaching a −3.46% over the 60-day

Table 4.3 Abnormal stock-market performance associated with firms announcing acquisitions
during 1982−6

| Category | Event Window | | | | |
	{0}	{−1,1}	{−5,1}	{−5,40}	{−20,40}
Entire Sample	−0.21**	−0.08	0.14	0.70	0.57
(n = 401)	(2.18)	(−0.45)	(0.53)	(1.05)	(0.75)
	42.39	46.63	50.37	54.11	53.12
Nontargets	0.09	0.49**	0.82**	3.32***	3.48***
(n = 232)	(0.66)	(2.19)	(2.42)	(3.80)	(3.46)
	44.83	48.71	56.03	62.93	62.07
All Targets	−0.78***	−0.93**	−1.27***	−3.38***	−3.46***
(n = 113)	(−4.59)	(−3.16)	(−2.82)	(−2.93)	(−2.60)
	39.82	39.82	38.05	38.05	38.94
Hostile Targets	−0.95***	−1.50***	−1.34**	−3.37**	−3.19**
(n = 70)	(−4.64)	(−4.22)	(−2.46)	(−2.42)	(−2.00)
	38.57	37.14	35.71	38.57	40.00
Friendly Targets	−0.50*	−0.01	−1.17	−3.39*	−3.91*
(n = 43)	(−1.68)	(−0.02)	(−1.47)	(−1.67)	(−1.67)
	41.86	44.19	41.86	37.21	37.21
Miscellaneous	−0.31	−0.69	0.14	−1.93	−3.33
(n = 56)	(−1.01)	(−1.32)	(0.17)	(−0.94)	(−1.42)
	37.50	51.79	51.79	50.00	44.64

Note: z-statistics are in parentheses and percent abnormal retuns that are positive are listed below z-
statistics.
* Significant at the 10 percent level.   ** Significant at the 5 percent level.
*** Significant at the 1 percent level.

event window. (All of these estimates, moreover, were highly statistically significant.) The fact that the returns become significantly more negative as the event window extends beyond the acquisition announcements suggests that, as the market learned more about these acquisitions during the succeeding weeks (about such things as the purchase price, definitiveness of the acquisition, and expected synergies), it took an increasingly dim view of the prospects for the acquisition and the acquiring company.

By contrast, the average stock price reaction to announcements of 232 acquisitions by companies that did not later become targets ranged from neutral to sharply positive – depending, again, on the event window chosen. The average announcement-day return for these nontarget companies was 0.09%, and became progressively larger with each extension of the window, reaching a high of 3.48% over the 60-day window. (With the exception of the announcement-day return, all of these estimates were significant at the 0.05 level or higher.) In sharp contrast to acquisitions by target companies, as more information became available to investors about acquisitions by nontarget companies, their reaction to the new business combination became more positive.

Finally, our results showed no statistically significant market reaction – regardless of the window chosen – to the 56 acquisitions made by the group of companies classified as "miscellaneous."

As summarized in figure 4.1, then, our findings demonstrate that the stock-market assigned a negative value to acquisitions by companies that later became takeover targets, especially targets of hostile offers. At the same time, it positively valued acquisitions by companies that were not subjected to takeover bids during the sample period.[9]

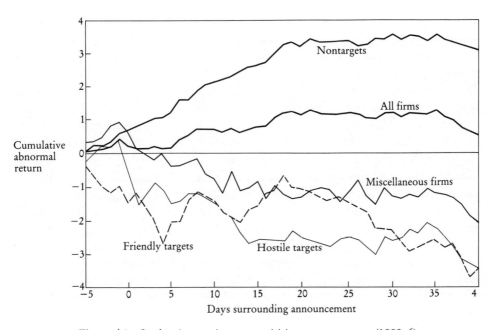

Figure 4.1   Stock price reactions to acquisition announcements (1982–6)

A Comparison of Divestiture Rates (Along With Some Striking Evidence on Market Efficiency)

The results presented so far show that, on average, acquisitions by targets – especially hostile targets – reduce their stock prices, whereas nontarget companies make acquisitions that increase their stock prices. Broadly speaking, there are two plausible explanations for the market's negative reaction to the acquisitions made by targets: (1) target companies tend to make acquisitions that the market expects to reduce the combined operating profitability of acquirer and acquired (what might be called "negative synergies"); and (2) targets tend to overpay for acquisitions the market believes will otherwise increase the combined profitability of the combined companies (so much so that the overpayment exceeds the expected synergies from the combination).[10]

These two explanations are by no means mutually exclusive since acquirers can both overpay and make otherwise poor acquisition choices. (In fact, many of the diversifying acquisitions of the 1970s and early 80s probably fit both categories.) And, technically, of course, any mistaken acquisition represents a form of overpayment – one in which the returns do not justify the investment. Both explanations, moreover, are consistent with the argument that takeovers function (ultimately) as a means of disciplining managers who fail to maximize stockholders' wealth.

But there is nonetheless an important difference between these two explanations – one that could lend itself to testing. Those acquisitions that prove to have "negative synergies" – or, alternatively, those that prove to have greater value to other potential acquirers – are much more likely to be divested than otherwise synergistic acquisitions for which the acquirer overpaid. In the case of "negative synergies," the motive behind many takeovers is to "undo" inefficient acquisitions previously made by the targets. In the case of overpayments for otherwise sound investments, takeovers can serve to restrain managers in target firms from further waste of stockholder capital through future overpayments; but, in such cases, there will be little opportunity to create value simply by divesting past acquisitions.

Although unable to devise a way of testing the overpayment explanation, we attempted to measure the extent of the "negative synergy" hypothesis by comparing the rate at which acquisitions made by targets were subsequently divested with the corresponding divestiture rate for nontargets during the sample period. Target divestitures were defined to be all acquisitions by targets that were divested during a period ranging from three months prior to the reception of their bid through the end of the sample period (June 1988). Such transactions thus included the following: (1) divestitures by targets to defend against a takeover; (2) divestitures as part of a restructuring program after defeating a takeover attempt; and (3) divestitures by acquiring firms following successful takeovers of the targets.

Nontarget divestitures, by definition, consisted of acquisitions that were divested voluntarily by the end of the sample period.

To the extent that "negative synergies," then, and not "overpayment," was motivating the takeovers of "bad bidders," we expected the divestiture rate to be significantly higher for targets than for nontargets. We also expected the stock-market reaction to announcements of acquisitions later divested to be significantly more negative than the price reactions to acquisitions that were retained. This relationship was expected to hold, moreover, not only for the sample of targets, but for the nontargets and miscellaneous companies as well.

The data   We were able to track subsequent divestitures of acquisitions from three sources: annual issues of *Mergers and Acquisitions*, *The Wall Street Journal Index* and Standard & Poor's *Directory of Corporate Affiliations* for each of the years 1982–8. We also relied on telephone conversations with representatives of the acquiring companies to confirm our findings.

The data revealed that 81 (or 20.2%) of our entire sample of 401 acquisitions over the period 1982–6 were subsequently divested during the period 1982–8. Moreover, there was a significant difference in the rate of divestiture by targets and nontargets. Whereas only 9.1% (21/232) of the acquisitions made by nontargets were later divested, over 40% (46/113) of the acquisitions made by targets were divested, either in response to or following successful or unsuccessful takeover attempts. (The z-statistic for this difference in divestiture rates was a highly significant 6.34.) There was, however, no significant difference in divestiture rates between hostile targets and friendly targets (the rates were 41.9% (18/43) for acquisitions made by friendly targets, and 40% (28/70) for acquisitions made by hostile targets). It is also noteworthy that *only two* of the friendly targets and none of the hostile targets divested previously acquired units *without the threat of takeover*.

The market response to acquisitions as a predictor of future divestiture

As shown in table 4.4, the stock price reaction to announcements of acquisitions later divested was significantly more negative than the market response to acquisitions not so divested. For the entire sample of 81 divested acquisitions, the average announcement-day return was -1.26% (significant at the 0.01 level). Using the longer 60-day window, the acquiring companies underperformed the market by 5.59%, on average (and, again, all of these estimates were significant at the 0.01 level for all windows).

By contrast, the announcement-day return for the acquiring companies of the 320 acquisitions that were not later divested was 0.05% (not statistically significant). As we used longer event windows, the returns became progressively more positive, reaching 2.13% for the 60-day window (significant at the 0.01 level).

This finding of a statistically significant negative market response to announcements of acquisitions that are later divested, together with a positive and significant price reaction to acquisitions that are retained, delivers a strong message of market efficiency. In essence, the market reaction to announcements of acquisitions amounts to an immediate unbiased forecast – that is, one that turns out to be right on average – of the likelihood that the assets now being acquired will ultimately be divested.

Table 4.4   Abnormal stock-market performance associated with firms announcing acquisitions during 1982–6 that are subsequently divested versus acquisitions during 1982–6 that are not subsequently divested

		Event Window				
	Category	{0}	{−1,1}	{−5,1}	{−5,40}	{−20,40}
Panel A: Acquisitions that are Subsequently Divested	Entire Sample (n = 81)	−1.26*** (−6.15) 35.80	−1.75*** (−4.93) 30.86	−1.53*** (−2.81) 38.27	−4.01*** (−2.88) 35.80	−5.59*** (−3.48) 32.10
	Nontargets (n = 21)	−1.16*** (−2.86) 42.86	−1.66** (−2.30) 28.57	−0.57 (−0.53) 47.62	2.55 (0.92) 61.90	2.48 (0.78) 57.14
	All Targets (n = 46)	−1.45*** (−5.58) 30.44	−1.56*** (−3.46) 30.44	−2.07*** (−3.01) 34.78	−7.04*** (−3.99) 23.91	−8.91*** (−4.38) 21.74
	Hostile Targets (n = 28)	−2.01*** (−7.13) 28.57	−2.59*** (−5.30) 21.43	−1.84** (−2.46) 32.14	−4.96*** (−2.59) 28.57	−6.35*** (−2.88) 28.57
	Friendly Targets (n = 18)	−0.58 (−1.19) 33.33	0.04 (0.05) 44.44	−2.44* (−1.89) 38.89	−10.27*** (−3.09) 16.67	−12.90*** (−3.37) 11.11
	Miscellaneous (n = 12)	−0.75 (−1.16) 50.00	2.38** (−2.11) 41.67	−0.45 (0.26) 41.67	−3.21 (−0.73) 33.33	−5.91 (−1.16) 25.00
Panel B: Acquisitions that are Not Subsequently Divested	Entire Sample (n = 320)	0.05 (0.50) 44.06	0.35** (1.90) 50.63	0.56** (1.99) 53.44	1.89*** (2.63) 58.75	2.13** (2.57) 58.44
	Nontargets (n = 211)	0.21 (1.59) 45.02	0.70*** (3.07) 50.71	0.96*** (2.78) 56.87	3.40*** (3.80) 63.03	3.58*** (3.47) 62.56
	All Targets (n = 67)	−0.32 (−1.47) 46.27	−0.50 (−1.33) 46.27	−0.72 (−1.26) 40.30	−0.87 (−0.59) 47.78	0.28 (0.17) 50.75
	Hostile Targets (n = 42)	−0.25 (−0.94) 45.24	−0.77* (−1.70) 47.62	−1.00 (−1.45) 38.10	−2.31 (−1.31) 45.24	1.08 (−0.53) 47.62
	Friendly Targets (n = 25)	−0.45 (−1.24) 48.00	−0.05 (−0.08) 44.00	−0.25 (−0.27) 44.00	1.56 (0.64) 52.00	2.56 (0.91) 56.00
	Miscellaneous (n = 44)	−0.18 (−0.56) 34.09	−0.23 (−0.40) 54.55	0.30 (0.34) 54.55	−1.58 (−0.71) 54.55	−2.63 (−1.02) 50.00

Note: z-statistics are in parentheses and percent abnormal returns that are positive are listed below z-statistics.
*Significant at the 10 percent level.   **Significant at the 5 pervent level.
***Significant at the 1 percent level.

In the case of the 46 acquisitions later divested by just the target companies, our findings strongly support the argument that many takeovers in the 1980s were designed primarily to reverse past acquisition mistakes. The average announcement-day return associated with these acquisitions was −1.45% (significant at the 0.01

level); and the average return fell to -8.91% when using a 60-day window. By contrast, the average announcement-day return associated with 67 acquisitions by targets that were not later divested was -0.32%; and estimates using longer event windows were also not reliably different from zero.

In short, the average negative stock price effect associated with acquisitions made by targets was largely the result of the subset of acquisitions later divested, whether in "bust-up" takeovers, or during or following an unsuccessful takeover attempt. Such evidence provides support for the "negative synergies" as opposed to the "overpayment" explanation for the market's negative reaction to acquisitions (although, as suggested earlier, it is impossible to distinguish completely between the effects of the two).

The results on divested acquisitions by the nontarget categories were also of interest. The average announcement-day return associated with 21 acquisitions made by nontargets that were later voluntarily divested was -1.16% (significant at the 0.01 level). In contrast, the announcement-day return associated with 211 nontarget acquisitions not so divested was 0.21 (not significant). Over the 60-day period, however, the return was a positive (and highly significant) 3.58%. On average, these results indicate that the nontarget companies eventually chose voluntarily to divest those acquisitions whose prospects the market pronounced from the outset to be poor.

The rate of divestiture by acquiring companies, as noted earlier, was significantly higher for targets (40.7%, 46/113) than for nontargets (9.1%, 21/232). And, perhaps equally telling, there were only two divestitures by target companies *prior* to a takeover threat. In this sense, the *voluntary* divestiture rate for targets (1.8%, 2/113) was actually considerably lower than the divestiture rate for nontargets (z-statistic = 3.23). The clear suggestion here is that many of the nontargets that sold off past acquisitions may have avoided takeover attempts precisely by voluntarily divesting less profitable acquisitions. Had the target companies done the same, or refrained from such acquisitions in the first place, they too may have avoided bids.

Conclusion

The evidence presented in this article supports economists' concept of the "market for corporate control" (specifically, takeovers) as a mechanism for disciplining managers who operate their companies in ways that do not maximize profits. It also provides support for Michael Jensen's more recent "free cash flow" theory, which views takeovers as a means of disciplining managers who "waste" excess corporate capital on value-reducing acquisitions instead of paying it out to stockholders.

The evidence also bears directly on popular objections to hostile takeovers.

First, although critics lament the rise of so-called "bust-up" takeovers during the 1980s – those that led to large divestitures – our findings are consistent with the argument that such bust-up takeovers promote economic efficiency by reallocating the targets' assets to higher-valued uses or more efficient users.

Second, our results cast new light on existing research into the effect of takeovers on the equity value of acquiring companies. Critics of hostile takeovers often argue that although target shareholders fare well in takeovers, such transactions frequently reduce the equity value of the acquirers. Our evidence illuminates this controversy by suggesting that takeovers can be at once a source of the problem of stockholder neglect and a solution to that problem. Although we find that the returns to acquiring companies are approximately zero *in the aggregate*, use of the aggregate data obscures the fact that the market discriminates very clearly between "good" bidders and "bad" bidders. Bad bidders, the evidence demonstrates, are far more likely to become the next takeover candidates.

Notes

This article is a shorter, less technical version of an article by the same title published in the *Journal of Political Economy* (1990). The views expressed herein are those of the authors and do not necessarily reflect the views of the SEC or of the authors' colleagues on the staff of the SEC.

1 See Michael C. Jensen and William H. Meckling, "Theory of the Firm: Managerial Behavior, Agency Cost and Ownership Structure," *Journal of Financial Economics* 3 (October 1976), pp. 305–60.

2 The seminal work on the market for corporate control (and indeed the origin of the phrase) is Henry Manne's article, "Mergers and the Market for Corporate Control," *Journal of Political Economy* 3 (April 1965), pp. 110–20. Another important early study is Robin Marris, "A Model of the Managerial Enterprise." *Quarterly Journal of Economics* 77 (May 1963), pp. 185–209. For more recent surveys of scholarship on the control market, see Michael C. Jensen and Richard S. Ruback, "The Market for Corporate Control: The Scientific Evidence," *Journal of Financial Economics* (April 1983), pp. 5–50; and Gregg A. Jarrell, James A. Brickley, and Jeffry M. Netter, "The Market for Corporate Control: The Empirical Evidence Since 1980," *Journal of Economic Perspectives* 2 (Winter 1988), pp. 49–68 (chapter 17 below).

3 See Michael C. Jensen, "Agency Costs of Free Cash Flow, Corporate Finance, and Take-overs," *American Economic Review* (May 1986), pp. 323–9. For a more extensive treatment of the argument that one of the primary causes of hostile takeovers may be "friendly" takeovers, see Amar Bhide, "The Causes and Consequences of Hostile Takeovers," *Journal of Applied Corporate Finance* (Summer 1989).

4 The S&P 500 index increased by about 60 percent from shortly before the first announcement of the Celeron acquisition in February 1983 through 20 days before the first announcement of Goldsmith's bid in October 1986. If the shareholder losses ($249 million [announcement day] and $573 million [−5,40 window]) associated with Goodyear's energy acquisition had instead been invested in the S&P 500 during this period, they would have increased to $401 million and $923 million, respectively. In this sense, the premium offered by Goldsmith can be seen as restoring much of the equity value in Goodyear that had been lost through acquisition.

5 Every quarter *Value Line* examines the financial prospects of about 1,500 firms in more than 65 industries.

6 Both the NYSE and the ASE require member firms to disclose to Dow Jones any information, such as news of an acquisition, that might be expected to significantly affect

their stock prices. Dow Jones transmits the disclosed information across the *Broadtape* to subscribers across the country. Subsequent editions of the Wall Street Journal carry most of the Broadtape stories.

7   It is tempting, but probably wrong, to infer from table 4.2 that nontarget firms make acquisitions more often than targets. This inference is unwarranted because the sample period is effectively longer for nontargets than for targets. For the target companies, we recorded only acquisitions made from January 1982 through three months prior to the first announcement of their suitor's interest in acquiring control. For example, if the first announcement of a bid for a target firm occurred in March 1984, we recorded acquisitions for only the two years 1982 and 1983.

One conclusion that does emerge unambiguously from table 4.2 is this: Because 79% of the hostile targets did not make a large acquisition during the sample period preceding the reception of their bids, our "bad bidder" explanation of hostile takeovers is at best a partial explanation for these transactions. As also shown in table 4.2, the relative size of the acquisitions relative to the acquiring firms do not vary much between the target and nontarget subsamples, thus allowing for comparison of the empirical results below.

8   See Paul Asquith, Robert F. Bruner, and David W. Mullins, Jr., "Merger Returns and the Form of Financing," (Manuscript. Cambridge: Harvard University, 1987). This study finds that, for a sample of 343 mergers and tender offers that occurred during 1973–83, there were significant positive stock price reactions to acquiring firms for cash offers and negative reactions for stock offers. We find a higher proportion of cash offers in our study than do Asquith et al. They focus on mergers and tender offers, whereas our study examines all acquisitions, including purchases of assets and divisions, which are generally cash offers.

9   Though the difference in the market's response to acquisitions by nontargets and the other groups is obvious from the exhibit, there is little apparent difference between the market reaction to the hostile target, friendly target and miscellaneous groups. As shown in table 4.3, however, the estimates are statistically significant in all event windows for the hostile target category, but not significant in two of the windows for the friendly target category or any of the windows for the miscellaneous category.

10 For theories of bidder overpayment, see Richard Roll, "The Hubris Hypothesis of Corporate Takeover," *Journal of Business* (April 1986), pp. 197–216 (chapter 3 above); and Bernard Black, "Bidder Overpayment in Takeovers," *Stanford Law Review* 41 (February 1989), pp. 597–660.

5

Operating Performance in Leveraged Buyouts: Evidence from 1985–1989

Tim C. Opler

This study investigates the consequences of leveraged buyouts (LBOs) on operating performance using a sample of 44 going-private transactions completed in the period 1985–9. Previous studies have documented increases in before- and after-tax cash flows following LBOs (see Bull [1], Kaplan [7], Kaplan and Stein [8], Kitching [9], Long and Ravenscraft [11], Muscarella and Vetsuypens [12], and Smith [17].[1] Kaplan [7] and Smith [17] have also shown that capital expenditures decline following LBOs. Kaplan [7] has argued that this decline represents reductions in wasteful investments. These authors have also shown that there are few changes in employment, R&D and maintenance expenditures following LBOs.

The Kaplan and Smith studies have been widely cited as evidence that leveraged buyouts result in efficiency improvements. However, these studies consider leveraged buyouts which occurred in the early and mid-1980s. Several observers have noted that, in the latter half of the 1980s, the leveraged buyout market evolved to the point where pricier and riskier transactions took place (see Kaplan and Stein [8], Jensen [6], and Summers [19]). Quite possibly, the returns from taking firms private declined over time as opportunities dried up for remedying agency problems easily through leverage and increases in management.[2] Thus, real operating gains may have been more difficult to achieve in later deals. Consistent with this account, Long and Ravenscraft [11] find that operating profit margins declined by an average of 2% following 107 leveraged buyouts which occurred in the 1985–7 period. This suggests that the dramatic operating improvements documented in earlier LBOs were due to an unusual abundance of attractive LBO targets and that "the number and type of firms that can be revitalized through LBOs is limited" (Long and Ravenscraft, p. 17).

Like Long and Ravenscraft, this paper documents changes in operating performance following LBOs of the mid- and late 1980s.[3] However, there are several differences between these studies. First, this study examines solely the largest LBOs of the late

1980s. In particular, this study documents changes in operating performance following all but two of the 20 largest LBOs which occurred between 1985 and 1990. The largest LBOs are likely to have the greatest impact on the economy and thus are naturally of the most interest to policymakers. Second, this study examines LBOs which occurred through 1989, whereas Long and Ravenscraft studied LBOs through 1987. The last two years, 1988 and 1989, are important in evaluating the LBO phenomenon since many of the largest LBOs (e.g., RJR/Nabisco) occurred in these years.

The main results of this study can be summarized as follows:

- Operating profits/sales rise by an average of 16.5% from one year before until two years after the LBOs in the sample. After adjustment for industry trends, operating profits divided by sales rise by an average of 11.6%.
- Operating profits per employee rise by an average of 31.8% in the two years following the LBOs in the sample. After industry adjustment, the rise is 40.3%.
- Cash flow net of investment rises even more significantly.
- LBOs have little impact on R&D, but result in sharp declines in capital expenditures and income taxes paid.

The results are broadly comparable with those of Kaplan [7] and Smith [17]. Kaplan finds that operating profits/sales rise by an average of 11.9% in the two years after LBOs. This rise goes to 23.3% after industry adjustment. This study shows a larger rise before industry adjustment and a smaller rise afterwards. Smith [17] shows that industry-adjusted operating cash flows per employee rise significantly after LBOs. The rise documented here is similar. While conclusions about changes in operating performance following LBOs will depend on the sample and the definitions of variables examined, the results presented in this paper suggest that the LBOs of the late 1980s produced positive operating improvements that are roughly the same as those observed by Kaplan [7] and Smith [17]. They are also significantly higher than those reported by Long and Ravenscraft [11] and somewhat higher than those reported in Kaplan and Stein [8].

The remainder of this paper is organized as follows. Section I describes the sample and performance measurement benchmarks. Section II presents results on operating performance and compares the results to those obtained previously. Section III summarizes and concludes.

Table 5.1   Distribution of sample leveraged buyouts by year

	Year				
	1985	1986	1987	1988	1989
Number of LBOs	1	4	7	21	11

I   Data and Performance Measurement

The sample consists of 44 large leveraged buyouts completed between 1985 and 1989 (see table 5.2). This sample contains all firms listed in the 1990 Forbes Private 400 that completed LBOs in 1985–9 and had financial information in *Compact Disclosure*, *Moody's Industrial Manual*, or the COMPUSTAT II PST, FC and research files for the year prior to the buyout until at least one year afterwards.[4] This financial information is provided by LBO firms because of SEC disclosure requirements associated with their issue of publicly traded bonds, preferred stock or warrants. The remaining 60 LBO firms in the Forbes 400 were not selected because they did not have publicly traded securities, because they had no pre-LBO financials, because they were a division of a larger firm, or because they were taken private in late 1989 or in 1990. Table 5.1 shows the distribution of sample firms by year. Roughly 75% of the LBOs were completed in 1988 and 1989.

The sample selection procedure may introduce biases of two sorts in the final results. The first arises because the sample excludes firms that went private since 1985 and went public before November 1990. Firms which go public again perform better than average (see Muscarella and Vetsuypens [12]), biasing the results downward.[5] In addition, firms which experienced marked declines in sales may have dropped out of the Forbes Private 400.[6] The second bias arises from excluding firms without publicly traded debt. However, only two of the 20 largest LBO companies in the 1990 Forbes Private 400 were excluded for this reason (NWA – Forbes Rank #11; and Montgomery Ward & Co. – Forbes Rank #14).[7] In addition, this exclusion criterion does not appear to have introduced important biases in past studies. Smith [17], for example, shows that firms excluded from her sample for similar reasons experienced nearly identical change in the employees-to-sales ratio, a good proxy for change in subsequent operating performance.

Several accounting measures of performance are employed in this study: (*i*) *Operating cash flow*, which is operating income or net sales minus cost of goods sold and selling, general and administrative expenses. This measures cash flow before depreciation, interest and taxes. (*ii*) *Net cash flow*, which is cash flow minus capital expenditures. This variable measures the cash produced by a firm that is available for discretionary expenditures, payment of taxes, repayment of debt or payment of dividends to equity holders.

Table 5.2 shows the identity of firms in the sample and their sales revenues one year before and two years after completing a leveraged buyout. The firms are ordered by their sales rank in the Forbes Private 400. The largest firms in the exhibit are RJR Nabisco, Southland, R. H. Macy and Supermarkets General. As stated earlier, this study focuses on the largest LBOs which occurred in the 1985–9 period. Most of the firms in the sample reported revenues exceeding $1 billion in their most recently available annual financial statement as of December 1990. Only one of the firms had revenues less than $500 million.

Table 5.2 Identity of sample firms, Forbes Private 400 Rank, sales revenues and growth in operating cash flow/sales $(T-1, T+2)$ before and after the leveraged buyout (dollar figures are in millions)

Firm	1990 Forbes rank	LBO Year	Sales T+2	Sales T−1	Growth in cash flow/sales
RJR Nabisco	4	1989	12,114	11,765	64.3%
Southland	6	1987	7,602	12,377	57.2%
R. H. Macy	9	1986	5,449	4,260	−0.8%
Supermarkets General	10	1987	5,962	5,123	17.2%
Trans World Airlines	20	1988	4,502	3,145	7.7%
Hospital Corp. of America	22	1989	4,631	4,676	−16.4%
Levi Strauss	28	1985	2,762	2,514	175.4%
Owens-Illinois	29	1987	3,572	3,674	30.2%
American Standard	31	1988	3,637	3,400	−9.3%
Jack Eckerd	32	1986	2,876	2,509	17.3%
Revco D S Inc.	49	1987	2,409	2,743	−12.5%
Alco Health Services Corp.	51	1989	2,564	1,733	−35.7%
Borg-Warner Corp.	53	1987	2,145	3,379	16.6%
Burlington Industries	57	1987	2,670	2,778	116.8%
Best Products Co., Inc.	61	1988	2,095	2,142	43.9%
Payless Cashways Inc.	64	1988	2,007	1,526	1.7%
Charter Medical Corp.	70	1988	1,228	813	−64.6%
York Holdings Corp.	94	1988	1,409	690	160.4%
Hillsborough Holdings Corp.	99	1988	1,344	2,368	35.0%
Tops Markets Inc.	131	1986	812	743	16.3%
Foodmaker Inc.	133	1988	875	541	31.6%
IBC Holding Corp.	135	1988	1,105	543	51.4%
Cullum Cos Inc.	137	1988	1,100	1,003	11.0%
Lear Seating Corp.	146	1988	1,068	900	52.1%
Essex Group Inc.	149	1988	1,054	737	10.3%
Fort Howard Corp.	150	1988	1,054	1,549	60.2%
Kash N Karry Food Stores	154	1988	1,038	840	−26.3%
Chicago & Northwestern	180	1989	961	899	146.7%
Super Rite Foods Holdings	205	1989	962	642	33.5%
Harvard Industries Inc.	211	1988	NA	559	NA
Insilco Corp.	229	1988	762	745	49.7%
International Controls Corp.	236	1989	693	153	−37.8%
Arkansas Best Corp.	250	1988	849	732	44.2%
Musicland Stores Corp.	264	1988	836	510	10.0%
AFG Industries Inc.	294	1988	648	406	13.2%
Dyncorp	295	1988	646	749	−58.4%
Bell & Howell Co.	297	1988	398	584	−94.2%
Horace Mann Educators Corp.	303	1989	639	620	13.3%
Edgcomb Corp.	317	1989	NA	556	NA
Silgan Holdings Inc.	326	1989	658	120	−9.1%
Joy Technologies Inc.	329	1987	521	800	24.4%
Florida Steel Corp.	348	1988	532	319	25.7%
Envirodyne Industries Inc.	356	1989	544	476	−2.1%
Warnaco Group Inc.	361	1986	590	561	−20.1%

Tim Opler

Table 5.3 reports summary statistics about the sample. The exhibit shows that the sample consists of firms with total sales of $89.9 billion and a total of 826,677 employees before their leveraged buyouts. The median firm had sales of $870 million before buyout and had 13,685 employees. The exhibit also shows that the total sales and total employees for the sample firms declined slightly in the first year after going private. However, total sales rose by two years after going private, and the median firm experienced an increase in sales even after the first year. Similarly, the total operating cash flow of the firms in the sample rose from $8.87 billion in the year before going private to $11.37 billion two years after going private. This represents a total increase in operating cash flow of $2.5 billion. This estimate obviously weights the largest firms in the sample more, particularly RJR/Nabisco, and is a good way to observe the overall effects of LBOs for investors. Table 5.3 also shows a significant decline in total taxes paid (roughly 80%) attributable to the increased interest expense on the debt taken on in LBOs. Total capital expenditures of the sample firms declined by slightly less than $2 billion. R&D expense for the sample firms was low to begin with and showed little appreciable change following buyout.

Table 5.3 Summary statistics for sales, operating cash flow, employees, leverage, taxes, capital expenditures, and research and development expense for 44 leveraged buyouts completed in the 1985–9 period (dollars in millions)

Variable	Mean	Total	First quartile	Median	Third quartile	N
Panel A: Firm One Year Before LBO						
Sales	2,006	88,280	591	870	2,628	44
Cash flow	202	8,869	44.4	84.4	193	44
Employees	23,619	826,677	7,400	13,685	37,000	35
Long-term debt	368	16,207	92.2	185	387	44
Taxes	52.2	2,243	5.7	17.5	54.4	43
Capital expenditures	129	4,655	16.2	54.2	193	36
R&D expense	1.46	64.2	0	0	0	44
Panel B: Firm One Year After LBO						
Sales	1,761	77,487	704	954	1,885	44
Cash flow	203	8,918	55.8	99.4	203	44
Employees	19,395	717,621	4,800	10,159	31,800	37
Long-term debt	1,580	67,937	334	770	1,803	43
Taxes	16.7	731	−2.0	5.4	13.6	43
Capital expenditures	81.5	3,424	10.3	32.0	98.0	42
R&D expense	1.74	78.4	0	0	0	45
Panel C: Firm Two Years After LBO						
Sales	2,127	89,321	762	1,084	2,670	42
Cash flow	271	11,373	63.7	105	256	42
Employees	20,908	815,424	6,300	10,407	32,895	39
Long-term debt	1,459	61,295	338	764	1,819	42
Taxes	12.6	516	−7.0	3.4	13.3	41
Capital expenditures	64.4	2,704	11.7	27.9	63.2	42
R&D expense	1.24	54.7	0	0	0	44

II   Empirical Results

A.   *Impact of LBOs on operating performance*

Post-LBO operating changes for representative firms can be observed by measuring the median change in operating performance variables before and after LBOs as shown in table 5.4. This exhibit provides the median change for two time windows (year −1 to +1 and year −1 to +2) before and after industry adjustment.[8] Statistical significance of changes in operating performance is assessed using Wilcoxon signed rank tests.[9]

Table 5.4 shows that median operating cash flow to sales rises by 16.6% from one year before until two years after the sample LBOs. After adjustment for industry trends, the operating profit margin rose by an average of 11.6%. Operating profits per employee rise by an average of 31.8% in the two years following the LBOs in the sample. After industry adjustment, this rise is 40.3%. The rise in operating

Table 5.4   Impact of LBOs on operating cash flow − median percentage change and industry-adjusted change in operating cash flow and in operating cash flow as a percentage of sales for 44 LBOs completed between 1985 and 1989

	From year i to year j	
Cash flow measure	*−1 to +1*	*−1 to +2*
A. Operating cash flow	N = 44	N = 42
Percentage change	10.2%	34.5%[a]
Industry-adjusted percentage change	−9.39%	0.0%
B. Operating cash flow/sales	N = 44	N = 41
Percentage change	9.74%[c]	16.6%[a]
Industry-adjusted percentage change	8.69%	11.6%[b]
C. Operating cash flow/employee	N = 30	N = 32
Percentage change	16.1%[b]	31.8%[a]
Industry-adjusted percentage change	11.8%	40.3%[a]
D. Net cash flow	N = 36	N = 34
Percentage change	19.3%[b]	80.7%[a]
Industry-adjusted percentage change	49.5%[c]	73.8%[a]
E. Net cash flow/sales	N = 36	N = 34
Percentage change	67.4%[c]	65.7%[a]
Industry-adjusted percentage change	58.1%[a]	49.6%[a]
F. Net cash flow/employee	N = 28	N = 30
Percentage change	53.7%[c]	59.6%[a]
Industry-adjusted percentage change	75.2%[b]	79.2%[a]

Notes: Operating cash flow is net sales less cost of goods sold and selling, general and administrative expenses. Net cash flow is cash flow less capital expenditures. Year −1 is the year before completion of the merger. Year +1 is the first full year afterwards. Significance tests are two-tailed Wilcoxon signed rank tests.
[a] Significant at the 1% level.
[b] Significant at the 5% level.
[c] Significant at the 10% level.

cash flow per employee suggests that LBOs are associated with significant improvements in labor productivity (also see Lichtenberg and Siegel [10]). Net cash flow also rises after LBOs. The median rise, before and after industry adjustment (66% and 50%, respectively), is greater than that documented in terms of operating cash flow and represents an economically and statistically significant rise in cash payout potential.

An important discretionary expense item is spending on new plant and equipment. LBO firms may decrease their capital expenditures after going private either because previous expenditures were wasteful (e.g., Jensen [5]) or because of the pressure to service debt (e.g., Myers [13]). Panel B of table 5.5 shows that the median capital expenditure to sales ratio declines by almost 40% by two years after an LBO.

Because of the tax deductibility of interest, LBO firms are likely to pay less taxes in the first years after going private. Table 5.5 gives evidence consistent with this view. The exhibit shows that median taxes, taxes/sales and taxes/employees all decline by more than 80% after LBOs. Most firms in the sample do not report R&D expense because it is negligible relative to sales. Panel F of table 5.5 shows the median

Table 5.5 Impact of LBOs on capital expenditures, taxes paid, and research and development expense – median percentage change and industry-adjusted change in expense item and in expense-item as a percentage of sales for 44 LBOs completed between 1985 and 1989

	From year i to year j	
Expenditure category	*−1 to +1*	*−1 to +2*
A. Capital expenditures	N = 34	N = 34
Percentage change	−28.5%[c]	−28.1%[c]
Industry-adjusted percentage change	−28.5%[c]	−28.3%[c]
B. Capital expenditures/sales	N = 34	N = 33
Percentage change	−25.9%	−42.2%[a]
Industry-adjusted percentage change	−30.0%[c]	−50.7%[c]
C. Income taxes paid	N = 42	N = 39
Percentage change	−85.4%[a]	−89.1%[a]
Industry-adjusted percentage change	−81.7%[a]	−76.7%[a]
D. Income taxes paid/sales	N = 42	N = 39
Percentage change	−84.3%[a]	−87.2%[a]
Industry-adjusted percentage change	−65.8%[a]	−57.3%[a]
E. R&D expenditures (nonzero R&D only)	N = 8	N = 8
Percentage change	6.61%	3.19%
Industry-adjusted percentage change	6.61%	3.19%
F. R&D expenditures/sales (nonzero R&D only)	N = 8	N = 8
Percentage change	15.4%	−7.20%
Industry-adjusted percentage change	15.4%	−8.13%

Notes: Only eight firms in the sample reported R&D expenditures in the year before their LBO. Change in R&D is shown only for these firms. Year −1 is the year before completion of the merger. Year +1 is the first full year afterwards. Significance tests are two-tailed Wilcoxon signed rank tests.
[a] Significant at the 1% level.
[b] Significant at the 5% level.
[c] Significant at the 10% level.

change in R&D intensity for those firms which do report positive R&D. This exhibit shows a small decline in R&D expense relative to sales two years after the sample LBOs.

B.   Comparison to previous studies

Table 5.6 compares changes in key operating ratios observed in this study to those observed in six previous studies. Kaplan [7] finds that operating cash flow to sales rises by 11.9% in the two years after 34 LBOs from the 1980–6 period. Muscarella and Vetsuypens [12] find that the median cash flow to sales of 28 firms rises by 23.5% from the completion of an LBO until after going public again (1976–87). The improvement of 16.5% observed for the firms studied here is in between the improvement observed in these two other studies. The improvement observed after industry adjustment is also comparable to that observed in Kaplan's study. Smith [17] finds that operating cash flow per employee rises by $1,369 (−1,+2 years) relative to a pre-buyout median of $8,793 for 12 firms which completed LBOs in the 1977–86 period. The equivalent improvement in this study is $1,188 relative to a base of $8,088. This improvement is quite similar and suggests that later LBOs did not result in smaller efficiency gains.[10] This pattern is not consistent with the argument that changes in the LBO market after 1985 dried up the supply of profitable LBO opportunities. This pattern is also different from that observed by Long and Ravenscraft [11] who find that operating cash flow in 107 post-1985 LBOs actually *decreases* by 2%. The difference in the results of this study and Long and Ravenscraft [11] are likely to be due to differences in sample composition; perhaps the smaller average size of the LBOs in their sample accounts for the difference.

In a particularly thorough study of post-LBO performance, Smith [17] finds that profit margins rise after LBOs, while taxes, capital expenditures and R&D expenses fall. She also finds little change in the level of employment. This study also finds sharp declines in taxes paid and capital expenditures. There appears to be little change in R&D expense. This study also shows no significant change in the level of employment after LBOs.

Table 5.6   Summary of studies of changes in firm operations after LBOs

Variable	This study	Kaplan	Kaplan & Stein	Kitching	Long & Ravenscraft	Muscarella & Vetsuypens	Smith
Operating cash flow/sales	16.5%	11.9%	12.1%	55%	9%	23.5%	NA
Taxes	−89.1%	NA	NA	−43%	NA	NA	NA
Investment/sales	−42.2%	−31.6%	NA	NA	NA	−11.4%	−31.5%
Employees	0.3%	0.9%	NA	NA	NA	−0.6%	2%
R&D	−7.2%	NA	NA	NA	NA	NA	−7.4%
Time period	1985–89	1980–86	1980–89	1980–87	1981–87	1976–87	1977–86
Number of LBOs	42	37	66	110	198	35	37
Window	(−1,+2)	(−1,+2)	(−1,+2)	(0,+3)	(−1,+1)	Variable	(−1,+2)

Notes: NA means statistic not available or computed.

III   Conclusion

This study investigates change in operating performance following 44 LBOs of the last half of the 1980s. The median post-LBO operating cash flow to sales ratio of firms in the sample rises by 11.6% after industry adjustment. This rise is comparable to that observed in earlier LBOs by Kaplan [7], Muscarella and Vetsuypens [12], and Smith [17], although some differences in sample selection criteria and variable definitions qualify this comparison. All told, the LBOs in this sample were followed by increases in operating cash flow in excess of $2 billion, suggesting that these transactions have yielded significant efficiency gains for investors. Increases in net cash flow were even higher. Because the analysis was limited to the first two years after LBOs, the results do not show the full impact of an LBO on operating performance. The total impact of an LBO over its lifetime is likely to change as new cost-cutting measures are undertaken in the years following a deal (see Muscarella and Vetsuypens [12]). This study also finds that capital expenditures, income taxes and R&D expense decline after LBOs are completed.

While improvements in cash flow following LBOs suggest that these transactions mitigate management–shareholder agency conflict and force disgorgement of free cash flow, it is possible that other factors account for the results observed here (see Palepu [16]). Possibly, improvements come from cutting "invisible" discretionary expenses important for long-run performance (see Stein [18]) or from factors having nothing to do with LBOs known to insiders prior to going private. This study has provided little evidence regarding these possibilities beyond that offered in Kaplan [7] and Smith [17].

The finding that LBOs in the 1985–9 period were not accompanied by smaller operating improvements than observed in earlier transactions suggests that these transactions were not "more marginal" as has been suggested by some observers. This casts doubt on the contention that the collapse of the LBO market in 1989 and 1990 evidenced the unusual and transitory nature of the leveraged buyout transaction. Rather, the combination of high prices in this market (see Kaplan and Stein [8]), the rise in interest rates in 1988 and 1989, the bankruptcy of the leading junk bond issuer, and heightened government pressure on banks and insurance institutions were likely to have contributed to the market collapse. This is not to say that all firms are well-suited for an LBO. Firms with expected financial distress costs make poor LBO candidates (see Opler and Titman [14]). Nonetheless, as interest rates decline, economic conditions improve and regulatory pressures on banks ease, it is quite possible that firms will continue to reap the benefits of LBOs in the 1990s.

Notes

I would like to thank Dan Asquith, Gerry Lawson, Julia Liebeskind, Louis Lowenstein, David Ravenscraft, Sheridan Titman, Mike Vetsuypens, and especially two referees and Tom

Copeland (the editor) for useful comments and suggestions. Tina McCarthy of *Forbes* magazine also generously provided assistance.

1   Similar studies which examine operating performance after corporate mergers include Healy, Palepu and Ruback [3], Jarrell [4], and Opler and Weston [15].

2   This view has been expressed often in the press. See, for example, Faltermayer [2], who suggests that deals in the latter half of the 1980s were particularly nonproductive.

3   A second study which examines returns on LBOs in the late 1980s is Kaplan and Stein [8]. These authors find that 18 LBOs in 1985–6 resulted in a growth in operating margins, from one year before until two years after, of −5.4%, and that 22 LBOs in the 1987–8 period were followed by operating margin growth of 19.2%. These growth rates are not industry-adjusted.

4   LBOs are defined as transactions where the equity of a separate, publicly traded firm was delisted and replaced largely with debt while the firm was not merged into another firm. In an LBO, management takes a significant dollar amount of equity in the new, private firm (this may not be large percentage-wise in big deals such as RJR/Nabisco). Cases where delisted firms are merged into shell organizations established by LBO sponsors (e.g., Hillsborough Holdings) are also classified as LBOs. This definition is similar to that used by Kaplan [7] and Smith [17].

5   For example, Safeway Stores, which experienced strong operating improvements, was not in the 1990 list because of its public offering.

6   I examined earlier Forbes 400 lists in search of large buyouts which were subsequently followed by sharp sales declines. Firms which became financially distressed (e.g., Revco, Hillsborough and Southland) were not removed from the list. However, Beatrice was not included in the list because it was fully broken up by the end of 1990. The firm's operating income had risen from US$169 million in 1985 to $343 million in 1989 with even sales revenue.

7   Qualitative credit review by Standard & Poor's suggest that the NWA buyout has not performed badly.

8   Industry-adjusted changes are computed by subtracting the median change for all firms in the same three-digit SIC code on COMPUSTAT over the same time period.

9   The test statistic is computed as

$$S = [\sum r_i^+ - n(n + 1)/4],$$

where r_i^+ is the rank of the absolute value of the ith observation of the variable studied after discarding zero values. n is the number of nonzero values of the variable and the summation is over positive values of the variable. Average ranks are used for tied values. The significance level of S is computed by treating $[S(n - 1)^{1/2}]/[(nV - S^2)^{1/2}]$ as a Student's t variate with $n - 1$ degrees of freedom. Here

$$V = [n(n + 1)(2n + 1) - .5\sum t_i(t_i + 1)(t_i - 1)]/24,$$

where the sum is calculated over groups tied in absolute value and t_i is the number of tied values in the ith group.

10 The results of this study and Smith [17] are not fully comparable because Smith used a measure of operating cash flows which removed accruals (e.g., pertaining to decreases in noncash working capital) and adjusted out inventory write-ups. All else being equal, nonremoval of changes in net noncash cash flow will bias the operating improvements in

this study downward since Smith [17] observes reduced working capital relative to sales. In addition, to the extent that firms include depreciation and amortization expenses in their cost of goods sold or selling, and general and administrative expenses, the approach used in this study may under-report operating improvements relative to Smith [17].

References

1   Bull, I., 1989, Management Performance in Leveraged Buyouts: An Empirical Analysis, in *Leveraged Management Buyouts: Causes and Consequences*, Y. Amihud (ed.), New York, New York University Press.

2   Faltermayer, E., 1991, The Deal Decade: Verdict on the '80s, *Fortune*, August, 26, 58–70.

3   Healy, P. M., K. G. Palepu, and R. S. Ruback, 1990, Does Corporate Performance Improve After Mergers?, NBER Working Paper No. 3348, May.

4   Jarrell, S. L., 1991, Do Takeovers Generate Value? Evidence on the Capital Market's Ability to Assess Takeovers, Working Paper, Southern Methodist University, July.

5   Jensen, M. C., 1986, Agency Costs of Free Cash Flow, Corporate Finance and Takeovers, *American Economic Review*, May, 323–9.

6   Jensen, M. C. , 1990, Discussion in LBO Conference, *Journal of Applied Corporate Finance*, Summer, pp. 6–37.

7   Kaplan, S. N., 1989, The Effects of Management Buyouts on Operating Performance and Value, *Journal of Financial Economics*, November, 217–54.

8   Kaplan, S. N. and J. C. Stein, 1991, The Evolution of Buyout Pricing and Financial Structure in the 1980s, Working Paper, University of Chicago, September.

9   Kitching, J., 1989, Early Returns on LBOs, *Harvard Business Review*, November–December, 74–81.

10 Lichtenberg, F. R. and D. Siegel, 1990, The Effects of Leveraged Buyouts on Productivity and Related Aspects of Firm Behavior, *Journal of Financial Economics*, September, 165–94.

11 Long, W. F. and D. J. Ravenscraft, 1991, The Aftermath of LBOs, Working Paper, University of North Carolina, April.

12 Muscarella, C. J. and M. R. Vetsuypens, 1990, Efficiency and Organizational Structure: A Study of Reverse LBOs, *Journal of Finance*, December, 1389–414.

13 Myers, S. C., 1977, Determinants of Corporate Borrowing, *Journal of Financial Economics*, March, 147–75.

14 Opler, T. C. and S. Titman, 1991, The Characteristics of Leveraged Buyout Firms, Working Paper # 9-91, University of California Los Angeles, May.

15 Opler, T. C. and J. F. Weston, 1991, The Impact of Mergers on Operating Performance, Working Paper, University of California Los Angeles, September.

16 Palepu, K. G., 1990, Consequences of Leveraged Buyouts, *Journal of Financial Economics*, September, 247–62.

17 Smith, A. J., 1990, Capital Ownership Structure and Performance: The Case of Management Buyouts, *Journal of Financial Economics*, September, 143–65.

18 Stein, J. C., 1989, Efficient Capital Markets, Inefficient Firms: A Model of Myopic Corporate Behavior, *Quarterly Journal of Economics*, November, 655–69.

19 Summers, L., 1990, Discussion in LBO Conference, *Journal of Applied Corporate Finance*, Summer, 6–37.

6

The Shareholder Gains from Leveraged Cash-outs: Some Preliminary Evidence

Robert T. Kleiman

In recent years, the market for corporate control has expanded at an astonishing rate. In 1986, for example, there were over 2,200 merger and acquisition transactions representing a total dollar volume in excess of US$200 billion – a 20 percent increase over 1985.[1] As a result of this growth in takeover activity, corporate managers have devised a number of defensive strategies to preserve their independence. Academic research, however, strongly suggests that actions that reduce the possibility of takeover are generally harmful to the target firm's shareholders – especially those measures not submitted for shareholder approval.[2]

The purpose of this study is to analyze the stockholder consequences of a recently developed defensive strategy, the leveraged recapitalization (also known as a "leveraged cash-out"). The changes in capital structure and equity ownership wrought by LCOs are similar to those brought about by leveraged buyouts (LBOs). In both cases, the firm significantly increases its financial leverage and management increases its proportional ownership of the company.

Recent research has shown that leveraged buyouts announcements are associated with material increases in shareholder wealth – on average, about 30 percent.[3] Because of the similarity of leveraged cashouts to LBOs, I begin with the hypothesis that leveraged cash-outs can be expected to produce stockholder gains of roughly the same order.

What Are Leveraged Cash-outs?

Although not originally conceived as such, leveraged cash-outs have become a popular defensive tactic that is used by target companies to ward off hostile takeovers. Such major recapitalizations provide existing shareholders with a large one-time payout in cash or debt securities while still allowing shareholders to maintain a significant equity interest in the restructured company. In these transactions, the firm replaces the majority of its equity (in fact, the *book* value of the firm's equity typically becomes negative) with a debt package consisting of both senior bank debt and subordinated debentures. The leveraging of the firm discourages corporate raiders who can no longer borrow against the assets of the target firm to finance an acquisition. Also, LCOs are often accompanied by a major restructuring in which the company, pressured by the debt, sells off assets and streamlines operations.

The most typical form of the LCO is that in which the company uses newly borrowed funds to pay its shareholders a large one-time dividend. There are variations on this formula (see appendix A for three cases); but, in all varieties of LCOs, management-owned shares do not participate in the distribution, so that management's proportional ownership significantly rises. (In effect, leveraged recapitalizations are stock splits in which only the insiders' shares are split.)

The firm's outside shareholders either retain their existing shares or exchange their old shares for new shares, called "stubs." In the first leveraged cash-outs, Multimedia. FMC, Colt Industries, and Owens–Corning issued cash plus new stock to outside shareholders in exchange for their old stock. In later LCOs – such as those by Holiday Corp., Caesar's World, and Harcourt Brace Jovanovich – the firms took on substantial additional debt to finance the cash dividends, while management received new shares in place of the dividend. In either instance, however, the firm's shares continue to be publicly traded and, as a result, shareholders continue to have the opportunity to share in the future gains (or losses) of the firm.

An alternative to the LBO . . .

LCOs, as pointed out earlier, have several important features in common with leveraged buyouts. In both types of transactions, the firm changes from an equity- to a debt-dominated capital structure. In order to support the large amount of debt incurred in financing these transactions, management suspends dividend payments, thus conserving cash that would otherwise flow to the firm's shareholders. In this manner, non-tax-deductible dividend payments are converted to interest payments which are fully tax-deductible; and, as a result, operating income for the next few years is almost entirely sheltered from taxation.

But possibly of greater benefit than the tax shields is the concentration of ownership in management's hands achieved by the use of leverage. In LBOs, management normally receives equity without making an investment. In LCOs, corporate managers' percentage ownership increases by virtue of the fact that executives receive new shares of (roughly) equivalent value instead of cash (again, see the appendix for the terms of exchange of three special cases). Shares in the newly recapitalized company (or, in the case of an LBO, the newly privatized company) may represent a significant portion of the wealth of the individual managers.

As in an LBO, the ownership structure that results from an LCO ties managerial rewards more closely to performance. Hence, LCOs, like LBOs, strengthen managerial incentives to operate efficiently through better management of working capital and smaller support staffs. Also, the high levels of financial leverage have a powerful disciplining effect since default or renegotiation of the debt can cost managers their independence and even their jobs. And finally, with discretionary cash flow dedicated to debt service requirements, management's temptation to reinvest corporate capital in low-return businesses (or, as potentially destructive, diversifying acquisitions) is largely removed.[4]

Given the strong similarities between LBOs and LCOs, then, it should come as no surprise that the best LCO candidates have much in common with LBO firms: namely, (1) a predictable earnings stream that can be used to service debt; (2) a "clean" balance sheet with little debt; (3) a strong market position in the firm's primary market; (4) mundane product lines not likely to become obsolete; (5) low requirements for future capital investment and research and development expenditures; (6) a heavy asset base which can be used as collateral for loans; (7) excess assets which can be sold off; and (8) experienced management with a proven track record. Companies undertaking these transactions are thus typically manufacturing companies having low levels of business risk.[5]

But an alternative with a difference

Now that we have discussed the similarities, what are the critical differences between LBOs and LCOs? The most important – and indeed the factor which spawned the first LCO (in the case of Multimedia) – is that LCO firms remain publicly-traded companies and thus avoid the potential managerial conflict of interest associated with LBOs. Critics of LBOs argue that senior executives negotiating the sale of the company to themselves could be engaged in self-dealing – that is, profiting at the expense of their shareholders by buying shares at too low a price. Apologists for LBOs reply, however, that a company that proposes a management buyout at an inside price must conduct an auction and sell the company to the highest bidder. By announcing a buyout offer, management effectively puts the company "in play," thereby inviting higher bids from other would-be acquirers.

In contrast to an LBO, an LCO does not formally put the company "in play." Since the same group of shareholders remains in control after the leveraged recapitalization, management is not technically selling the company. It is, therefore, not compelled by law to respond to competing bids by virtue of the fact that an LCO does not actually establish an explicit value for the firm's shares. Rather, that value is equal to the per share amount of the shareholder distribution plus the *ex post* trading value of the "stub" shares. Hence, the appeal of LCOs as an antitakeover strategy.

To be sure, LCO companies retain one of the disadvantages of public ownership which LBOs avoid: the costs of disseminating information to shareholders and satisfying SEC disclosure requirements. But continued public ownership also confers the benefit of access to the public capital markets with their attendant liquidity. This access to capital markets should enable LCO firms to raise capital on more attractive terms than private companies because investors are typically better able than private lenders to diversify away firm-specific risks. Also, whereas LBOs impose costs on managers by forcing them to hold poorly diversified and illiquid portfolios, LCOs can offer compensation packages that are better suited to the preferences of individual managers because of the marketability of the common stock. And, finally, since the public trading of a company's shares allows shareholders to readily sell their holdings if they disagree with corporate policies, there is less potential in LCOs for costly disagreements among stockholders.

Current Research on Defensive Tactics

According to most creditable research, antitakeover actions typically impose significant losses on the target firm's shareholders. Much of this evidence is thus consistent with the "managerial entrenchment" hypothesis – the argument that actions which eliminate actual or potential takeover bids further managerial interests at the expense of shareholders.

For example, shareholders experience negative wealth effects from "greenmail" transactions – those in which a firm negotiates the repurchase of a block of its common stock at a significant premium above the market price in exchange for the block-holder's promise not to seek control of the firm.[6] Moreover, public stockholders also experience significant losses in the following situations: when the managers of the target firm terminate merger negotiations;[7] when managers indicate their opposition to open market share accumulation;[8] when managers attempt to eliminate cumulative voting provisions (which enable outsiders to gain board representation);[9] when managers issue securities with poison pill provisions;[10] when the target firm and a substantial shareholder enter into a standstill agreement which limits the holdings of the shareholder to some maximum percentage for a specified number of years;[11] and when managers respond to hostile takeovers with defensive adjustments in their ownership and asset structures.[12] On the other hand, stockholders are typically not affected when managers bring litigation to stop or delay a tender offer or when firms adopt antitakeover charter amendments.[13]

In contrast to most of the defensive tactics listed above, there are good reasons, as we have seen, to believe that leveraged cash-outs should work to increase shareholder wealth. Like some leveraged buyouts, LCOs can be viewed as defensive reactions to market pressures to change the corporate financial structure, while at the same time permitting incumbent management to remain in control. Like LBOs, because these transactions provide managers with greater equity ownership, organizational efficiency should improve. And, as in LBOs, the debt taken on in LCOs, besides providing valuable tax shields, effectively bonds managers' promises to pay out future free cash flows. In so doing, it reduces management's temptation to waste corporate capital on low-return projects and diversifying acquisitions.[14]

Finally, unlike most of the defensive strategies listed above, LCOs require shareholder approval, and it is unlikely that shareholders would consistently approve transactions contrary to their interests.[15]

Table 6.1 List of leveraged recapitalizations

Firm	Date	US$ Amount	Prior hostile bid
1. Multimedia	5/3/85	$890 million	YES
2. FMC	2/24/86	$1.8 billion	NO[a]
3. Colt	7/21/86	$1.5 billion	NO
4. Owens Corning	8/29/86	$1.5 billion	YES
5. Holiday Corp.	11/13/86	$2.7 billion	NO[b]
6. Harcourt Brace Jovanovich	5/27/87	$3.0 billion	YES
7. Caesar's World*	5/19/87	$960 million	YES
8. Allegis**	5/29/87	$3.0 billion	YES
Mean		$1.92 billion	

* Recapitalization plan was subsequently rejected by the New Jersey Casino Commission.

** Recapitalization was subsequently cancelled in favor of a restructuring proposal involving a special dividend paid from the proceeds of the sales of the firm's hotel and rental car units.

[a] FMC was concerned about the emergence of an unfriendly suitor but no actual bid was announced in the *Wall Street Journal*.

[b] There was speculation concerning a possible bid by Donald Trump but no bid actually surfaced.

Source: The *Wall Street Journal*

Shareholder Gains from LCOs

In order to determine the shareholder consequences of leveraged recapitalizations, I examined the market reaction to announcements of LCOs by eight companies. These firms, the announcement dates, and the reported dollar value of the transactions are shown in table 6.1. The average dollar value of the payouts to shareholders was close to $2 billion, a figure significantly greater than the level of the average management buyout.[16] In five of the eight cases, there was a previous announcement of a hostile takeover bid; and in one other case a *Wall Street Journal* article indicated that management was concerned about the possibility of an unfriendly bid. Only in the cases of Colt Industries and FMC did there appear to be no public indication of a takeover threat.

Table 6.2 displays the changes in the firms' capital structures that resulted from these transactions. The increases in financial leverage are substantial and are even greater than those associated with leveraged buyouts. In each case, the firm has a *negative* net worth and book value per share upon completion of the recapitalization. Although the book value of the equity is negative, the market capitalization for each of the LCO firms remained substantially positive after completing the transaction. For example, FMC Corporation had a book value of negative $507 million and a market value in excess of $700 million just after completing its LCO.[17]

Table 6.3 shows the changes in insider ownership that result from the LCOs. Prior to the transactions, management and employees, on average, owned only 6.4 percent of the company's common stock. (In comparison, previous research has found an average managerial ownership of 13.9 percent for the 30 companies that comprised the

Table 6.2 Capital structure changes resulting from the leveraged recapitalizations (US$ millions)

		Before recapitalization	After recapitalization
Multimedia	L-T debt	73.2	877.7
	Net worth	248.7	d576.4
	Book value/share	14.91	d52.4
FMC Corp.	L-T debt	303.2	1,787.3
	Net worth	1,123.1	d506.6
	Book value/share	7.54	d11.25
Colt Industries	L-T debt	342.4	1,643.1
	Net worth	414.3	d1,078
	Book value/share	2.55	d36.91
Owens Corning	L-T debt	543.0	1,645.2
	Net worth	944.7	d1,025
	Book value/share	31.70	d25.94
Holiday Corp.	L-T debt	992.5	2,500
	Net worth	638.7	d850
	Book value/share	27.07	d31.15
Harcourt Brace Jovanovich	L-T debt	790.3	2,550
	Net worth	531.5	d1,050
	Book value/share	13.48	d21.00

Note: (1) *d* denotes deficit.

(2) This table includes only those 6 companies that actually completed the leveraged recapitalizations.

Table 6.3 Changes in share ownership of insiders for firms announcing leveraged recapitalizations

Firm	Before recapitalization	After recapitalization
1. Multimedia	13%	43%
2. FMC Corp.	19%	40%
3. Colt Industries	7%	38%
4. Owens Corning	1%	16.2%
5. Holiday Corp.	1.5%	10%
6. Harcourt Brace Jovanovich	7%	30%
7. Caesar's World	1.5%	1.5%*
8. Allegis	1%	1%*
Means*	6.4%	29.5%

* Note that the percentage ownership of insiders for Caesar's World and Allegis does not change. In the case of Caesar's World, the New Jersey Casino Control Commission rejected the leveraged recapitalization after it had been approved by stockholders. In the case of Allegis, the leveraged recapitalization was subsequently cancelled in favor of a restructuring. Hence, the mean value for the "after recapitalization" column excludes these two companies.

Sources: Proxy Statements and the Value Line Investment Survey

Table 6.4   The market response to LCO announcements

	2-day returns	60-day returns
1. Multimedia	−1.2%	10.4%
2. FMC	8.0%*	21.0%
3. Colt	40.1%	28.5%
4. Owens Corning	−1.3%	37.7%
5. Holiday Corp.	0.0%	26.0%
6. Harcourt Brace Jovanovich	20.7%	55.6%
7. Caesar's World	6.5%	37.4%
8. Allegis	9.1%	50.0%
Mean	10.2%	33.3%
Mean (excluding Colt & FMC)	5.6%	—

* The three-day return is 16.1%.

top, middle, and bottom ten of the Fortune 500 for 1975.)[18] However, after the completion of the LCOs, the average percentage of insider ownership increased to 29.5 percent. As argued earlier, the greater insider ownership stake (combined with the necessity of meeting the debt service requirements) can be expected to encourage greater organizational efficiency and value-maximizing behavior on the part of management.[19]

The stock market response to LCO announcements

One of the major implications of the efficient markets hypothesis is that stock prices respond rapidly and in an unbiased manner to the announcement of new information. A large body of empirical evidence indicates that stock price changes provide the best estimate of the effect of a specific event on the value of the firm. Accordingly, this study compares the returns to companies announcing LCOs with the returns to the overall market over the same time period (adjusted for the risk of individual companies). The resulting market-adjusted returns may be interpreted as the stock market's assessment of the long-term value consequences of these recapitalizations.

Because five of the eight LCO companies had already received takeover bids (and one of the other three firms had publicly expressed awareness of an impending takeover bid), the market response to the announcement alone of an LCO would significantly understate the total gains to shareholders; a better measure would also incorporate the run-up caused by the possibility of takeover. I accordingly calculated the price changes both during the two-day period surrounding the announcement of the LCO and over a 60-day period prior to, as well as 40 days after, the day of announcement.

Consistent with previous merger studies, my study indicates that stock prices begin to rise approximately two months prior to the announcements of leveraged cashouts – primarily, in most cases, because of the presence of a hostile bidder. But even without including the substantial run-up in prices prior to the announcements, my results indicate that LCO announcements are associated with material increases in shareholder

wealth. The average market-adjusted (or "abnormal") return on the day of announcement (day 0) was a positive 8 percent; and on day −1 the return was a positive 2.2
percent, amounting to a 2-day abnormal return of more than 10 percent. Over the
60-day period (−59,0) prior to and including announcement day, the eight LCO firms
experienced an average positive return of 33.3 percent. And, as shown in figures 6.1
and 6.2, there does not appear to have been any material change in the pattern of the
abnormal returns in the 40 trading days following the announcements.

In analyzing the returns of the eight firms in the sample, it is useful to distinguish
between "pre-emptive" LCOs (those cases in which there was no prior public indication of an outstanding or an expected takeover bid) and "defensive" ones. As indicated
previously, the LCOs of Colt Industries and FMC can be viewed as pre-emptive, and
the other six as defensive.

Of all the firms in the sample, Colt Industries achieved the largest positive market
response during the two-day announcement period – roughly 40 percent. In the Colt
case, there was no significant run-up in price prior to the announcement, and thus the

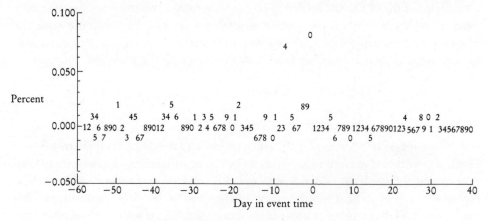

Figure 6.1 Plot of daily average abnormal returns

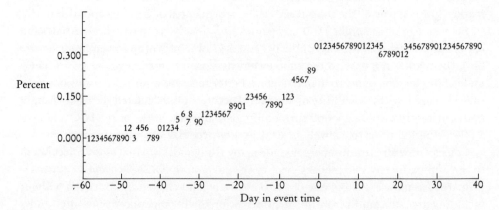

Figure 6.2 Plot of cumulative average abnormal returns

immediate 40 percent price increase arguably reflects the *entire* capitalized value of the benefits expected from the recapitalization.

The case of FMC provides further evidence of the value of a largely, although perhaps not wholly, pre-emptive recapitalization. FMC's shareholders earned net-of-market returns of 16 percent over the three-day period (−2 to 0) leading up to and including the announcement day. There had, however, been some run-up in FMC's price (on the order of 5 percent) in the two months prior to announcement of the LCO. Moreover, perhaps as if to explain this run-up, press accounts announcing the transaction contain statements by FMC's management that the recapitalization was motivated in part by the general possibility of hostile takeover.

The other six LCOs, by contrast, may be characterized as unambiguously "defensive" recapitalizations. The two-day announcement returns ranged from −1.3 percent (in the Owens-Corning case) to a startling 20.7 percent for Harcourt-Brace-Jovanovich – surprising in that this 20 percent came on top of an earlier 35 percent stock price increase upon announcement of a takeover bid. The average two-day return to these six takeover targets was a positive 5.6 percent. Thus, in contrast to most other defensive maneuvers, leveraged cash-outs do not appear to harm shareholders. In fact, on average they appear to hold out benefits to shareholders that are commensurate with, if not greater than, those promised by takeover.

Summing Up

This paper has examined the characteristics and valuation consequences of a recently developed antitakeover defense – the leveraged cash-out. These transactions involve a recapitalization in which the company moves from an equity- to a debt-dominated capital structure. The firm uses the proceeds from the debt to make a large one-time distribution of cash to the firm's shareholders. Management-owned shares do not participate in the distribution, so that management's proportional ownership rises significantly.

In contrast to a leveraged buyout, the firm remains publicly traded and the firm's shareholders have the opportunity to share in future gains. Like leveraged buyouts, leveraged recapitalizations may be viewed as a response to market pressures to change the firm's financial structure while permitting incumbent management to remain in control. Management receives a substantial equity stake in the recapitalized companies, which raises their personal benefits from enhancing organizational efficiency. In addition, the substantial increase in financial leverage reduces management's discretion over the firm's free cash flow since the cash must be devoted to meeting the debt payments.

Consistent with the gains to shareholders in LBOs, this study finds significant positive abnormal returns around the announcements of eight leveraged recapitalization transactions. In contrast to many other antitakeover devices, leveraged cashouts appear to lead to a greater convergence of interests between managers and shareholders, thereby increasing shareholder wealth.

Appendix: review of terms of exchange

1 FMC Corporation: There were three different parties to the transaction and three associated exchange offers:

1) public shareholders – $70+1 new share
2) the thrift plan – $25+4 new shares
3) management and the PAYSOP – $0+5 2/3 new shares

The share price of FMC 60 days prior to announcement of the LCO was roughly $70. The value of each of the three offers could be different, depending on the initial trading price of the new shares. If the new shares sold for $15, all three parties to the transaction would have held $85 in total value. After the transaction took place, the actual share price of the new shares was $16, thus giving shareholders $86 in total value and management over $90.

2 Colt Industries: In Colt's exchange offer, there were two parties – public shareholders and the Retirement Savings Plan; and the deal was structured so as give both a claim of equal value immediately *after* the trading value of the new shares was established. Public shareholders received $85 in cash and one share of new Colt stock for each share held prior to the offering, whereas each share of stock held in the Colt Retirement Savings Plan received no cash and a number of new shares equal to one plus $85 divided by the initial trading price of the stub $(1+85/P_{stub})$. That price turned out to be $11.50, and thus the management group received 8.39 shares of the new Colt stock.

3 Owens-Corning: The outside shareholders in this recapitalization received $52 cash, $35 face amount (roughly $19 market value) of junior subordinated discount debentures, and one new share in exchange for each old share. Each of the common shares held by four of the company's employee benefit plans were converted into 7 new shares. Thus, as in the FMC deal, there is an implied value for the new shares ($11.80) at which the value of outsiders' and insiders' holdings would be equal.

Notes

Dr. Kleiman wishes to acknowledge the partial financial support of Interactive Data Corporation and the helpful comments of Donald Chew, Editor of *The Continental Bank Journal of Applied Corporate Finance*.

1   The source of these statistics is *Mergers & Acquisitions*, September/October 1987.
2   A recent study by Gregg Jarrell, James Brickley, and Jeffrey Netter distinguishes between two broad categories of defensive measures – those receiving voting approval by shareholders and those adopted unilaterally by management without shareholder approval. On average, those defensive tactics which require shareholder approval do not harm shareholders. However, those defensive actions which are adopted unilaterally by management are in most cases harmful to target shareholders. For further details see G. Jarrell, J. Brickley, and J. Netter, "The Market for Corporate Control: The Empirical Evidence Since 1980," *Journal of Economic Perspectives* (1988; chapter 17 above).
3   See Harry DeAngelo, Linda DeAngelo, and Ed Rice, "Going Private," *Midland Corporate Finance Journal* (Summer 1984). See also Khalil Torabzadeh and William Bertin, "Lever-

aged Buyouts and Stockholder Wealth," *Journal of Financial Research*, (Winter 1987), pp. 313–21.

4   The argument for the control function of debt was first presented formally by Michael Jensen in "Agency Costs of Free Cash Flow, Corporate Finance, and Takeovers," *American Economic Review* (May 1986), pp. 326–9. Free cash flow is the cash flow in excess of that required to fund positive net present value projects. For a less formal, but wider-ranging exposition of Jensen's "free cash flow" theory, see M. Jensen, "The Takeover Controversy: Analysis and Evidence," *Midland Corporate Finance Journal* (Summer 1986), pp. 6–31.

5   The characteristics of leveraged buyouts described in this section are based on the discussion in DeAngelo and DeAngelo (1987).

6   For documentation of the negative stock market reaction to targeted share repurchases, see Larry Dann and Harry DeAngelo, "Standstill Agreements, Privately Negotiated Stock Repurchases, and the Market for Corporate Control," *Journal of Financial Economics* (April 1983), pp. 275–300; and Michael Bradley and L. Macdonald Wakeman, "The Wealth Effects of Targeted Share Repurchases," *Journal of Financial Economics*, April 1983, pp. 301–28.

7   For evidence on the rejection of takeover proposals, see Peter Dodd, "Merger Proposals, Management Discretion and Shareholder Wealth," *Journal of Financial Economics* (June 1980), pp. 105–38.

8   On the market response to opposition to open market share accumulation, see Wayne Mikkelson and Richard Ruback, "An Empirical Analysis of the Inter-firm Equity Investment Process," *Journal of Financial Economics* (December 1985), pp. 523–53.

9   On the market response to the elimination of cumulative voting, see Sanjai Bhagat and James Brickley, "Cumulative Voting: The Value of Minority Shareholder Voting Rights," *Journal of Law and Economics* (October 1984), pp. 339–65.

10 See Paul Malatesta and Ralph Walking, "Poison Pill Securities: Stockholder Wealth, Profitability, and Ownership Structure," forthcoming in the *Journal of Financial Economics*, 1988; and Michael Ryngaert, "The Effect of Poison Pill Securities on Shareholder Wealth," *Journal of Financial Economics* (1988).

11 On standstill agreements, see Dann and DeAngelo (1983) cited in note 8.

12 On defensive adjustments in ownership and capital structure, see L. Dann and H. DeAngelo, "Corporate Financial Policy and Corporate Control; A Study of Defensive Adjustments in Asset and Ownership Structure," in the *Journal of Financial Economics*, 1988.

13 On the market response to antitakeover charter amendments, see Harry DeAngelo and Ed Rice, "Antitakeover Charter Amendments and Shareholder Wealth," *Journal of Financial Economics* (April 1983), pp. 329–59, and Scott Linn and John McConnell, "An Empirical Investigation of the Impact of 'Antitakeover' Charter Amendments on Common Stock Prices," *Journal of Financial Economics* (April 1983), pp. 361–99.

14 Consistent with this line of reasoning, previous research has found that exchange offers of debt for common stock are associated with significant increases in common stock returns. See Ron Masulis, "The Impact of Capital Structure Change on Firm Value: Some Estimates," *Journal of Finance*, March 1983, pp. 107–26.

15 See note 2 earlier on the difference between the market's response to defensive transactions approved by management and those not so approved.

16 See Harry DeAngelo and Linda DeAngelo, "Management Buyouts of Publicly Traded Corporations," *Financial Analysts Journal*, May/June 1987, pp. 38–49 for evidence regarding the average size of management buyouts.

17   The large levels of financial leverage resulting from the leveraged recapitalization may have potentially offsetting negative valuation consequences. In particular, FMC Corp., Colt Industries, Caesar's World, and Allegis were placed on Standard & Poor's Credit Watch list for possible downgrading. Robert Holthausen and Richard Leftwich (in "The Effect of Bond Rating Changes on Common Stock Prices," *Journal of Financial Economics* 1986) have shown that firms which are added to the S&P Credit Watch list for possible downgrading experience significant negative abnormal returns. However, the results of this study indicate that these negative effects are overwhelmed by the positive benefits of the recapitalization.

18   See Harold Demsetz, "The Structure of Ownership and the Theory of the Firm," *Journal of Law and Economics, June* 1983, pp. 375–90.

19   Randall Morck, Andres Shleifer, and Robert Vishny (in "Management Ownership and Corporate Performance: An Empirical Analysis," forthcoming in the *Journal of Financial Economics*) argue that performance declines as management's stake increases beyond the point where control challenges are effective. Clearly, this is the case with leveraged recapitalizations. However, with leveraged recapitalizations, the high levels of debt severely reduce management's discretion over the firm's free cash flows since the excess cash must be devoted to meeting the debt service requirements. Consequently, it is likely that management will follow value-maximizing behavior subsequent to the leveraged recapitalization.

7

Leveraged Buyouts: Wealth Created or Wealth Redistributed?

Kenneth Lehn and Annette Poulsen

Public controversy concerning corporate takeovers now proceeds from an almost universal recognition that these transactions create substantial wealth for shareholders of target companies. Numerous studies have documented this fact, including a recent Securities and Exchange Commission (SEC) analysis which found that approximately US$40 billion in premiums were paid to target shareholders in corporate takeovers during 1980–5.[1] Although the takeover debate persists, it no longer involves serious controversy about the plight of target shareholders in these transactions.

The current dispute centers around the question of whether shareholder value also represents the social value created by corporate takeovers. Defenders of corporate takeovers generally argue that the premiums paid in these transactions reflect increases in social wealth resulting from more efficient resource allocation. Although little is known about the source of this increased value, the defenders often suggest that takeovers create wealth because of economies of scale, synergistic gains, or replacement of inefficient management. In contrast, many critics argue that takeover premiums do not reflect newly-created wealth. These premiums, it is argued, consist almost exclusively of existing wealth that is redistributed from other claimants on the firm's assets, including bondholders, taxpayers, employees, and local communities.

The "wealth creation" versus "wealth redistribution" controversy pertains not only to hostile takeovers, but also to highly leveraged, going-private transactions. In going-private transactions, shareholders of a publicly-held corporation are bought out, typically at a large premium, by a bidder who wishes to take a concentrated ownership position in the reconstituted, privately-held firm. Frequently, these transactions are referred to as "management buyouts," because incumbent management is often the bidder, or "leveraged buyouts," because these transactions usually are financed heavily by debt. Hereafter, we refer to going-private transactions as leveraged buyouts.

During the past several years, both the number and dollar value of leveraged buyouts have substantially increased. Table 7.1 lists the annual number, mean equity value, and total equity value of these transactions during 1980–4. This sample will be described more fully later. For now, note that both the number and average size of leveraged buyouts increased steadily during this period. Eight leveraged buyouts were consummated in 1980 involving firms with a pretransaction mean equity value of approximately $24.5 million. In 1984, the corresponding numbers were 35 transactions and a mean equity value of about $156.8 million. Hence, the total equity value of firms that went private during this period increased from $195.8 million in 1980 to $5,488.6 million in 1984, a 27-fold increase. Since 1984, several Fortune 500 companies have gone private via a leveraged buyout, including Uniroyal, Levi Strauss, RH Macy, Beatrice Companies, and Jack Eckerd.

The premiums paid in leveraged buyouts have evoked conflicting interpretations. Defenders of these transactions generally argue that the premiums derive from a socially desirable reorganization of the firm that results in better alignment of managerial incentives. Critics argue that the premiums come largely at the expense of bondholders and taxpayers. This paper empirically examines a sample of leveraged buyouts during 1980–4 in hopes of contributing to this debate. Before addressing these issues, we first describe leveraged buyouts in more detail.

Structure of Leveraged Buyouts

Leveraged buyouts can be structured in several ways. Typically, the investor group wishing to take the firm private, hereafter referred to as the bidder, forms a shell corporation that becomes the legal entity making the acquisition. In reverse mergers, the shell corporation is merged into the target firm; in forward mergers, the target firm is merged into the shell corporation. Shareholder approval of mergers generally is required under state law, with the minimum percentage approval varying by state. Some states have short-form merger statutes that allow the owners of a "large" percentage of the outstanding shares of a corporation to enter into a merger without the approval of the other shareholders. As an alternative to a merger, the shell corporation can make a tender offer for the target firm's shares, or it can simply buy the target firm's assets and issue a liquidating dividend to the target firm's

Table 7.1   Number and size of leveraged buyouts (1980–4)

Year	No.		Mean equity value ($000)	Total equity value ($000)	
1980	8	(7.5%)	$ 24.5 million	$ 195.8 million	(1.8%)
1981	9	(8.5%)	80.5 million	724.5 million	(6.6%)
1982	22	(20.8%)	71.5 million	1,572.4 million	(14.4%)
1983	32	(30.2%)	91.3 million	2,922.4 million	(26.8%)
1984	35	(33.0%)	156.8 million	5,488.6 million	(50.3%)
	106*	(100.0%)	$102.9 million**	$10,903.7 million	(100.0%)

* Relevant COMPUSTAT data missing for two firms.
** Mean value for entire sample.

shareholders. However the transaction is structured, shareholders in the target firm receive cash, debt securities, or some combination of the two in exchange for their shares.

Typically, the financing of a leveraged buyout entails the use of senior debt, subordinated debt, and common equity. The proportions of each type of security vary, but usually senior debt accounts for the largest proportion of financing in these transactions. The senior debt typically is advanced by a commercial bank, insurance company, leasing company, or limited partnership that specializes in venture capital investments and leveraged buyouts. Frequently, commercial banks enter into a revolving-credit agreement with the going-private firm and secure their loans against the firm's accounts receivables, plant and equipment, and inventories. Senior debt held by insurance companies and leasing companies typically is secured against the firm's fixed assets and has a fixed repayment schedule, usually five to seven years.

Subordinated debt, referred to as "mezzanine money," is provided most frequently by pension funds, insurance companies, venture-capital/leveraged-buyout limited partnerships, venture-capital subsidiaries of commercial banks, and foundations and endowments. Three legal changes have fostered the growth in this type of financing of going-privates and are considered to be important in explaining the recent increase in leveraged buyouts. First, the 1978 change in capital gains tax that encouraged the formation of venture-capital limited partnerships led to the creation and expansion of numerous funds that specialize in leveraged buyouts. These funds have become the

Table 7.2 Average long-term debt, shareholders' equity, and debt–equity ratio, before and after a leveraged buyout (for 58 LBOs, 1980–4)

	Before LBO	*After LBO*	*Percentage change*
Avg. long-term debt	$45.6 million	$165.1 million	262%
Avg. shareholders' equity	99.7 million	29.9 million	−70%
Avg. debt–equity ratio	0.457	5.524	1,109%

Table 7.3 Number and size of leveraged buyouts by industry

	No.		*Mean equity value ($000)*	*Total equity value ($000)*	*Percent of total equity*
Apparel	7	(6.6)	$ 67.4 million	$ 471.6 million	(4.3%)
Bottled & canned soft drinks	5	(4.7)	153.3 million	766.7 million	(7.0%)
Food	9	(8.5)	50.9 million	458.3 million	(4.2%)
Publishing	3	(2.8)	231.8 million	695.4 million	(6.4%)
Retail	16	(15.1)	90.5 million	1,447.9 million	(13.3%)
Rubber & misc. plastics	5	(4.7)	22.0 million	110.2 million	(1.0%)
Textiles	12	(11.3)	163.7 million	1,965.2 million	(18.0%)
Other	49	(46.2)	101.8 million	4,988.4 million	(45.7%)
	106	(100.0)	$102.9 million	$10,903.7 million	(100.0%)

principal vehicle by which pension funds, insurance companies, and foundations and endowments have invested in leveraged buyouts. Second, the US Department of Labor, by its authority under the Employee Retirement Income Security Act of 1974 (ERISA), has promulgated regulations that classify leveraged buyout investments as "prudent" and thus eligible for investment by pension funds. This decision, along with the substantial growth of pension funds, undoubtedly facilitated the financing of leveraged buyouts. Third, a 1984 change in the US tax code encouraged the use of employee stock-ownership plans (ESOPs), which supposedly has accounted for a significant percentage of financing in post-1984 leveraged buyouts.

The equity capital used in leveraged buyouts is most often provided by the managers of the target firm and/or the outside investor group that provides some of the debt financing. Inevitably, the common equity in all leveraged buyout firms is more tightly held after the transaction than it was before.

Table 7.2 contains data that illustrates the dramatic change in capital structure that results from leveraged buyouts. These data were obtained from proxy statements filed with the SEC for 58 firms in our sample. These firms were selected because pro forma data on the change in capital structure were included in the proxy filing. The average book value of long-term debt in the quarter preceding the leveraged buyout proposal was approximately $45.6 million and the corresponding book value of shareholders' equity was approximately $99.7 million, resulting in an average debt-to-equity ratio of 0.457. The pro forma statements revealed that following the leveraged buyout the average book value of long-term debt would increase by 262 percent to $165.1 million, the average book value of shareholders' equity would contract by 70 percent to $29.9 million, and that the average debt–equity ratio would increase by more than eleven-fold to 5.524. The average sum of long-term debt and shareholders' equity increased 34 percent from $145.3 million before the leveraged buyout to $195 million after the leveraged buyout.

Wealth Creation or Wealth Redistribution?

Wealth-creation hypothesis

Proponents of the wealth-creation hypothesis frequently argue that leveraged buyouts create value by realigning managerial incentives in a way that enhances the productive efficiency of the firm. Economists and legal scholars have long recognized that a potential conflict exists between managerial incentives and shareholder interests in publicly-traded companies that are characterized by diffuse ownership structures and relatively small shareholdings of corporate managers. This potential conflict derives from the fact that managers in these firms do not bear the full wealth consequences of their decisions; their decisions affect the value of all outstanding equity, yet they own relatively little equity. If the "outside" (i.e., nonmanagement) equity is held diffusely, then monitoring by outside shareholders is "incomplete," because no individual shareholder receives the full value created by his or her costly monitoring activity.

Some scholars argue that the principal reason for leveraged buyouts is to reconstitute the firm's capital structure in order to mitigate managerial incentive problems. Since management buyouts result in concentration of most, if not all, of the firm's equity in the hands of management, the wealth consequences of their decisions are more effectively internalized. In nonmanagement buyouts, the equity will be tightly held by a specialist who presumably will closely monitor managerial performance, efficiently structure executive compensation, and thereby improve the productive efficiency of the firm. According to the wealth-creation hypothesis, the premiums paid in leveraged buyouts largely reflect the minimum amount by which the bidder expects to increase the value of the firm (i.e., the discounted value of future cash flows) through improved managerial efficiency.

Jensen (1986) has extended the wealth-creation hypothesis by elevating the role played by debt in mitigating managerial incentive problems.[2] A frequent characteristic of leveraged buyout candidates, Jensen argues, is the simultaneous presence of low-growth prospects and substantial cash flow. Jensen says:

> Free cash flow is cash flow in excess of that required to fund all projects that have positive net present values when discounted at the relevant cost of capital. Conflicts of interest between shareholders and managers over payout policies are especially severe when the organization generates substantial cash flow. The problem is how to motivate managers to disgorge the cash rather than investing it at below the cost of capital or wasting it on organization inefficiencies.[3]

Low-growth prospects suggest that opportunities to reinvest the cash flow profitably in the firm's current lines of business are limited. If the firm's management is specialized in its current lines of business, then it is unprofitable to invest the cash flow in acquisition of new lines of business. Leveraged buyouts effectively result in the "disgorging" of cash flow to the firm's securityholders, which Jensen contends is the value-maximizing use of this cash flow. The substantial debt resulting from leveraged buyouts serves as a bonding device; management is committed to pay out a substantial portion of the cash flow in the form of coupon payments on the debt, rather than reinvest it unprofitably. Since the penalty for defaulting on a coupon payment is presumably greater than the penalty for reducing dividend payments, debt more effectively compels management to pay free-cash flow to the firms' security-holders.

Empirical results. Casual inspection of the frequency distribution of leveraged buyouts by industry confirms Jensen's observation that these firms typically operate in "mature" industries with apparently limited growth opportunities. Table 7.3 lists the number and size of leveraged buyouts by industry for a sample of 106 leveraged buyouts. (This sample was collected from three sources: COMPUSTAT; Drexel, Burnham, Lambert; and Thomas H. Lee Co.) Sixteen of the firms, or 15.1 percent of the sample, were in the retail industry, accounting for $1.5 billion, or 13.3 percent of the value of the firms that went private via a leveraged buyout. Twelve firms, or 11.3 percent of the sample, were textile firms, accounting for approximately $2 billion, or 18.0 percent, of the value of leveraged buyouts. Also represented heavily in the sample were food processing firms (8.5 percent of the sample accounting for 4.2 percent of the value), apparel firms (6.6 percent and 4.3 percent, respectively), and bottled and canned soft drinks (4.7 percent and 7.0 percent, respectively). These five industries account collectively for 46.2 percent of the sample and 46.8 percent of the value of the leveraged buyouts.

Table 7.4 shows the average cumulative abnormal returns associated with the first announcement of a leveraged buyout proposal in the *Wall Street Journal* for 92 leveraged buyouts in our sample. The announcements vary from contemplating a leveraged buyout proposal to a board of directors' approval of a leveraged buyout proposal. Conventional event-study methodology was used to extract market-induced effects from the firms' stock price movements on the event date. The average net of market stock price reaction to these announcements is 20.10 percent when measured over a period of twenty days before the announcement to twenty days after the announcement. The cumulative t-statistic is 12.8, which indicates that the cumulative abnormal returns are significantly different from zero. Measured over a "twenty day window," that is, ten days before the announcement through ten days after the announcement, the average net of market stock price reaction is 20.76 percent, with a t-statistic of 18.5. Measured over a two day window – one day before the announcement through the day of the announcement – the average net of market stock price reaction is 13.93 percent with a cumulative t-statistic of 41.1. Although these results are somewhat less dramatic than results that DeAngelo, DeAngelo and Rice (1984) found for a sample of going-private transactions in the 1970s,[4] they nonetheless indicate that shareholders benefited greatly from leveraged buyouts during 1980–4.

Table 7.5 contains summary statistics on the premiums paid in leveraged buyouts. The row in this table labeled "Cash Premium Offered" provides statistics for the difference between the offer price and the market price of the firm's common stock

Table 7.4 Cumulative daily abnormal returns associated with first announcement of a leveraged buyout proposal for 92 leveraged buyouts (t-statistics in parentheses)

Number of trading days (before, and after) announcement	*Cumulative daily abnormal return*
(−20,20)	20.10%
	(12.8)
(−10,10)	20.76%
	(18.5)
(−1,0)	13.93%
	(41.1)

Notes: Where possible, all daily stock returns were obtained from CRSP (Center for Research in Securities Prices) tapes. For stocks that are traded over the counter, returns were obtained from the ISL (Investment Statistical Listing) tapes of Interactive Data Services, New York. The stock returns of 82 firms in our sample were contained on the CRSP tape and the stock returns of 20 firms in our sample were contained on the ISL tape. The stock returns of 6 firms were not contained on either tape. 9 additional firms were dropped due to insufficient returns data.

Table 7.5 Premiums paid in leveraged buyouts, 1980–4

	Number of LBOs	Mean	Std. deviation	Minimum	Maximum
Cash premium offered	72	41.0%	23.2%	2.0%	120.0%
Market-valued premiums	89	39.5%	23.2%	1.7%	120.0%

twenty trading days prior to the first announcement of the leveraged buyout, divided by the latter price. The average value of the offered premium is 41 percent and it ranges from 2 percent to 120 percent. This variable was calculated only for the 72 leveraged buyouts in the sample that were all-cash offers, since no direct measure of the market value of non-cash offers was available.

A good approximation of the value of cash and non-cash offers can be obtained, however, from the final price at which the firm's common equity traded before it became private. Hence, we calculated a second measure of the premiums paid in leveraged buyouts – the "Market-valued Premium." This premium is the difference between the final price at which the company's equity traded and its market price 20 days prior to the first going-private announcement, divided by the latter price. The average value of the market-valued premium for the 89 firms in the sample for which we obtained these data was 39.5 percent, ranging from 1.7 percent to 120.0 percent. Since the market-valued premium can be calculated for more firms, we use this measure in the analysis that follows.

To empirically probe Jensen's hypothesis, we collected COMPUSTAT data on the cash flow for 66 firms in the sample. These firms represent all firms in the sample for which COMPUSTAT had data on both earnings and depreciation expense for the year preceding the leveraged buyout. We created two measures of cash flow: the ratio of operating income plus depreciation expense to the market value of equity $[(CF/EQ)_1]$ and the ratio of income before extraordinary items, plus depreciation expense to market value of equity $[(CF/EQ)_2]$. Although these are not proxies for "free" cash flow, because we have not yet proxied the firms' growth prospects, we posit that a direct relationship between each of these measures of cash flow and premiums is consistent with Jensen's hypothesis.

The data reveal a direct and significant relationship between the two cash flow measures and the market-valued premiums paid. Table 7.6 contains the mean premium for firms with low and high ratios of cash flow to equity. Shareholders in the 33 firms with the lowest values of $(CF/EQ)_1$ received an average premium of 33.4 percent, whereas shareholders in the 33 firms with the highest values of $(CF/EQ)_1$ received an average premium of 49.0 percent, a difference that is significant at the 0.99 level. The average premiums increase from 31.0 percent for the 22 firms with the lowest values of $(CF/EQ)_1$, to 39.5 percent for the 22 firms with the median values of $(CF/EQ)_1$, to 53.1 percent for the 22 firms with the highest values of $(CF/EQ)_1$.

The same regularities characterize the relationship between the second measure of cash flow, $(CF/EQ)_2$, and premiums. The average premium for the 33 firms with the lowest values of $(CF/EQ)_2$ was 33.8 percent, whereas the average premium was 48.6 percent for firms with the highest values. The average premium increases steadily with

Table 7.6 Mean cash flow to equity ratio (CF/EQ) and mean market-valued premiums for firms with low cash flow to equity ratios and high cash flow to equity ratios

Sample	Number of firms	Mean cash flow equity	Mean market-valued premiums
A. *Cash flow = operating income & depreciation expense (CF/EQ)$_1$*			
50% Lowest (CF/EQ)$_1$	33	0.291	33.4%
50% Highest (CF/EQ)$_1$	33	0.637	49.0%
33% Lowest (CF/EQ)$_1$	22	0.250	31.0%
33% Median (CF/EQ)$_1$	22	0.399	39.5%
33% Highest (CF/EQ)$_1$	22	0.727	53.1%
B. *Cash flow = income before extraordinary items & depreciation expense (CF/EQ)$_2$*			
50% Lowest (CF/EQ)$_2$	33	0.137	33.8%
50% Highest (CF/EQ)$_2$	33	0.303	48.6%
33% Lowest (CF/EQ)$_2$	22	0.117	33.2%
33% Median (CF/EQ)$_2$	22	0.190	38.8%
33% Highest (CF/EQ)$_2$	22	0.341	51.6%

Table 7.7 Ordinary least squares estimates of market-valued premiums as a function of cash flow to equity measures and as a function of equity value (t-statistics in parentheses)

Intercept	0.192	0.119	0.212	0.177
	(3.1)	(1.5)	(3.4)	(2.2)
(CF/EQ)$_1$	0.473	0.558		
	(3.9)	(4.1)		
(CF/EQ)$_2$			0.888	0.962
			(3.5)	(3.5)
EQUITY		0.0000002		0.0000001
		(1.4)		(0.7)
Number in sample	66	66	66	66
R^2	0.193	0.216	0.161	0.168
F-statistic	15.3	8.7	12.3	6.4

(CF/EQ)$_2$, from an average of 33.2 percent for the 22 firms with the lowest values, to 38.8 percent for the 22 firms with the median values, to 51.6 percent for the 22 firms with the highest values of (CF/EQ)$_2$.

Table 7.7 contains estimates from an ordinary least squares regression in which premium is regressed on each of the two measures of cash flow. When entered separately, the coefficient estimates on (CF/EQ)$_1$ and (CF/EQ)$_2$ are 0.473 and 0.888 respectively, and both of these estimates are statistically significant (t-statistics of 3.9 and 3.5, respectively). (CF/EQ)$_1$ alone explains more than 19 percent of the variation in premiums and (CF/EQ)$_2$ alone explains more than 16 percent of the variation in premiums.

To standardize for firm size, the ordinary least squares regression was run with the market value of equity (EQUITY) also included as an independent variable. When equity value is included, the coefficient estimate on $(CF/EQ)_1$ actually increases to 0.558 and its t-statistic increases to 4.1. Similarly, the coefficient estimate on $(CF/EQ)_2$ increases to 0.962 and its t-statistic increases marginally. The coefficient estimate on EQUITY was not significant in either equation.

Although we have not yet controlled for growth prospects, the data contained in tables 7.6 and 7.7 are consistent with the wealth-creation hypothesis and more specifically with Jensen's version of this hypothesis.

Wealth-redistribution hypotheses

Critics of the view that leveraged buyouts create wealth argue that the payment of premiums in hostile takeovers and leveraged buyouts does not necessarily imply increased social efficiency. Indeed, some argue that it is even incorrect to infer that firm value, let alone social value, is increased simply because premiums are paid to target shareholders in these transactions.

An alternative explanation offered by some critics is the wealth-redistribution hypothesis. They suggest that because these transactions are so highly leveraged, it is likely that at least part, and possibly all, of the increased value in common equity will be offset by a reduction in the value of the firms' outstanding bonds and preferred equity. Empirical support for this hypothesis is found in an article by Masulis (1980), who found that the announcement of a debt-for-common stock exchange offer generally results in diminution in the value of the issuer's outstanding non-convertible bonds.[5]

Redistribution from bondholders and preferred stockholders

The argument that the shareholder wealth created by leveraged buyouts consists largely of redistribution from bondholders and preferred stockholders has appeared frequently in law articles and the popular press. In a supplement to his article in *The Business Lawyer* (1986), Morey McDaniel wrote.[6]

> The bondholder ripoff has become front-page news. For a vivid account of how stockholders in leveraged takeovers have profited at bondholder expense see . . . "Merger Wave: How Stocks and Bonds Fare," *N.Y. Times*, Jan. 7, 1986 . . . "shareholders of the acquired company do great," said Michael S. Hyman, managing director of First Boston Corporation. "Bondholders on both sides are often left holding the bag. It's horrible." . . . *Business Week* has discovered the bondholder ripoff, too. "The takeover and leveraged buyout craze may be a boon for shareholders, but it is slaughtering owners of high grade corporate bonds" [states] Farrell. "Takeovers and Buyouts Clobber Blue Chip Bondholders," *Business Week*, November 11, 1985. . . . Barron's also has reported on the bondholder's plight. "Takeovers, mergers, stock repurchases, and leveraged buyouts are a good news–bad news story." Good news for stockholders as share prices soar. Bad news for bondholders whose bonds are "turned instantly from gems to junk by the swelling of

debt taken on to finance the transactions," [states] Forsyth. "Bad Grades: Takeovers Teach a Costly Lesson to Bondholders." *Barron's*, February 24, 1986.

If the central tendency of leveraged takeovers is to diminish bondholders' and preferred stockholders' wealth by the degree suggested in the articles quoted above, then potentially these transactions could leave firm value unaffected, or they could actually diminish firm value.

This version of the "wealth-redistribution" hypothesis, even if empirically valid, suffers from a conceptual weakness that attenuates its importance for public policy. A market for bondholder (and, presumably, preferred stockholder) protection exists in the form of covenants that provide bondholders with protection in the event of changes in control, debt issues, and so forth. Presumably, bondholders pay a price for this protection in the form of lower coupon rates. Bondholders who forgo this protection presumably receive a premium in exchange for bearing some increased risk that their wealth may be expropriated by managerial decisions, or a change in control. McDaniel notes that the market for bondholder protection is adapting to the new takeover environment.[7]

> Bond investors are beginning to demand protection against the ravages of the takeover wars. "Industrial corporations are finally becoming aware that their bonds aren't attractive without protections for bondholders against takeovers," says William Gross, managing director of Pacific Investment Management Co., which runs a $9.5 billion bond portfolio.

Unless significant transaction costs exist that impair the efficiency of the market for bondholder protection, it is difficult to provide an economic justification for a public policy remedy to this supposed problem.

Empirical results. Inspection of the data suggests that although bondholders and preferred stockholders have suffered wealth losses in some leveraged buyouts, this does not appear to be the central tendency. To examine the effect of leveraged buyouts on the wealth of bondholders and preferred stockholders, we consulted *Moody's Bond Record* for a list of firms in our sample that had bonds or preferred stock listed on the New York Stock Exchange or the American Stock Exchange. After compiling this list, we recorded the daily prices of the bonds and preferred stock over a 20-day window centered on the date of the first *Wall Street Journal* announcement of the leveraged buyout, the same date used in examining the common-stock price reaction to the leveraged-buyout announcement. Bond prices were obtained from daily editions of the *Wall Street Journal*, and preferred stock prices were obtained from Standard & Poor's *Daily Stock Price Record* for the New York Stock Exchange, American Stock Exchange, and the Over-the-Counter market.

It should be noted that the inferences which can be drawn from these bond price data are quite limited, since only "odd-lot" trades (i.e., trades of nine bonds or fewer) must be executed through the exchanges. Nonetheless, if the central tendency of leveraged buyouts is to redistribute wealth from bondholders to common stock-

Table 7.8 Bond and preferred stock price reaction to announcement of leveraged buyout

	Average price 10 days prior to announcement	Average price 10 days after announcement	Average pct. change in price
13 Bonds traded	$83.375	$82.192	−1.42%
9 Non-convertible bonds	77.694	75.778	−2.46%
4 Convertible bonds	96.156	96.625	0.49%
Bond index	69.815	64.778	−7.21%
10 Preferred issues traded	48.288	59.575	23.37%
3 Nonconvertible preferred	42.417	59.667	40.67%
7 Convertible preferred	50.804	55.250	8.75%

holders, some evidence of this should be found in these reported bond-price data.

The data refute the hypothesis that leveraged buyouts result in significant redistribution of wealth from bondholders and preferred stockholders to common stockholders. In fact, for the sample of 92 LBOs that we studied, 68 firms, or nearly three-quarters of the sample, did not have any listed bonds outstanding; 85 firms, or 92.4 percent of the sample, did not have any listed preferred stock outstanding. Twenty-four firms in our sample had 37 listed bonds outstanding and 7 firms had 10 listed preferred stock issues outstanding.

Table 7.8 contains price data for the listed bonds and listed preferred-stock around the date of the LBO announcement. Thirteen of the 37 listed bonds traded on the exchange during the 20-day period centered on the LBO announcement date. The average bond price declined 1.42 percent from $83.375 to $82.192 during this period. The average price of the 9 nonconvertible bonds decreased by 2.46 percent during this period, from $77.694 to $75.778. The average price of the 4 convertible bonds increased by 0.49 percent.

Although the relatively few bonds that traded on the exchange during the period declined in price, this decline was considerably smaller than the average decline in the 20-bond index reported daily in the *Wall Street Journal*. This index declined from an average of $69.815 to an average of $64.778, a decline of 7.21 percent, over this same period. Hence, the data strongly suggest that there was no "net-of-market" decline in the value of the 13 bonds. These results are consistent with results found by Dennis and McConnell for a sample of 94 takeovers during 1962–80.[8]

Price data on the 10 preferred stock issues that traded during the period surrounding the leveraged buyout announcement also refute the hypothesis that leveraged buyouts entail considerable wealth redistribution from preferred stockholders to common stockholders. The average price of the 10 issues increased by 23.37 percent from $48.288 to $59.575. The 7 convertible preferred issues increased in value by 8.75 percent from $50.804 to $55.250. The 3 nonconvertible preferred issues that traded on the exchange increased in value by 40.67 percent, from $42.417 to $59.667. Although these numbers are not market adjusted, they strongly suggest that preferred stockholders have generally not suffered wealth losses in leveraged buyouts.

Redistribution from taxpayers

Some scholars have argued that the principal source of premiums paid in leveraged buyouts are tax benefits that accrue at both the corporate and personal level. For example, Lowenstein (1985) has written:[9]

> How can managers and their buying consortia pay so much? Until recently, we could only speculate as to the answer, because once a company went private, a veil dropped. A small but growing number of these firms, however, have returned to the public market. What emerges from the study of one such firm, Fred Meyer, Inc., and of twenty-seven recent buyout proposals is that the single most important factor explaining the pricing of these deals, though not their existence, is taxes. Management often can, with suitable backing, purchase the business from the public and finance the premium portion of the purchase price entirely out of tax generated cash flows.

If leveraged-buyout premiums are financed exclusively by reduction in the firm's tax liability, then leveraged buyouts may increase the value of the firm. But this increase in firm value also diminishes social wealth, assuming that the costs of arranging these transactions are nonzero. The after-tax cash flows of the firm increase under this scenario, but the leveraged buyout indirectly raises the tax liability of other taxpayers.

In this paper, we ignore the personal tax benefits associated with leveraged buyouts. The two most frequently cited corporate tax incentives for leveraged buyouts are the tax deductibility of interest expense and the "step up" of assets to take advantage of liberalized accelerated depreciation deductions permitted by the 1981 change in federal tax law. The US tax code encourages corporate debt financing by allowing interest payments on debt to be deducted from taxable income, while dividend income is taxed at both the corporate and personal level. According to many critics of leveraged buyouts, the premiums paid in these transactions are largely financed by the tax savings associated with the dramatic change in capital structure.

Some scholars have argued that the principal source of premiums in leveraged buyouts is the ability of firms to take advantage of a tax change in 1981 that simplified rules for "stepping up" assets and liberalized the accelerated depreciation schedule, both of which created an incentive for some firms to step up the value of their assets. In order to increase the value of a firm's assets that is used for deducting depreciation expenses from the firm's tax liability, a transaction that establishes the market value of the assets is necessary. Because of recapture taxes, this incentive is greatest for firms that have assets whose tax basis is significantly below their market value and that are relatively undepreciated.

In leveraged buyouts, the US Internal Revenue Service allows assets to be stepped up only when certain acquisition techniques are employed. Step-ups are disallowed when a one-tier reverse cash merger is employed, that is, when the bidding shell corporation is merged directly into the target firm. In these mergers, the assets have a carryover tax basis since the IRS considers the corporate identity of the acquired firm to be unchanged. These mergers are treated as recapitalizations, however, which do confer personal tax benefits to managers in management buyouts. Sometimes step-ups are permitted in two-tier reverse cash mergers, which are mergers in which a subsidiary of the shell corporation is merged into the target firm, and then the target firm is merged into the shell corporation. Step-ups are permitted in these mergers, provided that at least 80 percent of the target firm's stock is acquired by the investor group making the merger proposal.

Step-ups also are permitted in leveraged buyouts that are structured as forward mergers or sales of assets. In sales of assets, the target firm either issues a liquidating dividend to its shareholders, or it remains in existence as a registered closed-end investment company. The latter course is chosen only when the assets are sold below tax basis, that is, below the value used for tax purposes. This provides target shareholders, including, of course, the managers, with a tax-free sale of assets and an opportunity to invest the proceeds of this sale in tax-exempt securities, which generally are exempt from corporate taxation as well as personal taxation. To accomplish this, the target firm must have more than 100 shareholders after both the sale of the assets and a self-tender offer designed to take the firm private.

Empirical results. To examine the tax benefits argument, we estimate a linear regression model in which LBO premiums were regressed on the firms' pretransaction tax liability. If tax benefits are a significant factor in leveraged buyouts, then these transactions should be most valuable for firms with relatively high-tax liability. To test this, we collected tax data from the COMPUSTAT tape; tax data were available for 87 firms in the sample. Since premiums represent a percentage change in the value of the common equity, we expressed pretransaction tax liability as the ratio of corporate income tax to market value of equity in the year immediately preceding the leveraged buyout.

The evidence strongly suggests that tax benefits do play a significant role in leveraged buyouts. Table 7.9 lists the mean tax–equity ratio (T/EQ) and mean premium for firms with low-tax liability and firms with high-tax liability. The average premium, for the 43 firms with the lowest tax-equity ratio was 32.1 percent; the corresponding average for the 43 firms with the highest tax-equity ratio was 47.7

Table 7.9 Mean tax-to-equity ratio and mean offered market-valued premium for firms with low tax-to-equity ratios and high tax-to-equity ratios

Sample	N	Mean tax-equity	Mean market-valued premium*
50% Lowest tax-equity	43	0.040	32.1%
50% Highest tax-equity	43	0.137	47.7%
33% Lowest tax-equity	29	0.022	32.1%
33% Median tax-equity	28	0.086	36.8%
33% Highest tax-equity	29	0.157	50.7%

*The t-statistic corresponding to the difference in the mean premiums for the two subsamples is 3.3. This difference is significant at the 0.99 level.

percent, a difference that is statistically significant. Similarly, the average premium increases from 32.1 percent for the 29 firms with the lowest tax-equity ratio to 36.8 percent for the 28 firms with the median tax-equity rates.

Table 7.10 contains a set of regression estimates of premiums as a function of both the ratio of cash flow to equity and the ratio of tax to equity, with and without the market value of equity also included as an independent variable. When entered simultaneously, both the cash-flow measures and the tax measure continue to enter the equation with positive and statistically significant coefficient estimates. $(CF/EQ)_1$ and (T/EQ) together explain almost 24 percent of the variation in premiums; $(CF/EQ)_2$ and (T/EQ) together explain more than 21 percent of the variation in premiums. When "equity" is added as an independent variable, the R^2s increase slightly, and both the cash-flow measures and the tax measure continue to enter with positive and statistically significant coefficient estimates.

Conclusion

Inspection of leveraged buyout premiums has revealed support for both the wealth-creation and the wealth-redistribution hypotheses, two hypotheses that are not, of course, mutually exclusive. Premiums are directly related to pretransaction cash flow, a result that is consistent with Jensen's version of the wealth-creation hypothesis. Premiums are also directly related to pretransaction tax liability, which supports Lowenstein's version of the wealth-redistribution hypothesis. However, no support was found for the argument that premiums in leveraged buyouts come largely at the expense of bondholders and preferred stockholders.

Future research will consist of further testing of these hypotheses. To examine the relationship between "free" cash flow and LBO premiums, several measures of the firms' growth prospects will be calculated and incorporated into the empirical analysis. Furthermore, the relationship between free cash flow and LBO premiums will be examined for two subsamples of firms: those in which managers owned a substantial

Table 7.10 Ordinary least squares estimates of market-valued premium as a function of $(CF/EQ)_1$, $(CF/EQ)_2$, T/EQ, and EQUITY (t-statistics in parentheses)

Intercept	0.169	0.087	0.184	0.137
	(2.7)	(1.1)	(2.9)	(1.7)
$(CF/EQ)_1$	0.401	0.490	0.739	0.829
	(3.2)	(3.6)	(2.9)	(3.0)
$(CF/EQ)_2$				
T/EQ	0.656	0.691	0.710	0.745
	(2.0)	(2.1)	(2.1)	(2.2)
EQUITY		0.0000002		
		(1.5)		
Sample size	66	66	66	66
R^2	0.239	0.267	0.216	0.228
F-statistic	9.9	7.5	8.7	6.1

percentage of equity in the firm before the LBO proposal, and those in which managers owned little equity in the firm before the LBO proposal. It would seem that the free-cash-flow theory of leveraged buyouts would predict a stronger relationship between free cash flows and LBO premiums for the latter subsample than for the former subsample. To further test the effect of LBO announcements on the value of the sample's outstanding bonds, data on bond rating changes will be collected. If a significant proportion of the sample sustained a decline in bond rating during the period surrounding the LBO announcement, then it is likely that the reported bond price data is masking a more significant effect on bond values. Finally, our present tax variable is a reported tax rate, not an "effective" tax rate. Although we have no reason to suspect that our present tax variable is biased, in the future we shall examine the relationship between effective tax rates and LBO premiums.

Notes

The SEC, as a matter of policy, disclaims responsibility for any private publication or statement by any of its employees. The views expressed herein are those of the authors and do not necessarily reflect the views of the Commission.

1 Office of the Chief Economist, US SEC.
2 Michael C. Jensen, 1986, "Agency Costs of Free Cash Flow, Corporate Finance and Takeovers," *American Economic Review* May, pp. 323–9.
3 Ibid., p. 323.
4 Harry DeAngelo, Linda DeAngelo, and Edward M. Rice, 1984, "Going Private: Minority Freezeouts and Stockholder Wealth," *Journal of Law and Economics* October, pp. 367–402.
5 Ronald Masulis, 1980, "The Effect of Capital Structure Change on Security Prices: A Study of Exchange Offers," *Journal of Financial Economics* 139.
6 Morey W. McDaniel, 1986, Bondholders and Corporate Governance – A Supplement, manuscript, 10 March.
7 Ibid., p. 36.
8 Debra K. Dennis and John J. McConnell, 1985, "Corporate Mergers and Security Returns," manuscript, 27 March.
9 Louis Lowenstein, 1985, "Management Buyouts," 85 *Columbia Law Review* pp. 730–1.

8

Original Issue High Yield Bonds: Aging Analyses of Defaults, Exchanges, and Calls

Paul Asquith, David W. Mullins, Jr., and Eric D. Wolff

The development of the original issue high yield bond market represents one of the most successful innovations in recent financial history.[1] From its inception, a major impetus behind the growth of the new issue high yield bond market has been the argument that risk-adjusted returns are high. Specifically, it is argued that defaults on high yield bonds, while higher than those on investment grade bonds, are low relative to their coupon rate, i.e., that their higher coupon rates more than compensate for the default risk. This apparent market inefficiency has been attributed to outdated conventions used by rating agencies and bond investors, both of whom supposedly fail to see the true risk/return characteristics of high yield bonds.

Attempts to verify empirically the risk/return characteristics of the original issue high yield debt market are difficult because of data limitations. Since 1977 marks the beginning of the original issue high yield debt market,[2] there is only a limited history of its performance through time and none through a full range of economic and capital market conditions. Second, corporate bonds are primarily an institutional market with little or no trading on organized exchanges. Most trading is done over-the-counter with only a few market makers, particularly with smaller issues. Thus, there is no reliable, centralized data source, and broker/dealers consider their over-the-counter, institutional trading data proprietary.

Notwithstanding these serious data limitations, Blume and Keim (1987, 1988) have studied the risk/return characteristics of high yield debt. They find that high yield debt produces higher realized returns and lower standard deviations of returns than either investment grade or Treasury bonds over the period 1977–87 but not over the period 1982–7. These mixed results may partially reflect the difficulty in obtaining accurate transaction-based return data on a large sample of bonds. While Blume and Keim provide important insights into the risk/return characteristics of high yield debt, this issue remains an important topic for future research.

Default studies of high yield bonds have generally supported a positive view of this market. A series of early studies (e.g., Altman and Nammacher (1985), Altman (1987), Altman and Nammacher (1987), and Weinstein (1987)) have documented low default rates for high yield bonds. These studies have reported annual default rates in the 1–3 percent range, with Altman and Nammacher (1987) finding an average default rate of 1.5 percent for 1978–86. These rates, while higher than the default rate on investment grade bonds, are offset by the 3–5 percent spread in yields between high yield and investment grade bonds. These studies showing consistently low default rates have convinced many of the proposition that the high yield debt market has low risk-adjusted default rates.[3]

There are, however, several problems which bias downward the reported default rates in these high yield studies. One source of bias is the failure to account properly for exchanges.[4] Some studies drop exchanged bonds from their high yield bond samples. If exchanges reflect increased risk, exchanged bonds should have a higher default rate than initial issues. Even if exchanged bonds are not eliminated from a sample, distressed exchanges may be used to avoid technical default, thereby reducing the reported rate of default. As a result, the reported default rate might understate the actual incidence of financial distress by issuers and losses by bondholders.

Second, traditional studies of high yield bond defaults have not properly considered the aging of the bonds. Studies such as those by Altman and Nammacher (1985, 1987), Altman (1987), and Weinstein (1987) measure the default rate by dividing the amount of defaults in a given year by the par value of all outstanding issues.[5] This definition of default rate ignores the important effect of bond age on default risk. If bond default rates are not stationary through time but rise with bond age, and if there is a rapid growth in new issue volume year to year, default rates are severely biased downward by this measure. An alternative way to measure default risk is to consider defaults over time within a cohort of bonds issued at the same time.

In his most recent paper on high yield debt, Altman (1989) employs an aging concept, "cumulative bond mortality," which utilizes cohort issue years. "Cumulative bond mortality" measures default rates on bonds that have been outstanding for equal periods of time and adjusts the size of the denominator for calls, maturities, previous defaults, and sinking funds. This technique avoids the aging bias of earlier studies, and Altman finds ten-year cumulative mortality rates of 6.64 percent for BB bonds and 31.91 percent for B bonds, and five-year rates of 31.17 percent for CCC bonds. These latter two cumulative rates are much higher than the rates that would result from cumulating the average yearly default rates cited above and in note 3. This mortality technique, because it divides defaults only by bonds still outstanding, may produce percentages somewhat higher than the total percentage defaulting on any original yearly sample.

The objective of this paper is to present an analysis of the high yield bond market which avoids the two methodological difficulties noted above: failure to consider exchanges and the aging of bonds. It specifically incorporates the concept of aging in an analysis of defaults, exchanges, and calls for an exhaustive data base of all original issue public high yield corporate bonds issued between January 1, 1977 and December

31, 1986. For these 741 bonds, all relevant events are examined through December 31, 1988.

The results are striking. A buy-and-hold investor who purchased a portfolio of all high yield bonds issued in 1977 and 1978 would, by December 31, 1988, experience a default rate of 34 percent. Of the bonds issued in the years 1979–83, between 19 and 27 percent default by December 31, 1988. Default rates for issue years 1984–6 range from 3 to 9 percent by December 31, 1988.

The effect of bond age on the default rate is clearly evident in these results. Default rates are lower immediately after issue and rise over time. By the time these defaults occur, the overall market is much larger due to the rapid growth in new issue volume. This growth makes the high default rates of old bonds appear small relative to the size of the overall market, which is dominated by recently issued bonds with low default rates.

This study also examines exchanges because of their potential use in avoiding default through a reorganization of claims. The results confirm that, by December 31, 1988, a significant fraction of bonds issued (up to 31 percent for some years) have been subject to exchanges. However, a significant proportion of exchanges are followed by default and are included in the default results reported above. Thus, these results do not support the argument that exchanges are completely effective in eliminating defaults for high yield bonds. They do, however, point to the importance of not dropping exchanged bonds and their successors from any study of the high yield market.

In addition to defaults and exchanges, this study examines calls of original issue high yield bonds. A significant percentage of the bonds issued were called by December 31, 1988. The percentage called for the earlier issue years 1977–82, where call protection can be considered to have expired, ranges from 26 to 47 percent.

Summing the aged results for defaults, exchanges, calls, and maturities gives a picture far different from the common perception of a stable market with low defaults. By December 31, 1988, only a relatively small fraction of high yield bonds originally issued in years 1977–82 remain outstanding. On the down side, approximately one third of bonds issued in these years have defaulted or have been exchanged. An additional one third have been called, requiring investors to reinvest. Only a small fraction of original issue high yield bonds has been paid off through sinking funds or at maturity. By December 31, 1988, the residual issues which have neither defaulted nor been called or matured represent only 28.1 percent of the original issues of 1977–82.

Results for these early years do not appear anomalous. Early year default results for issue years 1983–6 are equal to or worse than those for issue years 1977–82. Of course, these early year results do not necessarily predict similar future default rates.

I　Data and Methodology

This paper examines all public original issue high yield corporate bonds, often called "junk bonds," issued between January 1, 1977 and December 31, 1986. These are bonds rated below investment grade, i.e., BB/Ba or below at time of issue. A starting date of 1977 was chosen as the first year since there were very few original issues of high yield bonds before that year. (In 1976 only five high yield bonds, par value US$105.0 million, were publicly issued. In the first half of 1977, only eight such bonds were issued; in the second half, eighteen bonds were issued.) Bonds that had been downgraded from investment grade, called "fallen angels," were not included.[6]

Moody's and Standard and Poor's ratings were used as a screen, with bonds rated BBB or above by S&P or Baa or above by Moody's not included. A bond not rated by one agency was included if the other agency rated it below investment grade. Thus, no bond in the sample was considered investment grade by either major rating agency.[7] Bonds not rated by either agency, double NR's, were not included in the sample even though some lists of high yield securities include some of these bonds. There are many double NR's, usually small issues, but there is no agreement among investment banks on which of these bonds should be classified as high yield. Banks include different double NR bonds in their high yield lists depending on whether those bonds were sold or are traded by that firm's high yield group.

The sample bonds were identified by examining the calendar of new securities issued in *Moody's Bond Survey* and *S&P's Bond Guide* over the period from 1977 to 1986. This list was checked against Securities Data Corporations's listing of high yield bonds.[8] Convertible bonds were also excluded from the sample because of their equity component.

After identifying the original issue high yield corporate bond universe, all bonds' histories were followed until December 31, 1988 for credit events including defaults, bankruptcies, exchanges, calls, repurchases, debt–equity swaps, mergers, and puts by holders.[9] These histories were obtained from several sources including each firm's *10K*'s and Annual Reports, *S&P Credit Week*, *Capital Changes Reporter*, *S&P Called Bond Record*, *S&P Bond Guide*, *Moody's Bond Survey*, the *Wall Street Journal*, Salomon Brothers' list of defaulted bonds, Drexel's list of defaulted and exchanged bonds, and First Boston's list of defaults and exchanges. Since none of these sources was complete, additional information for some of the bond histories was obtained by contacting the firm or the bond's trustee.

Table 8.1 presents summary data on the sample of original issue public high yield bonds for the period 1977–86.[10] As Table 8.1 shows, this market has grown rapidly in total issues, dollar amount, and average size of issue. The amount of original issue high yield debt per year was relatively stable until 1981, averaging slightly over $1 billion per year. It then grew rapidly to almost $31 billion in new issues in 1986. In fact, 1986 represents 27 percent of all issues and 43 percent of all par value issued since January 1, 1977. New issues in 1985 and 1986 together constitute 47 percent of issues and 64 percent of par value issued through December 31, 1986. The average size (in par value) of new issues increased from approximately $30 million per issue in the late 1970s to $155 million in 1986. Average yield to maturity rose steadily from 1977 to its peak of 17.4 percent in 1981 and declined to 12.6 percent by 1986. The 741 new public issues of high yield corporate debt during 1977–86 had an aggregate par value of $71.5 billion.

Table 8.1 New issuances of high yield bonds by number of bonds and par amount for issue years 1977–86. High yield bonds are all bonds rated below investment grade at issue date by Moody's and Standard & Poor's. Par value is the customary method used to state the size of the high yield market

Issue year	Number issued	Amt. issued ($ millions)	Average issue amount ($ millions)	N	Average coupon %	N	Average YTM %	N
1977	26	908	34.08	26	10.466	26	10.714	17
1978	51	1,442	28.28	51	11.416	51	11.631	34
1979	41	1,263	30.81	41	12.284	41	12.633	32
1980	37	1,223	33.05	37	13.596	36	14.709	28
1981	24	1,240	51.67	24	14.793	21	17.395	18
1982	41	2,490	60.73	41	13.772	40	16.832	29
1983	74	6,003	81.12	74	12.049	72	13.928	35
1984	102	11,552	113.26	102	14.349	74	15.577	61
1985	145	14,463	99.75	145	13.773	127	14.290	110
1986	200	30,949	154.75	200	12.471	188	12.636	173
Total	741	71,533	96.54	741	12.917	676	13.653	537

II   Results

A.   Defaults

Table 8.2 presents cumulative defaults through December 31, 1988 for high yield bonds issued from 1977 through 1986. Default is defined as declaration of default by the bond trustee, the filing of bankruptcy by the issuing firm, or the assignment of a D rating by S&P for a missed coupon payment. If the bond has been exchanged for other securities, default is also defined as a default of the securities for which the original bond was exchanged.

The results presented in table 8.2 document that default percentages are high for "older" bond issues. An investor who bought and held all high yield bonds issued in 1977 and 1978 would experience, by December 31, 1988, cumulative defaults of 34 percent. Buying and holding all new issues in the years 1979–83 would, by December 31, 1988, produce cumulative defaults ranging from 19 to 27 percent. Cumulative defaults are much lower for "younger" bonds. The issue years of 1984–6 produced cumulative defaults of 3–9 percent through December 31, 1988.[11]

The importance of aging on default rates is illustrated clearly in table 8.3. This table reports year by year default rates and cumulative default percentages for each issue year.[12] Default rates are low for the first several years after issue. In fact, for seven of the ten issue years, there are no defaults in the first year after issue, and, for three of the issue years, there are no defaults in the first two years. These low early year default rates lead to low cumulative default percentages, ranging from 0 to 8 percent three years after issue, with the majority in the 3–6 percent range.[13]

Yearly default rates increase with time, and, thus, older bonds have much higher cumulative default percentages. Seven years after issue, cumulative defaults rise to 18–26 percent for the issue years 1978–82 although no 1977 issues had defaulted seven

Table 8.2 Cumulative defaults for original issue high yield bonds until 12/31/88 by year of issue. High yield bonds are all bonds rated below investment grade at issue date by Moody's and Standard & Poor's. Defaults are defined as a declaration of default by the bond's trustee, filing of bankruptcy by the firm, or assignment of a D rating by S&P for a missed coupon payment

Issue year	Total issued		Total defaulted[a]		Cumulative % of total defaulted	
	Number	Amount ($ millions)	Number	Amount ($ millions)	Number	Amount ($ millions)
1977	26	908	6	308	23.08	33.92
1978	51	1,442	17	494	33.33	34.26
1979	41	1,263	12	312	29.27	24.70
1980	37	1,223	12	337	32.43	27.56
1981	24	1,240	4	260	16.67	20.97
1982	41	2,490	11	646	26.83	25.94
1983	74	6,003	16	1,153	21.62	19.21
1984	102	11,552	15	1,084	14.71	9.38
1985	145	14,463	10	510	6.90	3.53
1986	200	30,949	17	2,519	8.50	8.14
Total	741	71,533	120	7,623		

[a] If the original bond has been exchanged for other securities and no longer exists, default is also defined as a default of the securities for which the bond was exchanged.

years after issue. Eleven and twelve years after issue date, cumulative defaults are 34 percent for the two relevant years, 1977 and 1978. Because a methodology which properly considers aging is employed, the default percentages presented in table 8.3 are much higher than those reported in many earlier studies.

Table 8.3 also indicates no trend toward improvement in aged default rates in more recent issue years. Issue years 1982–6 have average early year default rates equal to or worse than issue years 1977–81. In fact, the most recent issue year in the sample, 1986, exhibits the highest first year default rate and is second among all ten issue years in cumulative default percentages two and three years after issue.

Table 8.4 gives unaged yearly default rates calculated by taking the amount of defaults in a given year and dividing by cumulative new issues since 1977. This is similar to the methodology[14] used to calculate default rates in Altman (1987), Altman and Nammacher (1985, 1987), Fridson et al. (1988a, b), and Weinstein (1987), and by Drexel Burnham Lambert.[15] Table 8.4 demonstrates that replicating this methodology on the sample here yields results similar to those reported elsewhere. Annual default rates calculated in this manner average under 2 percent from 1980 to 1986, and the "unaged" cumulative default percentage, calculated as cumulative defaults divided by cumulative new issues, is 10.66 percent by December 31, 1988. This clearly demonstrates that it is the use of the aging methodology, not differences in the database, which causes our higher default percentages.

Table 8.5 provides further insight into the reason for these low unaged default rates. This table presents the average issue age of the original issue public high yield

Table 8.3 Aged defaults for high yield bonds grouped by year of issue. In this table an nth year default is defined as a default within $n \times 365$ days of the issue date. High yield bonds are all bonds rated below investment grade at issue date by Moody's and Standard & Poor's. Defaults are defined as a declaration of default by the bond's trustee, filing of bankruptcy by the firm, or assignment of a D rating by S&P for a missed coupon payment

Issue year	1st	2nd	3rd	4th	5th	6th	7th	8th	9th	10th	11th	12th	Total
				Panel A: % of Par Amount Defaulted in nth Year After Issue									
1977	0.00	0.00	0.00	0.00	0.00	0.00	0.00	7.71	3.63	19.27	3.30	0.00[a]	33.92
1978	0.00	8.32	0.00	1.39	0.00	7.91	4.85	3.12	5.55	1.39	1.73[a]	—	34.26
1979	0.00	0.00	5.54	1.11	2.38	6.73	1.98	0.00	5.78	1.19[a]	—	—	24.70
1980	0.00	0.57	2.45	0.00	0.00	13.90	6.30	1.88	2.45[a]	—	—	—	27.56
1981	0.00	6.05	0.00	8.06	6.85	0.00	0.00	0.00[a]	—	—	—	—	20.97
1982	1.00	2.41	1.61	11.49	0.00	9.44	0.00[a]	—	—	—	—	—	25.94
1983	0.00	0.00	6.08	7.83	4.80	0.50[a]	—	—	—	—	—	—	19.21
1984	2.29	1.99	2.03	3.06	0.00[a]	—	—	—	—	—	—	—	9.38
1985	0.00	0.80	2.28	0.45[a]	—	—	—	—	—	—	—	—	3.53
1986	2.73	3.84	1.57[a]	—	—	—	—	—	—	—	—	—	8.14
				Panel B: Cumulated % of Par Amount Defaulted for x Years After Issue									
1977	0.00	0.00	0.00	0.00	0.00	0.00	0.00	7.71	11.34	30.62	33.92	33.92[a]	33.92
1978	0.00	8.32	8.32	9.71	9.71	17.61	22.47	25.59	31.14	32.52	34.26[a]	—	34.26
1979	0.00	0.00	5.54	6.65	9.03	15.76	17.74	17.74	23.52	24.70[a]	—	—	24.70
1980	0.00	0.57	3.03	3.03	3.03	16.93	23.22	25.10	27.56[a]	—	—	—	27.56
1981	0.00	6.05	6.05	14.11	20.97	20.97	20.97	20.97[a]	—	—	—	—	20.97
1982	1.00	3.41	5.02	16.51	16.51	25.94	25.94[a]	—	—	—	—	—	25.94
1983	0.00	0.00	6.08	13.91	18.71	19.21[a]	—	—	—	—	—	—	19.21
1984	2.29	4.28	6.32	9.38	9.38[a]	—	—	—	—	—	—	—	9.38
1985	0.00	0.80	3.08	3.53[a]	—	—	—	—	—	—	—	—	3.53
1986	2.73	6.57	8.14[a]	—	—	—	—	—	—	—	—	—	8.14

[a] May be incomplete; i.e., entire sample may not have been outstanding for x years.

Table 8.4 Yearly default percentages for original issue high yield bonds calculated without aging. High yield bonds are all bonds rated below investment grade at issue date by Moody's and Standard & Poor's. Defaults are defined as a declaration of default by the bond's trustee, filing of bankruptcy by the firm, or assignment of a D rating by S&P for a missed coupon payment. Default percentages are calculated as the number (or $ amount) of defaults in a given year divided by the universe of all high yield bonds issued through that year

Year	Number defaulted	Amount defaulted ($ millions)	Total number issued since 1/1/77	Total amount tissued since 1/1/77 ($ millions)	Defaults % Number	Defaults % $ Amount
1977	0	0	26	908	0.00	0.00
1978	0	0	77	2,350	0.00	0.00
1979	1	20	118	3,613	0.85	0.56
1980	1	100	155	4,836	0.65	2.08
1981	2	107	179	6,076	1.12	1.77
1982	7	145	220	8,566	3.18	1.69
1983	4	125	294	14,569	1.36	0.86
1984	8	303	396	26,121	2.02	1.16
1985	13	821	541	40,584	2.40	2.02
1986	37	2,104	741	71,533	4.99	2.94
Total[a]	120	7,623	741	71,533	16.19	10.66

[a] From 1/1/77 to 12/31/88.

bond market. Average issue age is defined as average time since issue date for all bonds in the sample.[16] Because of the rapid growth in new issue volume, the average age of the overall market actually declined for several years and has hovered around two years.

As a result, default rates which do not consider bond age, such as those in table 8.4, produce biased results. As the aging analysis in table 8.3 demonstrates, default rates do not increase until several years after issue. By then, the larger default rates on old bonds appear small relative to the size of the overall market, now dominated by bonds issued in the previous year or two. An aging methodology is necessary to produce a clear view of the default experience of a buy-and-hold investor.

The illusion of low unaged default rates calculated as in table 8.4 can be sustained only as long as the explosive growth in new issues continues. Once growth slows, as it inevitably must, the overall market will no longer be dominated by recently issued bonds with lower default rates. With slower growth in new issue volume, the average age of the overall high yield bond market will grow, revealing higher aged default percentages such as those reported in table 8.3.[17]

Finally, it should be noted that the aged default rates reported in this paper are not necessarily indicative of future default rates. The sample studied here covers a period of generally falling interest rates, rising stock prices, and good economic conditions (except for a brief 1982 recession). Further adversity in capital markets and/or economic conditions could produce higher default rates. In addition, because of the youth of this market, few of the issuers were required to make principal payments during the sample period. With the added burden of sinking fund and maturity payments, future

Table 8.5 The average issue age[a] of all high yield bonds issued after January 1, 1977, until the date given. High yield bonds are all bonds rated below investment grade at issue date by Moody's and Standard & Poor's. Average issue age is defined as the amount of bonds issued multiplied by the time since issue date divided by the total amount issued

Bonds issued after 1/1/77 until the date below	Average issue age weighted by par value of issues
12/31/77	0.48 years
12/31/78	0.85 years
12/31/79	1.36 years
12/31/80	1.87 years
12/31/81	2.39 years
12/31/82	2.50 years
12/31/83	2.28 years
12/31/84	2.01 years
12/31/85	2.07 years
12/31/86	1.94 years

[a] Formally, the par amount of each bond is multiplied by the number of days since issue. This weighted amount is summed and then divided by the cumulative par amount issued. For example, if an equal amount of bonds is issued every year for ten years, the average age at the end of ten years is five years. If more bonds are issued at the beginning of the period, the average age is > five years. If more are issued at the end of the period, the average is < five years.

default rates could be higher even without a worsening of the economy. On the other hand, more underwriter and investor experience with the credit-worthiness of high leverage or low rated firms, greater liquidity in the secondary market for high yield bonds, and a more active role for exchange offers may lower future default rates.

B.   Exchanges

Exchanges are important in analyzing high yield bonds since they may be used to avoid the event of default by a reorganization of claims. In a distressed situation, a firm may offer bondholders the opportunity to exchange the bond for securities with less current service burden (e.g., by a lower coupon rate, a delayed sinking fund, or a combination exchange of bonds and common stock).[18] Such distressed exchange offers, if not properly considered, might understate the incidence of firm financial distress as well as the size of losses experienced by bondholders since the terms of the exchange should reflect a significant probability of default on the old debt. Furthermore, if exchanges are not followed afterwards, defaults on the newly issued bonds (and on any residual amount of untendered old bonds) will be ignored.

The results in table 8.6 confirm that, by December 31, 1988, a significant percentage of the bonds issued in the early sample years have been subject to exchanges. Four of the first five issue years have cumulative exchange percentages in excess of 17

Table 8.6 Cumulative successful exchanges for original issue high yield bonds until 12/31/88 by year of issue. This table does not include exchanges subsequent to default or bankruptcy. It also does not include debt–equity swaps. High yield bonds are all bonds rated below investment grade at issue date by Moody's and Standard & Poor's. Defaults are defined as a declaration of default by the bond's trustee, filing of bankruptcy by the firm, or assignment of a D rating by S&P for a missed coupon payment

Issue year	Number of issues exchanged[a]	Amount of issues exchanged ($ millions)	% of total issues exchanged		% of total issues exchanged with no subsequent default[b]	
			Number	Amount	Number	Amount
1977	6	281	23.08	30.95	11.54	15.75
1978	10	290	19.61	20.11	7.84	9.02
1979	4	56	9.76	4.43	2.44	1.11
1980	7	212	18.92	17.33	8.11	6.13
1981	6	365	25.00	29.44	20.83	24.19
1982	4	180	9.76	7.23	4.88	0.80
1983	8	820	10.81	13.66	5.41	7.58
1984	7	555	6.86	4.80	6.86	4.80
1985	7	470	4.83	3.25	4.83	3.25
1986	3	480	1.50	1.55	1.00	1.07
Total	62	3,709	8.37	5.19	5.13	3.48

[a] For an additional eleven issues in the sample (par value $581 million), the issue was exchanged after a default or bankruptcy.

[b] As of 12/31/88. This is the percentage of all issues in the sample that have been exchanged without any subsequent default. A high percentage of exchanged bonds subsequently default. (See table 8.7.) A small percentage eventually mature or are called. (See table 8.7.)

percent. Cumulative exchanges for more recent issue years are between 2 and 14 percent.

The results presented in table 8.7 illustrate, however, that exchange offers have not always been successful in avoiding default. For all issue years, excluding 1984 and 1985, a significant fraction of exchanges, 18–89 percent, are followed by default on the securities received in the exchange offer. These defaults are included in the default results reported in tables 8.2, 8.3, and 8.4. Of all exchanges, slightly less than one third are followed by default, more than half are followed by no other event by December 31, 1988, and the remaining 9 percent are called or are paid off at maturity. Table 8.6 shows that exchanges not followed by default are a small fraction of total issue amount for most issue years. Thus, these results do not support the argument that exchange offers succeed in eliminating defaults, although they may reduce their number or change their timing.

C. Calls and maturity

Table 8.8 reports cumulative call percentages for high yield bonds. Between 26 and 47 percent of the bonds issued in the first six years, 1977–82, have been called by

Table 8.7 Amounts and percentages of successful exchanges that have defaulted, matured, or been called from the exchange until 12/31/88 by year of issue. This table does not include exchanges made subsequent to a default or bankruptcy. Percentages are calculated for the sample of total successful exchanges

Issue year	Exchanges/no other events				Exchange/default				Exchange/call or maturity			
	Number	Amount ($ millions)	% Number	% Amount	Number	Amount ($ millions)	% Number	% Amount	Number	Amount ($ millions)	% Number	% Amount
1977	0	0	0.00	0.00	3	138	50.00	49.11	3	143	50.00	50.89
1978	4	130	40.00	44.83	6	160	60.00	55.17	0	0	0.00	0.00
1979	1	14	25.00	25.00	3	42	75.00	75.00	0	0	0.00	0.00
1980	2	50	28.57	23.58	4	137	57.14	64.62	1	25	14.29	11.79
1981	3	240	50.00	65.75	1	65	16.67	17.81	2	60	33.33	16.44
1982	1	10	25.00	5.56	2	160	50.00	88.89	1	10	25.00	5.56
1983[a]	4	455	50.00	55.49	4	365	50.00	44.51	0	0	0.00	0.00
1984	6	455	85.71	81.98	0	0	0.00	0.00	1	100	14.29	18.02
1985	7	470	100.00	100.00	0	0	0.00	0.00	0	0	0.00	0.00
1986	2	330	66.67	68.75	1	150	33.33	31.25	0	0	0.00	0.00
Totals[b]	30	2,154	48.39	58.07	24	1,217	38.71	32.81	8	338	12.90	9.11

[a] One of the defaulted bonds in 1983, par value $85 million, was later called when the issuing company was acquired by another firm. To avoid double-counting, the bond is only classified as a default.

[b] Total percentages are of total exchanges and are not the average of the yearly percentages.

Table 8.8 Cumulative calls for all high yield bonds until 12/31/88 by year of issue. High yield bonds are all bonds rated below investment grade at issue date by Moody's and Standard & Poor's

Issue year	Number of issues called	Amount of issues called ($ millions)	Cumulative % of total issues called	
			Number	Amount
1977	9	296	34.62	32.60
1978	13	373	25.49	25.87
1979	13	414	31.71	32.78
1980	11	368	29.73	30.09
1981	8	345	33.33	27.82
1982	15	1,174	36.59	47.15
1983	12	790	16.22	13.16
1984	14	1,059	13.73	9.17
1985	16	2,024	11.03	13.99
1986	5	937	2.50	3.03
Total	116	7,780	15.65	10.88

December 31, 1988. This partially reflects the sharp decline in interest rates beginning in 1982. It may also reflect required calls associated with asset sales or an improvement in some bonds' credit ratings. Thus, for a large percentage of the high yield market, lower interest rates and/or good performance by the issuers are translated into calls, requiring bondholders to reinvest. In contrast, only 3–14 percent of the bonds issued in 1983–6 have been called by December 31, 1988. Given normal call protection periods and lower coupon rates (see table 8.1), this is not surprising.

The high cumulative call percentages for early issue years raise the question of whether call provisions were correctly priced for these issues. In view of the possibility of upgrading lower grade bonds, and the larger inherent equity component, one would expect the call options on such bonds to be more valuable than call options on investment grade debt.[19] Exploring the issue of upgrades, of the 116 calls in our sample, 42.2 percent came after upgrades, 13.8 percent came after downgrades, and 44.0 percent had no change in rating since issue. For A rated bonds issued in 1977–86, the percentage of calls after upgrade was 29.4 percent, 38.1 percent came after downgrades, and 32.5 percent had no change.[20]

Maturity results are given as part of table 8.9. The original issue high yield bond market has been primarily long term, and only 2.19 percent of the total value of all issues in the sample had reached maturity by December 31, 1988. For three of the early years, 1978–80, no bonds have yet matured.

D.   Summary results on defaults, exchanges, calls, and maturity

Table 8.9 contains summary aged results for defaults, exchanges, calls, and maturities and presents a more detailed picture of this market than previous studies. By December 31, 1988, about one third (32.5 percent) of the high yield bonds issued in years

Table 8.9 Cumulative disposition of original issue high yield bonds by percentage of par amount issued until 12/31/88 by year of issue. In this table an *n*th year default is defined as a default within $n \times 365$ days of the issue date. High yield bonds are all bonds rated below investment grade at issue date by Moody's and Standard & Poor's. Defaults are defined as a declaration of default by the bond's trustee, filing of bankruptcy by the firm, or assignment of a D rating by S&P for a missed coupon payment

Issue year	Total issued ($ millions)	Defaults %	Exchanges (still outstanding) %	Calls %	Maturities %	Residual outstanding[a] %
1977	908	33.92	0.00	32.60	9.59	24.12
1978	1,442	34.26	9.02	25.87	0.00	30.86
1979	1,263	24.70	1.11	32.78	0.00	41.41
1980	1,223	27.56	4.09	30.09	0.00	38.27
1981	1,240	20.97	19.35	27.82	2.42	29.44
1982	2,490	25.94	0.40	47.15	10.84	15.66
1983	6,003	19.21	7.58	13.16	5.83	54.22
1984	11,552	9.38	3.94	9.17	4.60	72.91
1985	14,463	3.53	3.25	13.99	0.00	79.23
1986	30,949	8.14	1.07	3.03	0.97	86.68
Total	71,533	10.66	3.01	10.88	2.19	73.27

[a] Does not adjust for sinking funds and partial repurchases. If these were included, the residual percentage would be lower.

1977–82 have defaulted or have been exchanged. Another third (34.7 percent) of the issues have been called and a small percentage (4.5 percent) have matured. Thus, by December 31, 1988, only 28.1 percent of the original issues of 1977–82 have not defaulted, exchanged, been called or matured.

Results for more recent issue years show fewer defaults and calls. However, the aging analysis of defaults in tables 8.3 and 8A.1 to 8A.3 demonstrates that cumulative defaults for later issue years are similar to those for bonds from early issue years at comparable ages. Call rates are lower, however, due presumably to call protection and a leveling off of interest rates. Thus, while a much larger percentage of recent issues remain outstanding without default, there is no evidence suggesting a fundamental change in the nature of the market.

The summary of aging results also underscores the extent to which the outstanding high yield market is dominated by recently issued "young" bonds. This dominance is due not only to the rapid growth in new issue volume but also to the attrition in outstanding issues due to defaults, calls, and principal payments.[21] This attrition accelerates with issue age, thereby diminishing the outstanding balance of older issues.

E.　Other results

Table 8.10 presents data, by S&P rating, on the composition of high yield bond issues and on cumulative defaults.[22] One notable result is the shift toward CCC rated issues in later issue years. Prior to 1983, the original issue public high yield corporate bond market was comprised almost exclusively of BB and B rates issues. This reduction in initial credit quality since 1983 raises the question of whether defaults may prove

Table 8.10 Distribution by issue year of original issue high yield bonds by S&P rating at time of issue and cumulative defaults from issue date until December 31, 1988 by issue year and S&P rating. High yield bonds are all bonds rated below investment grade at issue date by Moody's and Standard & Poor's. Defaults are defined as a declaration of default by the bond's trustee, filing of bankruptcy by the firm, or assignment of a D rating by S&P for a missed coupon payment

| Issue year | Total issued ($ millions) | Share of market by rating class as % of total issues | | | Cumulative default % | | | |
| | | | | | Total market | By rating class | | |
		BB	B	CCC or below		BB	B	CCC or below
1977	908	42.62	55.95	1.43	33.92	6.46	55.71	0.00
1978	1,442	28.29	70.87	0.83	34.26	35.54	34.15	0.00
1979	1,263	27.95	65.80	6.25	24.70	33.99	21.42	17.72
1980	1,223	26.00	71.95	2.04	27.56	16.67	32.27	0.00
1981	1,240	24.27	75.73	0.00	20.97	0.00	27.69	NA
1982	2,490	44.38	54.02	1.61	25.94	22.62	26.47	100.00
1983	6,003	27.90	63.85	8.25[a]	19.21	0.00	24.99	39.39[a]
1984	11,552	29.48	59.34	11.18	9.38	2.94	10.80	18.89
1985	14,463	31.72	54.62	13.67	3.53	4.36	3.92	0.00
1986	30,949	13.24	69.05	17.71	8.14	0.00	9.08	10.57
Total[b]	71,533	23.26	63.58	13.16	10.66	5.37	12.44	11.39

[a] One bond issue for $35 million was rated below CCC. This CC bond issue defaulted during its first year out.

[b] This is the total amount and percentages for all years together. It differs from an average yearly percentage with each year weighted equally since later years represent a larger share of all issues.

higher in future years. Cumulative default percentages by S&P rating demonstrate that B rated issues exhibit higher default percentages than BB rated issues for seven of the ten issue years. While inferences in early issue years about CCC rated issues are limited by the small issue amounts, their cumulative defaults are higher than BB or B rated issues for four of the last five issue years. For the entire sample, the default percentage is 5.37 percent for BB bonds, 12.44 percent for B bonds, and 11.39 percent for CCC bonds. This lower percentage for CCC bonds is probably explained by their lower average age. The average issue age is 2.45 years for BB bonds, 1.90 years for B bonds, and 1.21 years for CCC bonds.

Stratifying the sample by industry shows that neither issues nor defaults are concentrated in a few industries. This is not surprising given the tremendous growth in the high yield bond market and the fact that economic conditions may differ by sectors of the economy. There are at least twenty-seven industries with over $1 billion in par value issued. In addition, there are twelve industries with over $200 million in defaults.[23] These twelve industries are energy, steel, industrial machinery and equipment, miscellaneous manufacturing, toys and sporting goods, ship transportation, utilities, credit companies, mortgage bankers, real estate, motion picture production, and hospitals/healthcare.

Table 8.11 presents underwriter market share and default percentages by issue year for original issue high yield bonds. The dominant underwriter, Drexel Burnham Lambert, increased its new issue market share from under one third during 1977–80 to 53–63 percent in 1981–5 before dropping to 45 percent in 1986. Of the total sample of high yield bonds, more than half were underwritten by Drexel. Table 8.11 also presents defaults by underwriter for each issue year. Issues underwritten by Drexel exhibit lower default percentages than do the aggregate issues of all other underwriters. In every year except for 1985, Drexel has a lower cumulative default percentage on its issues than all other underwriters taken together. If the defaults are further categorized by rating class and year of issue, Drexel has lower or equal default rates in each year for all CCC's and for nine of the ten years for both B's and BB's. These differences may be explained by Drexel's experience and expertise in the high yield market and by other underwriters' attempts to penetrate the market by underwriting less creditworthy issues.

Finally, after 1980, high yield debt increasingly began to be used for funding mergers and leveraged buyouts.[24] LBO high yield debt constitutes 24.2 percent, 24.6 percent, and 21.0 percent of the total par value issued in 1984, 1985, and 1986, respectively, and totals $12.9 billion. This LBO debt is 18.6 percent of the total 1977–86 sample. Three LBO bonds, totalling $704 million par value, have defaulted by December 31, 1988. All are associated with one transaction, the 1986 LBO of

Table 8.11 Share of original issue high yield bonds issued and cumulative default percentages by underwriter measured in par value of issue by year of issue with the entire issue allocated to the lead underwriter. High yield bonds are all bonds rated below investment grade at issue date by Moody's and Standard & Poor's. Defaults are defined as a declaration of default by the bond's trustee, filing of bankruptcy by the firm, or assignment of a D rating by S&P for a missed coupon payment

Year	Total issued ($ millions)	Share of market as % of total issues[a]		Cumulative defaults %		
		DBL[b]	Non-DBL[b]	Total market	DBL issues[c]	Non-DBL issues[c]
1977	908	14.98	85.02	33.92	22.06	36.01
1978	1,442	26.35	73.65	34.26	29.74	35.88
1979	1,263	32.30	67.70	24.70	23.53	25.26
1980	1,223	34.18	65.82	27.56	20.33	31.30
1981	1,240	63.23	36.77	20.97	20.41	21.93
1982	2,490	54.42	45.58	25.94	3.32	52.95
1983	6,003	54.02	45.98	19.21	17.21	21.56
1984	11,552	60.10	39.90	9.38	4.68	16.47
1985	14,463	60.87	39.13	3.53	3.92	2.92
1986	30,949	44.90	55.10	8.14	0.79	14.13
Total	71,533	50.84	49.16	10.66	5.13	16.37

[a] DBL is Drexel Burnham Lambert.
[b] The average issue age (as defined in table 8.5) is 1.85 years for DBL issues and 2.03 years for non-DBL issues.
[c] The cumulative defaults for DBL and non-DBL are the percentages of DBL and non-DBL issues for a given year that default by December 31, 1988. The weighted average (not the sum) of these two percentages gives the total market cumulative default percentage for each year.

Revco Drug Stores. This makes the default percentage for all LBO debt 5.47 percent, but even fewer implications can be drawn from this subsample given its short history and single defaulting firm.

III Return Implications

While our results do provide some insight into high yield bond returns, we do not explicitly calculate returns here. The best evidence to date on high yield bond returns is presented in Blume and Keim (1988), and their results are mixed. For the sample period 1977–87, they find that monthly realized returns on high yield bonds (0.89 percent) exceed returns on both Treasury bonds (0.76 percent) and investment grade bonds (0.78 percent). However, their data source (the S&P Bond Guide) for the first five years of this sample period, 1977–81, likely includes a significant number of "fallen angels," bonds issued as investment grade and subsequently downgraded. These bonds might be expected to have different return characteristics than original issue high yield bonds. Furthermore, the prices in the S&P guide are a combination of transaction prices, bid and ask prices, and matrix prices.

For the sample period 1982–7, Blume and Keim (1988) find that high yield bonds underperform both Treasury bonds and investment grade bonds by a substantial margin. The monthly realized return average is 1.26 percent for high yield bonds, 1.39 percent for Treasuries, and 1.46 percent for investment grade bonds. Their data sources for this sample period are Drexel Burnham Lambert and Salomon Brothers. While this database is not as likely to be dominated by fallen angels and there is no matrix pricing, only bonds included in Drexel's and Salomon Brothers' high yield bond indices are used. This may introduce selection bias since these indices are not composed of randomly selected bonds. Instead, bonds are periodically selected to enter and leave the indices. When bonds are selected to leave the indices, Blume and Keim find substantially negative returns for the following two months.

Thus, Blume and Keim's work illustrates a significant problem – the difficulty in obtaining accurate transactions-based return data on a complete (or random) sample of original issue high yield bonds.

One potential solution to this problem is to use return simulations, but these have other weaknesses. Inputs for simulations include coupon spreads between high yield bonds and a benchmark bond (e.g., Treasury bonds); sequences of defaults, exchanges, calls, sinking funds, and maturities; high yield bond prices (i.e., retention values) at default, exchange, and call; reinvestment prices and strategies for all "mortality" events; and, finally, a hypothetical cash-out terminal value for the portfolio of high yield bonds.

There are problems with most of these inputs. For example, coupon spreads compare callable high yield bonds with Treasury bonds, many of which are noncallable or callable only after a long call protection period. High yield coupons include compensation for the probability that rates decline and/or the bond is upgraded and the issuer calls the bond. The effect is to truncate the upper tail of the callable bond's return distribution, while there is no such truncation for noncallable Treasury bonds.

Two possible adjustments are to subtract the call option value from high yield bond coupon rates to produce a coupon comparable to Treasury yields or to compare spreads of high yield bonds to callable corporate bonds.[25] However, without some adjustments, simulations based upon stated coupon spreads do not capture the option characteristics of call provisions.

There are also problems with the assumed sequences of mortality events (defaults, exchanges, calls). First, this is still a young market. The realized incidence of defaults, exchanges, calls, and the like represents only one draw from the distribution, and there is little reason to believe that this draw is the mean – the expected result. Also, many of the events are affected by interest rate changes. It is internally inconsistent to use historical incidences produced under one set of interest rate changes in simulations which assume no interest rate volatility.

However, the most serious deficiency in using simulations is the lack of real price data as inputs for reinvestment strategies and for the end-of-period cash-out terminal value of the bond portfolio. For example, Altman (1989) and Goodman (1989) in their corporate bond return simulations assume that all bonds that do not default (or are not subject to any other mortality event) sell at par. This is a critical assumption which has an important impact on simulated returns. Their justification is that, because interest rates are not assumed to vary, all nondefaulting bonds should sell at par. This assumption is not correct for bonds subject to low early-year and higher later-year default probabilities. Even with no change in interest rates, if the bonds are callable, such bonds should sell below par in their early years. It is these price declines in the early years that constitute the mechanism through which realized returns below stated coupon rates are achieved. In later years, higher default incidences reduce the stated yield.

Were such bonds not to sell below par in the earlier years, a "free money" game would exist. Investors could buy newly issued bonds, pocket most of the high coupons while early-year defaults were low, and then sell the bonds at par before the higher later-year defaults appeared.

Thus, even in the absence of interest rate volatility, the default sequence itself produces bond prices below par. Terminal value assumptions that all nondefaulting bonds sell at par can substantially overstate the simulated return on high yield bonds. Moreover, high yield bond prices are obviously affected not only by the default sequence and interest rate changes but also by changes in the value of the firm.

As an empirical matter, despite generally falling interest rates during the 1980's, our sample bonds were selling at an average price of about 90 percent of par in late 1987 and 1988. A comparable sample of Treasury bonds was priced at 106 in late 1988.[26] Lower terminal values for high yield bonds and higher values for Treasuries suggest that simulations based upon the assumption of par values overstate the relative returns on high yield bonds.[27]

Even if transaction returns can be calculated, or if realistic inputs are entered for return simulations, there are still difficulties in deciding how to interpret them. As noted earlier, this market is still new, and historical incidences represent not the mean but only one draw from the distribution. As with stock price performance, a full range of economic and capital market conditions will be required to assess accurately high yield performance. In addition, few of the bonds issued to date have entered a period requiring repayment of principal – another reason for caution.

Further, it is not true that, after adjusting for defaults, "return spread results [of corporate bond returns versus Treasury returns] should be insignificantly different from zero."[28] Default risk is only one type of risk. Even after adjusting for defaults, returns on high yield bonds may require a risk premium over Treasury returns. Whether one characterizes this risk premium as a systematic risk premium or as an interest rate risk premium, expected high yield bond returns should include compensation for this market risk as well as for default risk. Blume and Keim (1987) estimate a beta of 0.30 for their sample of high yield bonds over the period 1982–6. Coupled with a market risk premium of 5–8 percent, this translates to an expected return spread of 150–240 basis points for high yield bonds versus risk-free bonds. High yield realized returns adjusted for default must therefore beat risk-free returns by more than this spread to produce superior risk-adjusted returns.

Finally, a liquidity-related premium may need to be included in high yield expected returns, a point Altman (1989) makes. This factor may be especially important in comparing high yield bonds to Treasury bonds due to the dramatic differences in liquidity in the two markets.

What does all this mean? Not much, we suspect. Simulated returns with hypothetical terminal values and numerous other hypothetical inputs are inferior to realized returns calculated from actual transactions. Furthermore, the best evidence to date, Blume and Keim (1988), reports mixed results on the performance of high yield bonds versus benchmark bonds. What is needed is accurate transactions-based return data over a full range of economic and capital market conditions and a complete (or random) sample of high yield bonds. In our view, the return performance of high yield bonds remains an important topic for future research.

IV Conclusions

This study incorporates the age of high yield bond issues and reveals default percentages substantially higher than those reported in most previous studies. Buying and holding a portfolio of all bonds issued in 1977 and 1978 produces cumulative defaults exceeding 34 percent by December 31, 1988. Also, by this date, cumulative defaults range from 19–27 percent for issue years 1979–83 and from 3–9 percent for issue years 1984–6.

Cumulative defaults also rise more quickly as the time since issue increases. Cumulative defaults are generally in the 3–6 percent range three years after issue, increase to 18–26 percent seven years after issue (for all but the first of the issue years), and reach 34 percent eleven years after issue.

An aging analysis is necessary to measure clearly the default rates experienced by a buy-and-hold investor. Cumulative defaults calculated without aging compare current defaults with the current size of the overall high yield bond market. However, current defaults actually reflect higher default rates on older bonds, and these defaults appear as a small fraction of the current market (which is dominated by the growth of newly issued bonds).

A significant portion of early high yield issues are also exchanged. However, many of these exchanges are followed by default on the securities received. Exchanges not followed by default are a small fraction of total issues for most issue years, so exchange offers do not eliminate all defaults, although they may reduce or delay them.

Moreover, a large percentage of high yield bonds from early issue years have been called by December 31, 1988. Cumulative calls for the issue years of 1977–82 range from 26 to 47 percent, reflecting the sharp decline in interest rates beginning in 1982, the expiration of call protection, and possibly an increase in credit quality for some of the bonds in the sample. In contrast, a smaller percentage of post-1982 issues have been called.

Summary data for the early issue years 1977–82 show that by December 31, 1988 about one third of these issues have defaulted or been exchanged, one third have been called, and only a small percentage have reached maturity. The residual issues, which have not defaulted, been exchanged, been called, or matured, represent only 28 percent, on average, of the original issues of 1977–82.

As for future defaults, there is no evidence that bonds from later issue years will perform any better than bonds from earlier issue years. Cumulative default percentages for the first several years after issue have been higher for later issue years. Later issue years also contain a higher proportion of lower rated (i.e., CCC) issues. Finally, the defaults reported in this paper result primarily from difficulty in meeting interest payments. Relatively few bonds have been outstanding long enough to incur the added burden of principal repayment. All of these factors suggest that future default rates could be different from those reported here. Other factors that may affect default rates include more experience with high yield bonds by underwriters and investors, and conditions on both the capital market and the economy.

Returns on high yield bonds need to be analyzed as well. In an efficient market, the expected return on high yield bonds should be sufficient to offset the expected default rate and should include premiums for market-related or systematic risk and for the value of the option to call the bond. Analysis of returns should provide insight into whether market participants correctly incorporated these factors, including high default rates, in the pricing of high yield bonds. Only after more return analyses are complete can judgments of the risk/return characteristics of the high yield debt market be made.

Notes

Mullins is on leave from the Harvard Business School at the US Department of the Treasury. This research was performed while Mullins was on the faculty of the Harvard Business School and represents his personal views and not those of the US Department of the Treasury. Wolff is at the US Department of Justice. This research was performed while Wolff was at the Harvard Business School and represents his personal views and not those of the US Department of Justice. We wish to acknowledge the assistance of First Boston, Drexel Burnham Lambert, Morgan Stanley, and Salomon Brothers for making default data available. Thanks are also due to the Division of Research, Harvard Business School for providing financial support. In addition, we wish to thank Ben Bisconti and Darquise Cloutier for their assistance with data collection and Paul Bonner for his computer analysis. We also wish to thank Steve Buser, Greg Hradsky, Michael Jensen, Tim Luehrman, Bob Merton, René Stulz, and the referee for the *Journal of Finance*, as well as the participants at the University of Chicago and Harvard University Finance Seminars, for their comments. Finally, special thanks are due to Bruce MacLennan for his research assistance.

1   The growth in this market can be viewed as a process of securitization. Low rated firms previously borrowed from insurance companies and banks. Development of the public high yield market allowed the securitization of these private placements.

2   1977 was the first year public high yield bond issues exceeded five issues or US$110 million.

3   These low annual default rates are also reported in research reports and in the financial press. For example, see Fridson, Wahl, and Jones in Morgan Stanley's January 1988 *High Performance* and in a Morgan Stanley March 1988 report titled "The Anatomy of the High Yield Debt Market: 1987," or Carney in *Business Week* (3/30/87), who quotes a default rate at 1.22 percent, and Douglas Hallett in the *Wall Street Journal*, who cites a junk bond default rate of 1.6 percent a year.

4   An exchange offer involves the holders of an existing bond accepting a new security in exchange for that bond. Nondistressed exchanges allow a corporation to readjust its capital structure quickly. A distressed exchange allows a corporation which may have trouble meeting its debt obligations to reduce them. The new security usually has lower coupons, or delayed sinking funds and principal payments. Sometimes the securities exchanged are equity or have an equity component. Exchange offers may be either registered with the SEC or unregistered if they meet requirements under Section 3(a)(9) of the Securities Act of 1933.

5   This is the cumulated new issue volume at par value over several years. This number is often adjusted by subtracting calls, maturities, and upgrades and by adding downgrades and registered private placements.

6   Fallen angels may behave differently from original issue high yield bonds since there has already been a negative "event" that caused downgrading. This event may either increase or decrease the likelihood of another such event.

7   Bonds rated BBB by one agency and below BBB by the other, "split triple B's," are sometimes considered high yield.

8   The universe of bonds collected from Moody's and S&P matched with Security Data Corp. (SDC) in 738 cases. There were four bonds listed by SDC that were not included in Moody's or S&P. Ratings may have come later after issue date. Also, three bonds listed in Moody's or S&P are not in SDC. They were left in the sample so that it contains the complete Moody's and S&P lists.

9   Exchanges involve the substitution of one or more securities for the original bond. These successor securities were also followed forward in time for future credit events.

10 Statistics on the size of the market and par value issue volume presented in table 8.1 closely parallel those of underwriters (such as Drexel Burnham Lambert) and researchers (such as Altman) once differences in sample definitions are accounted for. In particular, the total is different from some studies because it excludes (1) issues not rated by both major rating agencies (double NR's) and (2) issues rated investment grade by one agency and below investment grade by the other rating agency (split triple B's). The sample also includes only original public issues, thus excluding "fallen angels" and private bond issues which are subsequently taken public.

11   These default rates are not directly comparable to Altman's (1989) cumulative mortality
      rates. This is both because Altman separates his sample by rating classes and because
      Altman reduces the denominator by calls, maturities, defaults, and sinking funds, thus
      increasing the annual mortality rate. Calculating Altman's cumulative mortality rates
      using our data base yields cumulative rates of 21.11 percent and 41.78 percent after ten
      years for BB and B rated bonds and 37.50 percent after six years for CCC bonds. These
      percentages are higher than Altman (1989). Our twelve-year cumulative mortality rates
      for BB and B bonds are 28.18 percent and 44.35 percent, respectively. A probable reason
      for our higher defaults is our tracking of exchanges.

12   Default within the nth year is defined as a default within $n \times 365$ days of the issue date.
      Thus, bonds are grouped by issue date within cohorts of issue years (January to Decem-
      ber), but credit events are defined in time elapsed since issue date.

      More detail on year-by-year default rates are included in tables 8A.1, 8A.2, and 8A.3.

13   Table 8A.3 shows that average aged default rates by years since issue date are their lowest
      in years 1, 2, and 3 (in that order).

      The average aged default rate for n years is defined as the average n-year default rate
      over all issue years; i.e., the average aged default rate for the first year is the weighted
      average number of defaults which occur during all first years. Table 8A.2 presents the
      year-by-year calculations.

14   See note 5.

15   Drexel (1989) using this methodology finds, "Between 1971–88, annual high yield
      default rates (including 'fallen angels') have averaged about 2%" (p. 7). Also, in figure 1.9
      of Drexel (1989), the "original issue high yield only" default rates average 0.95 percent
      for 1977–88.

16   Average issue age is calculated by summing the par amount of the bond times the days
      since issue data and dividing that sum by the par amount of all bonds issued times 365
      days. There is no adjustment made here for bonds which are called, mature, default, or
      exchange. If there were, the average issue age would presumably decrease since "older"
      bonds would be more likely, on average, to have experienced these events.

17   The defaults presented in table 8.3 are given as a percentage of par amount issued. Table
      8A.1 also gives defaults as a percentage of bonds issued. A third way to calculate defaults
      is as a percentage of firms issuing. This approach would be important if a disproportionate
      number of firms with multiple issues defaulted, particularly in the early sample years
      when issue numbers were smaller. In fact, this is not the case; the 741 issues are by 499
      different firms, and the 120 defaults are by 81 different firms. This makes the per-bond
      default percentage of 16.19 percent almost identical to the per-firm default percentage of
      16.23 percent. Furthermore, since most firms with multiple bonds issue in several
      different years, the yearly per-firm default rate is higher than the per-bond default rate for
      eight of the ten sample years, including 1977, 1978, and 1979 (with per-firm default
      rates of 24.00 percent, 34.69 percent, and 30.00 percent, respectively).

18   Such distressed exchanges might represent a more efficient method of reorganizing claims
      than default and/or bankruptcy. See Jensen (1989) for a fuller discussion of this issue.
      Exchanges which occur after bankruptcy and default, and which represent a formal
      reorganization of claims are not included in the results. There are eleven such exchanges,
      representing $581 million in par value of bonds.

19   For example, the value of the call option on AA utility bonds has been estimated as 50–
      70 basis points. For high yield debt, both sensitivity to interest rate changes and the
      possibility of improving credit quality of the firm may lead to a higher call option spread.

Blume and Keim (1987), however, find lower price volatility for high yield debt, perhaps because of shorter duration.

20 A selection process identical to that for high yield bonds (as described in section II) was performed for all original issue bonds rated A/A by Moody's and S&P in order to serve as a comparison. There were 1224 such bonds issued between 1977 and 1986, representing $134.46 billion in par value at issue. Complete results on this sample are not presented in this paper.

21 Sinking funds and partial repurchases would reduce the amount of older bonds even further.

22 S&P ratings were used except in cases where S&P did not rate the bond. For these bonds, the comparable Moody's rating was used.

23 This second set of industries are not all contained in the first set. Four of the industries with over $200 million in defaults have less than $1 billion in par value issued. They are miscellaneous manufacturing, toys and sporting goods, ship transportation, and hospitals/health care.

24 The following statistics are only for LBO debt and contain no merger and acquisition debt not related to an LBO.

25 However, as noted above in section II.C, the value of call options on high yield bonds may not be the same as their value on investment grade bonds.

26 These prices are taken from a sample of 288 high yield bonds that had neither defaulted nor exchanged. Prices are desk prices supplied by First Boston, Drexel Burnham Lambert, Morgan Stanley, and Salomon Brothers. Treasury bond prices are from a sample of thirty Treasury bonds selected to match issue dates and maturities over the period 1977–86. Treasury bond prices were collected from the *Wall Street Journal*.

27 Our sample data allow us to illustrate a hypothetical simulation. Assume the following: a spread of high yield coupon to Treasuries of 400 basis points, our historical sequence of defaults with retention values at 40 percent of par, calls at an average premium of 104 percent of par, exchanges at a retention value of 70 percent of par, and a terminal cash-out value at 90 percent of par for high yield bonds and 106 percent of par for the Treasury bonds. The spreads and call prices above are both averages from our sample of high yield bonds. The retention values are taken from a sample of ninety-one defaulted and seventeen exchanged bonds with desk prices supplied by First Boston and Drexel Burnham Lambert. The terminal values are as described in note 26 above.

    The result is a simulated ten-year return advantage of only 115 basis points for high yield bonds over Treasuries. These return spreads may be far below the basis point premium required to offset other types of risk such as systematic risk and the value of the call option. Simulations performed in an analogous manner on our sample of A rated bonds (see note 20) produce simulated return spreads to Treasury bonds roughly the same as our simulated high yield return spreads.

28 From Altman (1989), section V, pp. 920–1.

References

Altman, Edward I., 1987, The anatomy of the high-yield bond market, *Financial Analysts Journal* 43, July–August, 12–25.

——, 1989, Measuring corporate bond mortality and performance, *Journal of Finance* 44, 909–22.

Altman, Edward I. and Scott A. Nammacher, 1985, The default rate experience on high-yield corporate debt, *Financial Analysts Journal* 41, July–August, 25–41.

—— and Scott A. Nammacher, 1987, *Investing in Junk Bonds* (John Wiley & Sons, Inc., New York).

Bianco, Anthony, 1986, Junk bonds are starting to live up to their names, *Business Week*, February 17, 64–5.

Blume, Marshall E. and Donald B. Keim, 1987, Lower-grade bonds: Their risks and returns, *Financial Analysts Journal* 43, July–August, 26–33.

—— and Donald B. Keim, 1988, Volatility patterns of fixed income securities (Wharton School working paper).

Drexel Burnham Lambert, 1989, *1989 High Yield Market Report*.

Fridson, Martin S., Fritz Wahl, and Steven B. Jones, 1988a, The Anatomy of the High Yield Debt Market (Morgan Stanley Credit Research).

——, Fritz Wahl, and Steven B. Jones, 1988b, New techniques for analyzing default risk, in: *High Performance* (Morgan Stanley Credit Research).

Goodman, Laurie S., 1989, High yield default rates: Is there cause for concern? (Goldman, Sachs & Co., Fixed Income Research).

Hallett, Douglas, 1987, Life insurance industry needs, *The Wall Street Journal* 29, July, 14.

Jensen, Michael C., 1989, Active investors, LBO's and the privatization of bankruptcy (Harvard Business School working paper).

Weinstein, Mark I., 1987, A curmudgeon's view of junk bonds, *Journal of Portfolio Management*, Spring, 76–80.

Appendix

Table 8A.1 Aged defaults for original issue high yield bonds grouped by year of issue. High yield bonds are all bonds rated below investment grade at issue date by Moody's and Standard & Poor's. Defaults are defined as a declaration of default by the bond's trustee, filing of bankruptcy by the firm, or assignment of a D rating by S&P for a missed coupon payment

		Aged Defaults for All Bonds Issued in 1977 (*Total issued, 26 bonds, $908 million par value*)				
Years after[a]	*Number defaulted*	*Amount defaulted* (*$ millions*)	*% Number defaulted*	*Cumulative % number defaulted*	*% Amount defaulted*	*Cumulative % amount defaulted*
1st Yr	0	0	0.00	0.00	0.00	0.00
2nd Yr	0	0	0.00	0.00	0.00	0.00
3rd Yr	0	0	0.00	0.00	0.00	0.00
4th Yr	0	0	0.00	0.00	0.00	0.00
5th Yr	0	0	0.00	0.00	0.00	0.00
6th Yr	0	0	0.00	0.00	0.00	0.00
7th Yr	0	0	0.00	0.00	0.00	0.00
8th Yr	1	70	3.85	3.85	7.71	7.71
9th Yr	1	33	3.85	7.69	3.63	11.34
10th Yr	3	175	11.54	19.23	19.27	30.62
11th Yr	1	30	3.85	23.08	3.30	33.92
12th Yr[b]	0	0	0.00	23.08	0.00	33.92
Total	6	308	23.08	23.08	33.92	33.92

Table 8A.1 *Continued*

Aged Defaults for All Bonds Issued in 1978
(Total issued, 51 bonds, $1,442 million par value)

Years after[a]	Number defaulted	Amount defaulted ($ millions)	% Number defaulted	Cumulative % number defaulted	% Amount defaulted	Cumulative % amount defaulted
1st Yr	0	0	0.00	0.00	0.00	0.00
2nd Yr	2	120	3.92	3.92	8.32	8.32
3rd Yr	0	0	0.00	3.92	0.00	8.32
4th Yr	1	20	1.96	5.88	1.39	9.71
5th Yr	0	0	0.00	5.88	0.00	9.71
6th Yr	4	114	7.84	13.73	7.91	17.61
7th Yr	3	70	5.88	19.61	4.85	22.47
8th Yr	2	45	3.92	23.53	3.12	25.59
9th Yr	3	80	5.88	29.41	5.55	31.14
10th Yr	1	20	1.96	31.37	1.39	32.52
11th Yr[b]	1	25	1.96	33.33	1.73	34.26
Total	17	494	33.33	33.33	34.26	34.26

Aged Defaults for All Bonds Issued in 1979
(Total issued, 41 bonds, $1,263 million par value)

Years after[a]	Number defaulted	Amount defaulted ($ millions)	% Number defaulted	Cumulative % number defaulted	% Amount defaulted	Cumulative % amount defaulted
1st Yr	0	0	0.00	0.00	0.00	0.00
2nd Yr	0	0	0.00	0.00	0.00	0.00
3rd Yr	4	70	9.76	9.76	5.54	5.54
4th Yr	1	14	2.44	12.20	1.11	6.65
5th Yr	1	30	2.44	14.63	2.38	9.03
6th Yr	2	85	4.88	19.51	6.73	15.76
7th Yr	1	25	2.44	21.95	1.98	17.74
8th Yr	0	0	0.00	21.95	0.00	17.74
9th Yr	2	73	4.88	26.83	5.78	23.52
10th Yr[b]	1	15	2.44	29.27	1.19	24.70
Total	12	312	29.27	29.27	24.70	24.70

Table 8A.1 *Continued*

Aged Defaults for All Bonds Issued in 1980
(Total issued, 37 bonds, $1,223 million par value)

Years after[a]	Number defaulted	Amount defaulted ($ millions)	% Number defaulted	Cumulative % number defaulted	% Amount defaulted	Cumulative % amount defaulted
1st Yr	0	0	0.00	0.00	0.00	0.00
2nd Yr	1	7	2.70	2.70	0.57	0.57
3rd Yr	1	30	2.70	5.41	2.45	3.03
4th Yr	0	0	0.00	5.41	0.00	3.03
5th Yr	0	0	0.00	5.41	0.00	3.03
6th Yr	6	170	16.22	21.62	13.90	16.93
7th Yr	2	77	5.41	27.03	6.30	23.22
8th Yr	1	23	2.70	29.73	1.88	25.10
9th Yr[b]	1	30	2.70	32.43	2.45	27.56
Total	12	337	32.43	32.43	27.56	27.56

Aged Defaults for All Bonds Issued in 1981
(Total issued, 24 bonds, $1,240 million par value)

Years after[a]	Number defaulted	Amount defaulted ($ millions)	% Number defaulted	Cumulative % number defaulted	% Amount defaulted	Cumulative % amount defaulted
1st Yr	0	0	0.00	0.00	0.00	0.00
2nd Yr	1	75	4.17	4.17	6.05	6.05
3rd Yr	0	0	0.00	4.17	0.00	6.05
4th Yr	1	100	4.17	8.33	8.06	14.11
5th Yr	2	85	8.33	16.67	6.85	20.97
6th Yr	0	0	0.00	16.67	0.00	20.97
7th Yr	0	0	0.00	16.67	0.00	20.97
8th Yr[b]	0	0	0.00	16.67	0.00	20.97
Total	4	260	16.67	16.67	20.97	20.97

Aged Defaults for All Bonds Issued in 1982
(Total issued, 41 bonds, $2,490 million par value)

Years after[a]	Number defaulted	Amount defaulted ($ millions)	% Number defaulted	Cumulative % number defaulted	% Amount defaulted	Cumulative % amount defaulted
1st Yr	1	25	2.44	2.44	1.00	1.00
2nd Yr	1	60	2.44	4.88	2.41	3.41
3rd Yr	1	40	2.44	7.32	1.61	5.02
4th Yr	3	286	7.32	14.63	11.49	16.51
5th Yr	0	0	0.00	14.63	0.00	16.51
6th Yr	5	235	12.20	26.83	9.44	25.94
7th Yr[b]	0	0	0.00	26.83	0.00	25.94
Total	11	646	26.83	26.83	25.94	25.94

Aged Defaults for All Bonds Issued in 1983
(Total issued, 74 bonds, $6,003 million par value)

Years after[a]	Number defaulted	Amount defaulted ($ millions)	% Number defaulted	Cumulative % number defaulted	% Amount defaulted	Cumulative % amount defaulted
1st Yr	0	0	0.00	0.00	0.00	0.00
2nd Yr	0	0	0.00	0.00	0.00	0.00
3rd Yr	6	365	8.11	8.11	6.08	6.08
4th Yr	4	470	5.41	13.51	7.83	13.91
5th Yr	5	288	6.76	20.27	4.80	18.71
6th Yr[b]	1	30	1.35	21.62	0.50	19.21
Total	16	1,153	21.62	21.62	19.21	19.21

Aged Defaults for All Bonds Issued in 1984
(Total issued, 102 bonds, $11,552 million par value)

Years after[a]	Number defaulted	Amount defaulted ($ millions)	% Number defaulted	Cumulative % number defaulted	% Amount defaulted	Cumulative % amount defaulted
1st Yr	4	265	3.92	3.92	2.29	2.29
2nd Yr	3	230	2.94	6.86	1.99	4.28
3rd Yr	3	235	2.94	9.80	2.03	6.32
4th Yr	5	354	4.90	14.71	3.06	9.38
5th Yr[b]	0	0	0.00	14.71	0.00	9.38
Total	15	1,084	14.71	14.71	9.38	9.38

Aged Defaults for All Bonds Issued in 1985
(Total issued, 145 bonds, $14,463 million par value)

Years after[a]	Number defaulted	Amount defaulted ($ millions)	% Number defaulted	Cumulative % number defaulted	% Amount defaulted	Cumulative % amount defaulted
1st Yr	0	0	0.00	0.00	0.00	0.00
2nd Yr	4	115	2.76	2.76	0.80	0.80
3rd Yr	4	330	2.76	5.52	2.28	3.08
4th Yr[b]	2	65	1.38	6.90	0.45	3.53
Total	10	510	6.90	6.90	3.53	3.53

Table 8A.1 *Continued*

Aged Defaults for All Bonds Issued in 1986
(Total issued, 200 bonds, $30,949 million par value)

Years after[a]	Number defaulted	Amount defaulted ($ millions)	% Number defaulted	Cumulative % number defaulted	% Amount defaulted	Cumulative % amount defaulted
1st Yr	6	845	3.00	3.00	2.73	2.73
2nd Yr	6	1,189	3.00	6.00	3.84	6.57
3rd Yr[b]	5	485	2.50	8.50	1.57	8.14
Total	17	2,519	8.50	8.50	8.14	8.14

[a] "Years after" is calculated from the issue day; i.e., a bond issued on June 1, 1977 that defaults in May 1978 defaults during the first year. If the same bond defaulted in July 1978, the default would be during the second year.

[b] May be incomplete; i.e., entire sample may not have been outstanding for x years.

Table 8A.2 Aged default rates[a] for high yield bonds by number of years since issue date. High yield bonds are all bonds rated below investment grade at issue date by Moody's and Standard & Poor's. Defaults are defined as a declaration of default by the bond's trustee, filing of bankruptcy by the firm, or assignment of a D rating by S&P for a missed coupon payment

	Aged default rates			1 Year out	% Defaulted	
Issue year	Number defaulted	Amount defaulted ($ millions)	Total issued	Issue amount ($ millions)	Number	Amount
1977	0	0	26	908	0.00	0.00
1978	0	0	51	1,442	0.00	0.00
1979	0	0	41	1,263	0.00	0.00
1980	0	0	37	1,223	0.00	0.00
1981	0	0	24	1,240	0.00	0.00
1982	1	25	41	2,490	2.44	1.00
1983	0	0	74	6,003	0.00	0.00
1984	4	265	102	11,552	3.92	2.29
1985	0	0	145	14,463	0.00	0.00
1986	6	845	200	30,949	3.00	2.73
Total[b]	11	1,135	741	71,533		
Average aged default rate[c]					1.48	1.59

	Aged default rates			2 Years out	% Defaulted	
Issue year	Number defaulted	Amount defaulted ($ millions)	Total issued	Issue amount ($ millions)	Number	Amount
1977	0	0	26	908	0.00	0.00
1978	2	120	51	1,442	3.92	8.32
1979	0	0	41	1,263	0.00	0.00

Table 8A.2 *Continued*

	Aged default rates				2 Years out	
		Amount		*Issue*	*% Defaulted*	
Issue	*Number*	*defaulted*	*Total*	*amount*		
year	*defaulted*	*($ millions)*	*issued*	*($ millions)*	*Number*	*Amount*
1980	1	7	37	1,223	2.70	0.57
1981	1	75	24	1,240	4.17	6.05
1982	1	60	41	2,490	2.44	2.41
1983	0	0	74	6,003	0.00	0.00
1984	3	230	102	11,552	2.94	1.99
1985	4	115	145	14,463	2.76	0.80
1986	6	1,189	200	30,949	3.00	3.84
Total[b]	18	1,796	741	71,533		
Average aged default rate[c]					2.43	2.51

	Aged default rates				3 Years out	
		Amount		*Issue*	*% Defaulted*	
Issue	*Number*	*defaulted*	*Total*	*amount*		
year	*defaulted*	*($ millions)*	*issued*	*($ millions)*	*Number*	*Amount*
1977	0	0	26	908	0.00	0.00
1978	0	0	51	1,442	0.00	0.00
1979	4	70	41	1,263	9.76	5.54
1980	1	30	37	1,223	2.70	2.45
1981	0	0	24	1,240	0.00	0.00
1982	1	40	41	2,490	2.44	1.61
1983	6	365	74	6,003	8.11	6.08
1984	3	235	102	11,552	2.94	2.03
1985	4	330	145	14,463	2.76	2.28
Total[b]	19	1,070	541	40,584		
Average aged default rate[c]					3.51	2.64

	Aged default rates				4 Years out	
		Amount		*Issue*	*% Defaulted*	
Issue	*Number*	*defaulted*	*Total*	*amount*		
year	*defaulted*	*($ millions)*	*issued*	*($ millions)*	*Number*	*Amount*
1977	0	0	26	908	0.00	0.00
1978	1	20	51	1,442	1.96	1.39
1979	1	14	41	1,263	2.44	1.11
1980	0	0	37	1,223	0.00	0.00
1981	1	100	24	1,240	4.17	8.06
1982	3	286	41	2,490	7.32	11.49
1983	4	470	74	6,003	5.41	7.83
1984	5	354	102	11,552	4.90	3.06
Total[b]	15	1,244	396	26,121		
Average aged default rate[c]					3.79	4.76

Table 8A.2 *Continued*

	Aged default rates			5 Years out		
		Amount		Issue	% Defaulted	
Issue year	Number defaulted	defaulted ($ millions)	Total issued	amount ($ millions)	Number	Amount
1977	0	0	26	908	0.00	0.00
1978	0	0	51	1,442	0.00	0.00
1979	1	30	41	1,263	2.44	2.38
1980	0	0	37	1,223	0.00	0.00
1981	2	85	24	1,240	8.33	6.85
1982	0	0	41	2,490	0.00	0.00
1983	5	288	74	6,003	6.76	4.80
Total[b]	8	403	294	14,569		
Average aged default rate[c]					2.72	2.77

	Aged default rates			6 Years out		
		Amount		Issue	% Defaulted	
Issue year	Number defaulted	defaulted ($ millions)	Total issued	amount ($ millions)	Number	Amount
1977	0	0	26	908	0.00	0.00
1978	4	114	51	1,442	7.84	7.91
1979	2	85	41	1,263	4.88	6.73
1980	6	170	37	1,223	16.22	13.90
1981	0	0	24	1,240	0.00	0.00
1982	5	235	41	2,490	12.20	9.44
Total[b]	17	604	220	8,566		
Average aged default rate[c]					7.73	7.05

	Aged default rates			7 Years out		
		Amount		Issue	% Defaulted	
Issue year	Number defaulted	defaulted ($ millions)	Total issued	amount ($ millions)	Number	Amount
1977	0	0	26	908	0.00	0.00
1978	3	70	51	1,442	5.88	4.85
1979	1	25	41	1,263	2.44	1.98
1980	2	77	37	1,223	5.41	6.30
1981	0	0	24	1,240	0.00	0.00
Total[b]	6	172	179	6,076		
Average aged default rate[c]					3.35	2.83

Table 8A.2 *Continued*

	Aged default rates			8 Years out		
Issue year	Number default	Amount default ($ millions)	Total issued	Issued amount ($ millions)	% Defaulted Number	% Defaulted Amount
1977	1	70	26	908	3.85	7.71
1978	2	45	51	1,442	3.92	3.12
1979	0	23	41	1,263	0.00	0.00
1980	1	0	37	1,223	2.70	1.88
Total[b]	4	138	155	4,836		
Average aged default rate[c]					2.58	2.85

	Aged default rates			9 Years out		
Issue year	Number default	Amount defaulted ($ millions)	Total issued	Issued amount ($ millions)	% Defaulted Number	% Defaulted Amount
1977	1	33	26	908	3.85	3.63
1978	3	80	51	1,442	5.88	5.55
1979	2	73	41	1,263	4.88	5.78
Total[b]	6	186	118	3,613		
Average aged default rate[c]					5.08	5.15

	Aged default rates			10 Years out		
Issue year	Number default	Amount defaulted ($ millions)	Total issued	Issued amount ($ millions)	% Defaulted Number	% Defaulted Amount
1977	3	175	26	908	11.54	19.27
1978	1	20	51	1,442	1.96	1.39
Total[b]	4	195	77	2,350		
Average aged default rate[c]					5.19	8.30

Table 8A.2 *Continued*

Issue year	Number default	Amount defaulted ($ millions)	Total issued	Issued amount ($ millions)	% Defaulted Number	% Defaulted Amount
		Aged default rates			*11 Years out*	
1977	1	30	26	908	3.85	3.30
Total[b]	1	30	26	908		
Average aged default rate[c]					3.85	3.30

[a] Aged default rates are defined as the number (or $ amount) of bonds issued in a particular calendar year that default within x years after the issue date, e.g., 1977's Aged Default Rate for 2 years out is the number (or $ amount) of bonds issued in 1977 that default between one year and two years after the issue day.

[b] The totals will not equal the totals in table 8.3 because only complete years (as of December 31, 1988) are used in calculating averages. For example, there have not been three complete years of history for all bonds issued in 1986, so the default rates for three years do not include 1986.

[c] The average aged default rate is defined as the number (or $ amount) of bonds that default in the nth year after issue date for all issue years. It is value weighted and is not the average of nth year rates for individual issue years.

Table 8A.3 Average aged default rates for high yield bonds by number of years since issue date. High yield bonds are all bonds rated below investment grade at issue date by Moody's and Standard & Poor's. Defaults are defined as a declaration of default by the bond's trustee, filing of bankruptcy by the firm or assignment of a D rating by S&P for a missed coupon payment

Years after	N[a]	Number of issues	Amount of issues ($ millions)	Yearly % Number	Yearly % Amount
1st Yr	10	11	1,135	1.48	1.59
2nd Yr	10	18	1,796	2.43	2.51
3rd Yr	9	19	1,070	3.51	2.64
4th Yr	8	15	1,244	3.79	4.76
5th Yr	7	8	403	2.72	2.77
6th Yr	6	17	604	7.73	7.05
7th Yr	5	6	172	3.35	2.83
8th Yr	4	4	138	2.58	2.85
9th Yr	3	6	186	5.08	5.15
10th Yr	2	4	195	5.19	8.30
11th Yr	1	1	30	3.85	3.30

[a] Number of issue years in the sample which have a complete nth year after nth issue year; i.e., all issue years since 1977 have complete 1st years, but only one (1977) has a complete 11th year.

9

Returns and Volatility of Low Grade Bonds, 1977–1989

Marshall E. Blume, Donald B. Keim, and Sandeep A. Patel

One of the most significant financial innovations in recent years has been the development of a public market for less-than-investment-grade debt. Prior to 1977 virtually all publicly traded bonds at the time of issue carried an investment grade rating. Of course, some of these bonds became "fallen angels" as their credit quality deteriorated, and some did default. Beginning in 1977 investment banking firms began to issue bonds with credit quality below investment grade. The growth in the market has been dramatic; according to Drexel Burnham Lambert, new issues of low grade bonds increased from US$1.1 billion in 1977 to $24.2 billion in 1989. Drexel estimates that at the end of 1989 the outstanding market value of low grade bonds was $205 billion, representing roughly one quarter of the total corporate debt market. Less than a quarter of the outstanding value of low grade bonds represents "fallen angels."

Given the size of this market, we know surprisingly little about the returns and risks of investing in it. Considerable research exists on the relation between original bond quality ratings and the incidence of default.[1] Such studies are of obvious interest to bondholders, but of more fundamental interest are the returns that these bonds actually realize.

A major hindrance to the analysis of the returns of low grade bonds has been the difficulty of obtaining reliable prices for calculating realized returns.[2] As an example, a price from the *Bank and Quotation Record*, a source used in some prior studies, may be a transaction price, an average of bid and ask prices, or either a bid or an ask price.[3] The returns computed from this source involve combinations of any four of these possible prices. Statistically, the use of this mixture of prices results in an upward bias in the calculated returns, and the bias increases as the bid-ask spread widens.[4] To remedy these problems, Blume and Keim (1987) assembled an extensive data base of dealer bid prices supplied by traders at Drexel Burnham Lambert and at Salomon Brothers.

The first section of this paper uses the Blume and Keim data, updated through 1989, to estimate summary statistics of the distribution of historical returns for low grade bonds and to compare the returns of low grade bonds with the returns of other classes of assets.[5] The other classes are long-term Treasury bonds, long-term high grade corporate bonds, the S&P 500, and small capitalization stocks.

The relative ranking of the realized returns of low grade bonds varies from one time period to another. For the longest period studied, 1977–89, the realized returns of these bonds are greater than those of long-term governments and long-term high grade corporates but less than those of the S&P 500 or small stocks. Unlike the realized returns, the relative ranking of the variance of the returns for low grade bonds is stable over time and is always less than the variance for any of the other asset classes. The lower variance of low grade bonds, relative to long-term Treasuries and high grade corporates, stems from the shorter duration of low grade bonds due to their larger coupons and greater probability of early call.

There is a possible caveat in interpreting these results as representative of the universe of low grade bonds. The market for low grade bonds is young and has experienced rapid growth, resulting in a heavier concentration of the market in recently issued bonds than would be the case if the market were more mature. If the probability of default increases or, more importantly, return characteristics change with the age of a bond, overall sample statistics from our data may be misleading if the original buyers of the bonds did not properly anticipate these risks.[6] To determine the importance of this caveat, the study examines the relation between the age of low grade bonds and their default rates and returns. Importantly, there is no observable relation between age and returns, and cyclical factors explain a large portion of the previously observed relation between age and default rates.

The second section of this paper contains an analysis of the covariability of low grade bond returns with returns on other assets. Some have described low grade bonds as hybrid securities; they have the appearance of fixed-income obligations but without an equity cushion An examination of the separate influences of unexpected changes in interest rates, equity returns, and seasonal effects on low grade bond returns supports this conjecture.

The third section addresses the issue of the efficiency of the low grade bond market and finds no evidence that low grade bonds are systematically mispriced.

The fourth section presents a brief summary of the main empirical results.

I   Characteristics of Low Grade Bond Returns

The summary statistics for low grade bonds in this section are based on three different sources. The primary source is a data base of low grade prices covering the years 1982–8. These prices are month-end bid prices from Drexel Burnham Lambert and Salomon Brothers.[7] The specific bonds included in the analysis satisfy the following criteria: (1) face value at time of issue is greater than $25 million; (2) the bonds are not convertible; and (3) time to maturity is at least 10 years from the date on which a return is calculated. As of December 1988, the average maturity of our sample is 14.7 years.[8]

To provide a longer perspective, we augmented our basis data with additional data prior to 1982 and after 1988. Prior to 1982 we collected month-end prices for the 1977–81 period for *all* bonds rated below BBB listed in the *S&P Bond Guide* satisfying the same three conditions as the 1982–8 sample. Although these data may not be as reliable as the Drexel and Salomon data, they do extend the sample back to 1977 – the beginning of the modern low grade bond market.[9] Despite the potential problems with the earlier data, the inferences from both sets of data are similar. For 1989 the monthly index returns are the returns of a long-term index developed by Drexel. Drexel (1989b) adopted virtually the same criteria that we imposed for the 1982–8 data in the construction of this index, and the Drexel index is thus comparable to the pre-1989 indices.[10] (The appendix contains the monthly returns of this index.)

For comparison, we also report results below for several stock and bond indices as published by Ibbotson Associates. The stock market indices are the S&P 500 and a value-weighted portfolio of stocks in the smallest quintile of NYSE common stocks.

Table 9.1 Summary statistics of returns for various asset categories. These statistics are based upon several indexes of monthly returns. From 1977 through 1988, the bonds underlying the low grade bond index are all nonconvertible with face value at time of issue of greater than $25 million and with time to maturity of at least 10 years from the date on which any return is calculated. The returns for the individual bonds from 1982 through 1988 are based upon bid prices from Drexel Burnham Lambert and Salomon Brothers and prior to 1982 upon prices from the *S&P Bond Guide*. The return indices from 1977 through 1988 are averages of these returns by month. For 1989 Drexel calculated a monthly return index using bid prices in virtually the same way as the 1977–88 indices were calculated, and this index was used to extend the sample through 1989. The returns for (1) the S&P 500, (2) a value-weighted portfolio of common stocks in the smallest size quintile on the NYSE, (3) the Salomon Brothers index of long-term high grade (rated A and above) corporate bonds, and (4) long-term (approximately 20 years to maturity) government bonds are from Ibbotson Associates

	Annual	Monthly		Adjusted standard deviation*		Autocorrelation		
	Geometric mean	Mean return	Standard deviation	1st Order	1st & 2nd Order	ρ_1	ρ_2	ρ_3
A. 1/1977 to 12/1989								
Long-term government bonds	9.3%	0.81%	3.76%	3.97%	3.91%	0.07	−0.02	−0.14
High grade bonds	9.7	0.83	3.46	3.91	3.85	0.15	−0.02	−0.10
Low grade bonds	10.2	0.85	2.70	3.15	3.05	0.20	−0.05	−0.12
S&P 500	14.6	1.25	4.56	4.69	4.31	0.03	−0.10	−0.08
Small stocks	19.1	1.65	5.88	6.46	6.19	0.11	−0.06	−0.13
B. 1/1977 to 12/1988								
Long-term government bonds	8.6	0.76	3.85	4.06	4.03	0.06	−0.01	−0.14
High grade bonds	9.1	0.79	3.56	3.99	3.96	0.14	−0.01	−0.01
Low grade bonds	11.3	0.93	2.74	3.16	3.04	0.18	−0.06	−0.13
S&P 500	13.3	1.16	4.63	4.80	4.45	0.04	−0.09	−0.09
Small stocks	19.4	1.68	5.97	6.59	6.22	0.12	−0.08	−0.13

Table 9.1 *Continued*

	Annual	Monthly		Adjusted standard deviation*		Autocorrelation		
	Geometric mean	Mean return	Standard deviation	1st Order	1st & 2nd Order	ρ_1	ρ_2	ρ_3
C. 1/1982 to 12/1989								
Long-term government bonds	16.3	1.32	3.40	3.55	3.66	0.05	0.04	−0.07
High grade bonds	17.1	1.36	2.98	3.33	3.49	0.13	0.08	−0.04
Low grade bonds	14.0	1.13	2.24	2.79	2.99	0.31	0.13	0.06
S&P 500	18.9	1.57	4.77	4.93	4.76	0.04	−0.05	−0.09
Small stocks	13.4	1.20	5.21	6.11	6.11	0.21	−0.00	−0.07
D. 1/1982 to 12/1985								
Long-term government bonds	20.9	1.65	3.37	3.61	4.01	0.08	0.16	−0.16
High grade bonds	23.1	1.80	3.47	3.85	4.12	0.13	0.11	−0.07
Low grade bonds	20.9	1.62	2.37	2.99	3.18	0.33	0.12	0.11
S&P 500	20.2	1.62	4.03	4.09	4.50	0.02	0.13	−0.16
Small stocks	20.1	1.64	4.59	5.48	5.92	0.23	0.14	0.01
E. 1/1986 to 12/1989								
Long-term government bonds	11.9	1.00	3.44	3.49	3.01	0.02	−0.16	−0.10
High grade bonds	11.4	0.93	2.36	2.56	2.33	0.10	−0.12	−0.13
Low grade bonds	7.5	0.63	2.00	2.33	2.35	0.19	0.01	−0.15
S&P 500	17.6	1.52	5.45	5.71	5.01	0.05	−0.15	−0.09
Small stocks	7.0	0.75	5.78	6.66	6.14	0.18	−0.12	−0.16

* Stale prices can induce positive but spurious autocorrelation in the indices of returns, biasing downward the estimated standard deviation of monthly returns. To examine the magnitude of this bias, the monthly standard deviations were adjusted in a two-step procedure: First, annualize the estimated monthly standard deviation, taking into account the autocorrelation. If σ^2 is the monthly variance and the first order autocorrelation is ρ_1 with all other autocorrelations zero, the variance of the sum of 12 monthly returns is $\sigma^2 (12 + 22 \rho_1)$. Thus, multiplying the monthly standard deviation by $(12 + 22 \rho_1)^{1/2}$ yields an annual standard deviation that takes into account the first order serial correlation. Second, divide by the $\sqrt{12}$ to re-express this annual standard deviation in monthly units. If the second order autocorrelation is ρ_2 and all high order autocorrelations are zero, the multiplying constant is $(12 + 22 \rho_1 + 20 \rho_2)^{1/2}$.

The long-term high grade corporate bond index is identical to the Salomon Brothers index of the same name. The long-term government bond index has a maturity of roughly 20 years and is derived by Ibbotson Associates from data in the *Wall Street Journal*.

A. Realized returns

From 1977 through 1989, low grade bonds realized a compounded annual rate of return of 10.2 percent (table 9.1 and figure 9.1). During these years, low grade bonds realized greater returns than long-term Treasury bonds (9.3 percent) and long-term high grade corporate bonds (9.7 percent), but lower returns than the S&P 500 (14.6 percent) and an index of small stocks (19.1 percent).[11]

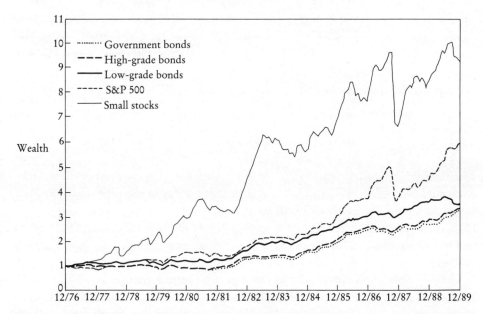

Figure 9.1 Major market indexes from December 1976 through December 1989. These indexes are all scaled to be 1.0 on December 1976 and are taken from various sources. From 1977 through 1988 the bonds underlying the low grade bond index are all nonconvertible with face value at time of issue of greater than $25 million and with time to maturity of at least 10 years from the date on which a return is calculated. The returns of individual low grade bonds from 1982 through 1988 are averages of these returns by month. For 1989 Drexel calculated a monthly return index in virtually the same way as the 1977–88 indexes were calculated, and this index was used to extend the sample through 1989. The returns for (1) the S&P 500, (2) a value-weighted portfolio of common stocks in the smallest size quintile on the NYSE, (3) the Salomon Brothers index of long-term high grade (rated A and above) corporate bonds, and (4) long-term (approximately 20 years to maturity) government bonds are from Ibbotson Associates. Linking these returns together yields the plotted index values.

From 1982 through 1989, the period for which we have Drexel and Salomon dealer bid prices and the new Drexel index, low grade bonds realized a compounded annual rate of return of 14.0 percent. During these more recent years, low grade bonds realized lower returns than the Treasury bonds (16.3 percent), long-term high grade corporate bonds (17.1 percent), and the S&P 500 (18.9 percent) but did realize greater returns than small stocks (13.4 percent). In either half of the 1982–9 period, the realized returns on low grade bonds are never the greatest nor the least. In both halves the returns on low grade bonds exceed those of small stocks. The average monthly returns lead to the same conclusions.[12]

The popular press in 1989 contained many reports describing the turbulence in the market for low grade bonds. The dominant underwriter and market maker Drexel Burnham Lambert was in serious financial trouble and would ultimately declare bankruptcy. Savings and loan associations were dumping their large holdings of low grade bonds. The returns realized by low grade bonds are consistent with these reports of turbulence. During 1989, low grade bonds realized a loss of −2.2 percent, while some other types of assets realized substantial positive returns.[13] Of the other four asset groups in table 9.1 the S&P 500 realized the greatest return of 31.5 percent and small stocks the lowest return of 10.2 percent. If one excludes the 1989 returns and examines the shorter 1977–88 period, the relative rankings of the realized returns of these asset groups remains unchanged (table 9.1). The gap between low grade bonds and the higher grade bonds widens, but equities still have the greatest returns.

B.　The relative volatility of low and high grade bonds

In each of the five periods reported in table 9.1, the estimated standard deviation of the monthly low grade bond returns is less than that for any of the other four categories of assets. A visual examination of the frequency distributions of returns for the 1977–89 period confirms this relative ranking (figure 9.2). If one excludes the 1989 returns and examines the 1977–88 period by itself, low grade bonds still have the least volatility.

One possible explanation for this perhaps unexpected result is statistical and is related to "stale" prices among the individual bond prices in the index. To illustrate, assume that the prices of all low grade bonds fall but that dealers mark down only half of the prices the first month and the remaining half the following month. Changes in an index of such prices will spread themselves across both months, inducing positive autocorrelation in the calculated returns for the index and a downward bias in the estimated standard deviations.[14]

The first order autocorrelations for all of the monthly indices of the five different types of assets are positive in each period (table 9.1), with the greatest values associated with low grade bonds and small stocks, a finding consistent with stale prices. Even so, after adjusting the estimated standard deviations of monthly returns for the observed autocorrelation, low grade bonds still display the lowest standard deviation (table 9.1).[15]

The remainder of this section explores the reasons for the lower volatility of low grade bonds in comparison to the higher grade bonds. To do this, consider the possible sources of the variance of the return of any individual low grade bond. There is no unique way to decompose this variance, but for the purposes of this paper it is useful to identify three sources of variance: factors unique to a specific bond, factors common to low grade bonds, and changes in the general level of interest rates. In an equally weighted portfolio of a large number of bonds, diversification virtually eliminates bond-specific risk, so the following analysis of low grade bond indices ignores this type of risk and concentrates on the other two sources of volatility.

The average time to maturity for the low grade bond index is slightly less than 15 years at the end of 1988, while the average time to maturity for the indices of long-term Treasury and long-term high grade corporate bonds is 20 years. Other things equal, the shorter maturity of low grade bonds compared with the higher grade bonds indicates that low grade bonds have a shorter duration and, therefore, will be less sensitive to interest rate movements.[16]

Even if the average time to maturity were the same for low grade bonds and either high grade corporate bonds or Treasury bonds, the low grade bond index will still have a shorter duration and hence less sensitivity to interest rates, for two reasons. First, the coupons on low grade bonds are greater than those on governments or high grade corporates. If the current prices and the time to maturity of two bonds are the same, the one with the greater coupon will have a shorter duration. Second, corporate bonds (both low and high grade) are often callable after a call protection period of a limited number of years, while governments are noncallable or only callable near maturity.[17,18] If interest rates drop, there is an increased probability that issuers of callable corporate bonds will call them, effectively shortening their duration. In addition, if the credit quality of a low grade bond issuer improves, it may be attractive to call and re-finance the bond with a higher quality bond even if there are no changes in interest rates. This possibility of credit improvement further shortens the duration of low grade bonds in comparison to both long-term governments and high grade corporates.

The shorter duration of low grade bonds reduces relative volatility, but offsetting this reduction is the possibility that additional factors common to all low grade bonds increase volatility. The spread between the yields on low grade and long-term government bonds is a measure of these additional factors. That the standard deviation of returns for the low grade bond index is less than that for the government bond index implies that the reduction in volatility due to shorter duration exceeds the increase in volatility stemming from unexpected changes in spreads.

To separate the volatility of low grade bonds due to unexpected changes in interest rates from that due to unexpected changes in spreads, we construct an equivalent "default-free bond" for each low grade bond and form an index of these equivalent bonds. Such an equivalent index mirrors the same call, coupon, and maturity features of the low grade bond index. Hence, any differences in volatility between our low grade index and the default-free equivalent portfolio can be attributed to volatility stemming from unexpected changes in spreads.

Our construction of an equivalent "default-free" bond involves two steps. First, identify a portfolio of government bonds that matches the promised cash flows from the coupons and principal repayment for each low grade bond at the time it first enters the sample.[19] Then, estimate the value of the call provision of the low grade bond and subtract this estimate from the price determined in the first step.[20] The returns from this adjusted series of prices mimic an equivalent callable default-free bond. Averaging these returns over all bonds in a specific month provides an equivalent monthly index.

The returns of this equivalent index, constructed of the "default-free" bonds having the same call and coupon features as the low grade bonds, are less volatile than the returns of the low grade bond index itself. The standard deviation of the index of equivalent default-free callable bonds is 1.93 percent, while the standard deviation of the low grade bond index over the same period is 2.21 percent (figure 9.3). Thus, the low standard deviation of low grade bonds in comparison to governments is due to the coupon levels of these bonds and their call features.

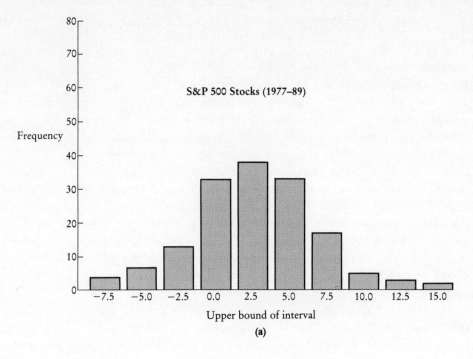

(a)

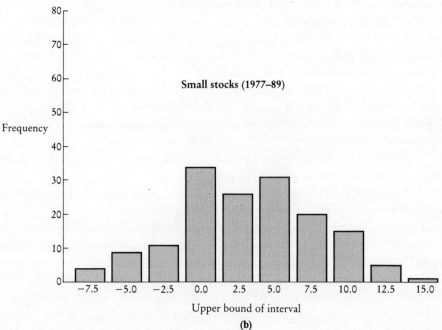

(b)

Figure 9.2 Frequency distributions of monthly returns for low grade bonds, long-term Treasury bonds, small stocks, and the S&P 500. This figure illustrates the lower volatility of low grade bonds. These histograms are based upon various indexes of monthly returns. From 1977 through 1988, the bonds underlying the low grade bond index are all nonconvertible with face value at time of issue of greater than $25 million and with time to maturity of at least 10 years from the date on which a return is calculated. The returns of individual low grade bonds from 1982 through 1988 are based upon bid prices from Drexel Burnham Lambert and Salomon Brothers, and prior to 1982 upon prices from the *S&P Bond Guide*.

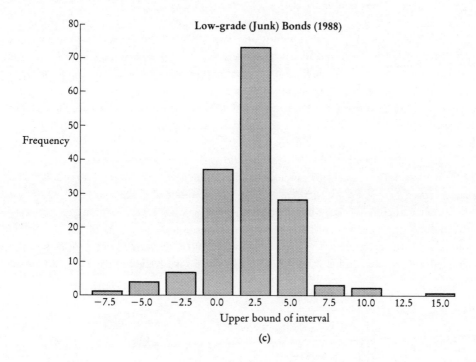

(c)

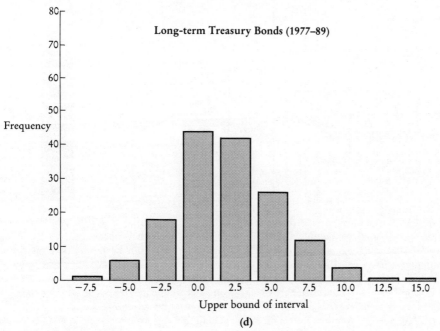

(d)

The return indexes from 1977 through 1988 are averages of these returns by month. For 1989, Drexel calculated a monthly return index in virtually the same way as the 1977–88 indexes were calculated, and this index was used to extend the sample through 1989. The returns for (a) the S&P 500, (b) a value-weighted portfolio of common stocks in the smallest size quintile on the NYSE, (c) the Salomon Brothers index of long-term high grade (rated A and above) corporate bonds, and (d) long-term (approximately 20 years to maturity) government bonds are from Ibbotson Associates.

The call features of low grade bonds are critical in explaining the low volatility of these low grade bonds. If one adjusts the governments only for coupon level *but not* for call features, the standard deviation of an index of such default-free bonds is 3.05 percent (figure 9.3). Thus, adjusting only for differences in coupons does not reduce the volatility of governments to a level below that of the low grade bonds. The further adjustment for call features is necessary to reduce the volatility of governments to a lever below that of low grade bonds.

In sum, the volatility of the low grade bond index is less than indexes for long-term governments, long-term high grade corporates, the S&P 500, and small stocks. The reasons for this lower volatility are the greater coupons and the call features of low grade bonds that reduce the duration of these bonds. A government index properly adjusted for these greater coupons and call features is less volatile than the low grade bond index. The difference between the volatility of the low grade bond index and the adjusted government index is the additional risk of low grade bonds. This additional

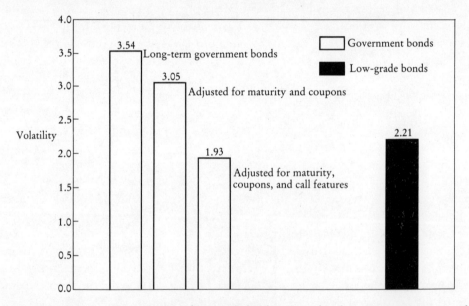

Figure 9.3   Relative return volatility of low grade bonds compared to long-term governments and governments adjusted for specific features of long-term low grade bonds for January 1982 through December 1988. This figure shows that the high coupons of low grade bonds and their call features account for the lower volatility of low grade bonds in comparison to long-term government bonds. For these years, the standard deviation of monthly returns for the low grade bond index used in this paper is 2.21 percent. The standard deviation for the Ibbotson returns for long-term government bonds is 3.54. Adjusted for the actual coupons and maturity of the bonds in the low grade index, the standard deviation drops to 3.05 percent. Adjusted further for the actual call features of the bonds in the low grade index, the standard deviation drops to 1.93 percent – a lower standard deviation than the low grade index. The text describes the specific procedures used in making these adjustments. The bonds underlying the low grade bond index are all nonconvertible with face value at time of issue of greater than $25 million and with time to maturity of at least 10 years from the date on which a return is calculated. The returns of individual low grade bonds themselves are based upon bid prices from Drexel Burnham Lambert and Salomon Brothers. The return indexes are averages of these returns by month.

risk is the risk associated with changes in the spread between the yields on low grade bonds and those on governments.[21]

C.   The relation between age, maturity, and returns of low grade bonds

The low grade bond market is a relatively young market that has experienced rapid growth. As a result, the current composition of the market is more skewed toward recently issued bonds than one would expect of a mature market that has reached "steady state" (figure 9.4). In addition newly issued bonds tend to have shorter maturities than in the past.

The empirical work of Altman (1989) and Asquith, Mullins, and Wolff (1989) suggests that the probability of default increases with the age of a low grade bond. If so, there will be a greater default rate in the future, compared to the recent experience, as the low grade bond market matures. Asquith, Mullins and Wolff (1989, p. 944) ask "whether market participants correctly incorporated these factors including high default rates, in the pricing of [low grade] bonds." Implicit in this question is the possibility that the realized returns on older bonds are less than on younger bonds.

A natural way to address this possibility is to divide the sample of low grade bonds into subindices cross-classified by maturity and age and examine the returns across subgroups. The maturity categories are two: 10 through 15 years, and 15 through 20 years. The age categories are three: 2 years old or less, 2 through 5 years, and 5 through 10 years. The calculation of the subindices for each category follows a two-step procedure: (1) for each month, assign each bond for which there is a monthly return to the appropriate subgroup; (2) for each month, average the returns for each subgroup to obtain equally weighted subindices.

There is little difference among the average returns as a function of the age of the bonds for the 1982–8 period (table 9.2), and formal tests of the equality of these average returns are unable to reject the hypothesis of equal expected returns.[22] As one would expect, the standard deviations tend to be larger for the bonds with longer maturity since these bonds are more sensitive to interest rate movements. There is no systematic relation between age of bond and standard deviation of the index, holding maturity constant.

Another way to evaluate the conjecture that the prices of older bonds did not properly anticipate the subsequent default rates is to compare the actual returns realized by older bonds with the low grade index itself. If the older bonds were overpriced initially, their subsequent realized returns should be less than the returns of the low grade index on the assumption that the more recently issued bonds are fairly priced.

In 1977 and 1978, the first two years of the modern low grade bond market, investment bankers underwrote 78 publicly traded low grade bonds with a total value of roughly $2.4 billion. Consider the following strategy: purchase each of the low grade bonds issued in 1977–8 in proportion to the value issued; sell defaulted bonds at the end of the month in which they default; reinvest all coupons, proceeds from

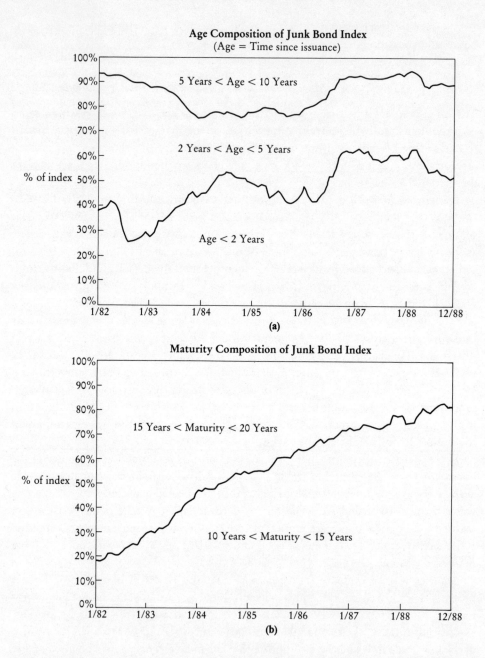

Figure 9.4 Age and maturity composition of the bonds in the low grade index from 1982 through 1988. The age composition (a) illustrates the growth over time of the number of new issues, and the maturity structure (b) indicates that the maturity of these newly issued bonds has been decreasing over these years. The low grade bonds used in plotting this figure are those used in constructing the low grade index and are all nonconvertible, with face value at time of issue of greater than $25 million and with time to maturity of at least 10 years from the date on which a return is calculated.

Table 9.2 Summary statistics for subindexes of low grade bonds based on years to maturity and age (years since issue) for the period January 1982 to December 1988. These subindexes for low grade bonds are derived from the monthly returns of individual low grade bonds from 1982 through 1988 calculated from bid prices from Drexel Burnham Lambert and Salomon Brothers. The bonds themselves are all nonconvertible with face value at time of issue of greater than $25 million. At the beginning of each month each bond was classified into one of six categories according to its age since issue and its then current years to maturity. Averaging the returns of these bonds by category provides the monthly indexes. The table presents the average monthly returns for each category and the monthly standard deviation. Since the number of bonds for each category varies from month to month, the table contains both the range of this number and its average over the 84 months

Age		Years to maturity	
(years since issue)		10 < Maturity ≤ 15	15 < Maturity ≤ 20
0 ≤ Age ≤ 2	Mean return (%)	1.27	1.38
	Standard deviation (%)	2.17	2.63
	Number of bonds		
	Range	7–88	5–44
	Average	45	24
2 < Age ≤ 5	Mean return (%)	1.35	1.11
	Standard deviation (%)	2.46	2.63
	Number of bonds		
	Range	10–38	17–59
	Average	18	34
5 < Age ≤ 10	Mean return (%)	1.29	—*
	Standard deviation (%)	2.38	—
	Number of bonds		
	Range	2–36	—
	Average	18	—

* There were only a few bonds in this category, and for some months no bond met the age and maturity requirements. Thus, it was not possible to construct a complete series of monthly returns for this category. As a consequence, the table reports no statistics for this category. When there were bonds that met the requirements, the number varied from 1 to 6 with an average of 3.

calls, exchanges, and sales of defaulted bonds in the low grade bond index presented in this paper; and liquidate the portfolio at the end of 1988.

By the end of 1988, the annual compounded realized return for this strategy was 10.63 percent.[23] For comparison, the compound annual rate of return for the low grade bond index from 1977 through 1988 is 10.3 percent – slightly less. Like the previous analysis, age does not appear to be a significant factor in explaining realized returns.

D.   *Do default rates actually increase with bond age?*

Both Altman (1989) and Asquith, Mullins, and Wolff (1989) conclude that default rates increase with the age of a low grade bond. The rank correlation between age and default rates, using the data in table 9.3 of Asquith, Mullins and Wolff, is 0.49 with a t-value of 4.58, supporting this conclusion.[24] Further analysis discloses, however, that a significant portion of the higher default rates, which appear related to the age of a bond, might better be attributed to general economic conditions. A closer examination of their data shows that the default rates were uniformly high across all age groups in several years, most notably 1985 and 1987, and uniformly low in other years, such as 1988.[25] This finding is not very surprising since general economic conditions contribute to the likelihood of default. There are more defaults in some years than others – regardless of age.

One way to remove this cyclical effect is to subtract from the raw default rate the mean default rate for the year in which the bonds defaulted. The rank order correlation between age and these mean-adjusted default rates drops from 0.49 to 0.22. The relation is weaker, but on the basis of a one-tail test is still significant at the 5 percent level ($t = 1.91$).[26] Thus, a substantial portion of the previously observed relation of age and default rates is due to cyclical effects.

II   Covariability of Low Grade Bond Returns

In addition to the analysis of the returns and volatility of the low grade bond index, we analyze the covariability of the returns of these bonds with the returns of other asset groups. This analysis shows that low grade bonds exhibit some of the characteristics of high grade bonds and some of the characteristics of stocks. From 1977 through 1989, the correlation between low grade bonds and long-term Treasury bonds is substantially less than the correlation between long-term high grade corporates and Treasury bonds – 0.68 and 0.95, respectively (table 9.3). The correlation between low grade bonds and small stocks is substantially greater than the correlation between long-term high grade corporates and small stocks – 0.52 and 0.19, respectively. The correlations for the other subperiods reported in table 9.3 behave similarly. This pattern of correlations implies that low grade bonds are less sensitive to interest rate movements and more sensitive to equity market movements than high grade bonds. As such, analysis of expected returns (and thus abnormal returns) for low grade bonds is complicated by the fact that the "risk" of these bonds must capture sensitivity to both interest rate and equity fluctuations, and we currently have no models that explicitly account for both of these influences.

Our objective is modest. We analyze the contribution of interest rate and stock market fluctuations to low grade bond return variance through a series of regressions using the monthly return on the low grade bond index as the dependent variable. The independent variables include returns from various combinations of the long-term government bond index and the small stock index.[27] Also included are two dummy variables to reflect temporal or seasonal patterns in the low grade bond returns. The first is a variable that has a value of one for January observations and zero otherwise. This variable reflects the mounting evidence that the process generating returns may be different in January from other months. For example, Keim and Stambaugh (1986) find a significant January seasonal in the risk premiums of low grade bonds as well as smaller stocks.[28] The second dummy variable has a value of one for October 1987 and zero otherwise. October 1987 was a month of considerable turbulence, and the normal relations between the different markets may have temporarily changed.

Table 9.3 Correlations of monthly returns for various asset classes. These statistics are based upon various indices of monthly returns. From 1977 through 1988, the bonds underlying the low grade bond index are all nonconvertible with face value at time of issue of greater than $25 million and with time to maturity of at least 10 years from the date on which a return is calculated. The low grade bond returns themselves come from several sources: the return of individual low grade bonds from 1982 through 1988 are based upon bid prices from Drexel Burnham Lambert and Salomon Brothers and prior to 1982 upon prices from the *S&P Bond Guide*; the return indices from 1977 through 1988 are averages of these returns by month; for 1989 Drexel calculated a monthly return index in virtually the same way as the 1977–88 indices were calculated, and this index was used to extend the sample through 1989. The returns for (1) the S&P 500, (2) a value-weighted portfolio of common stocks in the smallest size quintile on the NYSE, (3) the Salomon Brothers index of long-term high grade (rated A and above) corporate bonds, and (4) long-term (approximately 20 years to maturity) government bonds are from Ibbotson Associates

	High grade bonds	Low grade bonds	S&P 500	Small stocks
A. 1/1977 to 12/1989				
Long-term government bonds	0.95	0.68	0.34	0.21
High grade bonds		0.75	0.32	0.19
Low grade bonds			0.48	0.52
S&P 500				0.81
B. 1/1982 to 12/1989				
Long-term government bonds	0.92	0.57	0.32	0.15
High grade bonds		0.66	0.31	0.16
Low grade bonds			0.52	0.51
S&P 500				0.86
C. 1/1982 to 12/1985				
Long-term government bonds	0.96	0.69	0.48	0.27
High grade bonds		0.77	0.48	0.28
Low grade bonds			0.60	0.48
S&P 500				0.83
D. 1/1986 to 12/1989				
Long-term government bonds	0.92	0.42	0.21	0.05
High grade bonds		0.47	0.17	0.02
Low grade bonds			0.49	0.55
S&P 500				0.88

The regressions for both the 1977–89 and the 1982–9 period lead to similar conclusions (table 9.4) and will be discussed together.[29] Both the government returns and the small stock returns, whether included together or separately, are significant. Replacing the government returns with the high grade corporate returns leads to greater values for R^2 (not presented in the table), suggesting that a component in the variation in low grade returns, in addition to the pure interest and equity effects, is in part captured by the returns for high grade corporate bonds. These results support the conjecture that low grade bonds are a hybrid security with features of both bonds and stocks.

The coefficient on the January dummy is consistent with a January seasonal of 1 to 2 percent. In the regressions that include only bond returns and the dummy variables,

Table 9.4 Regressions of low grade bond returns on bond and stock-market returns and dummy variables for various dates. In these regressions the low grade bond index is based upon nonconvertible bonds with face value at time of issue of greater than $25 million and with time to maturity of at least 10 years from the date on which a return is calculated. The returns themselves for the individual low grade bonds from 1982 through 1988 are based upon bid prices from Drexel Burnham Lambert and Salomon Brothers and prior to 1982 upon prices from the *S&P Bond Guide*. The return indices from 1977 through 1988 are averages of these returns by month. For 1989 Drexel calculated a monthly return index in virtually the same way as the 1977–88 indices were calculated, and this index was used to extend the sample through 1989. The returns for long-term government bonds and the value-weighted portfolio of common stocks in the smallest size quintile on the NYSE come from publications of Ibbotson Associates. The dummy variable for October 1987 has a value of one for this month and zero otherwise. The dummy variable for January has a value of one for these months and zero otherwise. The numbers in parentheses are t-values

	Intercept	October 1987 dummy	January dummy	Government bond total return	Small stocks total return	$\bar{R}^2$
A. 1977–89	0.31	−6.26	1.88	0.51		0.53
	(2.04)	(−18.76)	(2.89)	(9.67)		
	0.33	4.53	0.72		0.26	0.28
	(1.72)	(3.95)	(1.21)		(6.86)	
	0.11	−0.75	1.31	0.45	0.17	0.62
	(0.75)	(−0.75)	(2.41)	(8.49)	(6.11)	
B. 1982–9	0.53	−5.73	1.57	0.40		0.41
	(2.95)	(−15.79)	(1.83)	(6.57)		
	0.70	4.08	0.94		0.26	0.28
	(3.21)	(2.38)	(1.41)		(4.62)	
	0.39	−0.11	1.05	0.33	0.17	0.50
	(2.12)	(−0.06)	(1.45)	(5.21)	(3.17)	

the coefficient is positive for both periods, but significant only for the 1977–89 period. In the regressions that include only small stock returns and the dummy variable, the coefficient on the dummy variable is less than 1 percent and is not significant at the usual levels. This suggests that the January dummy is redundant when combined with the small stock returns that already contain a significant January seasonal. However, in the regressions including both bond returns and stock returns, the coefficient on the January dummy variable is significant in the overall period. This behavior of the coefficients suggests that there is an interaction among the bond returns, the stock returns, and the month of January that the regressions do not fully capture – a possible subject for future research.

The coefficient on the dummy variable for October 1987 is negative and significant in the regressions that exclude equity returns but is positive and significant in the regressions that include only equity returns. This pattern in the values of the coefficients on this dummy variable is consistent with an interpretation of low grade bonds as hybrid securities. In October 1987 the return on the low grade bond index is less than predicted by the normal relation of these bonds to governments and high grade corporates but greater than that predicted by their normal relation to small stocks. In the regressions that include both bond returns and stock returns the coefficient on the dummy variable is no longer significant.

Thus, low grade bonds are complex securities having some of the characteristics of higher grade bonds and some of the characteristics of equities. Any model for pricing low grade bonds needs to capture both fixed income and equity characteristics.

III   Are Low Grade Bonds Fairly Priced?

Prior to 1989, much discussion (mostly in the popular press) focused on the "inefficiency" of the low grade bond market. The popular story was that the returns of low grade bonds were well in excess of that required to compensate for their relatively low "risk" as measured by the historical volatility of well-diversified portfolios of such bonds.

A limited number of studies have examined whether low grade bond returns provide fair compensation for the risks involved. Weinstein (1987) examines a sample of "fallen angels" for the 1962–74 period. Before adjusting for interest rate volatility, he finds that these "fallen angels" have low betas (0.023) and significant abnormal returns (alphas) relative to a value-weighted CRSP stock market index. After adjusting for interest rate volatility, the abnormal returns are no longer significant. Weinstein concludes that low grade bonds are "fairly priced."

Turning to the more recent period, Blume and Keim (1987) estimate a market model regression for the sample of low grade bonds used in this paper but for the 1977–86 period. They find insignificant alphas and, in contrast to Weinstein's sample of fallen angels for the earlier period, an estimated beta of 0.34 relative to the S&P 500. Cornell and Green (1991) estimate multiple regressions similar to those reported in section III above, and conclude that low grade bonds are sensitive to both interest rate and stock-market fluctuations, but they do not directly address whether the bonds are fairly priced.

Kaplan and Stein (1990) employ a clever technique to extract the beta (relative to the stock market) for low grade bonds associated with highly leveraged recapitalizations from stock betas estimated before and after the recapitalization. They estimate the beta for their sample of low grade bonds to be 0.57. After making assumptions about the stock-market risk premium and default experience in the low grade bond market, Kaplan and Stein (1990 p. 6) conclude that the low grade bonds in their sample "do not receive adequate compensation for the risk they bear." Since their sample contains only twelve bonds and covers the limited period 1985–8, one should view this conclusion as tentative and subject to further verification.

This section addresses the efficiency of the low grade bond market in a very specialized and limited context. Consider an investor who holds a portfolio consisting of risky assets and a risk-free asset. The risky-asset portion is a portfolio of stocks and both high grade and low grade corporate bonds, weighted roughly in proportion to their market weights. If the expected return on low grade bonds exceeds that justified by their systematic risk, the investor could obtain a more efficient portfolio by shifting the composition of the risky-asset portion of the portfolio toward additional investment in low grade bonds, and thus, overweight this segment of the risky portfolio in comparison to market weights. Of course, such a shift might require an adjustment in the investment in the risk-free asset to readjust the overall risk of the portfolio.

Blume (1984) shows that the standard "alpha" coefficient can be used to determine whether an investor who currently holds a portfolio, say P, could obtain a more efficient portfolio by shifting some of P into an alternative asset group, say A. Consider the portfolio problem of minimizing the variance of a portfolio consisting of P and A subject to a wealth constraint and an expected return constraint. With some manipulation, the proportion to place in A is

$$x_A = k_{AP}[E(r_A) - \beta_{AP}E(r_P)] = k_{AP}\alpha_{AP} \tag{1}$$

where $E(r_P)$ and $E(r_A)$ are the expected returns of P and A in excess of the riskfree rate, k_{AP} is a positive number determined by the moments of P and A, and β_{AP} is $Cov(r_A, r_P)/Var(r_P)$. Thus, if α_{AP} is not zero, the sign of α_{AP} determines whether an investor who currently holds P should take a long or short position in A. The alphas associated with different alternative assets cannot be directly compared since k_{AP} varies from one alternative to another.

If the expected returns on low grade bonds are substantially in excess of that warranted by their systematic risk, an investor who currently holds a market-weighted portfolio of equities, high grade corporates, and low grade corporates would want to shift a portion of the investment in the first two asset categories into low grade bonds, thereby overweighting the low grade category. If so, α_{AP} would be positive.

Our estimate of α_{AP} assumes that the risky-asset portion of the portfolio P consists of 75 percent stocks, 20 percent high grade bonds, and 5 percent low grade bonds.[30] The indices used to measure the returns of the three asset categories are the same as those in table 9.1. The alternative portfolio (i.e. dependent variable) is the low grade bond index. Thus, a positive α_{AP} indicates that the investor should overweight low grade bonds; with a negative α_{AP} the investor should underweight low grade bonds.

To account for the possibility of nonsynchronous or stale prices, the regression estimates of α_{AP} and β_{AP} use the Scholes–Williams (1977) adjustment. The results without this adjustment are for the most part similar (table 9.5). For the entire period 1977–89, the alpha coefficient for low grade bonds is negative but not significant at the usual level of 5 percent. For comparison, table 9.5 contains a replication of this analysis but uses long-term high grade corporates as the alternative investment. The alpha coefficient for high grade corporates is also statistically indistinguishable from zero.

The estimated alpha coefficients vary substantially across subperiods for both low grade and high grade corporate bonds. From 1982 through 1989, the alphas for both types of bonds are positive but again insignificant. In the first half of this period, 1982–5, the alpha for low grade bonds is positive, while in the second half, 1986–9, the alpha is negative. In contrast, the alpha for long-term high grade corporates is positive in both subperiods, 1982–5 and 1986–9.

If low grade bonds were significantly underpriced relative to a portfolio of equities, one would expect to see consistently large alpha coefficients, and if overpriced, large

Table 9.5 Regression of excess returns of low grade and high grade bonds on the excess returns of a reference portfolio consisting of 75 percent stocks, 20 percent high grade bonds, and 5 percent low grade bonds, various dates. In these regressions all returns are measured in excess of the Treasury Bill rate as given in the publications of Ibbotson Associates. From 1977 through 1988, the bonds underlying the low grade bond index are all nonconvertible with face value at time of issue of greater than $25 million and with time to maturity of at least 10 years from the date on which a return is calculated. The returns of individual low grade bonds from 1982 through 1988 are based upon bid prices from Drexel Burnham Lambert and Salomon Brothers and prior to 1982 upon prices from the *S&P Bond Guide*. The return indices from 1977 through 1988 are averages of these returns by month. For 1989 Drexel calculated a monthly return index in virtually the same way as the 1977–88 indices were calculated, and this index was used to extend the sample through 1989. The returns for long term government bonds and the S&P 500 come from publications of Ibbotson Associates. As demonstrated in Blume (1984), the alpha coefficient of an alternative portfolio with respect to a reference portfolio has the following interpretation: a positive alpha indicates that an investor who currently holds the reference portfolio as the risky portfolio in conjunction with an investment in a risk-free asset could increase expected utility by shifting some of the risky portfolio into this alternative portfolio with a further adjustment to the risk-free investment; a negative alpha indicates that the investor should take a short position in the alternative portfolio; and an alpha of zero indicates no change. The table reports OLS regressions and also OLS regressions using the Scholes–Williams (1977) adjustment for nonsynchronous trade prices. The numbers in parentheses are t-values

Date	Alternative bond portfolio	Scholes–Williams		OLS Regression		
		α	β	α	β	$\bar{R}^2$
1/1977 to 12/1989	Low grade	−0.109	0.538	−0.039	0.435	0.376
		(−0.55)	(12.96)	(−0.23)	(9.65)	
	High grade	−0.089	0.529	−0.074	0.470	0.274
		(−0.33)	(9.26)	(−0.31)	(7.62)	
1/1977 to 12/1981	Low grade	−0.315	0.640	−0.253	0.568	0.400
		(−0.81)	(6.19)	(−0.76)	(6.13)	
	High grade	−0.607	0.622	−0.662	0.609	0.321
		(−1.21)	(4.67)	(−1.56)	(5.16)	
1/1982 to 12/1989	Low grade	0.089	0.490	0.187	0.348	0.374
		(0.41)	(11.60)	(1.00)	(7.60)	
	High grade	0.333	0.484	0.410	0.362	0.230
		(1.13)	(7.76)	(1.50)	(5.39)	
1/1982 to 12/1985	Low grade	0.270	0.707	0.453	0.469	0.506
		(0.96)	(10.99)	(1.80)	(6.96)	
	High grade	0.291	0.838	0.479	0.629	0.434
		(0.77)	(8.39)	(1.22)	(6.02)	
1/1986 to 12/1989	Low grade	−0.165	0.323	−0.116	0.256	0.300
		(−0.58)	(5.95)	(−0.46)	(4.43)	
	High grade	0.260	0.196	0.256	0.166	0.093
		(0.70)	(2.71)	(0.77)	(2.17)	

negative alpha coefficients. Instead, the alpha coefficients for low grade bonds are insignificant and fluctuate between positive and negative numbers. This evidence provides little support for the notion that these bonds are systematically under- or overpriced relative to a market-weighted portfolio of equities and bonds.

IV   Conclusion

This paper examines the risk and return characteristics of low grade bonds with a new data file of dealer bid prices for the most actively traded bonds in the market. The following three findings characterize the low grade bond market for the period 1977–89:

(1) A diversified portfolio of low grade bonds with more than 10 years to maturity exhibits less volatility than indices of long-term Treasury bonds, long-term high-yield corporate bonds, S&P 500 stocks, and small stocks. This perhaps unexpected result is attributable in large part to the lower sensitivity of low grade bonds to unexpected changes in interest rates. A comparison of the volatility of low grade bonds to the volatility of equivalent government bonds (equivalent in terms of coupons, call features, and maturity) shows that low grade bonds are more volatile.

(2) Previous research has intimated that differences in the age of low grade bonds may be associated with significant differences in their returns. Examination of subsamples of our data based on age and maturity reveals no evidence of a relation between the age of low grade bonds and their return distributions. Further, analysis of the default data suggests that at least part of the observed tendency for the probability of default to increase with the age of a bond is due to cyclical conditions in the credit market that affect all bonds regardless of their age. Thus, the relation of default to the age of a bond is weaker than previous studies suggest.

(3) The returns of low grade bonds display properties of both bonds and stocks and thus are more complex than for high grade corporate bonds. Any model used to explain the expected returns of these bonds should reflect both interest rate and equity factors. Despite this complexity, there is no evidence that low grade bonds are significantly over- or underpriced.

Appendix

Table 9A.1 Monthly returns (percent) for low grade bond index. These returns are based on several indices. From 1977 to 1988, the bonds underlying the index are all nonconvertible with face value at time of issue of greater than $25 million and with time to maturity of at least 10 years from the date on which a return is calculated. The returns for the individual bonds from 1982 through 1988 are based on bid prices from Drexel Burnham Lambert and Salomon Brothers and prior to 1982 on prices from the *S&P Bond Guide*. The return indices from 1977 through 1988 are averages of these returns by month. For 1989 Drexel calculated a monthly return index using bid prices in virtually the same way as the 1977–88 indices were calculated, and this index was used to extend the sample through 1989

	Jan	Feb	Mar	Apr	May	June	July	Aug	Sept	Oct	Nov	Dec
1977	2.20	1.90	0.00	0.90	1.80	3.30	−0.30	0.30	−1.60	0.20	2.30	0.10
1978	−1.30	0.30	1.30	0.00	−1.10	1.00	1.20	2.90	0.70	−5.80	0.80	−1.20
1979	5.10	−0.10	2.00	0.50	0.50	1.80	0.90	0.80	−2.10	−8.10	3.20	−1.20

Table 9A.1   *Continued*

	Jan	Feb	Mar	Apr	May	June	July	Aug	Sept	Oct	Nov	Dec
1980	−1.30	−6.00	−5.70	13.00	6.60	3.30	−1.90	−2.30	−1.30	0.40	−1.20	−1.00
1981	2.80	−1.20	2.00	−0.70	0.50	3.80	−3.10	−2.20	−2.90	3.50	8.40	−2.50
1982	−1.85	1.36	0.63	2.47	2.11	−1.08	4.30	8.67	3.76	4.62	2.71	1.29
1983	5.48	4.09	4.07	3.99	−2.32	−0.51	−1.61	0.94	2.42	1.10	1.29	−0.41
1984	3.76	−1.30	−1.05	−0.94	−4.60	1.20	3.05	2.05	4.00	2.88	0.67	−0.09
1985	3.91	1.17	0.81	1.38	4.43	0.87	0.23	1.55	0.56	0.30	2.44	3.17
1986	0.64	3.33	2.57	2.36	−0.89	3.06	−2.90	1.68	1.08	1.36	0.30	0.43
1987	4.04	2.15	0.23	−3.00	−0.27	0.65	−0.27	1.61	−3.82	−2.74	2.14	1.65
1988	4.10	3.59	−1.03	0.67	0.70	3.09	1.10	0.39	2.27	1.29	0.14	0.39
1989	2.03	0.21	−0.47	−0.05	1.24	2.26	0.00	−0.39	−1.79	−5.70	0.38	0.31

Notes

This paper was previously titled "The Components of Lower-Grade Bond Price Variability." We thank Stephen Foerster, George Pennacchi, René Stulz (editor), Mark Weinstein, an anonymous referee and participants in presentations at the Berkeley Program in Finance, the Garn Institute Symposium, Harvard, the NYU Conference on the High Yield Debt Market, the University of Western Ontario, and Wharton for helpful comments. Neelu Agrawal, Suzanne Barrett, and Todd Rosentover provided excellent research assistance. Remaining errors are ours.

1   Hickman (1958), Fraine and Mills (1961), and Atkinson (1967) are examples of early studies of the relation of original quality ratings and defaults. Altman (1987, 1989) and Asquith, Mullins and Wolf (1989) have extended these types of studies to the low grade bond market as it has developed since 1977.

2   See Nunn, Hill, and Schneeweis (1986) for a discussion of the potential problems in using published prices to measure bond returns. Some researchers (e.g., Altman (1989) and Goodman (1990)) have attempted to simulate the returns for a diversified investment in low grade bonds. These simulations rely on assumptions about such critical variables as: coupon spreads between low grade and Treasury bonds; the path of interest rates over the simulation period (most often assumed to be constant); the temporal profile of defaults, calls, and other events that affect the age, maturity, and composition of the index; the percent of par value of the bond recovered at liquidating events such as defaults and exchanges; and reinvestment rates. In addition to the imprecision arising from such assumptions, these simulations suffer foremost from lack of actual prices for the bonds being studied.

3   For example, Weinstein (1983, 1987) and Chang and Pinnegar (1986).

4   See Blume and Stambaugh (1983) for a discussion of such a bias in the context of stock returns.

5   Cornell and Green (1991) use returns for low grade bond (open end) mutual funds to estimate the risks and returns of low grade bonds. Their results are comparable with those reported below.

6   Altman (1989) and Asquith, Mullins and Wolff (1989) discuss the relation between default rates and age of low grade bonds.

7   See Blume and Keim (1987) for a detailed description of the construction of this data base, which at the time covered the years 1982–6. In that article, they find that there are sometimes significant differences in the prices of individual bonds from Drexel and

Salomon, but the differences between the prices tend to offset one other in an index. Thus, the index is more reliable than the prices of individual bonds.

    Until recently Drexel and Salomon stopped reporting the month-end bid prices in the month before a bond defaulted, something that could only be done with hindsight. Moreover, they sometimes retroactively dropped a bond for other reasons. To avoid this hindsight bias, the Drexel and Salomon data are augmented with total returns derived from prices in the *S&P Bond Guide* for the two months *following the deletion* of a bond from either the Drexel or Salomon sample unless it was called or exchanged. Subsequent to the 1987 study, Salomon and Drexel adopted similar procedures to avoid hindsight bias, and following these changes, we stopped augmenting their bond prices.

8   Recently-issued low grade bonds tend to have shorter maturities than those issued in the earlier years of this market. For example, Drexel (1989a) estimated that 59 percent of the straight low grade debt issued in 1988 had a maturity less than 10 years and that 57 percent of the straight low grade debt outstanding at the end of 1988 had a maturity less than 10 years. Because of our requirement of a maturity greater than 10 years, our sample of low grade bonds may not be representative of the overall market, and our average maturity of 14.7 years undoubtedly overstates the maturity for the market as a whole. Retaining this requirement preserves a degree of comparability with other long-term bond indexes.

9   A price from the *S&P Bond Guide* represents the closing price on the New York Bond Exchange or, if not available, the average bid price from one or more market makers or, if neither is available, a "matrix" price. As a consequence, and as mentioned above, monthly returns calculated from this source may be upward biased. To examine the extent of this bias, Blume and Keim (1987) collected prices from the *S&P Bond Guide* for the same bonds in the primary sample for this study for the 1982–6 period. The correlation between the indices constructed from these two data sources is 0.92. In view of this high correlation, the text reports some results going back to 1977.

10   The only major difference is that Drexel does not require that the issue size be equal to or greater than $25 million. Since the average issue size has grown over time, this difference is not likely to be substantial in 1989.

11   Cornell and Green (1991) report an average monthly return of 0.77 percent for their index of low grade bond funds over the same 1977–89 period. This is lower than our average monthly return of 0.85 percent because: (1) their return is reported net of management fees; (2) the funds in their index hold cash reserves which will tend to dampen the average returns during periods like the 1980s when low grade bonds achieved higher returns than money market instruments; and (3) it is likely that our sample of long-term low grade bonds has a longer average maturity (and duration) than the bonds contained in the managed funds in their index. As a result, the average return for their index of low grade funds is lower than the long-term high grade corporate and Treasury bonds for this period.

12   Since the low grade bond prices for 1982–8 are bid prices, there should be no bid-ask bias in the equally-weighted index of low grade bonds reported in the text. The logic of Blume and Stambaugh (1983) implies that an index representing the return from holding a single bond of each issue virtually eliminates the bid-ask bias. The estimate of the returns on this latter index is the ratio of the sum of the bond prices at the end of one month to the sum of the bond prices for the same bonds at the end of the prior month, all adjusted for accrued income and coupon payments. The average monthly return on this alternative index for 1982–8 is 1.33 percent, and the annual geometric mean is 16.8 percent. These

estimates compare to 1.31 percent and 16.6 percent for the 1982–8 period for the low grade bond index discussed in the text, respectively. That these two methods of constructing indices lead to virtually the same numbers implies the absence of any bid-ask bias, as should happen if the bond prices are really bid prices.

13   In their December release, Drexel Burnham Lambert reported an annual loss of 0.95 percent. This number was in error and was corrected in subsequent releases.

14   Fisher (1966) is perhaps the first to analyze the effect of stale prices on the autocorrelation of returns in an index.

15   The adjustment process first annualizes the estimated monthly standard deviations, taking into account the autocorrelation, and then re-expresses these annualized standard deviations in monthly units. If σ^2 is the monthly variance and the first order autocorrelation is ρ_1 with all other correlations zero, the variance of the sum of 12 monthly returns is $\sigma^2 (12 + 22\rho_1)$. Thus, multiplying the monthly standard deviations by $(12 + 22\rho_1)^{1/2}$ yields an annual standard deviation that takes into account the first order serial correlation. Dividing by $\sqrt{12}$ re-expresses this annual standard deviation in the monthly units reported in table 9.1. If the second order autocorrelation is ρ_2 and all high order autocorrelations are zero, the multiplying constant is

$$(12 + 22\rho_1 + 20\rho_2)^{1/2}.$$

16   There are many possible mathematical definitions of duration, each making slightly different assumptions about the way in which interest rates move. The present text will use the term loosely. One would need to postulate a specific bond pricing model and a stochastic process for interest rates to prove rigorously the statements in the text.

17   At the end of 1988, the average time to first call for our low grade bond sample is 3.50, resulting in an average duration measured to first call of 1.99 years.

18   Some low grade bonds provide considerably less call protection than high grade bonds. Some low grade bonds are callable after only three years, and there are some that are callable immediately. Most high grade bonds provide a five- or a ten-year call protection period. If the call protection provisions of low grade bonds are less stringent than high grade bonds, the call features of low grade bonds would lead to a relatively greater reduction in volatility than of high grade bonds.

19   We use a backward iterative algorithm to match the cash flows of the low grade bond with the cash flows of a portfolio of government bonds. First, identify a government bond that matures at the same time as the low grade bond. Second, determine the number of government bonds to buy in order to match the cash flow at maturity of the low grade bond. Third, reduce all the previous payments on the low grade bond by the coupon payments on the government bond. We repeat these three steps, but with the "maturity" redefined as the date of the last uncovered cash flow until we identify a portfolio of the government bonds that mimics the cash flows of the low grade bond. In the first step, if we cannot identify a government bond that matures at the same time as the low grade bond, we identify a government bond that matures before the low grade bond. We then assume that the payments on the government bond are reinvested at the coupon rate on the government bond.

20   The Black–Scholes formula is used to estimate the value of the call provision on a bond. This estimate values the call provision up to the end of the call protection period only and thus implicitly assigns a zero value to the call after the call protection period. Explicitly valuing this additional call protection would only lead to a further reduction in the

volatility of the comparable default-free bonds. The risk-free rate used in this calculation is the six-month Treasury Rate provided by Salomon Brothers. Also, the Black–Scholes formula does not take into account the possibility of early call due to an improvement in credit rating. Again, if it were possible to evaluate this reason for early call, there would be an even greater reduction in the volatility of the comparable default-free index.

21   As mentioned in the text, the possibility of credit improvement increases the likelihood that an issuer will call a low grade bond, which reduces the duration of the low grade bond. The default-free equivalent index does not adjust for the possibility of credit improvement. If it were possible to adjust the default-free equivalent index for this factor, the volatility of this default-free equivalent index would be further reduced, leading to a greater estimate of the yield-spread risk of low grade bonds.

22   We conducted tests of differences in means using portfolio returns and also with individual bond returns. For the latter, we adjusted the monthly returns for each bond by subtracting the overall low grade bond index return from the individual bond return for the respective month. This removed influences common to all low grade bonds (interest rate movements, co-movement with the equity market, etc.) that may potentially confound a test of differences across bonds that is measured over time. We then estimated a panel regression of the market-adjusted returns on separate dummy variables for the age and maturity classifications. The coefficients on all the dummy variables were jointly insignificantly different from zero.

       In the test using portfolio returns, we computed pairwise differences between the portfolio returns described in the text, adjusting the standard errors for potential heteroskedasticity induced by the changing number of bonds in the portfolio through time. We computed tests of the hypothesis that the differences in returns are significantly different from zero. Again, we were unable to reject the hypothesis.

23   Blume and Keim (1989) report a detailed analysis of the returns of these 78 bonds. The internal rate of return of the cash outflows in 1977 and 1978 and the cash inflow at the end of 1988 are used to approximate the realized rate of return. Blume and Keim show that this return is robust to a number of different assumptions. Of particular interest, they find that this return is not sensitive to variation in the assumptions about the liquidation value of defaulted bonds. Two extreme assumptions – a final liquidating price reported in the *S&P Bond Guide* at the end of the month of announced default, or zero – produced insignificantly different results. It is not surprising that the return on an index of low grade bonds does not vary much with the final price attributed to defaulted bonds. Even if a bond defaults and then has no value, the realized return will still be positive if the coupons are large enough and the bond pays the promised coupon a sufficient number of times before default. For example, the annual realized return of a bond that pays coupons for eight years and then becomes valueless is -1.0 percent if the coupon is 12 percent, 2.7 percent if the coupon is 14 percent, and 6.2 percent if the coupon is 16 percent.

24   See Blume and Keim (1989) for a more detailed discussion of this test. Briefly, they tested the null hypothesis that the rank correlation between bond age and default rate is equal to zero. To do this, first determine the age of the bonds and the ranking of default rates for each year within each cohort. For example, the 1977 cohort has twelve age categories – 1 year old (i.e., 1977) through 12 years old (1988) – and twelve rankings for the magnitude of default rate in each year – one for the lowest default rate (0.0%) and twelve for the highest (19.27%). Then pool these values for each of the ten cohorts examined by Asquith et al., resulting in a sample of 75 observations. The computed Spearman rank correlation is 0.49, and the Fisher z-transform provides the test statistic.

25   The specific analysis was to rearrange their default rates by calendar years and age of bonds rather than by year of issue and age of bond as in table 9.3.

26   The details of this test are the same as those described in note 25, except that the default rankings are now based on the mean-adjusted default rates.

27   We also estimated regressions using the S&P 500 index in place of the small stock index and the long-term high grade corporate index in place of the long-term government index. The results are very similar.

28   In addition to this relation in January, Keim and Stambaugh (1986) find that the premium of low grade over high grade bonds and the premium of small over large stocks are correlated for all months over the 1928–77 period. We confirm this for the 1977–89 period with a correlation of 0.45. This is further evidence that equity price movements, and in particular price movements of small stocks, may influence low grade bond price volatility.

29   The same regressions are estimated for each half of the 1982–9 period and lead to conclusions similar to the overall period. These results are not reported to conserve space.

30   As of the end of 1989, SEI estimates that the typical balanced institutional portfolio contained 49.5 percent in equities. The portfolio used in the text slightly overweights equities in terms of this statistic and underweights bonds. The effect is to bias the alpha coefficients upwards, favoring the conclusion that low grade bonds are underpriced.

References

Altman, E. I., 1987, The anatomy of the high-yield bond market, *Financial Analysts Journal*, July–August, 12–25.

——, 1989, Measuring corporate bond mortality and performance, *Journal of Finance* 44, 909–22.

Asquith, P., D. W. Mullins, Jr., and E. D. Wolff, 1989, Original issue high yield bonds: Aging analysis of defaults, exchanges and calls, *Journal of Finance* 44, 923–52 (see chapter 8 above).

Atkinson, T. R., 1967, *Trends in Corporate Bond Quality* (National Bureau of Economic Research, New York).

Blume, M. E., 1984, The use of "alphas" to improve performance, *Journal of Portfolio Management* Fall, 86–92.

—— and R. F. Stambaugh, 1983, Biases in computed returns: An application to the size effect, *Journal of Financial Economics* 12, 387–404.

—— and D. B. Keim, 1987, Lower-grade bonds: Their risks and returns, *Financial Analysts Journal*, July–August, 26–33.

—— and D. B. Keim, 1989, Realized returns and defaults on lower-grade bonds, Unpublished manuscript, Wharton School of the University of Pennsylvania.

Chang, E. and M. Pinnegar, 1986, Return seasonality and tax-loss selling in the market for long-term government and corporate bonds, *Journal of Financial Economics* 17, 391–416.

Cornell, B. and K. Green, 1991, The investment performance of low-grade bond funds, *Journal of Finance* 46, 29–47.

Drexel Burnham Lambert, 1989a, *High Yield Market Report: Financing America's Future* (Drexel Burnham Lambert, Beverly Hills, CA).

——, 1989b, *The Drexel Burnham Lambert High Yield Market Index* (Drexel Burnham Lambert, Beverly Hills, CA).

Fisher, L., 1966, Some new stock market indices, *Journal of Business* 29, 191–225.

Fraine, H. G. and R. H. Mills, 1961, Effect of defaults and credit deterioration on yields of corporate bonds, *Journal of Finance* 16, 423–34.

Goodman, L. S., 1990, High-yield default rates: Is there cause for concern?, *Journal of Portfolio Management*, Winter, 54–9.

Hickman, W. B., 1958, *Corporate Bond Quality and Investor Experience* (Princeton University Press, Princeton, N.J., and the National Bureau of Economic Research, New York).

Kaplan, S. N. and J. C. Stein, 1990, How risky is the debt in highly leveraged transactions? Unpublished manuscript, University of Chicago.

Keim, D. B. and R. F. Stambaugh, 1986, Predicting returns in the stock and bond markets, *Journal of Financial Economics* 17, 357–90.

Nunn, K. P., J. Hill, and T. Schneeweis, 1986, Corporate bond price data sources and return/risk measurement, *Journal of Financial and Quantitative Analysis* 21, 197–208.

Scholes, M. S. and J. Williams, 1977, Estimating betas from nonsynchronous data, *Journal of Financial Economics* 5, 309–27.

Weinstein, M. I., 1983, Bond systematic risk and the option pricing model, *Journal of Finance* 38, 1415–29.

——, 1987, A curmudgeon's view of junk bonds, *Journal of Portfolio Management*, Spring, 76–80.

10

The Decline in Credit Quality of New-issue Junk Bonds

Barrie A. Wigmore

The expansion of the junk bond market since 1985, particularly its use in funding merger-related transactions such as acquisitions, leveraged buyouts (LBOs) and recapitalizations, has raised the question whether increased defaults in this area are likely. To date, scholarly analyses of the default risk of junk bonds have focused on either annual defaults as a proportion of the total junk bond market or junk bond defaults in successive years after issuance.[1]

These studies do not measure the default likelihood of bonds issued in 1986–8, when volume quadrupled to finance merger-related transactions. Measurement of default experience requires a period at least long enough to exhaust the liquidity reserves built into the original financing plan and ideally long enough to capture the effects of some cyclical adversity. While it may be too soon to measure the default experience of the 1986–8 issues, we can compare their credit ratios with those of prior issues and thereby gain insight into changing default risk.

Decline in Credit Ratios

Table 10.1 outlines the annual averages for five *pro forma* credit ratios at time of issue for all underwritten junk bonds issued between 1980 and 1988 (other than issues of financial institutions and electric utilities). These credit ratios declined substantially over 1986–8.

Coverage of interest by *pro forma* earnings before interest and taxes (EBIT) averaged 0.72 for 1986–8, versus 1.19 for 1983–5. Coverage of interest by *pro forma* earnings before interest, taxes and depreciation (EBITD) averaged 1.26 in 1986–8, versus 1.74 for 1983–5. The average for *pro forma* debt as a percentage of net tangible assets rose to 159 percent from 116 percent between the same periods and peaked at over 200 percent in 1988.[2] *Pro forma* cash flow as a percentage of total debt averaged 3.3 percent

Table 10.1 Pro forma credit ratios for junk bond issuers, 1980–8 (weighted by principal; standard deviations in parentheses)

Year	EBIT cvg. of int.[a] (1)	EBITD cvg. of int.[b] (2)	Debt as a % of net tang. assets[c] (3)	Cash flow as a % of debt[d] (4)	Common equity as a % of cap.[e] (5)	Number of issues[f] (6)	Total volume (US$bill)[g] (7)	Merger-related volume (US$bill)[h] (8)	% of total volume[i] (9)
1980	1.99 (1.27)	2.73 (1.40)	60 (12)	17 (11)	39 (11)	26	0.9	0.1	11
1981	1.96 (1.06)	2.89 (1.07)	62 (12)	22 (11)	35 (14)	20	1.2	0.1	5
1982	2.07 (1.46)	3.00 (1.63)	65 (15)	18 (11)	35 (15)	17–19	1.5	0.2	13
1983	0.78 (2.54)	1.72 (3.20)	72 (27)	13 (24)	35 (23)	46	3.6	0.8	22
1984	1.14 (0.90)	1.69 (1.18)	175 (159)	7 (11)	21 (21)	68–70	7.4	3.3	45
1985	1.35 (1.27)	1.81 (1.50)	100 (83)	9 (10)	22 (20)	89–93	8.1	6.1	75
1986	0.77 (0.94)	1.38 (0.98)	123 (102)	5 (11)	16 (22)	147–151	24.4	18.4	75
1987	0.69 (0.63)	1.18 (0.69)	151 (116)	2 (8)	3 (32)	130–134	25.9	21.2	82
1988	0.71 (0.56)	1.23 (0.66)	202 (193)	3 (6)	4 (31)	132–135	27.0	25.0	93

[a] Latest nine or 12 months' pro forma earnings before interest and taxes divided by pro forma interest.
[b] Latest nine or 12 months' pro forma earnings before interest, taxes and depreciation divided by pro forma interest.
[c] Pro forma total debt divided by pro forma total assets minus goodwill, other intangibles and current liabilities excluding current debt.
[d] Net income plus depreciation and amortization divided by total debt.
[e] Common equity divided by capitalization including current debt.
[f] Number of issues providing data for Columns (1)–(5).
[g] Principal amounts of all publicly underwritten junk bond issues including those for which no credit data were available, but excluding issues by financial institutions and electric utilities.
[h] Principal amounts with use of proceeds for acquisitions, leveraged buyouts or recapitalizations.
[i] Column (8) divided by column (7).
Sources: IDD Information Services Inc., microfiche prospectuses, 10Ks and annual reports

in 1986–8, versus 9.7 percent in 1983–5. Common equity ratios declined steadily; these averages became useless in 1987–8, however, when standard deviations were 900 percent of the means, largely because of recapitalizations. (Accounting practice calls for the creation of large negative common equity accounts in the case of recapitalization, versus writing up assets if the same company were acquired.)

Glossary

Interest Coverage: Earnings before interest and taxes (EBIT) or else earnings before interest, taxes and depreciation and amortization (EBITD) divided by latest 12 months' interest adjusted for annualization of interest on known financing within the 12 months.

Cash Flow: Net income plus depreciation and amortization.

Junk Bonds: Bonds rated Ba1/BB+ or lower by Moody's and Standard & Poor's.

The averages in table 10.1 mask large variations within each year. For example, standard deviations averaged 98.2 percent for EBIT coverage of interest in 1986–8 and 250 percent for cash flow as a percentage of total debt. (Significance tests were not performed, as the population means were known rather than estimated.) A few issues had a large impact on the standard deviations – Tesoro Petroleum and Republic Steel in 1983, Metromedia in 1984, Comdata and Seven-Up in 1987, and Seven-Up, Dr Pepper and Playtex in 1988. Media companies (cable, cellular, newspaper and radio-TV) especially affected the 1984–8 standard deviations for debt as a percentage of net tangible assets, which were increased 50 percent by 79 media financings. The wide standard deviations of the credit ratio averages suggest the potential for wide variations in investment performance.

The data were tested to see whether, for a given issuer, a weak credit ratio in one area was offset by stronger credit ratios in other areas. The most obvious instance would be where low EBIT and EBITD coverage of interest was compensated for by low debt as a percentage of net tangible assets. Correlations of EBITD coverage of interest and debt as a percentage of net tangible assets for the years 1984 to 1988 ranged from 0.006 to 0.28. Low EBITD coverage of interest did not tend to be coupled with low debt as a percentage of net tangible assets.

The credit ratio averages in table 10.1 are based on all of the issuers' debts, including senior debt, whereas junk bond issues in 1986–8 were predominantly subordinated issues, making up approximately 30 percent of capitalization. The credit protection indicated by these averages thus substantially overstates the credit protection for junk bonds.

The decline in credit ratio averages contrasts with Altman's finding of a "slight improvement" in Zeta scores for a small sample of junk bond issuers over an earlier period ending in 1986.[3] The decline also contrasts with the stability of the three-year moving averages of three similar ratios, given in table 10.2. These are published by

Standard & Poor's for extant issues rated BBB (the lowest level of investment grade debt) between 1980 and 1988.

Database and Derivation of Table 10.1

Table 10.1 is based on data from 694 publicly underwritten bond issues rated Ba1/BB+ or lower, as reported by IDD Information Services Inc. The sample represents all such bonds issued between January 1, 1980 and December 31, 1988, excepting those issued by financial institutions or electric utilities. Financial issuers of junk bonds, such as bank holding companies, savings and loans, and credit companies, were excluded because of their unique financial ratios (or at least what used to be their unique ratios). Electric utilities were excluded because of their unique accounting.

The database does not include debt issued in exchange offers and privately placed issues (although some of these, such as the Macy's LBO issues, were significant). Nor are previously issued junk bonds or bonds downgraded to junk status included.

Data were obtained from the prospectus for each issue. When this source was inadequate, 10Ks or annual reports were used.

The ratios for each issue were calculated on a *pro forma* basis at the time of issuance. Many of the prospectuses carried a complete set of *pro forma* financial statements – income statement, balance sheet, and sources and uses of funds. While *pro forma* adjustments differed across companies, in general the adjustments involved applying higher debt levels, interest costs, depreciation and amortization of goodwill, and lower income taxes, to the income statements for the last 12 months, as if the transactions had taken place at the beginning of the period. *Pro forma* balance sheets reflected the latest data available, restated for additional debt, less equity, written-up assets, changes in tax accounts and, usually, capitalized fees and goodwill. Whenever the prospectus presented two sets of *pro forma* statements, with one reflecting planned divestitures, statements prevailing after the divestitures (i.e., the ones

Table 10.2 Standard & Poor's credit ratios for BBB industrial issuers (three-year moving averages)

	EBIT cvg. of int. (1)	Funds from oper. as % of total debt (2)	Total debt as % of cap. incl. STD (3)
1980–2	3.26	33.60	38.02
1981–3	2.87	36.34	36.30
1982–4	2.91	38.07	34.80
1983–5	3.05	39.44	34.00
1984–6	3.19	40.45	34.81
1985–7	3.63	34.20	38.30
1986–8	3.69	37.10	39.50

Sources: Credit Week, Sept. 5 1988; S&P Debt Ratings Criteria Industrial Overview, 1986, p. 51; S&P Credit Overview, 1983, p. 26; S&P Credit Overview, 1982, p. 26; CreditStats, 10/9/89, p. 1

producing the more favorable ratios) were used. An attempt was made to eliminate nonrecurring charges from the *pro forma* calculations. In a few cases, ratios had to be estimated.

The ratios selected for calculation provide a multifaceted view of each issuer's status. The ratios measuring EBIT and EBITD coverage of interest, derived from the income statement, directly measure ability to pay interest. They were based on the latest 9 or 12 months' statement, whichever was the more current. No effort was made to calculate fixed charges such as rents and preferred stock dividends.

The interest coverage calculations used differ from those mandated by the SEC [the US Securities and Exchange Commission] in two ways – (1) lease charges were excluded and (2) when a company issued a relatively large amount of debt for an unnamed (and unknown) acquisition, the full amount of *pro forma* interest was used. (Pantry Pride, Triangle Industries, Vagabond Hotels, Wickes and E-II Holdings provide prominent examples of the second case.) *Pro forma* fixed charges per SEC regulations do not include interest on any new debt attributed to cash left on hand. The result is a distorted impression of favorable interest coverage. The interest coverage calculations for table 10.1 assumed a 12 percent interest cost on all debt whenever suitable *pro forma* information was not available. No provision was made for earnings generated by surplus cash.

It should be pointed out that various debt instruments that accrue interest due as additional debt, such as zero-coupon, payment-in-kind or deep-discount bonds, are not treated differently from debt that pays cash interest. Accrued interest is no different from cash interest under generally accepted accounting rules.

EBITD coverage of interest is a useful short-hand ratio for expressing both interest coverage and cash flow availability. An EBITD ratio over one leaves a margin for income taxes, capital expenditures and principal repayments. To offer any perspective, however, that margin must be expressed as a percentage of total debt. For example, EBITD coverage of 1.25 times 12 percent interest leaves cash equal to 3 percent of principal for taxes, capital expenditures or debt repayment. This figure corresponds to cash flow as a percentage of total debt, provided there are no income taxes.

I did not use adjusted EBITD interest coverage ratios, which many prospectuses make available in an indirect fashion and which are frequently used in discussing new issues. The adjusted EBITD ratio adds non-cash expenses such as pension expense to the EBITD numerator and excludes payments in kind and interest accretion on zero-coupon or deep-discount issues from the interest denominator. This measures current liquidity, but it treats deferred payment of operating expenses and additional borrowings such as payment in kind and interest accretion as a means of paying current interest. Such a measure provides no insight into the long-term sustainability of a company's debt burden.

The ratios measuring debt as a percentage of net tangible assets and common equity, derived from the balance sheets, measure the debt-holders' asset protection, directly and indirectly. Capital leases, pension obligations and contracts payable were treated as debt, but did not include deferred taxes. The averages for debt as a percentage of net tangible assets would have risen more, on the basis of historical asset costs, had it not been for the accounting practice of writing up the value of acquired assets to current costs. This practice also creates an unavoidable distortion in comparisons of acquisition financings with recapitalizations, because assets are not written up to current costs in the latter. The same practice "overstates" the decline in the average common equity ratios in 1987–8, because the recapitalizations enter the averages as negative equity.

The ratio measuring cash flow as a percentage of total debt represents combined earnings (or losses) plus depreciation and amortization from the sources and uses of funds statement. It measures ability to repay principal. No deduction was made for capital expenditures. Deferred tax and working capital changes were not included in cash flow, but extraordinary charges were added back.

Historical trend analysis for each issuer was not undertaken, because over three-quarters of junk bonds issued between 1985 and 1988 were issued in conjunction with some highly discontinuous event, such as an acquisition, LBO or recapitalization. For the same reason, I did not calculate such broadly accepted credit-quality measures as working-capital ratio, Z score and return on assets. It goes without saying that trend analyses since the discontinuous event would be extremely valuable, even if there were only one or two years of data.

Changes in Junk Bond Rating Standards

The annual percentage of new-issue junk bonds rated Ba by Moody's or BB by Standard & Poor's declined steadily from over 40 percent in 1982 to single digits in 1987–8 (see table 10.3). This simple measure of the decline in the credit quality of new-issue junk bonds understates the actual decline, however, because the credit ratios within credit-rating categories also declined for new issues in 1986–8.

Consider, for example, Moody's and Standard & Poor's B-rated issues, which represent 579 and 498, respectively, of the 694 new issues studied. The first panel of table 10.4 outlines the average credit ratios for issues rated B (irrespective of + or − designations) by Moody's. These declined steadily throughout the period. The average *pro forma* EBIT coverage of interest was 32 percent lower in 1986–8 than in 1983–5; the average EBITD coverage of interest was 18 percent lower; the average for debt as a percentage of net tangible assets was 57 percent higher; the average for cash flow as a percentage of total debt was 50 percent lower. Based on the two years 1987–8, the declines in average credit ratios were even worse.

New issues rated B by Standard & Poor's also experienced substantial decline in their average credit ratios between 1983–5 and 1986–8, as indicated by the second panel of table 10.4. EBIT coverage of interest declined 30 percent; EBITD coverage of interest declined 22 percent; debt as a percentage of net tangible assets rose 37 percent; cash flow as a percentage of total debt declined 49 percent.

The averages cited in table 10.4 for new issues rated B by Standard & Poor's differ markedly from those published by Standard & Poor's.[4] Their ratios for issues rated B are not based on *pro forma* financial statements (so past favorable ratios are reported,

Table 10.3   New-issue junk bond ratings*

	Ba		Moody's B		Caa		
	$ billion	*%*	*$ billion*	*%*	*$ billion*	*%*	*Total*
1980	0.2	22	0.7	78	0.0	0	0.9
1981	0.3	25	0.9	75	0.0	0	1.2
1982	0.6	43	0.8	57	0.0	0	1.4
1983	1.2	33	2.3	64	0.1	3	3.6
1984	1.3	18	6.1	82	0.0	0	7.4
1985	1.4	18	6.6	83	0.0	0	8.0
1986	4.7	19	19.0	78	0.7	3	24.4
1987	1.7	7	23.8	91	0.6	2	26.1
1988	2.0	7	24.5	91	0.5	2	27.0

	BB		Standard & Poor's B		CCC		
	$ billion	*%*	*$ billion*	*%*	*$ billion*	*%*	*Total*
1980	0.2	22	0.7	78	0.0	0	0.9
1981	0.3	25	0.9	75	0.0	0	1.2
1982	0.7	47	0.8	53	0.0	0	1.5
1983	0.8	22	2.4	67	0.4	11	3.6
1984	1.2	16	5.2	70	1.0	14	7.4
1985	1.2	15	5.0	63	1.8	23	8.0
1986	2.1	9	17.6	72	4.6	19	24.3
1987	3.2	12	18.2	70	4.7	18	26.1
1988	1.2	4	19.5	72	6.4	24	27.1

* Excludes electric utilities and financial issuers.
Source: IDD Information Services Inc.

despite an event that changed the credit), and they exclude 101 privately owned issuers (in particular, 85 LBOs).

The Relation Between Merger Prices and Credit Ratios

Between 1986 and 1988, 75 to 93 percent of the principal raised by new junk bond issues was for merger-related transactions such as acquisitions, leveraged buyouts and recapitalizations (see table 10.1). This allows us to relate merger prices to junk bond credit ratios, interest rates and capitalization ratios.

Table 10.5 relates EBIT coverage of interest to prices (expressed as a multiple of EBIT to eliminate leverage differences) paid for acquisitions of companies in the S&P 400 index, used as a proxy for junk-bond-financed merger prices. (An analysis of EBIT multiples for all junk-related merger transactions would be preferable but is beyond the scope of this study.) I assume that the average S&P merger transaction was financed with junk bonds and that the average annual interest rate and equity ratio were those for issues rated B by S&P in that year. The EBIT coverage of interest for those

Table 10.4 Credit ratios for issuers of B-rated junk bonds

	EBIT cvg. of int. (1)	EBITD cvg. of int. (2)	Moody's Debt as a % of net tang. assets (3)	Cash flow as a % of debt (4)	Common equity as a % of cap. (5)	Number of issues (6)
1980	1.64	2.27	64	14	37	22
1981	2.05	2.77	61	18	35	16
1982	1.66	2.25	68	14	33	12–13
1983	0.98	1.64	73	10	30	33
1984	1.13	1.63	126	8	29	57–58
1985	1.14	1.54	121	8	26	70–72
1986	0.77	1.50	144	7	22	118–122
1987	0.70	1.21	158	3	10	118–122
1988	0.73	1.26	203	3	5	119–121

	EBIT cvg. of int. (1)	EBITD cvg. of int. (2)	Standard & Poor's Debt as a % of net tang. assets (3)	Cash flow as a % of debt (4)	Common equity as a % of cap. (5)	Number of issues (6)
1980	1.67	2.33	62	14	38	22
1981	2.05	2.77	61	18	35	16
1982	1.70	2.36	66	17	34	12
1983	1.04	1.87	70	13	31	31
1984	1.08	1.59	129	8	30	53–54
1985	1.45	1.97	120	10	23	65–67
1986	0.93	1.67	93	9	25	105–107
1987	0.72	1.21	136	3	12	91–95
1988	0.84	1.35	207	4	8	91–94

Sources: IDD Information Services Inc., microfiche prospectuses, 10Ks and annual reports

Table 10.5 EBIT coverage of interest and acquisition prices

	S&P B-rated new-issue rates (1)	1 Minus B-rated equity ratios[a] (2)	EBIT multiple for 1.0 coverage[b] (3)	EBIT multiple of S&P 400 acqs.[c] (4)	Implied junk bond EBIT cvg.[d] (5)	Actual B-rated junk bond EBIT cvg.[e] (6)
1986	12.3	0.75	10.8	11.3	0.96	0.93
1987	13.1	0.88	8.7	17.5	0.50	0.72
1988	13.0	0.92	8.4	12.1	0.69	0.84

[a] One minus the annual average common equity ratio for all issues rated B by S&P (excluding electric utilities and financial issuers); i.e., the portion of the capitalization that is leveraged.
[b] The necessary EBIT multiple of col. (1) times col. (2) for one times interest coverage, assuming debt capitalization equal to col. (2); i.e., 100 divided by col. (1) times col. (2).
[c] Average acquisition price of all S&P 400 companies acquired each year, expressed as a multiple of earnings before interest and taxes.
[d] Implied EBIT coverage of interest if all S&P 400 acquisitions were financed at col. (1) rate with col. (2) percentage of debt; i.e., col. (3) divided by col. (4).
[e] From table 10.4, col. (1).

Sources: IDD Information Services Inc., microfiche prospectuses, 10Ks and annual reports

transactions follows from the EBIT multiple paid, as outlined in the table. Table 10.5 reveals that merger pricing throughout 1986–8 entailed junk bond EBIT coverages of interest systematically below 1.0.

The low average credit ratios for new junk bond issuers in 1986–8 raises a general question about the diversification of portfolios of these bonds. A portfolio of bonds of many companies in many industries would normally offer diversification under different economic conditions, and the wide standard deviations of the average credit ratios for these issues suggest that widely divergent portfolio returns are to be expected. The population of junk bonds issued in 1986–8, however, may have suffered a meaningful reduction in diversification, because the financing for 75 to 93 percent of these bonds stemmed from the merger market. The merger market in this period effectively constituted, directly or indirectly, a highly refined auction process, with an unprecedented amount of cash for acquisitions available from domestic companies, foreign companies, LBO funds and public recapitalizations. As a result, both merger prices and credit ratios tended to be pushed to the limit the market would bear.

Future Default Rates

Academic work on bankruptcy has tended to focus on bankruptcy predictors that look 6 to 24 months ahead and utilize time-series trend data. Quite appropriately, given the past objects of these studies, the bankruptcy predictors tend to relate to publicly-owned companies that have experienced a decline in their fortunes but have liability patterns that, to a significant degree, reflect earlier, better times. These circumstances do not fit the 1986–8 junk bond issues well, however, because we are concerned with results over a 5 to 10-year horizon for issuers that are often privately owned and that have debt structures crafted to specific cash flow expectations.

Some insight into these expectations can be gained from the highly simplified model in table 10.6. This is the type of model market professionals use to evaluate LBO equity investments. Issuers often share these models, or the projections derived from them, with junk bond investors. The model therefore serves as a simplified version of bond investors' expectations and can be used equally well for any highly leveraged junk bond issuer.

Table 10.6 illustrates the model using parameters prevailing in 1987–8: 13 percent interest, debt equal to 90 percent of capitalization, initial EBITD coverage of interest equal to 1.25, EBITD growth of 8 percent annually, and capital expenditures (including working capital growth) equal to 3 percent of acquisition cost. For simplicity, bank debt, which would normally constitute 60 percent of capitalization and be senior in status, and junk bond debt, which would normally constitute 30 percent of capitalization and be subordinated in status, have been combined into one factor at one interest rate. The model calculates a resale price – in this case, the approximate initial purchase price of eight times EBITD – which can be used as a cross-check on the target returns advertised by LBO advisers (usually over 30 percent). This example produces a consistent 30 percent pretax internal rate of return to the equity investors.

Table 10.6   LBO return model ($100 investment; 8% EBITD growth)

Year (1)	Principal[a] (2)	Int. at 13%[b] (3)	EBITD ratio[c] (4)	8% growth EBITD (5)	4% cap. exp. (6)	Free cash[d] (7)	Sale proceeds at 8 × EBITD[e] (8)	Balance for equity[f] (9)
0	90.00							10.00
1	90.00	11.70	1.25	14.63	4	−1.07	117.00	27.00
2	91.08	11.84	1.33	15.80	4	−0.04	126.36	35.29
3	91.12	11.85	1.44	17.06	4	1.21	136.47	45.35
4	89.91	11.69	1.58	18.42	4	2.74	147.39	57.48
5	87.17	11.33	1.76	19.90	4	4.56	159.18	72.01
6	82.61	10.74	2.00	21.49	4	6.75	171.91	89.30
7	75.86	9.86	2.35	23.21	4	9.35	185.66	109.81
8	66.51	8.65	2.90	25.06	4	12.42	200.52	134.01
9	54.09	7.03	3.85	27.07	4	16.04	216.56	162.47
10	38.05	4.95	5.91	29.24	4	20.29	233.88	195.83
11	17.76	2.31	13.67	31.57	4	25.26	252.59	234.83
12	−7.50	−0.98	−34.97	34.10	4	31.08	272.80	280.30
13	−38.58	−5.01	−7.34	36.83	4	37.84	294.63	333.20
14	−76.42	−9.93	−4.00	39.77	4	45.71	318.20	394.61
15	−122.13	−15.88	−2.71	42.96	4	54.83	343.65	465.78

[a] Original principal of 90% reduced by prior year's cash flow in col. (7).
[b] 1987−8 junk bond average yield.
[c] First entry of 1.25 is the 1986−8 average; thereafter col. (5) divided by col. (3).
[d] Col. (5) minus cols. (3) and (6).
[e] The same multiple as the original purchase price.
[f] Col. (8) minus col. (2).

    The model is greatly simplified. Importantly, it ignores corporate income taxes. In those instances where asset values are written up for tax purposes and tax-loss carryforwards are built up in the early years, income taxes are not likely to be payable for 8 to 10 years. The model assumes that capital expenditures include increases in working capital, and it ignores asset sales, incremental financing (through the use of zero-coupon bonds, payment in kind bonds, or bank lines of credit) and fees. Furthermore, EBITD growth, a factor crucial to credit-worthiness in the model, is not dependent solely on economic growth. Most LBOs expect to make substantial cost reductions to increase EBITD.

    The model highlights several factors that are important to making long-term judgments about default risk. (1) Investors are dependent upon growth for the repayment of principal; this is especially true for junk bond investors, who at 30 percent of capitalization would not receive principal payments under this model until the 11th year. Nonetheless, the attractiveness of an LBO that works is evident. Judging from free cash (which is roughly equivalent to the common equity build-up), principal and the EBITD ratio, the issuer has returned to investment grade credit ratios by the 8th or 9th year.

    (2) In the first two years, even with growth, there is no free cash flow. Most LBOs thus use some form of incremental borrowing in the early years, such as zero-coupon

bonds, payment in kind bonds or bank lines, or they generate cash for debt service through asset sales.

(3) The sales proceeds in the model provide important protection for the senior (presumably bank) lenders, but this protection is also highly dependent upon growth and upon a sustainable merger market multiple. Growth and the merger market multiple are closely related, of course. A multiple of eight times EBITD may be justified for 8 percent EBITD growth, but the lower the growth rate, the lower the resale multiple. In a distress situation, this relationship erodes the resale protection for lenders at the same time their debt service is failing.

(4) The crucial variables for credit health are EBITD growth, capital expenditures and free cash. With assumptions of 90 percent debt and 1.25 initial EBITD coverage of interest, debt reduction needs to be combined with growth in EBITD if long-term debt obligations are to be met. Stability is not good enough. Under this model, for example, an issuer that had 3 percent EBITD growth, as in table 10.7, would require 14 years to retire half of its bank debt, if bank debt was 60 percent of capitalization, and would retire none of its junk bond debt (assuming that constitutes 30 percent of capitalization) within the 15-year model.

While most LBOs sell assets and cut capital expenditures in the early years in order to create free cash, this is a two-edged sword for junk bond investors, who are

Table 10.7 LBO return model ($100 investment; 3% EBITD growth)

Year (1)	Principal[a] (2)	Int. at 13%[b] (3)	EBITD ratio[c] (4)	3% growth EBITD (5)	4% cap. exp. (6)	Free cash[d] (7)	Sale proceeds at 5 × EBITD[e] (8)	Balance for equity[f] (9)
0	90.00							10.00
1	90.00	11.70	1.25	14.63	4	−1.07	73.13	−16.87
2	91.08	11.84	1.27	15.06	4	−0.78	75.32	−15.76
3	91.85	11.94	1.30	15.52	4	−0.42	77.58	−14.27
4	92.28	12.00	1.33	15.98	4	−0.01	79.91	−12.37
5	92.29	12.00	1.37	16.46	4	0.46	82.30	−9.99
6	91.83	11.94	1.42	16.95	4	1.02	84.77	−7.06
7	90.81	11.81	1.48	17.46	4	1.66	87.32	−3.50
8	89.15	11.59	1.55	17.99	4	2.40	89.93	0.78
9	86.76	11.28	1.64	18.53	4	3.25	92.63	5.88
10	83.51	10.86	1.76	19.08	4	4.23	95.41	11.90
11	79.28	10.31	1.91	19.65	4	5.35	98.27	18.99
12	73.93	9.61	2.11	20.24	4	6.63	101.22	27.29
13	67.30	8.75	2.38	20.85	4	8.10	104.26	36.96
14	59.20	7.70	2.79	21.48	4	9.78	107.39	48.19
15	49.42	6.42	3.44	22.12	4	11.70	110.61	61.19

[a] Original principal of 90% reduced by prior year's cash flow in col. (7).
[b] 1987–8 junk bond average yield.
[c] First entry of 1.25 is the 1986–8 average; thereafter col. (5) divided by col. (3).
[d] Col. (5) minus cols. (3) and (6).
[e] The appoximate multiple for successful refinancing under the model.
[f] Col. (8) minus col. (2).

dependent upon sustained growth for 10 to 15 years if the issuer is to be able to make relatively large lump-sum principal repayments in that time horizon. This long time horizon, especially when cash and assets are basically being shrunk to service senior lenders, points out the long perspective necessary for evaluating the wisdom of and returns from junk bond financing.

"Early" defaults by some 1986–8 issuers have been due to inability to pay interest. The broader question for companies still paying interest is the ability to repay principal. Indeed, emphasis on default rates in the short term, before the bulge of principal related to 1986–8 new issues comes due in 1996–2003, may miss the main weakness in junk bond credit.

Default Thresholds

The crucial credit factors of interest charges, capital expenditures and free cash can be combined into a single expression of EBITD coverage of interest, which explains why the ratio is popular. For example, 1.40 EBITD coverage of 13 percent interest when debt is 90 percent of capitalization can be translated as follows:

$$
\begin{aligned}
\text{Interest coverage} &= 13/13 & &= 1.00 \\
\text{Capital expenditures} &= (3/0.90)/13 & &= 0.25 \\
\text{Free cash} &= 1.95/13 & &= 0.15 \\
\text{Total} & & &= 1.40
\end{aligned}
$$

In turn, the LBO model can be run through various iterations of EBITD growth, capital expenditure requirements and resale values to evaluate the generation of free cash, the progress in paying down bank debt and the likelihood of principal repayment to junk bond holders at maturity. Such iterations should provide some general threshold levels of EBITD growth – levels that call for either bankruptcy or reorganization.

For example, reorganization would seem to be necessary under a scenario of a 3 percent EBITD growth rate and capital expenditures equal to 4 percent of capitalization, as in table 10.7. In this case, bank lenders have less than 10 percent of their principal repaid over 10 years, there are no principal payments to junk bond holders (assuming these bonds are 30 percent of capitalization) in the 15-year time horizon, and sale proceeds do not equal remaining debt until the eighth year. Note that, at 3 percent growth, the resale multiple is only 5 times EBITD – a multiple that could be successfully refinanced under the model.

Predicting the exact timing of default under the model is impractical and artificial, even if we assume many factors are held constant, because we cannot estimate the point up to which banks might be willing to reschedule principal payments or lend to make interest payments, especially if the borrower is unable to pay principal on a looming junk bond maturity. In practice, inability to meet a scheduled junk bond liability leads to default or reorganization of all debts, hence bank lenders force asset sales in advance of such a situation in order to delay bankruptcy or reorganization of debts. The most important credit issue for junk bonds is thus the ultimate repayment of principal; issuers have various ways to juggle current interest payments. Measuring just the ability of issuers to pay interest could significantly underestimate the ultimate default risk of junk bonds.

Default Rates

To date, the only effort to *project* junk bond default rates used a "cash flow" predictor identical to EBITD projected over 1988–93.[5] Wyss linked various projected scenarios from an econometric model to 573 junk bond issuers grouped into specific industries. The test for default required EBITD coverage of interest far enough below one over four quarters to exhaust all working capital, with no allowance for capital expenditures and no debt repayments. It is not clear how Wyss treated interest that accrued but did not have to be paid, but his assumptions appear inconsistent with junk bond issuers' emphasis on debt retirement and with the importance of capital expenditures to EBITD growth and the eventual repayment of junk bond principal. The five-year horizon used also artificially reduces the default rate versus a 10 to 15-year period, into which most junk bond maturities fall. The test thus becomes a test of ability to pay current interest, with no reference to paying principal.

No doubt companies that cannot meet this test will default, but as we have seen from the LBO model above, an issuer on track to being able to pay its bank and junk bond principal should probably have EBITD coverage of interest of 1.40 to 1.50 by the fifth year. Wyss found that, even with EBITD interest coverage of less than one, his model produced cumulative defaults in five years of 13.14 to 18.82 percent, depending upon the specific economic scenario.[6] If Wyss set bankruptcy tests of EBITD interest coverage levels from 0.70 to 1.50, it would provide a very interesting spectrum of default predictions, even within the constraint of a five-year horizon.

We can make an intuitive judgment about future default rates in light of prior research by Altman, Asquith and Wyss and the decline in the credit ratios of 1986–8 new issues outlined in this article. Asquith generally found cumulative default rates of 31 percent for junk bonds issued since 1977 and outstanding 10 years or more.[7] Altman found a 32 percent default rate for a similar sample.[8] Using a five-year horizon, Altman and Asquith found cumulative average default rates of 11.9 and 10.9 percent, respectively, while Wyss predicted rates of 13.14 to 18.82 percent, depending upon the specific economic scenario.[9] Inasmuch as credit ratios have declined significantly relative to the issuers that produced Altman's, Asquith's and Wyss's default rates, and as Wyss's EBITD coverage ratio test is too low, we appear justified in making the intuitive judgment that default rates over time for the 1986–8 junk bond issuers will probably rise significantly above prior issuers' levels.[10]

Notes

1 See, for example, E. I. Altman and S. A. Nammacher, *Investing in Junk Bonds* (New York: John Wiley, 1987); E. I. Altman, "The Anatomy of the High-Yield Bond Market," *Financial Analysts Journal,* July/August 1987; M. E. Blume and D. B. Keim, "Lower-Grade Bonds: Their Risks and Returns," *Financial Analysts Journal*, July/August 1987 for the former; and E. I. Altman, "Measuring Corporate Bond Mortality and Performance," *Journal of Finance*, September 1989; P. Asquith, D. W. Mullins, Jr. and E. D. Wolff, "Original Issue High Yield Bonds: Aging Analysis of Defaults, Exchanges and Calls," *Journal of Finance*, September 1989; and M. E. Blume and D. B. Keim, "Realized Returns and Defaults on Lower-Grade Bonds: the Cohort of 1977 and 1978" (Working Paper 31-89, Rodney L. White Center for Financial Research, the Wharton School of the University of Pennsylvania, 1989) for the latter.

2 Net tangible assets are defined as total assets less the sum of (1) goodwill, (2) costs assigned to rights, patents, licenses, etc., (3) financing expenses and (4) current liabilities (excluding debt due within one year).

3 See Altman, "The Anatomy of the High-Yield Bond Market," p. 24.

4 Standard & Poor's, *Credit Stats*, October 9, 1989, pp. 3, 13.

5 D. Wyss, C. Probyn, and R. de Angelis, "The Impact of Recession on High-Yield Bonds" (Washington, D.C., July 11, 1989).

6 Ibid., pp. 63, 65, 68, 72.

7 Asquith et al., "Original Issue Bond Mortality," p. 930.

8 Altman, "Measuring Corporate High Yield Bonds," p. 915.

9 Ibid., p. 915 and Asquith et al., "Original Issue High Yield Bonds," p. 930.

10 The author thanks Edward Altman and Peter Temin for their helpful comments.

11

Setting the Record Straight on Junk Bonds: A Review of the Research on Default Rates and Returns

Edward I. Altman

The yields on various fixed-income securities are determined by the market's assessment of three major risks in holding a given issue: (1) its sensitivity to changes in interest rates, (2) its illiquidity, and (3) its probability of default. Such yields are set by the market to provide investors with realized total returns that increase with the level of each of these three risks.

The most risky debt securities, at least in terms of illiquidity and default risk, are of course the lower-rated corporate bonds – better known as "junk" bonds.[1] And, until quite recently, high yield junk bonds indeed provided the highest returns to investors among all fixed-income securities.[2] But, with recent increases in default rates and general illiquidity in the junk bond market, the expected hierarchy of returns has (at least temporarily) been overturned. Investment grade corporate bonds, it turns out, outperformed high yield bonds during the decade of the 1980s.[3]

The number and size of recent defaults has raised widespread doubt about the future of this US$200 billion market. In 1989, $8.1 billion of corporate debt issued by 37 companies either defaulted or was exchanged for lower yielding and lower priority securities. (This amounts to 4% of the dollar value of all outstanding high yield securities, almost double the average annual rate of default over the period 1978–88.) Another $4.8 billion has already defaulted in the first six months of 1990; and several billion dollars of additional securities are in a severely distressed state, with exchange offers pending.

The current problems in the junk bond market – or, more precisely, the problems of a number of specific junk bond issues – have resulted in record yield spreads over Treasuries in 1990. Investors are now requiring more than 700 basis points over Treasury notes with comparable maturities. As suggested above, these spreads reflect increased concerns about both the liquidity and default risk of a large number of issues.

As a consequence, the amount of new issuance in 1990 has dropped to a trickle (under $400 million in the first half of 1990). And publicly-financed, leveraged corporate restructurings – which account for roughly half of all the junk bonds currently outstanding – have essentially disappeared.

At the same time, however, there are signs of a recovery. Total realized junk bond returns for the second quarter of 1990 were just reported (as this article went to press) to have been a positive 4.3 percent. Such returns probably reflect in part the growing institutional interest in investing in distressed (or just depressed) securities resulting from highly leveraged transactions. It is also worth noting that a number of financial institutions, including commercial banks, are now creating their own junk bond underwriting and trading departments – presumably based on the conviction that the market's current problems are temporary. And although there have been large re-demptions by the public of open-end, high yield mutual funds, the number of these funds remains large – approximately 84 as of March 1990. Assets under management of these public mutual funds at this time were $24.2 billion, down from a high of $35 billion in June 1989.

Much ado about nothing?

Ever since the classic study of corporate bonds published by Braddock Hickman in 1958, economists have been measuring and reporting default rates.[4] Despite this considerable scholarly lineage, early in 1989 well-established academic methods for measuring default rates (including my own) suddenly became the subject of intense controversy in the financial press. Articles appeared announcing the results of suppos-edly "new" research that led to a much more negative view of junk bonds than that projected by existing work. There were suggestions not only that the "new" methods were more reliable as a gauge of future default rates (and the articles neglected to mention that I pioneered the research technique that was used by others to "discredit" my own past studies), but that use of the traditional default measurement methods was motivated by financial ties between academic researchers and Wall Street firms.

After several respected analysts submitted letters to the editors protesting the implication, I pondered the question: How is it that long accepted research methods – methods that have been subjected to a peer review process far more rigorous than the standards imposed by most newspaper editors – now find themselves challenged in a news column? And, equally disturbing, why are long established reputations of academic scholars for conducting disinterested research being impugned by journalists?

The answer is actually fairly obvious. Junk bonds, because of their role in the highly leveraged and often hostile buyouts of the 1980s, have aroused enormous opposition. Change breeds resistance and, thus, controversy. And, for the media, controversy is of course their daily bread. The unfortunate consequence of this spur toward controversy is that the work of some journalists serves only to add to the popular confusion.

One prominent journalistic line of attack has been to question the soundness of the securities used to finance the objectionable transactions. And the recent rise in default rates has been seized upon as the sign of rottenness at the core of the financial restructuring movement.

In this article I will attempt to shed some light on the lingering debate over the proper measurement of default rates – one that, although an all but dead issue in the academic and scholarly community, continues to be revived in the financial press. I will start by explaining the traditional method for measuring defaults of junk bond portfolios and then compare the results of using this method with the default rates produced by the more recent "mortality" or "aging" concepts that have sparked such controversy in the press. The bottom line here is that the new default studies, however much their differences with the old have been exaggerated by the press, are really quite consistent in their findings with existing work (including much of my own). And, finally, I will attempt to use the existing research on junk bonds as a basis for speculating about future default rates and investor returns in the high yield market.

Traditional Measures of Default Rates and Losses

Accurate measurement of default risk is, of course, critical to the task of evaluating both the required risk premiums on bonds of different credit quality and the returns on those securities. The traditional method of measuring annual default rates is to calculate the dollar amount of all issues defaulting in a given year and divide that number by the dollar value of all bonds outstanding as of some point during that year. For any given category of bonds, the annual default rates are then added up over some longer time horizon to provide an estimate of the average yearly rate of default.

Historical default rates

Table 11.1 shows the average annual default rate, calculated using the method described above, for below investment grade debt for the period 1970–89, as well as for selected intervals within that 20-year period. The average annual default rate for the period 1970–89 was 2.5%. For the shorter period from 1978 to 1989, the average rate was 2.1%. In the most recent five years (1985–9), however, the average default rate increased to 3.4%.

Note also that, although the yearly default rate is dollar-weighted, each year is usually given equal weighting in calculating the average. This procedure implies that investors make a constant annual investment in junk bonds. But, if the investor's portfolio is instead expected to grow proportionally with the size of the market, then a size-weighted average of the individual annual rates is a more appropriate measure.

Default losses

The more relevant default statistic for most investors is not the rate of default, but rather the amount lost from defaults. The use of default rates alone effectively assumes that the value of defaulting bonds turns out to be zero. In reality, however, defaulting debt has sold for slightly less than 40% of par, on average, at the end of the month in which the default occurs. This 40% figure can in turn be interpreted as the market's

Table 11.1 Historical default rate low rated, straight debt only
1978–89 (US$ millions)

Year	Par value outstanding	Par value default	Default rate
1989	$201,000	$8,110.30[1]	4.035%[1]
1988	159,223	3,944.20	2.477%
1987	136,952	7,485.50[2]	5.466%[2]
1986	92,985	3,155.76	3.394%
1985	59,078	922.10	1.679%
1984	41,700	344.16	0.825%
1983	28,233	301.08	1.066%
1982	18,536	577.34	3.115%
1981	17,362	27.00	0.156%
1980	15,126	224.11	1.482%
1979	10,675	20.00	0.187%
1978	9,401	118.90	1.265%
Total	$790,271	$25,300.45	

Arithmetic average
default rate
1970–89 = 2.485%
1978–9 = 2.096%
1983–9 = 2.706%

Weighted average
default rate
1970–89 = 3.179%
1983–9 = 3.201%
1983–9 = 3.383%

[1] Not including Allied and Federated Stores.
[2] $1.841 million without Texaco, Inc., Texaco Capital, and Texaco Capital N.V. The default rate without these is 1.345%.

best guess, based on extensive experience with past defaults, about the eventual recovery of value in defaulting securities.

In 1987, Scott Nammacher and I published a study that attempted to measure the amounts lost from defaults.[5] In making these calculations, we assumed investors had purchased each defaulting issue at par value and sold it at the end of the month in which the default occurred, losing one coupon payment as well as any capital depreciation.

The average annual default loss over the sample period 1978–89 was approximately 1.5% per year, as compared to a default rate of 2.1% over the same period. For the most recent five years (1985–9) – when the average default rate rose to 3.4% – the actual loss rate was only 1.86%. And in 1989, our estimate of the loss rate was about 2.75%, as compared to the earlier reported default rate of 4.0%.

As suggested above, the fact that loss rates have averaged only about 60 percent of default rates stems from the fact that defaulting bonds are typically expected by the market to maintain about 40 percent, on average, of their market value in default. For example, as shown in table 11.2, the expected average recovery rates on defaulting bonds in 1988 and 1989 were 43.6% and 38.3%.[6]

It is also important to mention here that bondholders lose not only from defaults, but also in other cases of financial distress that do not result in default but rather in exchange issues.[7] One recent study of just original issue high yield debt – one that takes account of bondholder losses from distress exchange issues as well as defaults – found average annual losses of 1.88% over the period 1978–87.[8] Another recent study of high yield bonds that considered distressed exchange issues reported that bondholder losses averaged 1.6% per year for the period 1977–88.[9]

Table 11.2 Default rates and losses, high yield debt market 1985–9

Year	Par amount of default (SMM)	Default rate (%)	Weighted price after default	Weighted coupon (%)	Weighted default loss (%)
1989	8110.3	4.03	38.3	13.40	2.76
1988	3944.2	2.48	43.6	11.91	1.54
1987	7485.7	5.47*	75.9	12.07	1.65*
1986	3115.8	3.39	34.5	10.61	2.40
1985	992.1	1.68	45.9	13.69	1.02
Average	4729.6	3.41*	47.6	12.34	1.87*

*Including Texaco. Without Texaco, default rate and default loss for 1987 would have been 1.34% and 0.89% respectively. The average default loss for the years 1985–9 would have been 2.58% and 1.72% respectively.

The Mortality, or Aging, Approach

Although the traditional method for assessing default rates and losses has considerable relevance for measuring bond performance, it also has potential biases. Because of such biases, the most recent default history – while immensely useful to portfolio managers and other investment officers in projecting near-term expected losses and setting aside adequate reserves to cover such losses – may turn out to have been an unreliable basis for assessing longer-term losses and returns.

Why is that so? First of all, as with all historical studies, it could be suggested that the future is not likely to repeat the past. Both the numerator (that is, the amount of annual defaults) and the denominator (the amount of bonds outstanding) in the default rate ratio will surely change in the future. And if the amount of "junk" bonds outstanding fails to increase as it has in the past (or even falls, as it has in the first half of 1990) while the amount of defaults continues to grow, then default rates and investor losses will rise above the historical levels reported using the traditional approach.

One could also argue, however, that the opposite trend will take place in the near future. That is, in 1992 and beyond, as new issues begin to rise from currently depressed levels and as the defaults arising from past excesses are purged from the market, default rates for 1990 and 1991 measured traditionally are likely to be overestimates owing to this same bias.

A related criticism of the traditional method for calculating default rates – and the one that was seized upon by the press – is its failure to consider the possibility that the likelihood of default rises with the age of the bonds. In putting all junk bonds outstanding at a given point in time in the same basket, the average annual method effectively assumes that the probability of default for a newly issued bond is identical with that of a bond that has been outstanding for, say, five years. But if it is true that the probability of default rises with age – especially in the case of junk bonds, which are often called after the early years – then default rates on currently outstanding issues will begin to rise. And if the rate of new issuance is expected to fall, then current annual default rates would provide a misleadingly low predictor of future expected default rates.

Briefly stated, the basic contention is this: because of the rapid growth of the junk bond market during the 1980s, use of the traditional methods for measuring defaults could have blinded investors to the reality that default rates were rising well above reported levels.

Two new studies – and much confusion

Two recent academic studies explored this possibility by attempting to determine whether the probability of default of individual high yield issues increases with time after issuance. The first of these was a working paper I produced at NYU in 1988 entitled, "Measuring Corporate Bond Mortality and Performance" (later published in the *Journal of Finance*).[10] The second – and the one whose circulation in early 1989 aroused such intense interest in the press – was a study by Paul Asquith, David Mullins, and Eric Wolff called "Original Issue High-Yield Bonds: Aging Analysis of Defaults, Exchanges, and Calls" (published in the same issue of the *Journal of Finance* and printed as chapter 8 below).[11]

Now, what exactly did these studies set out to do? And what did they find?

In my 1988 working paper, I examined all corporate bonds issued between 1971 and 1986 (later updated through 1989) in an attempt to determine whether the probability of default increases with age (a trait I referred to as bond "mortality"). In so doing, I classified all bonds into one of seven individual bond rating cohort groups, including the four investment grade as well as the three non-investment grade ratings. I then sought to estimate what proportion of the par value of bonds originally issued in a given year in a given rating were still outstanding after the elapse of different periods of time. The original group of bonds was therefore reduced by calls, sinking funds, and maturation, as well as by defaults and exchanges.

My findings are summarized in table 11.3, which shows marginal annual default rates calculated in the traditional manner as well as the cumulative rates of default over a horizon extending ten years from the date of issue.

Before elaborating on the results of my own study, let me mention the approach taken by Asquith et al. They too calculated cumulative default loss ratios (shown in table 11.4) by tracking the "aging process" in specific year cohort groups. Unlike my study, they focused exclusively on junk bonds without attempting to distinguish among the three different classes of junk bonds (although there is some data presented by individual ratings within the junk bond segment).

Comparison of the results

As compared in table 11.5, the results of the two studies are quite similar. For example, in calculating the default rates five years after issuance of all B-rated bonds issued in the years 1977–84, I found the cumulative mortality rate for this dominant

Table 11.3   Adjusted* mortality rates by original S&P bond rating covering defaults and issues from 1971–88

Original rating		*Years after issuance*									
		1	2	3	4	5	6	7	8	9	10
AAA	Yearly	0.00%	0.00%	0.00%	0.00%	0.00%	0.15%	0.05%	0.00%	0.00%	0.00%
	Cum.	0.00%	0.00%	0.00%	0.00%	0.00%	0.15%	0.21%	0.21%	0.21%	0.21%
AA	Yearly	0.00%	0.00%	1.39%	0.33%	0.20%	0.00%	0.27%	0.00%	0.11%	0.13%
	Cum.	0.00%	0.00%	1.39%	1.72%	1.92%	1.92%	2.18%	2.18%	2.29%	2.42%
A	Yearly	0.00%	0.39%	0.32%	0.00%	0.00%	0.11%	0.11%	0.07%	0.13%	0.00%
	Cum.	0.00%	0.39%	0.71%	0.71%	0.71%	0.82%	0.93%	1.00%	1.13%	1.13%
BBB	Yearly	0.03%	0.20%	0.12%	0.26%	0.39%	0.00%	0.14%	0.00%	0.21%	0.80%
	Cum.	0.30%	0.23%	0.35%	0.61%	1.00%	1.00%	1.14%	1.14%	1.34%	2.13%
BB	Yearly	1.40%	0.65%	2.73%	3.70%	3.59%	3.86%	6.30%	3.31%	6.84%	3.70%
	Cum.	1.40%	2.04%	4.72%	8.24%	11.54%	14.95%	20.31%	22.95%	28.22%	30.88%
CCC	Yearly	1.97%	1.88%	4.37%	16.35%						
	Cum.	1.97%	3.81%	8.01%	23.05%						

* Adjusted for changes in population (cohort groups) due to defaults, call, and sinking fund redemption.

Table 11.4   Aged defaults for high yield bonds grouped by year of issue

Issue year	1	2	3	4	5	6	7	8	9	10	11	12	Total
Panel A: % of par amount in nth year after issue													
1977	0.00	0.00	0.00	0.00	0.00	0.00	0.00	7.71	3.63	19.27	3.30	0.01[1]	33.92
1978	0.00	8.32	0.00	1.39	0.00	7.91	4.85	3.12	5.55	1.39	1.73[1]	—	34.26
1979	0.00	0.00	5.54	1.11	2.38	6.73	1.98	0.00	5.78	1.119[1]	—	—	24.70
1980	0.00	0.57	2.45	0.00	0.00	13.90	6.30	1.88	2.45[1]	—	—	—	27.56
1981	0.00	6.05	0.00	8.06	6.85	0.00	0.00	0.00[1]	—	—	—	—	20.97
1982	1.00	2.41	1.61	11.49	0.00	9.44	0.00[1]	—	—	—	—	—	25.94
1983	0.00	0.00	6.08	7.83	4.80	0.50[1]	—	—	—	—	—	—	19.21
1984	2.29	1.99	2.03	3.06	0.00[1]	—	—	—	—	—	—	—	9.38
1985	0.00	0.80	2.28	0.45[1]	—	—	—	—	—	—	—	—	3.53
1986	2.73	3.84	1.57[1]	—	—	—	—	—	—	—	—	—	8.14

[1] May be incomplete, i.e. entire sample may not have been outstanding for *x* years.
Source: P. Asquith, D. Mullin, and E. Wolff. "Original Issue High Yield Bonds: Aging Analysis of Defaults, Exchanges, and Calls," *Journal of Finance* (June 1989)

Table 11.5 Comparative junk bond mortality/aged default statistics: four recent studies

Rating	Mortality (Altman) 1971–88[1]	Aging (Asquith et al.) 1977–88	Original issuer (Moody's) 1970–88
5-year cumulative default rate			
BA/BB	1.9%	NA	8.3%
B/B	11.5%	NA	22.3%
Caa/CCC	24.6%	NA	47.3%
Total (wgt. avg.)	8.1%	12.2[2]	11.8%
10-year cumulative default rate			
Ba/BB	10.7%	NA	14.2%
B/B	30.9%	NA	29.3
Caa/CCC	NA	NA	51.3%
Total (wgt. avg.)	NA	29.3%[2]	17.4%

[1] 1971–89 mortality results are as follows:

5-Year	Ba/BB	5.2	10-Year	Ba/BB	15.0
	B/B	11.6		B/B	32.9
	Caa/CCC	24.6		Caa/CCC	NA

[2] Based on combined 1977–9 issuance.

junk bond category to have been 11.5% (although the weighted average result was a somewhat lower 8.1 percent).[12] By comparison, the aging approach of Asquith et al. produced a 5-year cumulative default rate of 12.2% when averaging across all three classes of junk bonds. The 10-year cumulative default rates reported by the two studies are also very similar: whereas Asquith et al. reported that 29.3% of all junk bonds issued in the three years 1977–9 had either defaulted or been exchanged ten years after issuance, I found a cumulative mortality rate of 30.9% for just the B-rated bonds issued in the same period. Asquith et al. also found that roughly a third of the bonds had been called.

Also summarized in table 11.5 are the results of one other recent study of junk bond mortality, by Scott Douglass and Douglas Lucas of Moody's (1989).[13] The Moody's study, which focused on default rates among issuers rather than issues, came up with results pretty much consistent with the others. For example, although Moody's does find somewhat higher 5-year cumulative default rates for single B and double B issuers, the total weighted average rate of 11.8% is quite comparable – as is the 29% 10-year cumulative default rates for single B issuers.

The meaning of the new results

Now, given this reasonable amount of scholarly agreement about the historical cumulative default rates on junk bonds, what do these numbers really have to tell us about future expected default rates?

Asquith et al. interpret their findings as "clear evidence" that the probability of junk bond defaults increases with the age of the bonds (while also asserting that their aging technique produces higher default rates than those found in any prior study). And, as mentioned earlier, to the extent this "aging" interpretation is correct, then a slowdown in the rate of new issuance must lead inevitably to a sharp rise in annual default rates.

My interpretation of the new evidence, however, is considerably more cautious. As I warned readers in my initial working paper, the "modern" junk bond market is still quite new, having gotten its real start only as recently as 1977. For this reason, the mortality results for the relatively longer (say, 7–10 year) horizons are based on at most three or four years of original issuance data. (For example, 10-year mortality rates could be calculated only for the group of high yield bonds issued in 1977 and 1978, 9-year mortality rates only for bonds issued in 1977–9, and so forth.) And making generalizations from a sample this small is, needless to say, a questionable research practice.

Finally, one cannot deny that, as you increase the horizon on any investment in risky bonds, the cumulative default rate will rise over time. But that is not the same thing as saying that a six-year bond with a BB rating has a higher probability of default in the next four years than a younger bond in the same risk category.

Having said this, though, I am partly sympathetic to the "intuition" behind an aging process for corporate bonds. That argument, as mentioned earlier, holds that because the probability of call increases with a bond's age, and because credit-worthy companies are more likely to call than their weaker counterparts, then the remaining group of bonds will have a greater probability of future default than the original population. The same is true, by the way, for firms that directly repurchase their debt in the open market when the bonds' prices become attractive.

This intuition, however, has been neither confirmed nor even tested by empirical research. Moreover, the argument has been vigorously disputed by Moody's and S&P, whose livelihoods come from assigning bonds to their proper risk categories. The representatives of such agencies, in fact, argue that the age of a bond has no systematic effect on its credit-worthiness provided the bond's current rating is the same as its initial rating, and provided the current rating remains an unbiased estimate of the future rating – that is, neither too high nor too low on average. For example, a BB bond at issuance should have the same probability of default in years one and two as a five-year-old BB bond in years six and seven. Only if BB bonds in the aggregate have a higher probability of slipping to a lower rating after, say, five years than rising to a higher rating will the expected default rate rise systematically over time.

As I stated earlier, however – and let me repeat it again – such a propensity for bond ratings to drift lower has neither been tested nor demonstrated by academic research.[14] The recent study by Moody's finds, moreover, that the default rate on issues of a given rating actually decreases over time.

Furthermore, when I look more closely at the year-to-year default rates reported in Asquith et al., I am hard-pressed to discern a clear pattern of aging. For example, the first seven years of the 1977 cohort group all had 0.00% default rates. And, 1978's cohort had an 8.32% second year rate that proved to be higher than the default rate in any subsequent year. 1979's cohort had a relatively high third year rate – one which was about equal to the default rates in years 6 and 9.

Evidence of an aging pattern is even less convincing in my own mortality results. As shown in table 11.3, the yearly (marginal) mortality rates for single Bs are relatively constant at around 2–3% from the third to the 10th year after issuance (except for higher rates in the 7th and 9th years). BB default rates are fairly constant for the 2nd through 5th years and then increase for the 6th and 7th years; however, they fall back thereafter and then finally rise again in the 10th year. These results, however, are fairly sensitive to some large defaults by individual issuers.[15]

To be sure, the results of Asquith et al. do imply that you find a clearer aging pattern when you average all the first years, all the second years, and so forth. But even here, the results are by no means compelling. The average second- and third-year default rates, for example, are not appreciably lower than default rates in years 5, 7, and 8. And all of these years show annual rates of default falling within the narrow range between 2.2% and 2.5%.

Furthermore, as pointed out by Marshall Blume and Donald Keim in their recent study of junk bonds, none of the new "mortality" studies cited above attempts to account for the possibility that default rates depend significantly on prevailing economic conditions.[16] According to Blume and Keim, a proper analysis of default rates – one that would be useful for projecting long-run expected default rates on junk bonds – must control for general economic effects. And, in fact, in their own study of the same years covered by Asquith et al., Blume and Keim find no evidence of an aging effect when default rates are adjusted for overall economic conditions.

In summary, then, while there does appear to be some evidence of an aging effect, it is not very consistent across or within rating classes. Also, although there may be some bias inherent in the traditional approach to default measurement, the bias is probably not sufficient to undermine its use, at least as a short-term forecaster of default rates. And, finally, although calls of the most creditworthy junk issues may reduce the overall credit quality of the outstanding portfolio, the premiums paid by corporations to investors for that call option, in the form of higher yields when first issued, should compensate investors for granting that option. Moreover, the fact that companies typically pay premiums to retire the bonds also compensates investors for calls.

Measuring the Returns

Up to now, we have considered only the risk dimension of investing in junk bonds (and, in fact, we have considered only one aspect of total risk – default risk – while ignoring other significant risks such as illiquidity and the sensitivity of junk bonds to general economic conditions). To complete the analysis, we must use our measures of default losses to estimate the total returns to junk bond investors. Such returns can then be weighed against the risks – default and otherwise – to assess the adequacy of such returns within the general risk–return hierarchy of corporate securities.

Among the various published studies of default risk, some have estimated net returns to junk bonds using the traditional approach. I have used a mortality approach, and still others have used an aging approach like the one designed by Asquith et al. (although the latter study itself does not measure returns). All such studies conclude that, after adjusting for default risk, the returns to junk bonds have exceeded the returns to long-term Treasury Bonds.[17]

Simulated returns

The traditional approach   In some of my own work that uses estimates of annual default losses based on the traditional measurement approach, I found that the compounded average return on junk bonds over the period 1978–89 exceeded the average return on long-term Treasuries by roughly 1% (as reported in table 11.6). Given an average promised yield spread over the same period of slightly over 400 basis points (4.16%) and average annual default losses of 1.5 percent, one might have initially expected junk bonds to have earned an actual average spread over Treasuries of almost 250 basis points. (And, indeed, measured through 1988, the actual average spread was 241 basis points.)

It is important to recognize, however, that the actual return spreads reported in table 11.6 reflect not only differences between promised yields and actual percentage default losses, but also significant differences in the duration of junk bonds and Treasuries, as well as differences in market liquidity. For example, in the years 1984–6 – a period of falling interest rates – long-term Treasuries significantly outperformed junk bonds in large part because of their longer durations, and also because a proportion of junk bonds were called by companies that wanted to reduce their borrowing costs. And when such bonds are called, investors are forced to reinvest at lower rates.

Also, because the sample of junk bond returns are available over a relatively short period of time (12 years is not a large sample by any statistician's measure), an

Table 11.6   Annual returns, yields, and spreads on long-term (LT) government and high yield (HY) bonds

Year	Return (%)			Promised yield (%)[3]		
	HY[1]	LT Govt[2]	Spread	HY	LT Govt	Spread
1989	1.62	15.99	(14.37)	15.41	7.93	7.48
1988	13.47	9.20	4.27	13.95	7.93	7.48
1987	4.67	(2.67)	7.34	12.66	8.75	3.91
1986	16.09	24.08	(7.99)	14.45	9.55	4.90
1985	22.51	31.54	(9.03)	15.40	11.65	3.75
1984	8.50	14.82	(6.82)	14.97	11.87	3.10
1983	21.80	2.23	19.57	15.74	10.70	5.04
1982	32.45	42.08	(9.63)	17.84	13.86	3.98
1981	7.56	0.48	7.08	15.97	12.08	3.89
1980	(1.00)	(2.96)	1.96	13.46	10.23	3.23
1979	3.69	(0.86)	4.55	12.07	9.13	2.94
1978	7.57	(1.11)	8.68	10.92	8.11	2.81
Arith. avg.: 1978–89	11.58	11.07	0.51	14.40	10.24	4.16
Comp. avg.: 1978–89	11.19	10.20	0.99			

[1] E. Altman's compilation of composite for 1978–84 generated from over 440 high yield issues. Composite of several indices for 1985–9.
[2] Shearson Lehman Long-Term Government Index and Composite of several indices in 1989.
[3] Promised yield as of beginning of year. It represents the internal rate of return based on the security's current price and scheduled payments of interest and principal.

extended period of falling interest rates or an unusually severe liquidity crisis could lead to a significant downward bias on the returns.

The mortality approach   The mortality rate concept is more useful in measuring returns (and in fact is indispensable in capturing any "aging" effect that might exist). Instead of calculating annual returns and then averaging them – as if investors took out their money at the end of every year and then reinvested at the beginning of the next – the mortality approach assumes that investors buy and hold over the entire time horizon measured. Unlike the traditional approach, it also assumes that investors reinvest all cash flows from coupons, calls, maturities, and default recoveries in the same risk class of bonds.

As shown in table 11.7, which measures return spreads of corporate bonds over Treasuries through 1988, all rating classes of corporate bonds earned a positive spread over long-term Treasuries (which in turn produced an average yield of 8.75%). The expected risk–return hierarchy, although strongly in evidence among investment grade issues, does not hold up among non-investment grade bonds. As you go beyond a three-year holding period after issuance, the returns from B-rated and CCC-rated bonds fall below those of BB-rated bonds. In the 9th and 10th years, the high mortality rates of B-rated bonds drive their total returns below those of BBB-rated issues (although the power of compound interest still allows the Bs to outperform all other investment grade classes). And, if you extend the calculations to include returns

Table 11.7 Return spreads earned by corporate bonds over Treasury bonds*

Years after issuance	Bond rating at issuance						
	AAA	AA	A	BBB	BB	B	CCC
1	45	76	105	171	313	370	572
2	100	169	222	367	666	849	1421
3	165	254	369	614	1097	1225	2312
4	246	373	558	901	1653	1583	1899
5	343	529	786	1229	2289	2077	3083
6	447	725	1051	1671	2714	2589	N/A
7	578	924	1370	2190	3164	2838	N/A
8	747	1215	1775	2856	4316	3515	N/A
9	954	1554	2259	3641	5639	3421	N/A
10	1201	1949	2853	4493	6233	4215	N/A

* Measured in basis points compounded over time.

Table 11.8 Implied annualized excess return spread over Treasury bonds

	Tenth Year	Implied excess annual return spread over the T-bond initial rate
AAA	1201 b.p.[1]	55 b.p.[1]
AA	1949	88
A	2853	127
BBB	4493	195
BB	6233	263
B	4215	184

[1] b.p. equals basis points.
Source: Table based on an initial T-Bond rate of 8.75%

through 1989 (table 11.7 runs only through 1988), the BBB-rated bonds outperform all other corporate bonds over a 10-year period.

These results, it should be pointed out, do not include the effects of losses on distressed exchange issues. But because a large percentage (roughly 2/3) of such issues eventually default, the failure to account for such losses should not affect our results materially.

As summarized in table 11.8, the mortality-based results imply annualized compound rates of return over the average 8.75% long-term Treasury return that range from 55 basis points per year for AAA debt issues to 263 basis points per year for the BB category. These estimates are based on the implied rate of return per year on the ten-year spreads in table 11.7.[18]

The Blume and Keim study: measuring actual returns

One could object, as have Asquith et al., that all of the above studies rely on the use of simulated rather than actual junk bond prices in calculating junk bond returns. For example, the mortality-rate-based returns listed in table 11.7 are not based on actual year-end prices, but instead assume the perspective of an investor who buys and holds until maturity. As such, this analysis effectively ignores price fluctuations caused by changes in interest rates or market conditions and assumes that the only risk attending junk bonds is default risk.

The 1989 study by Blume and Keim, cited earlier, attempted to overcome these limitations by gathering actual, month-end prices over a ten-year period for all junk bonds issued in 1977 and 1978 (using Asquith et al.'s own sample). Much like the results of my study reported in table 11.7, Blume and Keim concluded that investors in all high yield bonds issued in 1977–8 outperformed intermediate-term Treasuries (with an average return of 7.6%) by almost one percent per year over the period 1977–88. The 8.51% actual yield earned by the 1977–8 group of bonds was about 2.6% less than the promised yield.

Moreover, when Blume and Keim made the assumption that all cash distributions to investors were reinvested in their own junk bond index, the total return rose to 10.37% (and was almost the same if reinvested in either high grade corporates or long-term Treasury bonds). Such returns, moreover, are adjusted for calls and distressed exchange issues.[19]

Summing up the past: positive spreads

Throughout much of the 1980s, original-issue high yield bonds were marketed to investors as promising "abnormal" returns – that is, returns that offered more in additional return than the higher default risk of the securities would justify. Today, of course, given the current depressed state of the junk bond market, the popular inclination is to denounce junk bonds as providing inadequate returns. The fact that the compounded return on Treasuries was actually greater than that of junk bonds over the period 1982–9 – and that BBBs outperformed B-rated securities over the 1980s – would seem to provide strong evidence in support of this argument.

But what does the current research really have to say to the critics and proponents of junk bonds? While just about every published analysis reports positive junk bond return spreads over Treasuries over long periods of time – even after adjusting for default risk – there is scant evidence today of "abnormal" returns. Those differences in returns that cannot be explained as a "default risk premium" can be reasonably accounted for as reflecting a number of other factors, such as differences in liquidity. Moreover, the equity-like features of junk bonds also make direct comparison of their returns (and the variances of those returns) with Treasuries and high grade corporates difficult.

To offer a useful guide to the future, research on junk bonds will require many more years of data than are now currently available. When we do reach the point where we have many years of experience, we will be able to say much more with far greater confidence about the expected returns from holding junk bonds – and about the various components, or risk "premiums," that investors require as a group for bearing the different risks associated with holding such bonds.[20]

The Future of Junk Bonds

Projecting the future

There has been only one study that attempts to project future default losses and rates of return on junk bonds. Published in 1989 by three researchers at DRI/McGraw-Hill, this study attempted to estimate the expected default frequency under four different economic scenarios of all 573 high-yield bond issuers with debt outstanding as of the end of 1988 (and for which balance sheet and income statement data was available from the Compustat data base).[21]

The economic simulations reflect four different degrees of general economic slow-down, including: (1) a "soft landing" with no recession but a moderate increase in prices; (2) a "mild recession" of two quarters in late 1989; (3) a "big recession" in 1990 with a peak-to-trough decline in real GNP of 3% but a decline in interest rates; and (4) an "inflationary recession" similar to the one we experienced in 1981–2.

Using projections of individual industry performance in each of these four scenarios as a basis for estimating specific company cash flows, the DRI researchers then calculated for each firm a measure of default risk – in this case, current assets less changes in cash flow – for each quarter over the period 1989–93. When this measure (which they call "available liquidity") is negative for four consecutive quarters, the company is judged to have defaulted. To calculate default rates for the entire sample of issuers, the DRI group then added up the defaulted issuers' outstanding long-term debt and divided by the total long-term outstandings of the entire 573 firms; it also divided the number of defaults by the total number of companies.

Returns on junk bond portfolios were projected by assuming that junk bonds yield a constant 350 basis point spread over 10-year US Treasury bonds and that defaulted bonds are sold at 40 cents on the dollar in the same quarter as the default. Any cash distributions (or noncash increases or decreases in the value of the portfolio) are assumed to be reinvested (or disinvested) in the same portfolio. The study also assumes that none of the debt outstanding at the beginning of the five-year period is redeemed.

Results

The default rates for the first three economic scenarios are remarkably similar, with projections of the cumulative five-year default running about 13% in each case. In terms of the number of companies, the estimates were that 67, 69, and 69 of the 573 firms would default in scenarios 1, 2, and 3 respectively. (These findings are quite similar to the historical findings reported in table 11.6 earlier.) The worst-case, inflationary-recession scenario results in a projected five-year cumulative default rate of about 19% (or about 4% per year in dollar terms), with about 81 companies defaulting.

Under all but the last scenario, moreover, high yield "junk" bonds outperform all other asset classes over the five year horizon, including long- and short-term governments, high grade corporate bonds, mortgages, domestic CDs and domestic equities.

And even in the worst-case condition, junk bonds outperform all asset classes other than short-term money market assets.

In short, the DRI study concludes that the projected risks associated with high yield bonds are roughly comparable to those experienced in the past 10 years, and that a well diversified portfolio of such bonds can be expected, even in a recessionary environment, to produce higher returns than most other asset classes.

There are, to be sure, a number of possible objections to the methods of the DRI study. The most potentially damaging is that the researchers do not attempt to simulate the kind of "contagion" effect, or liquidity crisis, that a series of defaults could have – and now appear to be having – on the rest of the market. On the other hand, by using a rather arbitrary "liquidity" measure as an indicator of default, the DRI study may also be underestimating the resilience of junk bonds. Use of such a measure effectively ignores the ability of companies to sell assets or raise new capital to meet its obligations. It thereby assumes bankers and other creditors also rely on liquidity measures in setting their credit standards.[22]

A different kind of simulation

A different approach is to simulate the theoretical "break-even" default rate on junk bonds that would result in a net return equal to an investment in risk-free government bonds. For example, a portfolio of 12% coupon junk bonds that experiences a default rate of 6.0% in a 12-month period and a consequent loss rate of 3.96% (assuming a 40% recovery rate) will "break even" when the promised yield spread between junk bonds and T-Bonds is 4.2%. The investor earns the 4.2% spread on the 94% of the portfolio that does not default which offsets the 3.96% default loss.

Presented in table 11.9 are various required yield spreads that result in break-even rates of return performance for a number of different default rate and recovery rate

Table 11.9 Break-even conditions for total returns on junk bonds vs. US Treasuries*

Default rate (%)	Default loss				Required yield spreads %			
	Recovery rates				Recovery rates			
	20%	30%	40%	50%	20%	30%	40%	50%
2.0	1.72	1.52	1.32	1.12	1.8	1.6	1.4	1.1
3.0	2.58	2.28	1.98	1.78	2.7	2.4	2.0	1.8
4.0	3.44	3.04	2.64	2.24	3.6	3.2	2.8	2.3
5.0	4.30	3.80	3.30	2.80	4.5	4.0	3.5	3.0
6.0	5.16	4.56	3.96	3.36	5.5	4.9	4.2	3.6
7.0	6.02	5.32	4.62	3.92	6.5	5.7	5.0	4.2
8.0	6.88	6.08	5.28	4.48	7.5	6.6	5.7	4.9
9.0	7.74	6.84	5.94	5.04	8.5	7.5	6.5	5.5
10.0	8.60	7.60	6.60	5.60	9.6	8.4	7.3	6.2
15.0	12.90	11.40	9.90	8.40	15.2	13.4	11.6	9.9

* Assuming a 12% junk bond coupon and various default recovery rates.

scenarios. (These rates, it should be kept in mind, are not necessarily acceptable or "economic" rates of return, since they offer investors no compensation over Treasury yields for bearing any risks other than that of default.) Even if the default rate exceeds the break-even yield spread amount, causing returns to be below those on risk-free opportunities, the absolute return to junk bond holders will still be positive in most cases. For example, in the event of a very large 10% default rate (which translates into $20 billion of par value defaults in 1989 numbers), a 5% promised yield spread would result in a return spread of −1.60%, but still a positive return of 5.40% in that year.

The results in table 11.9 also allow recovery rates to vary between 20%–50% to allow for the possibility, predicted by some market observers, that historical recovery rates will decrease in the future as the market evolves and default rates increase. And, indeed, we find that the recovery rate on the most junior straight debt defaulting in 1989 was only about 23 percent.

Incorporating other sources of risk   The results presented in table 11.9 are based on simple subtractions of expected default losses from yield spreads and thus reflect no attempt to incorporate the effect of other influences on returns such as interest rate changes or liquidity problems. To illustrate, once again, how such other factors can affect returns, consider that in 1988 the yield spread was 4.95% at the beginning of the year and the default losses turned out to be 1.65%. The return spread was not 3.30% (4.95%–1.65%), but rather 4.30% (see table 11.6) – mainly because rising rates had a disproportionately negative effect on Treasury prices. In 1986, by contrast, despite a promised yield spread of 4.90% and a 2.4% default loss rate, governments ended up outperforming junk bonds by a whopping 80% as interest rates fell dramatically and long term Governments reacted more positively than junk bonds.

In 1989, the main causes of the relatively poor junk bond performance have been market liquidity problems and the contagion effect of a large absolute amount of defaults (most notably, the Campeau experience) on the prices of other junk bond prices. This effect was further exacerbated by the dramatic flight to quality in reaction to the stock market decline of October 13, 1989.

The present   As of May 1990, the yield spread between junk bonds and Treasuries of comparable duration had risen to the range of 700 to 800 basis points, depending on what index you use.[23] As shown in table 11.9, if one assumes a 30% recovery after default, a default rate of about 9.0% would provide investors with a realized return equal to that of Treasuries (again, excluding the effect of interest rate changes and further liquidity problems). To the extent investors believe that such a high default rate (which would amount to over $18 billion in defaults) is unlikely, then junk bonds priced at current yields will appear to offer attractive investment opportunities.

If an additional risk premium of 1–2% is required by investors to compensate them for the risk of illiquidity, then a 7–8% default rate expectation is implied in today's yield spreads. And, if junk bond investors require an even greater yield spread – that is, greater than the premiums for bearing default and liquidity risks – then the implied default rate is probably below 7%. The junk bond market's vulnerability in a recessionary period is also of concern to many investors and to them the current yield spread may seem reasonable. Finally, the historic 40% recovery rate may not be achieved in the future. With the larger presence of lower-priority, subordinated securities, the senior debt holders, primarily commercial banks, should become more successful in upholding their priority status over subordinated issues in cases of either formal bankruptcy or private reorganization.

And, in fact, recovery rates on defaulted debt, as measured by the price just after default, have declined in recent years. As shown in table 11.10, secured debtholders have received 66% of par value, on average, after default; the senior debt has received 55%; and both the senior subordinated and the subordinated debt have averaged just 32% of par.[24] The relatively low recoveries in 1989 reflect higher debt levels relative to asset values and the expectation of relatively lower values following reorganizations.

Concluding Remarks

In this article I have tried to summarize and integrate the findings of a number of different studies on the measurement of junk bond default rates, default losses, and returns to investors. The results of these studies are important to investors, to under-writers, and, thus ultimately, to potential issuers that contemplate using this form of financing to grow or restructure their operations. The actual and anticipated default experience of corporate bonds will affect the cost of debt capital of new borrowers and their ability to take on new investment projects. Not only will financing rates be affected by changes in risk perceptions, but the number of leveraged restructurings will no doubt depend in large part on the resulting cost of finance. In this sense, expected default rates and the yields required by investors would appear to be a key to this market's future.

The future of the junk bond market is still uncertain. The system needs to be "cleansed" of the excesses of the past few years, especially with respect to highly leveraged restructurings and failed innovations such as deferred interest securities (DIBs and PIKs) and reset provisions. The market has shown signs of recovery in the

Table 11.10   Recovery rates* on defaulted debt by seniority (1985−9)

Year	Secured	Senior	Sen.subordin.	Subordin.
1989	$82.69 (9)	$53.70 (16)	$21.53 (18)	$24.56 (29)
1988	67.96 (13)	41.59 (20)	29.23 (11)	36.42 (18)
1987	12.00 (1)	70.52** (29)	51.22 (9)	40.54 (7)
1986	48.32 (7)	40.84 (7)	31.53 (8)	30.95 (33)
1985	74.25 (2)	34.81 (2)	36.18 (7)	41.45 (13)
Arith Avg.	66.451 (32)	55.292** (74)	31.614 (53)	32.118 (100)
Std. Dev.	18.722	26.457	19.87	15.423

* Price per $100 of par value at end of default month.
** Without Texaco, 1987 Recov. = $29.77/Arith. avg. sen. recov. = $43.11/Std. dev. of sen. recov. =
   20.781 (Compilation by E. Altman & D. Chin, New York University.)
( ) = Number of issues

second quarter of 1990, but liquidity problems are still manifest. The next wave of junk bond issues – and there will almost certainly be one (although whether the issues will be public or privately placed is not at all clear) – will reflect more conservative capital structures and financing strategies. Prices of leveraged transactions will come down, and the proportion of equity underlying such deals will rise.

Notes

1 Junk bonds are issued by three types of issuers. About 25 percent of the market is comprised of "fallen angels" – securities originally issued as investment grade bonds that have seen their credit profile deteriorate and their bond ratings reduced to categories below BBB (or Baa). Corporate bonds originally issued with below investment grade ratings for "normal business purposes" make up about another 25 percent of the market. The remaining 50 percent – and the principal cause of the fierce controversy over junk bonds – consist of high yield (mainly B-rated) bonds issued to finance large corporate restructurings, particularly in the period 1986–9.

2 This has been true whether one measures returns using changes in portfolio indexes or the performance of fixed income mutual funds.

3 For a more complete discussion of this change in hierarchy of returns and the consequent yield spreads available in the market in the first half of 1990, see my recent article. "How 1989 Changed the Hierarchy of Fixed Income Security Performance." *Financial Analysts Journal* (May–June 1990).

4 Braddock Hickman. *Corporate Bond Quality and Investor Experience* (Princeton University Press and the National Bureau of Economic Research, 1958).

5 Edward Altman and Scott A. Nammacher. *Investing In Junk Bonds: Inside the High Yield Debt Market* (John Wiley, NY, 1987).

6 This average recovery rate of about 40% is amazingly similar to those reported for 1900–43 defaults by Braddock Hickman in his classic study (see note 4).

7 Over the period 1900–43, for example, 105 (or almost 20%) of 549 reported "defaults" never experienced a legal default because the contracts were modified before failure took place. See Irwin T. Vanderhoof, F. Albert, A. Tenenbein, and R. Verni, "The Risk of Asset Default," Report of the Society of Actuaries, C1 Task Force of the Committee on Valuation and Related Areas (1989).

8 See Martin Fridson, Fritz Wahl, and Stephen Jones. "High Yield Performance," Morgan Stanley (1988).

9 See Gregory Hradsky and Robert Long, "High Yield Default Losses and the Return Performance of Bankrupt Debt," *Financial Analysts Journal* (July–August 1989), pp. 38–49.

10 Edward I. Altman, "Measuring Corporate Bond Mortality and Performance", Working Papers, New York University, (February and June 1988) and published in the *Journal of Finance* 44. no. 4 (September 1989).

11 Paul Asquith, David Mullins, and Eric Wolff, "Original Issue High-Yield Bonds: Aging Analysis of Defaults, Exchanges, and Calls," *Journal of Finance* 44, no. 4 (September 1989).

12 One could object to my use of just single-B issues by arguing that they have not always dominated the junk bond market as they clearly do today. The weighted average results shown in table 11.5, however, are clearly less meaningful for 10 years since original issue

triple-C's have not really been in existence for such a long period. For five years, the mortality rates for all junk bonds falls somewhat to 8.1% due to the relatively low double-B results.

13 See Scott Douglass and Douglas Lucas, "Historical Default Rates of Corporate Bond Issuers 1970–88," Moody's *Structured Finance* (July 1989).

14 In fact, I am presently involved in research to determine the extent of any such drift in bond ratings over time.

15 In the case of investment grade defaults, moreover, there appears to be even less of an aging effect, at least up to 10 years after issuance.

16 See Marshall E. Blume and Donald B. Keim. "Realized Returns and Defaults on Low-Grade Bonds: The Cohorts of 1977 and 1978," University of Pennsylvania working paper (1989). See also by the same authors. "Risk and Return Characteristics of Lower Grade Bonds." *Financial Analysts Journal* (July–August 1987), pp. 26–33.

17 This is consistent with Hickman (1958) and with T. R. Atkinson, "Trends in Corporate Bond Quality," National Bureau of Economic Research, NY (1967).

18 In a study forthcoming in the *Journal of Portfolio Management*, Laurie Goodman simulates both Asquith et al.'s and my own cohort groups by assuming various call rates, interest rate spreads, and recovery rates on defaults. She concludes that the mortality/aging studies are quite similar in terms of the simulated returns and that the return spreads of junk bonds are uniformly positive.

19 Asquith et al. estimate that about one-third of the 1977–8 cohorts had defaulted or been exchanged and that another one-third had been called.

20 For two thoughtful commentaries that add to our understanding of the similarities and differences of the aging/mortality results, see Duen-Li Kao, "The Default Risks of US High Yield Bonds." *Journal of Cash Management* (July/August 1989), p. 56; and Harry S. Marmer, "Junk Bonds, When Fact and Opinion Collide," *Risk* (September 1989), pp. 66–7.

21 David Wyss, Christopher Probyn and Robert de Angelis, "The Impact of Recession on High Yield Bonds," DRI/McGraw Hill, Washington (July 1989).

22 Other observers have estimated the future based on a qualitative "feel" for the market-place after observation of past default rates. Examples are 1989 reports by S&P and Moody's that postulate possible default rates as high as 10 to 15%.

23 Indeed, many analysts feel that the junk bond market today consists of three different groupings of issuers – the better quality issues, with lower yield spreads, the so-called average junk bond issues, and extremely high-risk issues selling at 1,000 basis points or more above T-bonds.

24 These are aggregate totals, with most defaults only involving one or two tranches of debt. For those companies with a complex capital structure involving several layers of debt priorities, the expected higher recovery rate for the more senior issues are manifest.

12

Proxy Contests and the Governance of Publicly Held Corporations

Harry DeAngelo and Linda DeAngelo

1 Introduction

The proxy contest is widely viewed as the ultimate vehicle enabling stockholders of publicly held corporations to discipline incumbent managers who fail to maximize firm value [Manne (1965), Alchian and Demsetz (1972)]. Despite its theoretical importance as a managerial disciplinary mechanism, however, we know little about whether or how proxy contests achieve this objective. For example, there is little systematic evidence explaining why dissident stockholders wage proxy contests rather than seek control through other methods. Similarly, with the exception of DeAngelo (1988), there has been little analysis of the process through which dissidents convince voting stockholders that the incumbents are indeed inefficient managers. Finally, while it is known that dissidents usually do not obtain majority control through a proxy contest [Dodd and Warner (1983)], the effect of dissident activity on the eventual ownership and management of target firms remains an unexplored empirical issue.

This paper provides evidence on these and related issues. Our empirical analysis yields several broad generalizations about the conduct and consequences of proxy contests. First, dissident stockholders typically campaign for votes by painting a simple "broad brush" picture of managerial inefficiency, using a variety of easy-to-convey criticisms such as poor operating profits or an allegedly inadequate dividend payout. Second, dissidents often possess industry, firm-specific, or take-over-related expertise that may help convince public stockholders of dissidents' ability to manage the firm or to effect beneficial changes in corporate policy. Third, resource limitations of the dissident group appear to encourage the choice of proxy contest as a takeover vehicle, since most dissident groups consist of individuals or private firms, with only one-fifth including participation by a publicly traded corporation.

Typically, whether or not the dissidents win the contested board election, members of the top management team lose their positions, either through the proxy contest itself or through other means shortly thereafter. Although the dissidents prevail in about one-third of our sample, another one-third of the firms experience resignations by top managerial personnel within three years of contest outcome, and most of these occur within one year. Moreover, roughly one-quarter of the sample firms are sold or liquidated shortly after the proxy contest. Taken together, these facts lead to the striking observation that less than one-fifth of sample firms remain independent, publicly held corporations run by the same management team three years after the proxy contest. This evidence indicates that, once a proxy contest materializes, incumbent managers face a serious threat to their tenure.

Viewed collectively, our evidence supports the perspective that proxy contests serve as a catalyst through which public stockholders initiate a referendum on major corporate policy shifts. Ancillary evidence supporting this perspective includes our finding that the overall stockholder wealth gains associated with proxy contests are largely attributable to gains by sample companies in which dissident activity leads to sale or liquidation of the firm. We also find that stockholder wealth falls when it is announced publicly that incumbents have successfully warded off the dissidents, but that these losses occur primarily when incumbent managers use corporate resources to induce the dissidents to abandon their takeover attempt. These latter two findings suggest that acquisition-related benefits and costs are an important component of the stockholder wealth effects of proxy contests.

The paper is structured as follows. Section 2 describes our sampling procedure, and provides evidence on the incidence of proxy contests and the public indications of dissident activity that typically precede them. Section 3 analyzes the campaign issues and the evidence cited by dissident stockholders in favor of the proposed change in board composition. Section 4 presents evidence on dissident and target attributes, and identifies two potentially important factors that encourage the use of vote solicitation as a takeover method. Section 5 reports the stockholder wealth consequences of dissident activity, and the relation between such activity and the subsequent sale or liquidation of the firm. Section 6 and the appendix document the relation between proxy contests and resignations by top management. Section 7 contains a brief summary.

2　Sampling Procedure and Proxy Contest Initiation

Our sample consists of 60 proxy contests for board seats on 60 exchange-listed corporations during 1978–85. Our source documents consist of the *Weekly Bulletins* of the New York Stock Exchange (NYSE) and American Stock Exchange (ASE) and the NYSE log of countersolicitations. These documents identify 70 proxy contests, but we exclude 10 contests for various reasons, largely because they are proxy solicitations by dissidents over specific corporate policy issues rather than attempts to obtain board representation.[1] Of the final sample of 60 target firms, 40 were NYSE-listed and 20 were ASE-listed at the time of the contest, with an annual profile of:

1978:	5 contests	1982:	7 contests
1979:	8 contests	1983:	9 contests
1980:	6 contests	1984:	6 contests
1981:	10 contests	1985:	9 contests

Dodd and Warner (1983) report a similar incidence of proxy contests for board seats on exchange-listed firms during the earlier 1962–77 period.

Over the last several decades, the incidence of proxy contests for board seats at exchange-listed firms has not differed markedly from the incidence of hostile tender bids. For example, over the period 1962–83, the MERC and Austin data bases identify 171 listed firms whose managers faced tender bids that could be confirmed as hostile in financial press reports [Dann and DeAngelo (1988)]. Combining our 1978–83 sample firms with those in Dodd and Warner (1983) for 1962–77 yields a total of 141 proxy contests for board seats at listed firms over the same period.[2] These facts run counter to the popular view that hostile tender bids greatly outnumber proxy contests. This view (perhaps encouraged by greater press coverage of tender bids) seems to be weakening, given that managers of very large and newsworthy firms such as Gillette and Texaco have recently faced proxy contests.

Dissident stockholders explicitly sought control of 48 of the 60 firms in our sample. In 36 of these 48 contests, the dissidents sought to elect a majority of the target board, which would give them the ability to determine the identity of top management and to set major corporate policies. In the other 12 control contests, the dissidents' intent to obtain control was evidenced by their offer to purchase the target firm outright.[3] These latter contests suggest a link between proxy contests and acquisition activity, and further evidence presented below clearly establishes the empirical importance of this relation. Finally, the dissidents' immediate goal in the last 12 contests was to obtain minority board representation, either to better monitor the policies of incumbent managers or to help managers identify and implement more profitable policies.

Publicly visible conflict between dissident stockholders and incumbent managers seldom begins with dissidents' announcement of their plans to wage a proxy contest. As table 12.1 documents, a contest announcement is the first visible sign of dissident activity in only 17 of our 60 sample contests. In 15 of the remaining 43 contests, dissidents first reveal an interest in board seats, which they hope to obtain through negotiation with the incumbents or in some unspecified way. In other cases, dissidents initially request a stockholder list (four contests), state an interest in control without indicating they would necessarily wage a proxy contest to obtain it (seven contests), disclose an intent to influence managerial policies (three contests), or propose to acquire the firm (six contests). In eight contests, the first indication of dissident activity comes from the incumbents, who charge dissidents with an illegal attempt to obtain control or who simply reveal dissidents' existence/interest in the target firm.

Likewise, for 14 of the 17 cases in which contest announcement was the first public indication of dissident activity, we find evidence of prior private disagreements between the dissidents and incumbent management. In seven of these contests, the

Table 12.1 Nature of first public announcement of dissident activity leading to a proxy contest for 60 proxy contests for board seats on New York and American stock-exchange-listed firms (1978–85)

Nature of first disclosure	Number of contests	Percent of full sample
Dissidents announce a proxy contest for board seats	17	28.3%
Initial public disclosure of dissident activity precedes proxy contest announcement	43	71.7%
Breakdown of disclosure types in subsample:		
Dissidents reveal interest in board representation	15	25.0%
Dissidents reveal attempt to obtain stockholder list	4	6.7%
Dissidents reveal interest in control, but do not specify particular takeover vehicle	7	11.7%
Dissidents reveal intent to influence corporate policies	3	5.0%
Dissidents propose to acquire target firm	6	10.0%
Incumbents reveal opposition to and/or existence of dissidents	8	13.3%

dissident leader is a former insider. In another seven, *Wall Street Journal* (*WSJ*) reports and proxy disclosures confirm that dissidents and incumbents had been in contact before the contest announcement. These observations suggest that proxy contests – unlike hostile tender bids in the widely held view – are not generally used as "surprise raiding vehicles" to catch the management of a publicly traded corporation unawares. Rather, proxy contests seem best viewed as a (radical) step in a continuing negotiation process in which the dissidents' inability to persuade incumbent management to implement their suggested policy shifts leads them to turn to outside stockholders for support.

3   The Nature and Conduct of Dissident Campaigns

To obtain the requisite support, dissidents must convince the other stockholders that a change in the board of directors is likely to increase the value of the firm. Dissidents typically wage these campaigns by publicizing multiple facts that collectively raise doubts about incumbents' performance, and that suggest a change in board composition is necessary to remedy the situation. Table 12.2 summarizes the managerial criticisms raised by the dissident stockholders of our 60 sample firms. We compiled this summary from the *WSJ* reports about each contest and all contest-related proxy statements available from Disclosure. The precise phrasing varies across campaigns, and we have therefore used our judgment to categorize the criticisms. The dissidents in a given contest typically raise a subset of these criticisms, and the specific combination of complaints varies across campaigns.

Dissidents most frequently argue that the incumbents have done a poor job either of managing the firm's current operations or of setting overall investment policy. In 41 of the 60 sample contests (68.3%), the dissidents claim that incumbents' operating performance is unsatisfactory. They cite a variety of performance indicators to support

Table 12.2 Dissidents' criticisms of incumbent managers in 60 proxy-contests for board seats on New York and American stock-exchange-listed firms (1978–85).[a]

	Number of contests	*Percent of sample*
Operating and investment policies:		
Poor operating performance	41	68.3%
Should consider sale of firm	28	46.7
Should consider asset mix change	16	26.7
Financial policies and ownership structure:		
Unsatisfactory dividend policy	17	28.3
Low stock ownership by board	17	28.3
Excessive debt	5	8.3
Managerial integrity and general competence:		
Inappropriate takeover resistance	30	50.0
Unwarranted compensation/perquisites	21	35.0
Incompetent/unreliable management	14	23.3

[a] These criticisms are compiled from all (i) dissident proxy statements available from Disclosure and (ii) *Wall Street Journal* reports about sample contests. The phrasing of dissidents' criticisms varies from case to case and the categories presented here reflect our judgment of their primary concerns in each particular case. The categories are not mutually exclusive, i.e., each dissident group typically raised multiple criticisms of incumbent management.

this claim, including low or declining earnings, a recent string of accounting losses, a low return on equity, a low market-to-book ratio, and/or a decline in the firm's stock price. In criticisms of incumbents' operating performance, dissidents tend to emphasize accounting rather than stock price measures of performance, perhaps because dissident activity itself typically results in material stock price increases. [See DeAngelo (1988) for an analysis of the use of accounting and stock price information in proxy fights.]

In 28 sample contests, dissidents argue that managers should consider sale or liquidation of the firm. A typical argument is that these transactions would create greater value for stockholders than would continued operation as an independent, publicly held entity under the direction of incumbent management. In 16 sample contests, dissidents argue that managers should consider a less radical change in the firm's asset structure, e.g., a partial divestiture of corporate assets, initiation of an acquisition program, or changes in certain divisional operations or product lines. Overall, dissidents' suggestions for changes in investment policy range from concrete proposals to sell or liquidate the firm and detailed plans to effect particular asset mix changes, to vague promises that the dissidents will investigate such possibilities, once elected to the board.

Dissidents also commonly claim that the firm's financial policies are inappropriate for its particular circumstances, and that these inferior policies are both the result and cause of incumbents' poor operating performance. In 17 contests, dissidents criticize the firm's dividend policy, frequently citing dividend omissions or cuts as evidence that incumbents are not generating adequate returns for stockholders, or that the firm's financial situation is more precarious than managers admit.[4] Also in 17 contests, dissidents claim that managers own too little stock in the target firm, a shortcoming they often blame for creating undesirable incentives that might help account for incumbents' substandard operating performance. In five contests, the dissidents claim incumbents have overleveraged the firm, thereby unadvisedly reducing its earnings and/or limiting the cash dividends available for stockholders.

Finally, dissidents often question incumbents' integrity by citing publicly visible managerial decisions that have overtones of self-dealing or conflicts of interest. In 30 contests, they challenge incumbent-initiated takeover defenses that allegedly decrease the likelihood that stockholders will receive a premium for their shares (and increase managerial control of the firm). In 21 contests, dissidents claim the incumbents have awarded themselves excessively generous compensation. In such cases, dissidents often contrast incumbents' "generous" compensation with the allegedly inadequate earnings or dividends they have generated for stockholders. In 14 contests, dissidents claim incumbents are simply incompetent or unreliable, e.g., because they have not delivered on past promises or because their forecasts have proved repeatedly to be biased.

In sum, dissidents typically campaign for board seats by citing multiple performance measures that collectively paint a "broad brush" picture of managerial inefficiency.[5] This approach probably reflects their perception that voting stockholders will be reluctant to view one or a few "poor realizations" as reliable evidence that incumbents are inferior managers. Dissidents uniformly avoid complex statistical analyses of the firm's earnings or stock price performance, but rather publicize simple, readily understood evidence of poor management. For example, they focus on particular outcomes that are obviously undesirable *ex post*, such as accounting losses or stock price declines (often from the all-time historical high). Dissidents sometimes quote articles in the financial press that portray incumbents in an unflattering light. Overall, their campaign strategies seem to reflect an assessment that voters have limited incentives to invest in detailed evaluations of incumbents' competence.

4   Dissident and Target Attributes

Proxy contests differ from other methods of corporate takeover in that voting stockholders must be convinced of dissidents' ability to identify and implement profitable policies. Although it may be difficult to forecast how dissidents would perform, the business background of the dissident leader serves as one indication of dissidents' ability to generate greater overall value for stockholders. Panel A of table 12.3 documents the expertise of dissident leaders according to information in proxy statements and *Wall Street Journal* articles. In 29 of the 60 contests, the dissident leader has prior experience in the target's line of business. In ten of these 29 cases, the dissident

Table 12.3 Expertise and composition of the dissident group in 60 proxy contests for board seats on New York and American stock-exchange-listed firms (1978–85)

	Number of contests
(A) *Expertise of dissident leader*	
Target company expertise	10
Target industry expertise	19
Alleged corporate raider[a]	11
Manufacturing expertise	6
Real estate expertise	6
Other private investor	8
(B) *Composition of dissident group*	
Dissident group includes no publicly traded firm	48
Dissident group includes a publicly traded firm	12
Cases in which the target's market value exceeds that of publicly traded dissident firm[b]	8
Mean (median) ratio of target's market value to that of publicly traded dissident firm[b]	2.05 (1.37)

[a] Parties that we so classified are the Belzberg brothers, Coniston Partners, Asher Edelman (two contests), Clyde Engle (two contests), Sir James Goldsmith, Carl Icahn (two contests), Leucadia National Corporation, and Harold Simmons.

[b] Each firm's market value is based on *Moody's Manual's* report of the number of shares of common stock outstanding and the average of the high and low share price for the calendar year prior to the contested board election.

leader was previously employed by the target firm or has served on its board. These facts suggest that expertise specific to the target's line of business is potentially useful in identifying poorly managed firms and/or in convincing voting stockholders that dissident board representation would substantially increase target firm value.[6]

Table 12.3 also contains a frequency count of other expertise possessed by dissident leaders which, in our judgment, might help convince voters to elect dissident directors. In 12 contests, the dissident leader has general experience in manufacturing (six contests) or real estate (six contests). Such expertise might help them better manage the target's resources, or convince voting stockholders of their ability to effect value-increasing changes in corporate policy. In 11 contests, dissident leaders have general capital market reputations as corporate raiders, suggesting that more than pure managerial or technological expertise affects a party's willingness to wage a proxy contest. This fact also suggests that proxy fight participation is determined at least in part by dissidents' ability to force a sale of the firm or other material policy shifts.

The apparent importance of dissidents' takeover-related expertise raises the question why dissidents seek board seats through vote solicitation rather than the purchase of voting stock. At this point, it is simply not possible to identify all of the economically relevant factors that determine why vote solicitation is used as a takeover method. However, ancillary evidence for our sample reveals two attributes of situations in which proxy contests are employed by dissidents. Specifically, proxy contests appear to be a more attractive takeover vehicle when (i) resource limitations make it difficult for the dissident group to purchase control and/or when (ii) takeover barriers impede the immediate purchase of control.

In the majority of contests (48 of 60), the dissident group consists only of individuals (acting on their own behalf or on behalf of a private firm or partnership). It seems reasonable to conjecture that such individuals choose to wage a proxy contest rather than lever their personal portfolios to the extent necessary to purchase control of an exchange-listed corporation. In such cases, there must also be some source of uniqueness between the particular wealth-constrained dissidents and the target firm. (Resource limitations cannot be the only important factor, since otherwise entry by wealth-constrained dissidents would simply serve to identify profitable takeover opportunities for less constrained bidders.) At present, the available evidence does not allow us to reliably identify the technological or informational factors responsible for uniqueness between particular target firms and takeover agents.[7] This issue is clearly important for future empirical work.

For the remaining 12 contests in which the dissident group includes a publicly traded corporation, the target firm is typically considerably larger than the dissident firm. Panel B of table 12.3 reports that the mean ratio of target to dissident equity value is 2.05, with a median of 1.37 (range 0.23 to 5.97). In eight of the 12 contests, the target firm's total equity value exceeds that of the dissident firm as of the year before the contested election. Targets of mergers and tender bids are, by contrast, usually much smaller than their bidder firms.[8] The size disadvantage of most dissident firms also suggests that the choice of proxy contest as a takeover vehicle reflects the dissidents' limited resources.

The ownership structures of the 12 publicly traded dissident firms provide further evidence that resource constraints affect the decision to wage a proxy contest. For 11 of these firms, proxy disclosures and financial press reports reveal a substantial consolidated share block (of at least 20% and often a majority) that is typically owned by parties who are also members of the dissident group. If these parties desire to maintain their vote ownership percentage, they should be correspondingly reluctant to expand the dissident firm's equity base to the extent necessary to purchase the target corporation. Accordingly, it seems plausible that their choice of proxy contest as a takeover vehicle at least in part reflects a desire to avoid dilution of their ownership position in the dissident corporation.

Finally, our evidence indicates that dissident stockholders tend to wage proxy contests when regulatory barriers and target takeover defenses restrict other methods of control transfer. Eleven of the 12 target firms for which dissidents both waged a proxy fight and made an acquisition proposal exhibit such takeover obstacles. These barriers include corporate charter and by-law provisions which specify staggered board terms that would delay election of a board majority by a new majority stockholder, poison pill securities and agreements to complete "friendly hands" stock placements that could make any large stake purchased by the dissidents less valuable, and regulatory constraints on the target firm that would impede a merger unless the incumbent board gave its approval.[9] These 11 cases provide especially clear evidence that proxy contests sometimes complement other methods of acquiring control of a publicly held corporation.

These 11 cases also suggest that proxy contests sometimes enable dissident stockholders to force a stockholder referendum on prospective mergers or liquidations supported by the dissidents but opposed by incumbent managers. The view that proxy contests sometimes facilitate the sale of a target company is consistent with Pound's (1988) findings that (i) dissidents' chances of winning an election are greater if they have made a formal offer to purchase shares, contingent upon their election victory, and (ii) dissident stockholders sometimes wage proxy contests not for board representation, but rather to defeat managerial proposals to adopt antitakeover charter amendments.

This takeover-facilitating view of proxy contests is also consistent with the circumstances of some of the more publicized and hotly contested proxy fights that postdate our 1978–85 sample period. Each of the three most dramatic contested elections of the 1988 proxy season – the battles for Texaco, Gillette, and Irving Bank – was a referendum forced by dissident stockholders over their proposals that management sell the target firm. Moreover, recent articles in the financial press cite the apparent increase in proxy contests during 1988 as a response to managers' implementation of stronger tender offer defenses such as poison pills, and to the adoption of tougher state takeover laws. In addition, many observers interpret these recent proxy contests as evidence of an evolution toward election campaigns that complement takeover bids and away from campaigns that emphasize replacement of management *per se*.[10]

5   The Wealth Effects of Dissident Activity

Our event-study analysis of stock price performance in part confirms the findings of Dodd and Warner (1983) in that dissident activity in sample firms typically generates gains for target stockholders. Our analysis also uncovers two interesting new empirical regularities about the stockholder wealth effects associated with dissident activity. First, incumbent managers' defensive actions play an important role in explaining the significant stockholder losses observed in contests in which incumbents successfully ward off the dissidents' challenge. Second, the average wealth gains experienced by target stockholders over the entire period of dissident activity are largely explained by gains to those target firms in which dissident activity leads to sale or liquidation.

We use the single-factor market model with equal-weighted index to assess each firm's stock price performance. For a given firm we estimate market model parameters using continuously compounded daily returns for the 200 trading days ending 100 days before initiation of dissident activity. These estimated parameters are used to calculate prediction errors (abnormal returns to target company stockholders) for various intervals during each firm's event period. We calculate z-statistics using the standardized prediction error approach detailed in Dodd (1980) and Patell (1976).

5.1   Stockholder wealth effects: full sample findings

For our full sample of 60 firms, we find an average abnormal stockholder wealth increase of 4.85% ($z = 10.83$) for the two-day period including the day before and the day of the first *Wall Street Journal* report of dissident activity, and of 18.76% ($z = 9.44$) when measured over the 40 trading days prior to and including the first public report. The announcement of a proxy contest is associated with an average two-day abnormal return of 3.82% ($z = 4.85$) for the 17 contests for which the contest announcement represents the first sign of dissident activity, and of 2.94% ($z = 4.74$) for the 43 contests with prior public indication of dissident activity. Over the full interval from 40 days prior to initiation through contest outcome, the average abnormal stockholder wealth increase is 6.02% ($z = 4.32$). For this interval, the market-adjusted returns approach [see Brown and Warner (1985)] reveals positive, but only marginally significant stock returns (mean = 2.99%, median = 2.70%, $z = 1.87$).

We find negative, but insignificant stock returns for (i) the period following the initiation of dissident activity through the contest outcome (-12.47%, $z = -0.77$) and (ii) the period following contest announcement through outcome (-6.32%, $z = -1.14$). These returns become significantly negative under the market-adjusted returns approach, consistent with the earlier findings of Dodd and Warner (1983). We conjecture that these negative returns reflect the market's imperfect ability to distinguish sample firms *ex ante* from other firms that are more likely to be acquired at a premium. Also, since firms experiencing a proxy challenge tend to exhibit poor pre-contest financial performance [DeAngelo (1988)], post-contest announcement returns may reflect the arrival of (previously uncapitalized) new information about sample firms' poor financial health. If such information effects are important, our event-study findings will underestimate the overall wealth impact of dissident activity.

5.2   Stockholder wealth effects by contest outcome

Table 12.4 reports the average stockholder wealth impact at initiation, outcome, and over the entire period of dissident activity for our sample partitioned by the nominal outcome of the dissidents' challenge to incumbent management. By "nominal" outcome, we mean the outcome of the proxy contest itself. The evidence reported below indicates that many sample firms experience major corporate policy shifts that can be linked directly to dissident activity. A broader view is that these policy shifts represent the economically relevant outcome of that activity.

The first outcome category in table 12.4 contains the 21 contests in which, according to *Wall Street Journal* reports, the dissidents obtain control of the target, either by acquiring a majority of board seats (18 contests) or by obtaining incumbents' explicit agreement to sell the firm to the dissidents (three contests). The second outcome category contains the 16 contests in which the dissidents obtain some board seats, but not enough to constitute a majority. For these 16 firms, *WSJ* reports do not

Table 12.4 Stockholder wealth effects (prediction errors, *pe*) at initiation of dissident activity and proxy contest outcome for 60 proxy contests for board seats on New York and American stock-exchange-listed firms (1978–85)

	Mean, median, z-statistic, and fraction of positive pe's for		
Sample category (number of firms)	2 days at initiation[a]	2 days at contest outcome[a]	40 days before initiation through contest outcome
(A) *Full sample (n = 60)*	4.85%	−1.17%	6.02%
	2.89	−0.43	6.62
	10.83	−2.71	4.32
	(0.78)	(0.42)	(0.59)
(B) *Sample partitioned by contest outcome*			
Dissidents obtain target board control (*n = 21*)	6.51%	2.60%	9.47%
	5.73	1.43	−3.47
	8.63	2.90	1.44
	(0.90)	(0.62)	(0.48)
Dissidents obtain some seats but not a majority of board (*n = 16*)	4.01	−0.24	30.12
	1.95	0.14	14.44
	4.88	0.34	4.77
	(0.81)	(0.50)	(0.69)
Incumbents successfully deflect dissidents' takeover attempt (*n = 23*)	3.91	−5.45	−14.80
	2.31	−2.63	8.33
	5.18	−7.56	1.59
	(0.65)	(0.18)	(0.64)

[a] Measurement interval includes the day before and the day of the first public report of the event in the *Wall Street Journal*.

reveal any explicit agreement to sell the firm to the dissidents, although we shall see that many of these firms were subsequently sold as a result of the dissidents' efforts. The third outcome category contains the 23 contests in which incumbents defeat the dissidents' challenge.

The data in table 12.4 reveal several interesting facts about the wealth consequences of dissident activity. First, regardless of the immediate outcome of the proxy contest, stockholder wealth increases materially – and by roughly the same amount – at the initiation of dissident activity. Although for brevity the data are not included in the table, the same inference applies when we measure abnormal stock returns from 40 days prior to initiation through initiation itself.[11] One plausible explanation for this finding (explored further below) is that an external challenge to managerial policies increases the likelihood that corporate resources will be reallocated to higher-valued uses.

Table 12.4 also indicates that stockholders experience average wealth losses of 5.45% (z = −7.56) in the two days surrounding contest outcome for the 23 contests in which incumbents defeat the dissidents' challenge. This finding appears to indicate that stockholders are systematically harming themselves by mistakenly choosing to retain the inferior management team. However, closer inspection reveals that this inference is unwarranted since, in most of these 23 contests, stockholders play no direct role in the resolution of hostilities. Specifically, in only seven of these contests does a stockholder vote actually determine the outcome. For these seven contests, the average return at announcement of contest outcome is an insignificant −1.73% ($z = -1.51$).

The outcomes of the remaining 16 contests are *not* determined by stockholder vote, but rather are effectively ended by incumbent managers' defensive actions. Specifically, 11 outcomes are settled by negotiations in which incumbents use corporate resources to induce the dissidents to abandon their takeover attempt. Another three outcomes are effectively determined when the dissidents withdraw because the courts uphold the validity of defensive restructurings announced by the incumbents. In the remaining two cases, the dissidents drop their takeover attempt because the incumbents agree to an acquisition by another party. For the 16 contests in which incumbents' defensive actions determine the outcome, the average stockholder return at outcome announcement is a significant −7.19% ($z = -8.13$). These circumstances suggest that the stock price decline at defeat of dissidents' challenge should not be attributed to voting stockholders' naiveté in distinguishing the superior management team.

5.3   *Relation to acquisition activity*

Another interesting empirical finding reported in table 12.4 is the wide variation in stockholder returns (by nominal contest outcome) over the full period of dissident activity. On average, we observe large overall wealth gains only for the 16 contests in which dissidents obtain a minority of the directorships. For the other outcome categories, average stockholder returns are not significantly different from zero; moreover, the mean and median return are of opposite sign.[12] The market-adjusted returns approach also indicates that stockholders experience significantly positive wealth effects only for the subsample in which dissidents obtain board representation, but not a majority of the directorships.[13]

It is puzzling that a compromise outcome in which *both* dissidents and incumbent managers obtain board representation generates especially large overall returns for stockholders. On the surface, such outcomes would seem to engender additional dissipation of resources in continued disagreements over the appropriate corporate policies. As table 12.4 reports, however, stockholders experience significant overall returns of 30.12% (median = 14.44%) in contests in which dissidents obtain a minority of directors. One possible explanation is that dissident board representation leads to improved monitoring of managerial decisions, hence to the implementation of higher-valued corporate policies. But given the size of these wealth gains, one is naturally curious about the types of policy shifts that might be generated through dissidents' minority board representation and/or through their public challenge of incumbent management.

The data in table 12.5 suggest there is an empirically important relation between dissident challenges and the decision to sell the target firm. We find that 17 (28.3%)

Table 12.5 Incidence and timing of company sales/liquidations for 60 proxy contests for board seats on New York and American stock-exchange-listed firms (1978–85)[a]

Outcome subsample	Number of firms	Announcement of sale or liquidation			
		Between initiation and contest outcome	First year after outcome	Second year after outcome	Third year after outcome
Dissidents gain board control via proxy contest	4	3	1	0	0
Dissidents obtain some seats, but not control	8[b]	1	5	1	1[b]
Dissidents obtain no board seats	5[b]	2	2	0	1[b]
Total	17	6	8	1	2

[a] These transaction timing dates refer to the initial announcement of an eventually completed plan or agreement to sell or liquidate the target firm.
[b] This category contains one firm whose sale or liquidation is not clearly linked to the dissidents' proxy challenge.

of our full sample of 60 firms are sold (15 firms) or liquidated (two firms), either during the proxy campaign or shortly thereafter. In 14 of these 17 cases, the sale or liquidation is announced within one year of contest outcome. All of these transactions and the additional company sale announced the following year (a total of 15 transactions) are clearly connected to dissident stockholders' proxy challenges.[14] Specifically, in six cases the dissidents themselves acquire the firm, in three cases acquisition by a third party effectively ends the contest, in five cases the dissidents' campaign places major emphasis on selling the firm, and in one case the firm is acquired by a party with which managers had privately placed shares to defeat the dissidents.

A closer look at the 15 firms whose sale or liquidation can be clearly linked to the efforts of dissident stockholders reveals that in seven cases the dissidents had obtained a minority of the board seats (see the second outcome category of table 12.4). These seven firms represent 43.8% of the 16 companies in which dissidents obtain a board minority. We find a much smaller fraction of target companies whose sale or liquidation is linked to the proxy contest in the other two outcome categories. Specifically, these firms comprise four (19.0%) of the 21 cases in which dissidents obtain target control, and four (17.4%) of the 23 cases in which the dissidents are defeated by incumbents. These findings suggest that minority representation *per se* can help dissident stockholders force the sale or liquidation of the target firm when it is valuable to do so, and when incumbents are reluctant to take the necessary steps.

Perhaps more importantly, these facts support a general empirical linkage between dissident activity and the eventual sale of the target firm. In fact, the data in table 12.6 reveal that the overall wealth gains associated with dissident activity (documented above) are largely driven by gains to those firms that were subsequently sold or liquidated as a result of the dissidents' efforts. For the 15 firms whose sale or liquidation is clearly linked to dissidents' efforts, the average wealth gain over the full period of dissident activity is a significant 15.16% ($z = 4.21$). For the remaining sample firms, the corresponding mean return is a considerably smaller 2.90% (z = 2.54). Similarly, the 21.96% median overall stockholder return in the 15 firms with a dissident-linked sale or liquidation is considerably greater than the 5.18% median overall return in the remaining sample firms.[15]

Table 12.6 also reveals that stockholders of firms in both subsamples experience significant wealth gains (on the order of 20%) around the initiation of dissident activity. A plausible explanation is that the initial run-up in target value is attributable to the market's perception that the dissidents' challenge increases the likelihood that firms in both subsamples will be sold at a premium. By this view, the market is not able to separate *ex ante* the subset of firms that will subsequently be sold or liquidated from the subset that will not be. For the latter firms, the lower returns over the period from initiation through outcome reflect a growing awareness, as the nature of the dissidents' challenge becomes clearer (and perhaps evolves in response to incumbents' actions), that the target firm will not be acquired.

6　Managerial Resignations and Dissident Activity

Dodd and Warner (1983) report that dissidents who wage proxy contests infrequently win majority control of the board. They find that dissidents successfully obtain a board

Table 12.6　Selected stockholder wealth effects (prediction errors, *pe*) for 60 proxy contests for board seats on New York and American stock-exchange-listed firms (1978–85), partitioned by whether sale of firm is linked to dissident activity

Sample category (number of firms)	Mean, median, z-statistic, and fraction of positive pe's for	
	40 days before contest initiation through initiation	*40 days before initiation through contest outcome*
(A) *Full sample (n = 60)*	18.76%	6.02%
	16.58	6.62
	9.44	4.32
	(0.78)	(0.59)
(B) *Sample partitioned by whether sale of firm is linked to dissident activity*		
Sale of target firm is linked to dissident activity[a] (*n* = 15)	22.36%	15.16%
	20.20	21.96
	5.90	4.21
	(0.93)	(0.80)
No evidence that any sale of target firm is linked to dissident activity (*n* = 45)	17.56	2.90
	14.04	5.18
	7.49	2.54
	(0.73)	(0.52)

[a] For these 15 cases, financial press reports clearly link the sale or liquidation of the target firm to dissident activity. In six of these cases the dissidents themselves acquire the firm, in three cases acquisition by a third party effectively ends the proxy contest, in five cases the dissidents' campaign placed major emphasis on selling the firm, and in one case the firm is acquired by a party with which managers had privately placed shares in an attempt to defeat the dissidents.

majority only 20–25% of the time, which is quite close to the finding (reported above) that dissidents win a board majority in approximately one-third of our sample of proxy contests. These relatively low nominal success rates seem to suggest that the advent of a proxy contest represents an ineffective threat to top management because these contests typically do not cost incumbents their positions.

A closer look at the impact of proxy contests – viewed broadly to include managerial resignations and company sales linked directly to dissidents' efforts – seriously challenges the view that incumbents have little to fear from a proxy contest. First, as discussed above, 17 of our 60 sample firms are sold or liquidated during the proxy contest or shortly thereafter, and 15 of these transactions are clearly linked to the dissidents' efforts. Second, as we next document, more than half the firms in which dissidents did *not* obtain board control experience resignations in top management [defined as a chief executive officer (CEO), chairman, and/or president], either during or shortly after the contest. Detailed case studies of these resignations (presented in the appendix and summarized here) reveal that at least three-quarters are directly related to the dissidents' attempts to replace incumbent managers.

To assess the frequency of managerial resignations for the 39 firms in which the dissidents did not obtain board control through the proxy contest, we inspect the *Wall Street Journal* for evidence of changes in CEO, chairman, and/or president around the time of the proxy contest. This search reveals resignations by individuals holding these titles in 20 of the 39 firms (51.3%), either during the proxy contest itself or within the three years of the contest outcome. In almost all (17 of 20) cases, the individual who resigned held the CEO position. All told, we observe resignations by 23 individuals of 38 managerial positions – 17 CEO positions, 11 board chairmanships, and 10 presidencies – in these 20 firms. The median age at resignation is 59, and the only two individuals who resigned close to the "normal" retirement age of 65 had personally been the subject of scathing attacks by the dissidents (see the case studies in the appendix for Condec and Kennecott Corp.).[16]

Some indication that the managerial resignations we observe are linked to the dissidents' proxy challenge can be found in panel A of table 12.7, which reports the timing of these resignations in relation to the outcome of the proxy contest. These data reveal that the resignations are bunched close in time to the election campaign, as one might expect if the dissidents' efforts influenced the management change. Fifteen of the 20 resignations occur either during the contest itself or within one year of the outcome. Viewed in relative terms, a full 38% (15 of 39) of the sample firms in which dissidents fail to obtain a majority of the directorships through the contested board election experience resignations by top managerial personnel within one year of the contest outcome.

This 38% resignation rate is much greater than the rates typically found in empirical studies of top management changes.[17] For example, Warner, Watts, and Wruck (1988) document an average annualized rate of 11.5% for arrivals or departures by top management (including retirements from the CEO, chairman, or president positions) reported in the *Wall Street Journal*. They find considerably lower management change rates (ranging from 1.4% to 6.0%, depending on company stock price performance) for changes they classify as forced by the board of directors. Weisbach

Table 12.7 Resignations by CEOs, presidents and/or board chairmen for the subsample of 39 exchange-listed firms in which dissidents did not obtain board control in a proxy contest (1978–85)

(A) *Timing of resignation*

	All cases	Between initiation and contest outcome	First year after outcome	Second year after outcome	Third year after outcome
Number of firms	20	2	13	2	3
Percent of subsample	51.3%	5.1%	33.3%	5.1%	7.7%

(B) *Nature of resignation*

	Number of firms	Percent of subsample
Resignation with replacement by dissident or buyer in "friendly hands" stock placement	6	15.4%
Resignation before contest outcome was resolved	2	5.1
Resignation amid continued signs of conflict with dissidents who now have board representation	3	7.7
Resignation with other signs of dissident involvement	4	10.3
All other resignations (all at other than normal retirement age)	5	12.8

(1988) documents an average rate for CEO departures (excluding retirements) of 4.8% for NYSE-listed firms, which is about half the retirement-inclusive departure rate for his sample. Coughlan and Schmidt (1985) find an average CEO departure rate of 12.7% (8.0% for CEOs younger than age 63) for firms listed in the *Forbes* compensation survey.

Thus, while the details of our sampling algorithm differ from those used in prior studies of top management changes, it seems reasonable to infer that the incidence of resignations documented here is not plausibly attributable to "normal" managerial turnover. Rather, the resignation frequency for the current sample appears more in line with the management change rates previously documented for other significant – and, for top management, also potentially traumatic – corporate events. The 38% resignation rate discussed above is roughly the same order of magnitude as the 33% management change rate reported by Gilson (1988) for firms experiencing financial distress, the 27% change rate reported by Klein and Rosenfeld (1988) for firms whose managers pay greenmail to deflect a possible takeover, and the 25% change rate reported by Walsh (1988) for firms that are acquired by another public corporation.[18]

Ideally, one would like to know whether the dissidents' proxy challenge significantly influenced the managerial resignations we document here. As Warner, Watts, and Wruck (1988) and Weisbach (1988) clearly establish, however, public sources rarely disclose the "true" reasons for a management change (probably because both the company and the executive involved suppress information they view as potentially embarrassing). Nevertheless, by piecing together information from financial press reports about the firm-specific circumstances surrounding each resignation in our sample, we are able to obtain qualitative evidence on the role played by the dissidents' challenge. This evidence is contained in the appendix, which provides detailed case studies of the managerial resignations that occur within three years of contest outcome at 20 sample firms in which dissidents fail to obtain a board majority through the contested board election.

A reading of these case studies uncovers evidence that, in 15 (75%) of the 20 firms, the managerial resignations are plausibly linked to the dissidents' efforts to unseat incumbent management. The nature and strength of this evidence varies from case to case and is summarized in panel B of table 12.7. Strong evidence of the importance of the dissidents' challenge is the replacement of the resigning manager in 6 of the 15 firms by a dissident or by a blockholder to whom the incumbents had sold shares in a "friendly hands" placement to diminish the dissidents' voting power. The identity of these managerial replacements leaves little doubt that the dissidents' efforts played a key role in effecting these resignations. Moreover, the case studies for these firms (American Bakeries, Condec, Deltona, FGI Investors, LLC Corporation, and Pantry Pride) provide confirmatory evidence of conflicts between the particular manager who resigned and the dissidents or the new blockholder (whose alliance with incumbent management evidently ended shortly after the contest).

In another five cases, the managerial resignation occurs during hostilities between the incumbents and dissidents, with three resignations taking place after the contest had apparently ended, but amid visible signs of renewed conflict with dissidents who had obtained board representation. (See the case studies for Canal Randolph, Chicago Rivet, Citadel Holding, Kennecott, and Management Assistance.) The fact that these resignations came during visible – and, as the case studies indicate, often quite heated – conflicts between the dissident and incumbent groups provides corroborative evidence of the dissidents' role in effecting these management changes. Moreover, in four of the five cases, financial press reports indicate that the particular individual who resigned had experienced direct personal conflicts with the dissidents.

In another four cases, other details reported by the *Wall Street Journal* suggest that dissident activity played a role in the managerial resignation, but the evidence is not as strong as for the eleven cases just discussed. In three of these four cases, the resignation occurs after the dissidents had obtained board representation and while the firm was experiencing significant financial difficulties as evidenced, for example, by large reported losses (Cook United, H. H. Robertson, and Saxon). In the remaining case (Pullman), the resignation came within six months of the dissidents' failure to obtain any seats, but followed a campaign that emphasized the alleged incompetence of the individual who ultimately resigned. During this campaign, the *Wall Street Journal* reported that the dissidents "are betting that even if they can't unseat Mr Casey (the firm's CEO) by a proxy contest, the questions they are raising will stir up enough adverse publicity to force him out of office".

The final five cases, by our judgment of *WSJ* reports, do not reveal a direct connection between the managerial resignation and the dissidents' proxy challenge (see the appendix entries for Chock Full O'Nuts, Louisiana Land & Exploration, New Jersey Resources, Texas International, and Tosco). All five resignations occur at other than "normal" retirement age, suggesting that some of these departures may be linked to the dissidents' efforts. Moreover, such linkage seems quite possible for the Louisiana Land and Tosco cases, since a reading of the appendix shows that our classification of the dissidents' role as unimportant in these resignations involved especially tough judgment calls, which another observer might reasonably reverse.

In sum, the case studies detailed in the appendix yield the overall impression that, even when dissident stockholders fail to obtain a board majority through a proxy contest, their efforts nonetheless frequently play a significant role in effecting a change in corporate top management. Of course, we have insufficient evidence to infer that the dissidents' efforts were the single critical factor in the managerial resignations we observe. For example, the possibility remains that other disciplinary forces (e.g., monitoring by the incumbent board) would have eventually led to the same managerial resignations. All we can reliably say is that the circumstances surrounding most of these resignations suggest that the dissidents' efforts were important in effecting the management changes.

Table 12.8 documents the cumulative survival rate for incumbent top managers of our sample firms for the period beginning with initiation of dissident activity and ending three years after contest outcome. The incumbent management team is treated as surviving intact as of a given date if (i) the dissidents fail to obtain board control through the proxy contest (per table 12.4), (ii) there are no top management resigna-tions (per table 12.7), and (iii) the firm is not sold or liquidated (per table 12.5). The striking empirical fact is that, in less than one-fifth of our sample, the same incumbent management team remains in control of the (still publicly held) target firm three years after the contest outcome. Moreover, as discussed above, the vast majority of this managerial attrition is directly connected to the dissidents' efforts.

The evidence accordingly suggests that, once a dissident challenge materializes, there is a considerably greater threat to incumbent managers than is implied simply by the frequency with which dissidents obtain a board majority through stockholder

Table 12.8 Cumulative survival rate for incumbent management for 60 proxy contests for board seats on New York and American stock-exchange-listed firms (1978–85)[a]

	Incidence of independent, publicly traded target firms with top management intact as of specified date	
Evaluation date	Number of firms	Percent of sample
As of initiation of dissident activity	60	100.0%
As of outcome of contest	34	56.7
As of one year after outcome	17	28.3
As of two years after outcome	14	23.3
As of three years after outcome	11	18.3

[a] We treat the incumbent management team as surviving intact as of a given date if (i) the dissidents fail to obtain board control through the proxy contest (per table 12.4), (ii) there are no resignations by CEOs, presidents, or board chairmen (per table 12.7), and (iii) the corporation is not sold or liquidated (per table 12.5). The cumulative survival figures reported here exceed those implied by the sum of the attrition figures documented in tables 12.4, 12.5, and 12.7 because some firms appear in more than one of these tables.

vote. Although this evidence indicates that dissident activity represents a more effective threat to incumbent management than is commonly thought, it does not imply that the "right" (i.e., economically efficient) number of proxy contests necessarily takes place. [See Pound (1988) for a discussion of factors that potentially affect the economic efficiency of stockholder voting as a mechanism for disciplining managers.]

Another important caveat is that our evidence does not imply that only poor managers are challenged in – or removed through – dissidents' proxy solicitations. On the contrary, because resources are expended in proxy solicitations when there are material information costs for outsiders to identify the superior management team, one would expect that some dissident challenges actually focus on (and ultimately remove) incumbent managers who are in fact better at operating the firm. Symmetrically, material information costs will sometimes enable relatively inefficient incumbents to survive a dissident challenge. In sum, given that proxy contests inherently arise because of positive information costs of evaluating alternative management teams, there is no reason to expect that they will always give control to the superior group.

7 Summary and Conclusions

This paper provides an empirical analysis of the conduct and consequences of 60 proxy contests for board representation on New York and American Stock Exchange-listed corporations during 1978–85. We find that dissident stockholders typically campaign for the public stockholder vote by painting a simple "broad brush" picture of managerial inefficiency, using a variety of easy-to-convey criticisms of managerial performance. Dissidents often possess industry, firm-specific, or takeover-related expertise that public stockholders might view as favorable indications of their ability to manage the firm or to effect beneficial changes in corporate policy. Resource limitations appear to affect the dissidents' choice of a proxy contest as a takeover vehicle, since most dissident groups consist of individuals or private firms, with only one-fifth including participation by a publicly traded corporation. Moreover, in these latter cases, the dissident firm is on average half the size of the target firm.

Consistent with Dodd and Warner (1983), we find that dissident activity is associated with overall stockholder wealth gains, and that stockholders typically experience losses at announcement that the dissidents have failed to obtain board representation. We also find, however, that the significant overall wealth gains associated with proxy contests are largely attributable to gains by those sample firms in which dissident activity leads to sale or liquidation of the corporation. Moreover, the wealth losses at the outcomes of unsuccessful proxy contests are due almost entirely to losses by those firms in which incumbents use corporate resources to induce the dissidents to abandon their takeover attempt. These latter two findings suggest that acquisition-related benefits and costs are an important – although not necessarily the only – determinant of the stockholder wealth consequences of proxy contests.

Our most striking finding is that less than one-fifth of sample firms remain independent, publicly held corporations run by the same management team three years after the proxy contest. This finding reflects the facts that (i) proxy contests are typically followed by managerial resignations, even when dissidents fail to obtain a majority of board seats, and (ii) proxy contests are often followed by sale or liquidation of the target firm. In short, a dissident challenge poses a serious threat to incumbent managers. This evidence suggests that proxy contests serve as a forum through which public stockholders can initiate a referendum on major corporate policy shifts, as well as a means of inducing the management changes that are apparently necessary to implement such shifts.

Appendix: *case studies of 20 top management resignations within three years of a proxy contest in which dissidents did not obtain majority control of the board*

This appendix contains brief case studies of resignations by top managers (defined as CEO, chairman, or president) for the 20 sample firms in which dissidents waged a proxy contest, but did not obtain a majority of board seats. Each case study describes the contest outcome and the circumstances surrounding the managerial resignation, including the position(s) of the officer(s) who resigned and any links to the dissident stockholders. *Wall Street Journal* (*WSJ*) articles are our primary information sources, but we also rely on information published in proxy statements, annual reports, and forms 10-K. The final entry for each firm is the classification of the managerial resignation (which underlies the aggregate data in panel B of table 12.7) and the length of time between contest outcome and the managerial resignation (which underlies the aggregate data in panel A of table 12.7).

American Bakeries Company   The dissidents elected four of the 12 directors on the classified board. Of the remaining eight directors, four represented management and four were to be outside directors acceptable to both management and dissident directors. The dissident leader immediately replaced Robert E. Grant (age 56) as chairman of the executive committee (which was the title given the firm's CEO position). Mr Grant, who had failed to be re-elected to the board, resigned from the company effective five months hence. The *WSJ* report quotes Mr Grant as saying he resigned "because I had no other choice. I'd been the key person in this company for several years, and I don't intend to be anything less than that". By the effective date of Mr Grant's resignation, both the chairman of the board (L. Arthur Cushman, Jr., age 51) and the president (George P. Turci, age 51) had also resigned their posts, although both men remained directors. The dissident leader assumed the duties of both positions, and the *WSJ* report quotes him as saying that events since the election of his slate have "been leading up to this [the two resignations]. I believe everyone wanted to end any possible strain and divisiveness in the company, and it was felt that this was the only way to do it". *Classification*: Resignation and replacement by dissident within one year of contest outcome.

Canal Randolph Corporation   The dissidents, led by Asher Edelman, settled with management in a compromise agreement that gave them three of the six board seats. The settlement came before the election was held and after the courts had ordered the company to reinstate cumulative voting, under which the dissidents' 28.7% stake would enable them to elect at least two of the six directors. Under the terms of the settlement, Mr Edelman was named vice chairman of the board and chairman of the executive committee, while Sir Walter Salomon (age 76) was to continue as chairman and Raymond French (age 63) was to continue as president and CEO. Mr Edelman emphasized to the *WSJ* that these titles were effective only until the compromise slate was approved by stockholders at the annual meeting, i.e., that the new board would reconsider these positions. He also expressed his interest in working with Mr French, since the primary target of his campaign against incumbent management had been Sir Walter. Specifically, Mr Edelman characterized Sir Walter as a "76-year-old chairman" who ran the company far too conservatively and "a foreign resident who spends little time in the US". Sir Walter resigned unexpectedly from the position of chairman and from the executive committee at the annual meeting, while retaining his directorship. Immediately after the meeting, the new board named Mr French to the additional post of chairman. Sir Walter's stated reason for his resignation was: "It's time to entrust the future of the company to the younger generation". The company was subsequently liquidated, as Mr Edelman's platform had recommended. *Classification*: Resignation within one year of contest outcome amid visible signs of conflict with dissidents who now have board representation.

Chicago Rivet & Machine Company   Ralph W. Jindrich (age 54), president and CEO, resigned and was replaced by John A. Morrisey, chairman (age 45) two months after the dissidents obtained board representation. John Morrisey and his brother were major stockholders, with a combined 6.1% of the common stock. At the time of Mr Jindrich's resignation, the dissidents had amassed a 10.6% stake and had obtained (via cumulative voting) one of the two board seats they sought, but hostilities between the incumbents and dissidents continued. The dissidents claimed that the board needed "a new outlook" because of the firm's ongoing poor earnings performance, and Mr Jindrich's resignation followed by three months the announcement of an annual loss. Four months after Mr Jindrich's resignation, hostilities were effectively resolved when the company repurchased the dissidents' shares at a premium, negotiated a standstill agreement, and the one dissident director resigned. *Classification*: Resignation before contest outcome was resolved.

Chock Full O'Nuts Corporation   The dissidents lost their initial proxy challenge, threatened a second contest, and accepted greenmail before mounting the second challenge. One of the dissidents' major criticisms of incumbent management was that they weren't using the company's valuable real estate in New York City efficiently. In part, they blamed this shortcoming on the firm's 80-year-old founder and chairman, who died subsequently (during the hostilities). His successor attempted to remedy some of the company's profitability problems by leasing the firm's restaurants to others and by developing the firm's (relatively high profit margin) business as a supplier of coffee to restaurants. In the process, the successor to the company founder acquired Chase & Sanborn and hired its president, Arthur R. Berman (age 45), as president and chief operating officer of Chock Full O'Nuts. Mr Berman resigned to "pursue other interests" two years later and could not be reached by the *WSJ* for comment on the reasons for his resignation. *Classification*: Resignation in third year following contest outcome at other than normal retirement age (age 45).

Citadel Holding Corporation   The company settled with the dissidents, naming their three representatives to an expanded ten-member board, when the dissidents continued to seek board representation after the company agreed to be acquired by another firm. The dissidents' original platform called for sale or merger of the company. Management had announced an agreement to be acquired by Great Western Financial Corp. the day before the scheduled stockholder meeting, at least partially in an attempt to delay the contested election. Following the merger announcement, the dissidents continued to seek board seats as "protection for all shareholders" if completion of the sale was delayed or terminated. In response, management switched the term of the CEO, Spencer Scott (who was currently up for re-election to the classified board), with the term of another director who was not up for re-election, and named the three dissidents directors. The acquisition was supported by Mr Scott and opposed by the dissident leader, Alfred Roven.

Two months after the settlement with the dissidents, the company terminated the acquisition agreement when its investment banker refused to issue the type of fairness opinion called for by the agreement. At that time, Mr Scott (age 63) resigned as chairman, CEO, and a director. He was to retain the title of chairman emeritus and serve as a consultant to the company. The *WSJ* report mentions Mr Scott's difficulties with Mr Roven, and quotes an unnamed executive as saying "Scott was his own man [as chairman]. Barrone [his successor as CEO] is a harmonizer". Six months after Scott's resignation, the company dismissed him from his consultant's position "for cause". The company refused to elaborate except to say it was disputing Mr Scott's claims for severance pay, and that it "believes that it may have substantial counterclaims against Mr Scott". A special committee of the board was formed to investigate the company's past relationship with Mr Scott, who could not be reached by the *WSJ* for comment. *Classification*: Resignation within one year of contest outcome amid visible signs of conflicts with dissidents who now have board representation.

Condec Corporation   The dissidents won seven seats on a 15-member board, running on a campaign to oust incumbent management and take the firm private. The dissident leader, William Farley, alleged that Condec management, led by Norman I. Schafler (age 66), was "weak", "confused", and had compiled a "miserable track record" by running the company "carelessly and without strategy". Moreover, he said, Condec was not a "Schafler family heirloom to be handed down from father to son" [Mr Schafler's 33-year-old son was vice president operations]. According to the *WSJ* report, the stockholder meeting was especially heated, with one stockholder saying that he intended to "crack the whip" on management and demonstrating his intention by "cracking a whip in the center aisle of the meeting room". Within four months of the contest outcome, Mr Schafler led a management group in a competing offer to take Condec private. Their offer was immediately topped by Mr Farley. Upon acceptance of his offer, Mr Farley was named chairman and CEO, succeeding Mr Schafler. Mr Schafler also sold the Schafler family stock in Condec to one of Mr Farley's companies, resigned his directorship, and "would have no further connection with the company". Gerald Rosenberg, the company president, resigned simultaneously. Stockholders approved new management's buyout offer three months later. *Classification*: Resignation and replacement by dissident within one year of contest outcome.

Cook United Corporation   The dissidents obtained three of the nine board seats they sought in the election, alleging that the company's earnings performance had been a "very sorry" one. The company's chairman and CEO, Martin M. Lewis (age 63), was criticized by the dissidents for his statement that 1978 was an "especially gratifying year". According to dissident proxy materials: "It is difficult to understand how a 2% return on total assets and less than a 1%

return on sales can be 'especially gratifying' to anyone with an interest in the company, let alone the chairman". Cook continued to experience repeated losses after the proxy contest, and was forced to substitute stock dividends for the cash dividends it had begun paying during the election campaign. Three years after the contest outcome, Mr Lewis resigned as CEO amid continued financial difficulties. He was replaced by the company president, George Jeffers (age 53), with Mr Lewis continuing as chairman. According to Mr Lewis, his resignation was part of "the orderly transfer of the lines of authority begun four years ago". The new CEO, Mr Jeffers, resigned eight months later without explanation and was replaced by a temporary management committee that included a dissident director. The individual who replaced the committee resigned the CEO position 14 months after his appointment. Meanwhile, the company had filed for bankruptcy protection under Chapter 11 because its lenders would not extend additional credit. *Classification*: Resignation in third year following contest outcome amid other signs of dissident involvement.

Deltona Corporation   The dissidents abandoned their efforts to unseat the board when management completed the sale of a 43% stake to Topeka Group Inc. in a "friendly hands" stock placement during the dissidents' solicitation attempt. Three months later Frank E. Mackle, Jr. (age 69), the founder, chairman and CEO, and Frank E. Mackle III (age 41), president and chief operating officer, resigned from the company. The Mackle family retained ownership of 5.8% of the voting stock, and Mr Mackle III expressed his intention to run for a directorship at the next annual meeting. He cited the "friendly hands" stock placement and differences in styles of management [between a family-run company and one managed by outsiders] as the reasons why he and his father resigned. According to the *WSJ* report, Mr Mackle III stated: "There were some style differences [between the Mackles and Topeka management]. Things will be smoother" if the Mackles leave the company. *Classification*: Resignation and replacement by buyer in a "friendly hands" stock placement within one year of contest outcome.

FGI Investors   After two attempts by the dissident group to elect trustees, management issued a large block (400,000 shares) to US Lend Lease Inc. The dissidents sued to stop the sale, alleging that management had engaged in "corporate ballot stuffing" and had breached its fiduciary duty to stockholders by failing to submit the matter to a vote, and by selling shares at too low a price. The dissidents lost both their suit and the election, the latter by a narrow margin of 26,000 votes (they had unsuccessfully sought to block US Lend Lease from voting its 400,000 shares). Three months later, amid continued litigation by both sides, the dissidents agreed to sell their shares to the company and US Lend Lease and to settle all litigation. Three months later, Arno Krumbiegel (age 37), president and CEO of FGI, resigned to start his own consulting firm. He was immediately replaced by the president of US Lend Lease, which at the time owned about 40% of FGI's stock. According to the *WSJ* report, the treasurer of FGI commented: "With the advent of US Lend Lease, and their eagerness to be active in the [trust's] management, Mr Krumbiegel was willing to step aside". *Classification*: Resignation and replacement by buyer in a "friendly hands" stock placement within one year of contest outcome.

Kennecott Corporation   After management had claimed victory in the contested board election and while the dissidents (Curtiss-Wright Corporation) were challenging that victory in the courts, Frank R. Milliken (age 65), chairman and CEO, announced he would retire effective almost immediately. [The US Supreme Court ultimately affirmed a lower court ruling that a new election be held because Kennecott's proxy materials were false and misleading.] Mr Milliken, who had been the subject of scathing personal attacks by the dissidents for alleged incompetence and mismanagement, had previously announced his intention to postpone his retirement for another eleven months. Mr Milliken was immediately replaced by Thomas D. Barrow (age 54), a senior vice president and director of Exxon Corporation. According to *WSJ* reports: "Industry sources see the . . . Kennecott decision to name a new CEO as a defensive move in the company's continuing proxy battle with Curtiss-Wright Corp. Kennecott insiders have been concerned with the company's ability to ward off another Curtiss-Wright challenge with two lame duck top executives [Mr Milliken and William Wendel, age 64, the company president]". In an interview, the new CEO cited the upcoming proxy fight with Curtiss-Wright as the "major situation" facing him at this time. T. Roland Berner, the Curtiss-Wright chairman, commented: "I'm talking about replacing the [Kennecott] board. This [the Barrow appointment] in no way vitiates the need to substitute for that board. They're trying to duck out, and we aren't going to let them". Despite these remarks, Curtiss-Wright settled on a compromise slate with new Kennecott management two weeks later. *Classification*: Resignation before contest outcome was resolved.

The Louisiana Land & Exploration Company   This situation is similar to Kennecott's – although management claimed victory in the election, the dissidents' challenged this outcome in the courts, claiming a new election should be held because management had misrepresented the firm's financial performance during the campaign. The dissident leader was particularly concerned because two million of the estimated 30 million shares voted in the election originally voted for the dissidents, but later switched to management. The dissident leader claimed that "if those votes hadn't changed, the dissidents would have won". The Louisiana Land proxy fight is notable because the company had several large blockholders – Carl Lindner's American Financial Corp. with a recently purchased 5% stake, the Hunt family's Placid Oil with 12.4%, Pioneer Corp. with 7.2%, Amerada Hess with 5.3%, and Boone Pickens' Mesa Petroleum with 1%. While awaiting the outcome of the dissidents' lawsuit, management caused the company to repurchase the combined 17% stake held by the Hunt family and American Financial. The Hunts had voted their 12.4% stake in favor of the dissidents, whereas American Financial had voted for management. Shortly after these repurchases, the firm was placed on Credit Watch (and eventually its bonds were downgraded).

During this period of continued uncertainty about the company's future direction, John G. Phillips (age 61) resigned as CEO. Mr Phillips, who retained the title of chairman, was expected to be replaced as CEO by the company president. Although the *WSJ* report describes the management change as coming "in the wake of a lawsuit brought by a group of dissidents . . . alleging that Louisiana Land's management misled shareholders about the company's financial position and other matters during a proxy fight", Mr Phillips claimed the change had "nothing whatsoever to do with the proxy fight". Fourteen months later, at age 62, Mr Phillips also resigned as chairman. In the interim, the company repurchased Pioneer Corp.'s stake (Pioneer had voted for the dissidents), and the dissidents lost their case in the courts. *Classification*: Resignation within one year of contest outcome at other than normal retirement age (age 61).

LLC Corporation   The dissidents, led by Harold Simmons, won six of the 15 board seats. Six months later, a dissident (the chief financial officer of Mr Simmons' Contran Corporation) was elected chairman, succeeding Stephen M. Friedrich (age 50), who was to continue as president and CEO. Four months later, following continued losses, Mr Friedrich was asked to resign all positions with the firm, including his directorship. According to the *WSJ* report, Mr Friedich's resignation was requested because "we've had several years of losses. A change was deemed [necessary] in order to turn the company around". At this time, Harold Simmons was elected chairman and Mr Friedrich's duties were assumed by an associate of Mr Simmons. *Classification*: Resignation and replacement by dissident within one year of contest outcome.

Management Assistance Inc.   The dissidents, led by Asher Edelman, won four of ten seats on the classified board. Within five months, Raymond P. Kurshan (age 60), chairman, president, and CEO, resigned from the company along with two directors. Mr Edelman named one replacement director, giving the dissidents five of nine board seats. The positions vacated by Mr Kurshan were to remain unfilled because, at the dissidents' urging, the company was in the process of liquidation. Although Mr Kurshan couldn't be reached for comment, the *WSJ* report quotes a company spokesman as saying that he believed Mr Kurshan resigned because he thought it "in the best interests of the company with all the divisiveness" as a result of the proxy contest and related lawsuits. Mr Edelman had filed suit against Mr Kurshan, asking compensatory, special, and punitive damages for Mr Kurshan's allegedly libelous, false, misleading, and defamatory statements about Mr Edelman during the proxy contest. This lawsuit was dismissed as part of the settlement agreement that accompanied Mr Kurshan's resignation from the company. *Classification*: Resignation within one year of contest outcome amid visible signs of conflict with dissidents who now have board representation.

New Jersey Resources Corporation   NUI Corporation, a competitor utility, made an unsolicited offer to purchase the company. After management rejected the offer, NUI announced that it would take its proposal directly to the stockholders through a proxy contest, which management claimed to win. However, NUI brought litigation challenging the fairness with which the election had been run and persuaded the courts to order a new election. Litigation between the two companies continued until New Jersey Resources agreed to a premium repurchase of its shares held by NUI, which then signed a standstill agreement. One year and four months later, the 76-year-old chairman retired and was succeeded by the firm's president and CEO. The *WSJ* report of the retirement makes no mention of the hostile takeover attempt by NUI. *Classification*: Resignation in second year following contest outcome at other than normal retirement age (age 76).

Pantry Pride, Inc.   Grant C. Gentry (age 60), the firm's chairman and CEO, was the target of the dissidents' campaign. For example, one *WSJ* article about the proxy contest is titled "Pantry Pride Chairman Gentry's Record, Personality Are Seen as Focus of Dispute". The article quotes the dissident leader as saying that incumbent management has "no incentive to operate the company efficiently because they have no stock to speak of, with the exception of the cheap warrants Gentry got". Although the campaign was especially heated, the dissidents obtained no board seats. Two months later, management agreed to issue sufficient shares to transfer effective control of the company to MacAndrews & Forbes, a private firm. According to Mr Gentry, one reason for the stock issuance was to "get a concentration of shares" in the hands of a single party and thus prevent future proxy battles. When the issuance was announced, the company claimed that Mr Gentry would continue to run Pantry Pride. Three months later, however, Mr Gentry resigned and was succeeded by Ronald O. Perelman, the CEO of MacAndrews & Forbes. *Classification*: Resignation and replacement by buyer in "friendly hands" stock placement within one year of contest outcome.

Pullman, Inc.   Samuel B. Casey (age 51), the firm's CEO and president, was the target of the dissidents' campaign. The dissidents, two former insiders, alleged that Mr Casey had mismanaged the company and sought to have him fired. According to *WSJ* reports, the dissidents "are betting that even if they can't unseat Mr Casey by a proxy contest, the questions they are raising will stir up enough adverse publicity to force him out of office". Even though management won the election by a wide margin, the annual meeting was heated, as the dissidents were joined by other dissatisfied stockholders who questioned Mr Casey "about his perquisites and the company". Mr Casey remarked at the meeting: "I don't know when I've stood up to so much minutiae and trivia from so many people who don't know business". Six months later, Mr Casey resigned as president and CEO, at age 51, and was named to the previously vacant position of chairman. *Classification*: Resignation within one year of contest outcome amid other signs of dissident involvement.

H. H. Robertson Company   The dissidents, led by Canada's Belzberg family in conjunction with Guardian Industries, were enjoined from voting their shares because of antitrust conflicts with Guardian. The Belzbergs made a second attempt to elect directors (without the participation of Guardian) after Robertson omitted its quarterly dividend for the first time since 1936. In the settlement that followed by three weeks a subsequent court ruling favorable to the Belzbergs, management agreed to place three Belzberg representatives on the board without a vote. The *WSJ* reports that analysts speculated the move could lead to a wholesale departure of top management. One analyst commented: "They may not leave immediately, but maybe they will after they get their toes stepped on a few times by Hyman [Belzberg] and the brothers". The Belzbergs (who held approximately 20% of the stock) were said to be especially anxious to influence management to increase company profitability because they had seen the market value of their investment drop by one-half since buying shares; Six months later, James L. Davis (age 59), president and CEO, took early retirement in a period of persistent losses and continued inability to resume the firm's regular quarterly dividend payments. *Classification*: Resignation within one year of contest outcome amid other signs of dissident involvement.

Saxon Industries, Inc.   Management settled with the dissidents the day before the scheduled stockholder meeting by agreeing to name two of their representatives to the 12-member board. The meeting was postponed indefinitely. After the settlement, management began to implement some of the dissidents' suggestions for change, e.g., they divested some assets and instituted a cost-cutting program. Despite these measures, the company filed for bankruptcy protection under Chapter 11 within the year. The company immediately named a new president/CEO who was "experienced in management under Chapter 11" to succeed Stanley Lurie (age 61). Mr Lurie was elected chairman. Two months later, Mr Lurie resigned as chairman and a director after massive accounting irregularities became apparent. The dissidents subsequently filed suit against Mr Lurie and subordinate officers, charging that the defendants had falsified the company's books, thereby making false and misleading statements about the company's financial condition during the proxy contest. Federal prosecutors found that the financial statements management released during the proxy contest had overstated the firm's inventory by some $53 million. According to the *WSJ*: "The company, which reported operating profit of $6.5 million that year, would have had to take large losses . . . if the fictitious inventory had been discovered". Mr Lurie eventually pleaded guilty to conspiracy and fraud charges. *Classification*: Resignation in second year following contest outcome amid other signs of dissident involvement.

Texas International Company Although management apparently won the contested election, a federal judge ordered that a new election be held because both sides had violated federal proxy rules. Additionally, stockholders defeated management's proposed stock appreciation rights plan, which the dissidents had criticized as providing excessive compensation to the five top managers if the company were sold or liquidated. One month later, the dissidents settled their dispute with management and, in return for expense reimbursement, agreed to become passive investors and dispose of their shares. Two weeks later, George Platt (age 57), who was one of the three management nominees up for re-election to the classified board, gave up the title of president to fellow incumbent Robert C. Gist, who was previously executive vice president. We did not treat this as a managerial resignation since Mr Platt retained the title of chairman and chief executive officer and since he simultaneously assumed operating responsibility for the company's oil and gas subsidiary, whose current president had resigned. However, 27 months later, Mr Platt announced his resignation to take retirement at age 59. *Classification*: Resignation in third year following contest outcome at other than normal retirement age (age 59).

Tosco Corporation A preliminary vote count showed that the dissidents had won no board seats although they attracted 37% of the votes cast, more than three times their own stake. The dissident leader commented at the time that "this is only one game in a World Series". He had earlier vowed that, even if his slate was not elected, he would "continue his efforts to gain control of Tosco and to oust Morton Winston", president and CEO. After the initial vote count was revealed, the dissident leader announced his intent to "challenge every vote" in court. While doing so, he increased his stake and retained an investment bank to find a buyer for the company "willing to acquire control through buying the [dissident] group's holdings". Less than three months later, hostilities between management and the dissidents ended when management caused the corporation to repurchase the dissidents' shares at a premium, the dissidents signed a standstill agreement, and both sides dropped all litigation. Five months after the greenmail transaction, Mr Winston (age 52) resigned as president and CEO and was named chairman, a position in which "he won't have any day-to-day management duties". The management change was apparently required by the company's lenders as part of Tosco's debt renegotiations. Mr Winston had been repeatedly questioned at the post-greenmail annual meeting about the firm's "erratic performance", i.e., the wide swings in reported earnings. The *WSJ* suggests: "Those wide swings created something of a credibility problem for Mr Winston, who in recent years has more than once had to revise overly optimistic earnings projections . . ." *Classification*: Resignation within one year of contest outcome at other than normal retirement age (age 52).

Notes

Helpful comments were received from Lisa Borstadt, James Brickley, Clifford Holderness, Wayne Marr, Ronald Masulis, Eric Noreen, Patricia O'Brien, Edward Rice, Roberta Romano, Katherine Schipper, Kenneth Scott, Dennis Sheehan, James Sington, Clifford Smith, Richard Smith, Joanne Turner, Jerold Warner, Michael Weisbach, J. Fred Weston, Jerold Zimmerman, Thomas Zwirlein, the referees, George Baker and John Pound, and the editor, Michael Jensen. This study received financial support from the J. Ira Harris Center for the Study of Corporate Finance at the University of Michigan, the Arthur Young Foundation, and the Managerial

Economics Research Center at the University of Rochester. We would like to thank Gita Rao and Douglas Skinner for their research assistance.

1   Specifically, we deleted one contest because we could find no mention of it in the *Wall Street Journal Index*, four contests because they were attempts to gain board seats for consumer advocate or employee groups, three contests because they were attempts to open-end a closed-end fund, one contest because it was a court-administered open election after CEO Robert Vesco fled the United States, and one contest because, contrary to the initial source document, the dissidents did not propose a slate of directors, but rather simply sought to delay the stockholder meeting.

2   The 141 figure understates the incidence of proxy contests since it excludes contested elections over particular corporate issues such as the desirability of an antitakeover charter amendment. Issue contests are also empirically important since, e.g., 36% of the proxy contests studied by Pound (1988) involved only a dispute over corporate policy and no attempt by dissidents to acquire board seats.

3   The dissidents' immediate proxy fight objective was to obtain minority board representation in nine of the 12 contests in which they also offered to purchase the firm. The probable reason is that, in seven of the nine cases, the target elected directors to staggered terms so that a new majority stockholder could not immediately elect a majority of the board. The dissidents apparently sought minority representation as a means of convincing the incumbents to seriously consider selling the firm.

4   Castanias and Johnson (1987) provide evidence that the dividend yields of firms whose managers were subsequently engaged in a proxy contest are lower than the dividend yields of (i) a random sample of publicly held firms and (ii) a sample of firms whose stockholders subsequently received a tender bid.

5   There is an important difference between presenting evidence that *portrays* the incumbents as inefficient, and establishing that they are in fact inefficient in some Nirvana (zero information cost) sense. Theoretically, proxy contests can be expected to occur when there is truly significant doubt about the relative managerial abilities of incumbents and dissidents. If it were easy to identify superior management talent, there would be little incentive for both sides to incur significant costs to persuade voting stockholders to elect their team.

6   This interpretation is reinforced by the observation that other members of the dissident slate have company and industry expertise in 9 and 23 cases, respectively. These facts are consistent with Dodd and Warner's (1983) finding that, in 42.7% of their sample contests, former insiders participate in the dissident group. See also Borstadt and Zwirlein (1987) for further analysis of the roles played by former insiders versus outsiders in proxy contests.

7   We note in passing the table 12.3 data, which indicate that many dissidents possess target-specific, industry-specific, and takeover-related expertise.

8   Asquith, Bruner, and Mullins (1987) document a 0.40 mean ratio of post-offer target equity value to bidder equity value for the merger proposals they study. Bradley, Desai, and Kim (1988) document a 0.31 median (and 0.95 mean) ratio of pre-offer target value to bidder value for the tender bids in their sample. (The median is more informative about the typical size relation, since the cross-sectional distribution exhibits considerable skewness due to a subset of very large tender bid targets.)

9   Some of these sample firms had more than one type of takeover barrier. The incidence of the various takeover deterrents is as follows: staggered board terms (nine firms), poison pill securities (two firms), "friendly hands" stock placements announced in response to

dissidents' takeover attempts (two firms), and regulatory obstacles linked to banking and public utility operations (two firms).

10 The complementary relation between proxy contests and takeover bids is neither limited to 1988, nor even to the last several years. In our sample of 1978–85 contests, 46.7% of the dissident groups propose a sale of the target firm as part of their election campaign, 50% cite inappropriate takeover resistance as a reason to replace incumbent management, and 28.3% are sold or liquidated within three years of contest outcome. In Dodd and Warner's (1983, n. 20) sample of 1962–77 contests, 15% of the firms are merged within three years of contest outcome.

11 For firms in which dissidents obtain control, the mean return from 40 days prior through initiation of dissident activity is 17.68% ($z = 4.46$). For firms in which dissidents win some seats, but not a majority, the corresponding return is 16.47% ($z = 4.44$), and it is 21.35% ($z = 7.28$) for firms in which incumbents successfully deflect the dissidents.

12 The differences between mean and median reflect the modest size of the subsamples and the long intervals over which stock returns are often cumulated. Accordingly, market model parameter estimation errors can generate outlier observations (via repeated cumulation) that unduly influence the mean return. This possibility is of second-order concern for the inferences drawn here since, regardless of whether one relies on means or medians (or uses the market-adjusted returns method whose results are reported in note 13), there is no indication that stockholders in the first and third outcome categories typically experience significant wealth gains.

13 For the three outcome categories, the mean, median, and z-statistic under the market-adjusted returns method are (i) 9.70%, 11.64%, $z = 1.45$; (ii) 12.67%, 17.89%, $z = 2.33$; (iii) -10.45%, -3.18%, $z = -0.34$.

14 All 15 proposed transactions were eventually completed. Two additional sales (also eventually completed) were proposed within three years of contest outcome, but we find no apparent link between these latter two transactions and the dissidents' proxy challenges.

15 The same picture obtains when we calculate cumulative returns based on the market-adjusted returns method. For the 15 firms whose sale or liquidation is linked to dissident activity, the mean return is 23.39%, the median is 26.50%, and the z-statistic is 3.60. For the remaining 45 firms, the corresponding figures are -3.96%, -2.91%, and $z = 0.06$.

16 The age distribution at resignation is as follows: less than 50 years old, three individuals; between 50 and 59, nine individuals; between 60 and 63, six individuals; 65 or 66, two individuals; 69 or older, three individuals.

17 It is difficult to specify on *a priori* ground the appropriate interval for measuring managerial turnover related to dissident challenges. Here we emphasize the resignation rate measured through one year after the contest outcome, since proximity to the contest seems a good indication that the dissidents' efforts played a significant role. We also study each managerial resignation for signs of dissident involvement – see the case study discussion below.

18 Although it does not alter the point made in the text, these studies use somewhat different management change definitions from ours. Gilson's data refer to the per-firm rate of arrivals or departures by the CEO, chairman, or president. Klein and Rosenfeld's data refer to the per-firm departure rate by the CEO, chairman, or president. Walsh's data refer to the departure rate per-position for members of "top management" and are based on a survey of successfully acquired merger targets (with a survey response rate of 39%).

References

Alchian, Armen A. and Harold Demsetz, 1972, Production, information costs, and economic organization, *American Economic Review* 62, 777–95.

Asquith, Paul, Robert F. Bruner, and David W. Mullins, Jr., 1987, Merger returns and the form of financing, Working paper (Harvard University, Cambridge, MA).

Borstadt, Lisa F. and Thomas J. Zwirlein, 1987, The role of proxy contests as a disciplinary mechanism: internal labor market competition versus external capital market competition, Working paper (University of Colorado, Colorado Springs, CO).

Bradley, Michael, Anand Desai, and E. Han Kim, 1988, Synergistic gains from corporate acquisitions and their division between the stockholders of target and acquiring firms, *Journal of Financial Economics* 21, 3–40.

Brown, Stephen J. and Jerold B. Warner, 1985, Using daily stock returns: the case of event studies, *Journal of Financial Economics* 14, 3–31.

Castanias, Rick and Herb Johnson, 1987, Proxy fight versus tender offer: the effect of dividend yield, Working paper (University of California at Davis, Davis, CA).

Coughlan, Anne T. and Ronald M. Schmidt, 1985, Executive compensation, management turnover, and firm performance: an empirical investigation, *Journal of Accounting and Economics* 7, 43–66.

Dann, Larry Y. and Harry DeAngelo, 1988, Corporate financial policy and corporate control: a study of defensive adjustments in asset and ownership structure, *Journal of Financial Economics* 20, 87–127.

DeAngelo, Linda Elizabeth, 1988, Managerial competition, information costs, and corporate governance: the use of accounting performance measures in proxy contests, *Journal of Accounting and Economics* 10, 3–36.

Dodd, Peter, 1980, Merger proposals, management discretion and stockholder wealth, *Journal of Financial Economics* 8, 105–38.

Dodd, Peter and Jerold B. Warner, 1983, On corporate governance: a study of proxy contests, *Journal of Financial Economics* 11, 401–38.

Gilson, Stuart C., 1988, Management-borne costs of financial distress, Unpublished Ph.D. dissertation (University of Rochester, Rochester, NY).

Klein, April and James Rosenfeld, 1988, Targeted share repurchases and top management changes, *Journal of Financial Economics* 20, 493–506.

Manne, Henry G., 1965, Mergers and the market for corporate control, *Journal of Political Economy* 73, 110–20.

Patell, James M., 1976, Corporate forecasts of earnings per share and stock price behavior: empirical tests, *Journal of Accounting Research* 14, 246–76.

Pound, John, 1988, The efficiency of shareholder voting: evidence from proxy contests, *Journal of Financial Economics* 20, 237–65.

Walsh, James P., 1988, Top management turnover following mergers and acquisitions, *Strategic Management Journal* 9, 173–83.

Warner, Jerold B., Ross L. Watts, and Karen H. Wruck, 1988, Stock prices and top management changes, *Journal of Financial Economics* 20, 461–92.

Weisbach, Michael S., 1988, Outside directors and CEO turnover, *Journal of Financial Economics* 20, 431–60.

13

Shareholder Activism and Share Values: The Causes and Consequences of Countersolicitations Against Management Antitakeover Proposals

John Pound

I   Introduction

Voting is the fundamental mechanism whereby shareholders accept or reject incumbent directors' proposals about the structure, strategy, ownership, and management of the corporation. Efficient shareholder oversight has generally been held to imply that, faced with such choices, shareholders should vote so as to maximize the value of their holdings, and hence the value of the corporation.[1] Voting should thus prevent incumbent management from proposing and securing changes in corporate structure, personnel, or strategy that further their interests at the expense of shareholders and, implicitly, of economic efficiency. For more than 50 years, however, there has been widespread agreement that this ideal is not met in practice. Rather, voting appears to be an imperfect and costly means of governance. Primary problems are rational ignorance on the part of dispersed shareholders, which occurs if per-shareholder information costs outweigh the benefits from informed voting,[2] and high costs of organization and communication in the proxy voting system. In recent years empirical work has confirmed that voting does not always ensure the maximization of share values.[3]

The problems that affect voting, however, should, in theory, hold only when voting choices have relatively low value consequences. When proposals placed before shareholders exceed a threshold level of potential harm, one or several large, informed shareholders should find it in their economic interest to organize and attempt to defeat the value-decreasing proposal. The higher the level of expected harm from the proposal, the more resources will be spent by dissidents. The mechanism used to conduct such contests is a proxy fight.

This article analyzes a sample of these countersolicitation proxy fights launched by outside dissident shareholders against management antitakeover proposals since 1980. Antitakeover proposals are chosen for the analysis for two reasons. First, they represent a particularly controversial type of managerial initiative that other literature suggests may strain the management–shareholder contract. Second (and consistent with this view), antitakeover amendments are the only type of routine management initiative that has provoked a significant number of shareholder countersolicitations in the past decade.

Three issues are examined in the analysis. The first is the value consequences associated with votes on contested amendments – the efficiency of shareholders' voting choices in the presence of informed and active shareholder-led opposition. The second issue is what conditions, including underlying ownership and control structure, lead to dissident countersolicitations in response to managerial initiatives. The third issue is the overall effect of these voting decisions on the structure and control of the corporation.

The main conclusions that emerge from the analysis are as follows.

1   Countersolicitations are unsuccessful more often than they are successful. Dissidents win countersolicitation campaigns about 25 percent of the time. This is a significantly higher defeat rate than obtains for uncontested antitakeover amendment proposals (98 percent of which pass) but is also a substantially lower dissident success rate than obtains in other types of proxy contests. This is consistent with the view that countersolicitation campaigns place dissidents at a strategic disadvantage relative to other types of proxy contests because the dissident's vote solicitation campaign must occur within a very short period of time.

2   When shareholders approve contested antitakeover provisions, the net-of-market share price of the target firm falls significantly. In the sample, the average is approximately 6 percent, and each individual amendment approval causes negative net-of-market returns. Across the cases, share price reactions to amendment approval range from −3 to −30 percent. When amendments are defeated, share prices rise. In the sample, the average is approximately 4 percent, and each individual amendment defeat causes a positive net-of-market return. This evidence suggests that, overall, these management-sponsored initiatives are against the interests of outside shareholders. It also shows that shareholders often approve initiatives that have significant negative value effects, even in the presence of an active campaign to inform them that the proposals are harmful.

3   Dissident countersolicitations are almost always preceded by a direct control challenge. In 8 of the 16 countersolicitations in the sample, the dissident made an outright acquisition offer or stated definite acquisition plans prior to the countersolicitation campaign. In another seven cases, the countersolicitation was preceded by the dissident's acquisition of a large stake in the firm and an apparent intent to seek control or a change in management. In only one case in the sample was the countersolicitation completely independent of control aspirations on the part of the dissident investor. This implies that antitakeover amendment proposals must have a large potential negative effect on an individual or group of shareholders, before the economic incentive exists for active opposition.

4   Of the seven firms where the dissident had clear control intent, and where management won the antitakeover amendment vote, only one was ultimately acquired by the dissident in the year following the outcome of the proxy vote. This one firm was acquired through a follow-on proxy contest for control of the board. In four cases, the target firm stayed autonomous, and in several of these cases management vetoed or defeated subsequent attempts by the dissident to buy or find a buyer for the firm. In the remaining two cases, management led a leveraged buyout over dissident opposition. Overall, this evidence suggests that the adoption of antitakeover provisions over dissident opposition has a significant effect on dissidents and ultimately serves to veto a number of acquisition attempts.

The article proceeds as follows. Part II describes the sample. Part III discusses the frequency of dissident and management success in these contests and the implications for the operation of the proxy voting mechanism. Part IV examines the value effects of votes in proxy contests over antitakeover proposals. Part V examines the broader motives of dissident investors and thus the potential costs conveyed on them by managements' antitakeover amendment proposals. Part VI analyzes the structure of share ownership in the target firms. Part VII examines the fate of the target firms in the period following contest resolution to determine the overall effect of the contested vote on control structure and corporate policy.

II   Sample

Cases in which antitakeover amendment proposals were greeted by active outside opposition were isolated using the computerized online Dow Jones (DJ) News Retrieval System, the *Wall Street Journal* News Index, and the *Wall Street Journal*. First, a keyword search was conducted using the DJ News Retrieval System. This search isolated firms with antitakeover amendment proposals pending, for which news accounts contained some mention of shareholder opposition. Approximately a dozen keyword search routines were run, using, for example, the criteria that the phrases "antitakeover amendment" and "opposition" or "countersolicitation" and "dissident" appear in the same article. The computerized data base searches selected articles from the *Wall Street Journal* and *Barron's* from 1979 to April 1987, the full news coverage of the *Wall Street Journal* since 1984, and selected articles from business weeklies since 1984. Also searched was the data base compiled by the Investor Responsibility Research Center of antitakeover amendment proposals since 1984. This database includes over 600 proposals.

The hard-copy News Index and the original *Wall Street Journal* articles were then used to further identify and isolate the level of outside opposition to each proposal. Opposition had to be organized and identifiable for the case to be included in the sample. Anonymous "rumblings of discontent" among shareholders were judged insufficient evidence of serious opposition. Also, the vote announcement had to be clean, reported immediately – on the day following the vote – in the *Wall Street*

Journal. Otherwise, the effects of the news of the vote would be too difficult to isolate and the tests would have little power.

Overall, this search regimen isolated 20 cases of active antitakeover amendment opposition by outside shareholders. This appears to be close to the universe of active oppositions during this period. Of these 20 cases, 16 were sufficiently well covered in news sources to isolate full information on the dissident countersolicitation and a clear vote-outcome announcement date. One of the cases occurred in 1981, two cases were in 1982, four cases were in 1983, two were in 1984, nine were in 1985, and two were in 1986. This small universe of cases suggests that dissident countersolicitation campaigns have been rare, relative to the frequency of antitakeover amendment proposals. (Over the period of the sample, over 600 antitakeover charter provisions were proposed and ratified at nationally listed corporations.)

Appendix A shows the firms in the sample and the type of amendment proposed at each. There is a wide variety of amendment types across the sample. Most amendments are types that might be expected to have negative value consequences for shareholders. Jarrell and Poulsen find negative value effects associated with amendments that require large majorities to approve mergers and that lock in boards.[4] Many of the amendments in this sample are of these types. Several, such as Pacific Realty Trust's provision limiting share ownership by any single investor, place particularly high amounts of veto power in the hands of incumbent management. None of the amendments in the sample are of the more benign price-and-procedural variety (so-called fair price amendments) that is ostensibly designed purely to insure against expropriation of minority shareholders.

III   The Frequency of Dissident and Management Success

Determining the success or failure of the countersolicitation campaigns in the sample was relatively straightforward because all 16 contests were ultimately resolved by shareholder vote. Dissidents thus unambiguously won or lost the contests. This outcome differs significantly from what has been shown to occur in other types of proxy contests. In contests for control and partial control, in which dissidents run directors against management slates, between 25 and 30 percent of all contests are ultimately settled prior to the vote.[5]

Appendix A separates the firms in the sample by contest winner. Overall, it shows that dissidents won 4 contests, while management won 12.[6] This is a lower success rate than is enjoyed by dissidents in other types of proxy contests, including those for control and partial control of the board. Other studies report dissident success rates for these contests ranging from 40 to 50 percent.[7] The low frequency of dissident victory in the sample suggests that dissidents face significant problems in mounting countersolicitation campaigns in response to management proposals. A central deterrent to dissident victory in countersolicitation efforts is state laws that give management control over the timing of the vote and the identity of voters. First, state law allows management to fix a date for annual or special meetings. Under the laws of

Delaware and most other states, shareholder meetings can be called by management on notice as short as ten days. Concurrently, state law places no burden on management to delay the meeting if opposing shareholders wish to countersolicit. Management may thus spend months preparing proposals, may convene a meeting on relatively short notice, and may give potential dissidents very little time to analyze the proposals, organize, and countersolicit votes. If dissidents are viewed as competing bidders for the firm, these laws stand in striking juxtaposition to federal tender-offer laws. Federal tender-offer regulations require extension of offer periods in the event of new, competing bids in order to give shareholders and all bidders time to evaluate all offers for the firm.

Similarly, under state law, management is accorded the right to determine who is allowed to vote by specifying the record date prior to a shareholder meeting. The record date establishes ownership for the purposes of voting. After the record date, votes are not transferred when shares are sold unless the owner of record engages in the costly and time-consuming process of granting an irrevocable proxy to the new owner. The record-date convention creates two significant problems for dissidents. First, because management typically freezes vote ownership at the time that they announce proposals, dissidents cannot amass votes through open-market purchases of shares, nor can votes gravitate into the hands of informed shareholders friendly to dissidents. Thus, the record-date convention helps management by effectively preventing the market mechanism from reallocating votes in light of management and dissident proposals. Second, because some shareholders sell shares after the record date, votes may become separated from shares. This leaves some voters with no economic incentive to vote at all, let alone vote efficiently.

The record-date convention is an archaic and unnecessary one in the modern market. It was originally conceived to ensure against vote fraud and provide all parties with knowledge about who owns the right to vote. But this was early in the century, prior to computerization of ownership records. Once again, the contrast between state law governing ownership for purposes of voting, and federal law governing ownership for purposes of tendering in acquisition offers, is striking. In an open tender offer, federal regulations allow shareholders to purchase shares and tender them until the close of the offer. Tendering of nonowned shares is, of course, grounds for legal prosecution. But federal laws thus place no restrictions on the reallocation of shares to informed market actors. As a result, there is typically a huge volume surge surrounding tender-offer announcements, as informed investors amass shares. A similar mechanism is precluded in proxy contests, to the detriment of informed voting by active investors.

IV   The Value Effects of Contested Antitakeover Votes

A.   *Methodology*

Dissident campaigns against antitakeover amendments should create substantial *ex ante* uncertainty about vote outcomes for several reasons. First, the dissidents' decision to organize should be a signal to shareholders that the issue to be voted on is not routine. Second, the dissidents' organizing efforts make it less costly for shareholders to become informed, and voting should thus be characterized by higher participation and more informed choice. Third, these changed dynamics themselves should make it difficult to predict beforehand how any specific contested vote will turn out. Most firms experience very few proxy contests. Thus for any individual contested vote there are almost no grounds for predicting how the firm's (largely fixed) voting pool will behave in the presence of dissident opposition.

This uncertainty makes the value effect of shareholders' voting decisions observable at the time that the vote outcome is announced. Before the results of the vote are known, there will be two possible outcomes – passage and failure – and two associated share values. At this point, the market value of the firm will be

$$(p)V^p + (1 - p)V^f \tag{1}$$

where p is the probability that the proposal will pass, V^p is the value of the firm contingent on passage, and V^f is the firm's value contingent on the amendment failing. When the vote outcome is announced, the uncertainty will be resolved, and value will be either V^p or V^f. If the lower-valued alternative has passed, market value will drop, while if the higher-valued alternative is ratified, value will increase.[8]

The uncertainty associated with contested votes, and the observable reaction to vote outcomes, makes measurement of the value effects of voting more accurate for contested antitakeover amendments than for uncontested amendment proposals. Uncontested amendments are virtually always approved by shareholders. Hence there is no meaningful *ex ante* uncertainty about vote outcomes and no observable reaction to vote results. Researchers have circumvented this problem by examining share-price reactions to announcements by management that they will place amendments before shareholders for ratification. But this approach may be subject to significant measurement error because amendment announcements may convey information not only about the value effects of the amendment itself but also about the probability of acquisition and the motive and quality of incumbent management.[9] Thus the *ex ante* uncertainty associated with contested amendments makes them particularly important for assessing the efficiency of voting on antitakeover amendments generally.

This article's tests for value effects of contested antitakeover amendment votes focus on two measurement periods. The first is the specific day (or days) on which the news of the vote became public. For several firms in the sample, news about the vote outcome emerged on more than one day. In a typical example, a report might emerge that an amendment "appears to have failed" five days prior to the official date on which the actual defeat is reported by the company. Both dates must be accumulated to capture the full effect of the announcement and the resulting resolution of uncertainty about firm value. Thus for each firm, the effect of the vote announcement is calculated by first isolating all dates on which identifiable news emerged about the vote outcome. The market reaction to each news event is then measured over the period from one day prior to one day after that date. These price reactions are then accumulated for each firm to determine the total market reaction to the news of the vote outcome.

The second measurement period is the time interval over which the dissident countersolicitation campaign was conducted. This is defined as running from the day after the dissident announced the countersolicitation campaign to the day after the vote outcome became known. This longer window is less reliable as a measure of the effects of the vote itself on share values due to the potential for other news to emerge. But it ensures that the measured price reaction will capture all news that emerges about the proxy contest outcome, including information that leaks out substantially in advance of the actual vote announcement date.[10]

I employ a series of tests to determine the economic and statistical significance of the price reaction over these periods. All the tests use the firms' net-of-market returns in the period surrounding the announcement of the vote outcome, defined as

$$ER_{it} = (R_{it} - R_{mt}) \tag{2}$$

where ER_{it} is the excess return to firm i in period t, R_{it} is the observed total return to firm i in the period examined, and R_{mt} is the return to the appropriate composite market index for the period.[11]

Using the net-of-market return, I first ask whether the average value change across the sample in each event period is different from zero. I pose this test using the event-period, cross-sectional standard error for the 16 individual returns. Second, using individual firms' net-of-market returns at the time of the vote outcome announcement, I test whether each of these returns is significantly different from zero, given the variance of each firm's net-of-market returns over the preceding 18 calendar months.

B.   Results

Table 13.1 presents the net-of-market returns for each of the 16 firms in the sample, over the two measurement periods described above. Panel A presents results for firms where the antitakeover amendment was ultimately adopted by shareholders, while panel B presents evidence for the four firms where the dissident prevailed and the amendment was ultimately defeated. In addition, each panel presents summary statistics on the average change over the relevant subsample.

The results in table 13.1 are quite striking. Each of the 12 firms in which amendments were ultimately approved experienced significant negative returns at the time that the vote outcome became public. The net-of-market return averages about −7 percent across the sample around the vote outcome announcement date. These results show unambiguously that shareholder approval of these amendments is the less valued outcome. The results in panel B, for the four firms in which amendments were defeated, confirm this conclusion. In each of these cases, news that the amendment was defeated caused a significant increase in the firm's market value.

Table 13.1 Value effects of shareholder votes and dissident campaigns

| Company | A. Amendments approved by shareholders | |
	% Price change at vote outcome announcement	*% Price change over proxy contest*
Munsingwear	−6.60*	−3.79*
Scherer (R.P.)	−30.98*	−33.04
Pacific Realty Trust	−4.67*	−2.16
County Tower Corp	−5.95*	−6.68
Amrep	−4.68*	−27.78
KDI Corp	−3.60*	−6.75
Hubco	−3.70*	11.62
Murphy (G.C.)	−4.08*	−6.70
Hilton Hotels	−6.12*	−6.28
Gannett	−3.52*	−7.63
Uniroyal	−6.53*	−3.73
Asarco	−6.48*	−14.98
Average net-of-market change, twelve cases	−7.24	−8.99
t-statistic for hypothesis that average return equals zero	−4.12	−2.77

	B. Amendments defeated by shareholders	
Patrick Industries	6.20*	14.81
Superior Oil	5.72*	2.23
Tandycrafts	2.69*	7.04
Informatics General	3.80*	8.34
Average net-of-market change, four cases	4.60	8.11
t-statistic for hypothesis that average change equals zero	6.47	3.61

Note: Net-of-market stock return for 16 firms that were the subjects of dissident countersolicitation campaigns against management antitakeover proposals during 1981–6, over two event periods. The price change at vote-outcome announcement measures net-of-market return over the days on which information about the outcome of the shareholder vote on the antitakeover proposal became public. Net-of-market returns for each day on which vote outcome news emerged are measured over the window from two days before to one day after news day. The price change over the proxy contest measures net-of-market return from the day after the announcement of the dissident countersolicitation to the day after the official announcement of the vote outcome. In both cases, firm-specific net-of-market returns are measured as

$$ER_{it} = R_{it} - R_{mt}$$

where ER_{it} is the net-of-market return to firm i in period t, R_{it} is the observed raw return to firm i in period t, and R_{mt} is the observed return on the market in period t. Market return was approximated with NYSE composite index for NYSE and ASE listed firms, and OTC composite index for OTC firms.
* Denotes a firm-specific announcement date return that is significant at the 5 percent level, given the variance of that firm's three-day net-of-market returns for the preceding 18 months.

The net-of-market price movements over the period of the countersolicitation campaign, from dissident announcement to vote outcome announcement, are consistent with the results for the vote announcement date. Firms in which amendment proposals were ultimately ratified lost value during this period, while firms in which amendments were defeated gained in value. As expected, given the longer time horizon, net-of-market returns are more variable. But in no case do they contradict or offset the results for the vote announcement date.

These results show that when shareholders approve management charter initiatives over the active opposition of an informed outside shareholder, the result is a value loss for the corporation. The size of the value loss is significant in economic terms, particularly given that the net-of-market returns in table 13.1 probably do not reflect the full value effect of the amendment proposals in the sample.[12] Many firms in the sample experience value decreases of 6–10 percent when the vote outcomes are announced. The combination of the frequency with which amendments pass, and the size of the losses when they do, is perhaps surprising. One might have expected fewer value-decreasing outcomes in this sample, given that an outside shareholder expended significant resources to attempt to inform shareholders about the efficient voting decision.[13]

V   Dissident Motives and the Incentives for Shareholder Opposition

The existence of organized dissident countersolicitations shows that, when management initiatives exceed a certain threshold of potential harm, outside shareholders respond. The crucial question is then what threshold must be crossed for organized opposition to surface. Clearly, a low-cost threshold for dissident opposition would imply that voting may prevent all but relatively minor self-seeking managerial initiatives, while a high-cost threshold would imply that voting may sometimes not prevent significant distortions of the management–shareholder contract.

The evidence in section IV, documenting the share-price effects of votes on these dissident initiatives, can be interpreted as providing a perspective on the cost threshold at which these dissident campaigns arise. But this may not be a completely accurate interpretation. Dissidents may be motivated to organize because management proposals impose on them unique costs that are higher than those experienced by other shareholders. If this is the case, the share-price response to the countersolicitation campaign will not reflect the wealth effect of the management proposal on the dissident.

Dissidents' losses are potentially largest, relative to those experienced by other shareholders, when the dissidents are motivated by clear and immediate intent to seek control of the company. In this case, dissidents' potential losses from the management proposal derive from the loss of proprietary gains that could be realized by acquiring control of the firm. Some, but not necessarily all, of these losses will be shared by other outside holders.

Dissident losses are more likely to be equivalent to those of other shareholders if the dissident is a large, informed, but passive investor with long-term holdings in the corporation. Primary candidates to mount such efforts would be institutional investors and corporations with long-standing ownership stakes. In these cases, it would be less likely for the individual countersoliciting shareholder to have any proprietary knowledge about true firm value. Rather, these types of solicitations would be more likely to be motivated by a desire to protect existing value, as measured by the preproposal market price.

To examine the potential cost of these management proposals further, evidence was gathered on dissidents' identity and control intent in the period surrounding the countersolicitation initiative. Evidence on intent was gathered by examining news reports and proxy filings covering the period running from six months prior to the date of the countersolicitation announcement, to the date of the vote outcome. Appendixes B and C contain this evidence. Appendix B contains evidence on dissident intentions and activities, while appendix C describes dissident identity.

Appendix B shows that, of the 16 contests in the sample, 14 involved dissidents that had either potential or clear control intent with respect to the target firm. In 8 cases, a clear-cut control intent was expressed by the dissident. In 5 of these cases, the dissident made an outright acquisition offer prior to the countersolicitation contest, while in 3 cases the dissident stated a clear intent to gain controlling interest and replace the current board. In another 6 cases, the dissident acquired a large block position immediately prior to the countersolicitation contest and stated that future alternatives included expanding these holdings or attaining control.

Appendix C's evidence complements that contained in appendix B. It shows that in only one case was the dissident shareholder a (fiduciary) institutional holder. In the other 15 cases, the dissident was either an active individual investor with a record of control-oriented investment activity, or a firm with a similar activity record.

These statistics do not suggest that dissident countersolicitations are typically undertaken by informed but passive long-term investors to protect the status quo value of a target firm. Rather, the evidence suggests that dissident countersolicitations typically occur when a large, active investor with control intent stands to suffer a substantial setback should the antitakeover provision pass. In some cases in the sample, management's proposal of antitakeover provisions serves to force the hand of the active investor, and thus smokes out a control bid. The best example is that of Hilton Hotels, where investor Carl Icahn made an acquisition offer for the company in response to management's antitakeover amendment proposal that was contingent on that amendment's defeat. In other cases, increasing activism on the part of the large holder, and either a clear or a possible control bid led management to propose the antitakeover provision as a defensive measure.

This evidence thus suggests that the losses faced by dissidents across this sample of amendment proposals were probably larger, on a per share basis, than those faced by other outside shareholders. This, in turn, implies that the threat of countersolicitation campaigns will be a less effective deterrent to value-decreasing management voting proposals. Had most countersolicitations in the sample been conducted by passive shareholders to protect existing value, this would imply that dissident campaigns could potentially arise in many firms with informed large shareholders, even in the absence of the large-wealth consequences associated with a control contest.[14] But the large portion of campaigns accompanied by clear control intent suggests that these campaigns will arise in a few restricted firms, where the management initiative generates unusually high costs.

One further quite striking finding emerges from combining the evidence in appendix B with that contained in table 13.1. Appendix B shows that, for eight firms in the sample, outright or pending acquisition bids were on the table at the time of the shareholder vote. Table 13.1 shows that shareholders voted to approve antitakeover initiatives at 7 out of these 8 firms despite the existence of a value-increasing bid tied to the vote. These 8 cases thus show that shareholders sometimes vote to approve managerial initiatives even when, by doing so, they are rejecting specific takeover offers.

VI Ownership Structure and the Value Effects of Votes

Several studies argue that the ownership structure of the firm should systematically affect management's ability to protect its interests through the voting system. One study suggests that high levels of inside ownership might make it possible for management to pass wealth-decreasing proposals over the objections of outside shareholders because, as management ownership becomes higher, defeat of these initiatives requires a higher and higher proportion of all nonmanagement votes.[15] A second study suggests that, for both strategic and substantive reasons, dissidents will be likelier to win proxy initiatives, the higher their ownership level in the firm.[16] The effects of a third class of shareholders – institutional investors – is the subject of a continuing controversy. The first study referenced above suggests that institutions should act as informed shareholders and increase voting efficiency,[17] but others have suggested that institutional holders will tend to vote against dissidents to preserve ongoing business relationships with management, even when doing so decreases share values. Empirical evidence is mixed, indicating that institutional holders tend to vote with management in proxy contests,[18] but that in voting on uncontested antitakeover amendment initiatives, some types of institutional holders tend to vote against management, while other types tend to vote with management.[19]

Table 13.2 presents summary evidence on the ownership structure of the 16 firms examined in this article, including dissident ownership, management ownership, and institutional ownership. The sample is too small to test for systematic relations between ownership structure and contest outcome, but the data on ownership structure are broadly consistent with several of the hypotheses described above.

Most firms in the sample show high levels of inside ownership for large, nationally listed corporations. In only 4 cases is ownership by management less than 5 percent. In a number of firms, management owns over 20 percent of shares outstanding. At this level of ownership, management must secure the vote of only 30 percent of all outstanding outside shares to secure passage of amendments. The high management-ownership levels may thus help to explain why management felt able to propose amendments that engendered active opposition by outside shareholders. The average

Table 13.2 Ownership structure of target firms, 1981–6

Company	% Ownership		
	Insider	Dissident	Institutional
Munsingwear	5.0	9.2	33.0
Scherer (R.P.)	22.0[a]	<1.0	22.7
Pacific Realty Trust	11.0	9.0	0.0
County Tower Corp	14.6	6.0	13.6
Amrep Corp	21.5	21.3	6.7
KDI Corp	<1.0	22.9	4.0
Murphy (G.C.)	5.0	7.5	25.0
Hubco	15.0	5.1	0.0
Hilton Hotels	30.0	<5.0	67.0
Gannett	1.0[b]	5.0	72.0
Uniroyal	<5.0	5.0	44.0
Asarco	18.0	9.0	21.0
Patrick Industries	15.6	9.4	0.0
Superior Oil	30.0	3.5	36.0
Informatics General	2.0	5.0	32.0
Tandycrafts	8.1	9.9	34.9
Sample average	12.8	7.8	25.7

Note: Ownership stake is measured (in % of total voting stock outstanding) for management and directors ("inside ownership"), dissidents,
and institutional investors.
[a] Noninsider family members own approximately 20% additional.
[b] Corporation foundation owns additional 10%.

management-ownership level in the sample is higher than that obtaining in other
types of proxy contests, including control or partial control initiatives.[20]

Institutional ownership figures for firms in the sample and for the subsamples of
firms where amendments were ratified and rejected are somewhat less clear. Overall,
institutional ownership is lower in these firms than across all nationally listed firms as
a whole by about one-third, but average institutional ownership is consistent with that
found in firms that are the targets of other types of proxy fights, including control and
partial control challenges, where management ultimately wins the contests. It is over
50 percent higher than the average level found in firms that are the targets of other
types of proxy contests, where dissidents ultimately win.

Finally, dissident-ownership levels are roughly consistent with those found in other
types of proxy fights, including those for control and partial control. This is not
surprising, given that most dissidents in the sample had clear or potential control
intent. Dissident ownership is more substantial, perhaps, than might be expected if
these initiatives were purely aimed at turning back an unnecessary management
charter change, absent immediate control plans for the firm.

Overall, the ownership structure of these firms is consistent with that found for
other firms that are the subjects of proxy fights, with the striking exception of
management ownership. High management ownership suggests a convincing reason
why management took the chance of pursuing these amendments despite shareholder

opposition. It may be that management chose these voting initiatives rather than other possible defensive measures as their main defense against takeover bids precisely because of the strategic advantage that their ownership stake accorded them in the voting arena.

VII   Vote Outcomes and the Ultimate Fate of the Firm

A final question about the contested votes in this sample is what effect they have on the ultimate ownership and control of the target firm. For those firms that were the subjects of direct control offers, the value effects of the votes clearly reflect significant changes in the probability that the outstanding offer for the firm would be successful. But equally clearly, for most firms that probability does not go to zero. Potential acquirers, who have already invested significant resources on countersolicitation campaigns, might well pursue other acquisition strategies. By examining the history of these firms after the amendment vote, these cases provide a perspective on the potential effects of antitakeover amendments on control bids.

To examine the post-vote control structure of the firms in the sample, each firm was followed in all publicly available news sources for one calendar year after the date on which the vote outcome became known. News sources were scanned for news of any outside control activity against the firm undertaken by the original dissident or other outside parties; any major change in financial structure or internal ownership structure (including management buyouts); and any news about the ultimate fate of the original dissident (for example, liquidation of ownership position). This evidence is summarized in appendix D.

The evidence shows several patterns. The first, and perhaps most important, is the fate of the 8 clear acquisition attempts that were outstanding at the time that the votes on the antitakeover amendment proposals occurred. In one of these cases, that of Informatics General, the proposal was rejected by shareholders. The target firm acquiesced to purchase by the dissident a short period later. In the other 7 cases, the antitakeover proposal passed despite the existence of a clear acquisition offer. In 6 of the 7 cases, the dissident offer was ultimately defeated. In 2 of these 6 cases, management ultimately took the firm private in a leveraged buyout. In the remaining 4 cases, management vetoed the dissident's unwanted bid and kept the firm autonomous. In the one case in which the dissident ultimately gained control of the firm despite the passage of the amendment, the vehicle was not an acquisition offer, but a follow-on proxy fight for control of the board.

This evidence suggests that ratification of these amendment effectively deterred a significant number of dissident bids and ultimately allowed management to maintain control. The evidence lends further support to the hypothesis that in these cases amendment ratification was against the interests of some, and potentially all, outside shareholders.

When the sample is broadened to include firms that were the subjects of both clear and potential control intent, the story remains much the same. Of the 16 firms in the sample, 14 were the subjects of either clear or potential control intent by dissidents. Of these 14, dissidents gained control in only 2 in the year following the proxy fight. This offers further evidence that the adoption of the antitakeover amendments in the sample rendered outright acquisition offers strategically difficult to execute.

In several cases in which amendments were ratified by shareholders, dissidents continued to expend resources organizing and pressuring management after the vote, only to ultimately admit defeat. In the case of Amrep, for example, the dissident group sought an outside buyer for the firm willing to make a bid despite the existence of the antitakeover amendment, but ultimately announced that it was abandoning its effort. In the case of KDI, the dissident attempted to form a group to go forward with a hostile tender offer, but once again ultimately announced that the effort was deemed futile by the group's participants. This is further evidence that the amendments that were ratified significantly reduced outside shareholders' ability to influence the firms' ownership and control structure.

This evidence suggests that in these cases, the market was clearly correct in its judgment that the adoption of these amendments lowered the probability of a control change and hence lowered expected shareholder wealth. The evidence also suggests that amendment adoption may have had particularly costly effects on dissidents. In only 6 of the 14 cases involving clear or probable dissident-control intent was the firm ultimately bought by any party. In only one case, moreover, is it reported that the dissident disposed of a strategic block of stock in a negotiated transaction involving management or a friendly third party. Had more firms ultimately been acquired, or had more negotiated settlements ultimately occurred, it could be argued that dissidents might have benefited regardless of whether they became owners of the corporation. But the widespread retention of autonomy and absence of post-vote negotiations suggests that in many of these cases dissidents as well as other shareholders suffered losses from amendment ratification.

VIII Conclusion

This article examines the causes and consequences of dissident countersolicitations against management antitakeover proposals. These countersolicitations should potentially serve as an important check on managerial discretion in setting the corporate agenda. In such countersolicitations, outside shareholders expend resources organizing other shareholders and informing them of costs of managerial initiatives. The threat of this type of activism should set a threshold that management cannot cross in proposing changes that carry adverse consequences for shareholders.

Overall, the article shows that relatively few such countersolicitations occur, despite the large number of antitakeover amendment proposals made by management. In those contests that do occur, dissidents lose more often than they win. When dissidents lose, share prices fall by an average of 6 percent, whereas when they win, share prices rise. These results imply that these dissident campaigns were in shareholders' interests, and that the management proposals in the sample were not. The results also suggest that it is difficult, for strategic reasons, for dissidents to mount successful countersolicitation campaigns.

The cases in the sample also show that dissidents mount countersolicitation campaigns against management antitakeover provisions largely when the management proposal threatens to veto their plans to gain control of the corporation. In 14 out of the 16 cases studied, dissidents had either existing or pending acquisition offers for the corporation. This suggests that dissidents stood to suffer high expected losses if the amendments in the sample passed. This, in turn, implies that expected losses must be high for a dissident countersolicitation campaign to be undertaken.

Finally, the results show that the passage of antitakeover amendments over dissident protest has a significant deterrent effect on control bids. Of the 7 firms in the sample in which dissident control bids existed or were pending prior to the dissident campaign, and in which the amendment ultimately passed, only one was ultimately taken over by the dissident. Six firms remained under management control. Thus dissidents are correct to perceive that ratification of the amendments will significantly reduce the probability that they will gain control of the firm.

These results support the conclusions of other recent studies of the voting process. The results show that shareholders sometimes vote to approve antitakeover provisions even when dissidents expend resources on organizing shareholders and informing them about the value consequences of initiatives. In some of these cases, shareholders approve the amendment despite the existence of a direct acquisition offer from the dissident that will be placed in jeopardy by approval of the management initiative. These cases represent fairly dramatic examples in which voting outcomes are questionable on efficiency grounds.

Some of the inefficiencies that appear to exist in the current voting system clearly derive from fundamental economic incentive problems. The most important of these is probably the "rational ignorance" problem affecting individual shareholders' voting decisions, which occurs if widely dispersed shareholders, with relatively little stake in the corporation, face higher costs than benefits from informed voting. The cases in this article suggest, however, that these incentive problems may not be the whole story. Problems may also be caused by federal and state laws governing proxy solicitation and proxy voting that make outside shareholder opposition to management particularly difficult. Correction of these problems would encourage shareholder responsiveness and the efficiency of the process of corporate governance and corporate control.

Appendix A: Summary of antitakeover amendment proposals

Type of antitakeover amendment proposed by management for 16 firms where amendment proposals engendered active dissident opposition. Sample covers the period 1981–6.

Panel A: Amendments Approved by Shareholders

Company name	*Type of amendment*
Munsingwear	Authorization to sell 30 percent to 3 Japanese banks
Scherer (R.P.)	80 percent supermajority

Company name	Type of amendment
Pacific Realty Trust	No owner can own more than 9.8 percent
County Tower Corporation	80 percent supermajority/shrink board from 23 to 9
Land of Lincoln S & L	End cumulative voting
Amrep	Two-thirds supermajority/double authorization shares/ staggered board
KDI Corporation	85 percent supermajority or majority of unaffiliated directors
Hubco	75 percent supermajority/staggered board
Murphy (G.C.)	80 percent supermajority for director or bylaw change
Hilton Hotels	75 percent supermajority/staggered board/blank check preferred
Gannett	80 percent supermajority
Uniroyal	Staggered board/80 percent supermajority
Asarco	Staggered board/double authorization common

Panel B: Amendments Defeated by Shareholders

Company name	Type of amendment
Patrick Industries	Staggered board/supermajority/blank check preferred
Superior Oil	Staggered board/50 percent to call special meeting
Tandycrafts	Staggered board/supermajority
Informatics General	Majority of nonaffiliated shares to approve merger

Appendix B: The goals of dissident investors

A summary of dissident initiatives against the firms that were the targets of dissidents' antitakeover amendment countersolicitation campaigns. Included is all activity – other than the antitakeover amendment campaign – that occurred during the period from six months prior to announcement of a countersolicitation campaign, to the date of the vote-outcome announcement. Sample includes 16 firms that were the subjects of antitakeover amendment countersolicitation campaigns during the period 1981–6.

Company	Dissident activity
Munsingwear	None
Scherer (R.P.)	Direct takeover bid by dissident (FMC Corporation) prior to beginning of countersolicitation
Pacific Realty Trust	Direct acquisition bid prior to beginning of countersolicitation
County Tower	Dissident acquires 5 percent prior to countersolicitation and intends to increase holdings
Amrep Corporation	Dissident acquires 20 percent prior to countersolicitation and intends to increase stake to 49 percent
KDI Corporation	Dissident boosts stake to 22 percent prior to countersolicitation and says it intends to gain control
Murphy (G.C.)	Dissident acquires 7.5 percent prior to countersolicitation and intends to increase holdings

Company	Dissident activity
Hubco	Dissidents hold 5.8 percent and seek board representation
Hilton Hotels	Dissident makes direct acquisition offer prior to countersolicitation
Gannett	None
Uniroyal	Dissident launches hostile acquisition offer in response to antitakeover amendment proposals
Asarco	Dissident acquires 9 percent stake and may seek control or board representation
Patrick Industries	Dissident acquires 8.3 percent prior to countersolicitation and may seek control
Superior Oil	Stakes acquired by several potential acquirers prior to countersolicitation. Dissident urges board to consider all offers from potential bidders
Informatics General	Dissident makes direct acquisition offer prior to countersolicitation campaign
Tandycrafts	Dissident acquires 9.3 percent stake prior to countersolicitation

Appendix C: The identity of dissident shareholders

Identity of dissident shareholder in 16 cases where dissident-launched countersolicitation campaigns against management antitakeover proposals over the period 1981–6. Dissident is categorized as institutional investor, corporate investor, or active individual investor.

Company	Dissident identity
Munsingwear	Institutional investor (Tweedy Browne)
Scherer (R.P.)	Corporate investor (FMC Corporation)
Pacific Realty Trust	Corporate investor (linked to individual active investors including Campeau Corporation)
County Tower Corporation	Active individual investor (Morrisey)
Amrep Corporation	Corporate investor (Unicorp)
KDI Corporation	Investment partnership led by Tactron Inc.
Murphy (G. C.)	Individual investor (Goldberg)
Hubco	Private partnership (Hudson Financial)
Hilton Hotels	Corporate investor (Golden Nugget Corporation)
Gannett	Active individual investor (Lindner)
Uniroyal	Active individual investor (Icahn)
Asarco	Active individual investor (Holms and Court)
Patrick Industries	Private partnership (Koether)
Superior Oil	Member of founding family (W. K. Day)
Informatics General	Corporate investor (Sterling Software Inc.)
Tandycrafts	Private partnership (Initio Partners)

Appendix D: Postvote control activity undertaken
against target firms

A summary of all control activity undertaken against firms that were the targets of
countersolicitations against management antitakeover proposals in the calendar year following
vote on the antitakeover proposal. Included are any offers or attempts to acquire the firm by the
dissident shareholder, other outside shareholders, or management.

Company	Control activity
Munsingwear	Gulf & Western boosts stake to 30 percent
Scherer (R.P.)	None
Pacific Realty Trust	Acquired by management group in LBO over continuing dissident objection
County Tower Corporation	Acquired by third party in unsolicited but friendly transaction
Amrep Corporation	Dissident attempts to find buyer for firm; abandons effort
KDI Corporation	Dissident forms alliance with other investors to make takeover bid; alliance falls apart and dissident abandons efforts
Murphy (G.C.)	Acquired by third party in friendly ("white knight") transaction
Hubco	Dissident wins proxy fight to replace board and takes control
Hilton Hotels	None
Gannett	None
Uniroyal	Acquired by management group in leveraged buyout
Asarco	Dissident sells shares to third party friendly to management
Patrick Industries	None
Informatics General	Acquired by dissident
Superior Oil	Acquired by friendly third party ("white knight") transaction
Tandycrafts	None

Notes

I would like to thank Gregg Jarrell, Robert Monks, and Richard Zeckhauser for comments and
suggestions on an earlier draft. This research was supported in part by Institutional Shareholder
Services, Inc.

1   See, for example, David Austen-Smith and Patricia O'Brien, Takeover Defenses and
    Shareholder Voting (Working Paper No. 1823-86, MIT, Sloan School of Management
    1987); Frank Easterbrook and Daniel Fischel, Voting in Corporate Law, 26 *J. Law & Econ.*
    395 (1983). Recent work on voting structures and corporate control, while complicating
    the picture somewhat, does not reject this simple hypothesis as applied to new managerial
    initiatives. See, for example, Sanford Grossman and Oliver Hart, One Share One Vote and
    the Market for Corporate Control, 20 *J. Fin. Econ.* 175 (1988); Milton Harris and Artur
    Raviv, Corporate Governance: Voting Rights and Majority Rules, 20 *J. Fin. Econ.* 203
    (1988).

2   Rationally ignorant shareholders may know the equilibrium expected value of all mana-
    gerial proposals, even if they do not know the costs (or benefits) of individual proposals.
    As long as the expected value of all proposals is positive, the cost-minimizing strategy

for shareholders will be to vote for each individual proposal without determining its individual consequences.

3   In particular, several studies have documented that management is able to secure passage of various types of initiatives (notably antitakeover amendment provisions) that have a negative effect on share values. Gregg Jarrell and Annette Poulsen, Shark Repellents and Stock Prices: The Effects of Antitakeover Amendments since 1980, 18 *J. Fin. Econ.* 435 (1987).

4   Ibid.

5   See Harry DeAngelo and Linda DeAngelo, The Role of Proxy Contests in the Oversight of Publicly Held Corporations (working paper, Univ. Rochester, Simon School of Business 1988); John Pound, Proxy Contests and the Efficiency of Shareholder Oversight, 20 *J. Fin. Econ.* 237 (1988).

6   In one additional case, the lead dissident shareholder attained a place on the board in the aftermath of the campaign. Including this case as a dissident victory changes the totals to five dissident and eleven management victories. Substantively, however, it is difficult to conclude that this case represents a true dissident victory. Management was successful in altering the structure of the corporate charter to make an outright acquisition more difficult. A single seat on the board offers the dissident little strategic ability to change the charter, force an acquisition, or even force significant change in corporate strategy.

7   See Pound, note 5 above; DeAngelo and DeAngelo, note 5 above.

8   The market reaction will not reflect the full value of the proposal, however, unless prior to the vote the market believed with certainty that the opposite outcome would occur.

9   See Austen-Smith and O'Brien, note 1 above; John Pound, The Effects of Antitakeover Amendments on Takeover Activity: Some Direct Evidence, 30 *J. Law & Econ.* 353 (1987).

10   Several other specific event dates might seem to be promising candidates for examination, including the date on which management first announces the antitakeover amendment proposal and the date on which the dissident announces the countersolicitation campaign. Two problems render these dates unreliable in the sample studied here, however. First, in several cases, these announcements are not reported in news sources, making it difficult to determine precisely when news became available to market participants. Second, as is seen in part IV, in a number of cases there is confounding news on or surrounding the date of the dissident announcement, including news about the probability of an acquisition offer for the company.

11   The net-of-market approach is used for two reasons. First, recent evidence suggests that the parameters derived from the empirical market model become misspecified in the presence of control activity. See Sanjai Bhagat, James Brickley, and Uri Lowenstein, The Pricing Effects of Interfirm Cash Tender Offers, 42 *J. Fin.* 964 (1987). Second, the results in Stephen Brown and Jerold Warner, Using Daily Stock Returns: The Case of Event Studies, 13 *J. Fin. Econ.* 3 (1985), show the net-of-market technique to be at least as powerful as the regression-base market model in the absence of cross-sectional dependence. Given the small sample, utilizing the most powerful approach and minimizing mis-specification are particularly important here. The index used as a proxy for the market is the New York Stock Exchange (NYSE) index for firms listed on the NYSE and American Stock Exchange (ASE), and the over-the-counter (OTC) composite index for OTC-listed firms. These indices are reported in Standard and Poor's Daily Stock Price Record for each exchange.

12   Only if the market were certain that the opposite outcome would occur prior to the vote-

outcome announcement would the market reaction to the vote reflect its full value implications.

13   One might also note that when all observations in the sample are pooled, the expected value of the vote outcome is negative. Across the sample, the expected gain when amendments are defeated does not offset the expected losses from amendment adoptions. It thus appears that it would be profitable to systematically short firms experiencing dissident countersolicitations after the dissident's campaign announcement. There are three important caveats that weaken this conclusion, however. First, the expected value of shorting is relatively small, and this effect is observed over 16 trading opportunities spanning 6 years. Second, the rarity of proxy contests and the idiosyncratic nature of each firm's voter pool may make it virtually impossible to predict firm-specific outcomes. Third, and most important there is likely to be a "peso problem" bias in the small sample of amendment defeats gathered for this article. One would expect to observe a number of very large positive returns around defeat dates, when the defeat has a strong effect on dissidents' acquisition plans. The sample of amendment defeats contains none of these events (while the sample of amendment approvals contains one such dramatic event). Thus the "true" expected value of amendment defeats is probably higher than that observed in this article's sample.

14   One would not need to observe a large number of contests for this conclusion to hold. Rational managements should design proposals falling below the cost threshold at which dissident opposition occurs to preserve their reputation.

15   Jarrell and Poulsen, note 3 above.

16   Pound, note 5 above.

17   Jarrell and Poulsen, note 3 above.

18   Pound, note 5 above.

19   James Brickley, Ronald Lease, and Clifford Smith, Ownership Structure and Voting on Antitakeover Amendments, 20 *J. Fin. Econ.* 267 (1988). Their evidence shows that banks and insurance companies tend to vote with management, while money managers tend to vote against management. They also show that institutions with ongoing business relationships with the corporation tend to support management.

20   Ownership structure for other types of proxy contests is reported in Pound, note 5 above.

14

Equity Carve-outs

Katherine Schipper and Abbie Smith

Late in 1981 Condec Corporation filed a prospectus describing a plan to sell to the public slightly over 20 percent of the equity in its wholly-owned subsidiary, Unimation, Inc. In this "equity carve-out" (also known as a "partial public offering"), Condec sold 1.05 million common shares of Unimation at US$23 each, thereby raising $22.5 million in new equity capital (after fees and expenses). The purpose of the offering, as stated in the prospectus, was to use "$19.4 million to repay all [of Unimation's] outstanding long-term indebtedness to Condec, and the remainder to provide working capital." The market's response to Condec's announcement resulted in a 19 percent stock price increase (after taking account of market movements).

Why did Condec choose this relatively unusual method of raising capital instead of, say, selling more of its own common equity? Why, furthermore, did the market respond so favorably to the announcement of the offering – especially since announcements of common stock offerings generally signal bad news to investors?

In this article, we attempt to provide answers to these questions based on our own recently published study of 76 equity carve-out announcements by New York and American Stock Exchange companies over the period 1965–83.[1] Our study finds, in brief, that the stockholders of parent companies earn on average almost 2 percent positive market-adjusted returns during the five-day period surrounding announcements of the carve-outs – and almost 5 percent if an additional two weeks preceding the announcement are included. In contrast, the stock prices of companies announcing seasoned equity offerings fall some 3 percent or more, on average, around the time of announcement; and announcements of convertible debt offerings provoke an average negative reaction of 1 or 2 percent. Thus, according to the findings of recent research, equity carve-outs represent the only form of new equity financing by public companies which results, on average, in an increase in shareholder wealth.

The popular argument

One popular explanation for the positive market reaction to equity carve-out announcements is that carve-outs allow investors to evaluate exceptional corporate
growth opportunities on a stand-alone basis. This explanation would imply that
Condec, a large, defense-oriented conglomerate, decided to carve out 20 percent of
Unimation, a robot manufacturer, to reinforce the market's perception of the value
of that subsidiary and thus, presumably, to increase the market's valuation of Condec
as a whole. As another example, MGM/UA's 1982 carve-out of its Home Entertainment Group has been described as a means of "cash[ing] in on the craving of investors
for a share in what may become an enormous market for pay television and home
videos."[2] Commenting on this same transaction, an analyst at Bear Stearns stated that
such a partial public offering provided "a way for studios to enhance their own
valuations and for investors to get a piece of the fast-growing market [for home
video]."[3]

The assumption underlying this explanation seems to be that investors are attracted
to subsidiary growth opportunities when these are isolated from the consolidated
entity (that is, available for separate purchase). By creating a separate public market for
Unimation's common stock, the popular argument seems to run, the carve-out
allowed Condec to benefit by allowing direct investment in the growth opportunities
of the robot subsidiary.

A variant of this popular argument holds that investors might value a specific
investment opportunity more highly when set apart from a conglomerate if and when
it offers them a scarce commodity: that is, a so-called "pure play." It might be difficult
for investors to invest in, say, stand-alone public robotics manufacturers. (Such an
advantage is likely to last only as long as there are few "pure plays" around.) This
variant is illustrated, in the case of Unimation, by the following analysis:

> The Unimation offering is among the first opportunities for substantial investment in
> the growing robot industry and it attracted considerable interest when it was announced
> last month. Most robotics companies that are publicly traded over the counter are too
> small to attract major investors. (*Wall Street Journal*, November 27, 1981)

In this article, we argue that although equity carve-outs may indeed create securities which have scarcity value, there are also other explanations for the market's
positive response to partial public offerings. First of all, equity carve-outs may overcome the problem of the information gap between insiders and investors that attends
all seasoned equity offerings. They may also provide more information to the market
about the subsidiary, thereby stimulating new investor demand (not to mention the
interest of potential corporate acquirers). Perhaps more important, however, is that
although the parent company generally retains a majority interest in the "carved-out"
subsidiary, equity carve-outs are often accompanied by important changes in management responsibilities and incentive contracts. Expected improvements in performance

from changes in managerial accountability and incentives may partially explain the market's positive reaction.

In the pages that follow we shall explain more precisely what an equity carve-out is, and how it differs from and resembles both spin-offs and seasoned equity offerings. We then review our own recent research on carve-outs, and discuss differences between equity carve-outs and conventional parent equity offerings that might account for the systematically negative response to the latter and the generally positive response to the former. Last, we take a look at what happens to subsidiaries after they have had partial public offerings. Seldom do carved-out subsidiaries remain unchanged for very long, with the public simply maintaining its minority interest in the firm. Instead they are generally either re-acquired by the parent, completely spunoff, acquired by management through an LBO, or acquired by some other firm. We attempt to make sense of these developments.

The Market Reaction to Related Events: Seasoned Equity Offerings and Spin-offs

An equity carve-out resembles a primary offering of seasoned stock in that cash is received from the investing public. Several recent studies of the market's response to seasoned equity offerings have confirmed average negative returns to stockholders of 2 to 3 percent over the two-day period surrounding the announcement of the issue.[4] In addition, our own study of carve-outs found that for those companies which had a seasoned common stock offering within five years of a carveout, the average price reaction to the parent stock offering was −3.5 percent over the five-day period ending with the announcement.

Many of the features which distinguish a subsidiary equity offering from a seasoned equity offering represent similarities with a voluntary spin-off.[5] In a spin-off, distinct equity claims of a wholly-owned subsidiary are distributed as a dividend to the consolidated entity's shareholders and begin to trade in public equity markets. Thus, in both spin-offs and equity carve-outs, a subsidiary's equity claims begin to trade separately from equity claims on the consolidated entity. Studies of the market reaction to announcements of corporate spin-offs all document positive abnormal returns of about 3 percent in the two-day period ending with the *Wall Street Journal* announcement date.[6]

A subsidiary equity offering differs in two respects from a corporate spin-off. First, as mentioned, whereas in a spin-off the subsidiary stock is distributed to the existing shareholders of the consolidated entity, the equity carve-out is a sale of subsidiary stock which raises new capital. Second, in a spin-off the parent company typically relinquishes control over the subsidiary by distributing all of the subsidiary stock. In an equity carve-out, the parent company typically does not relinquish control over the subsidiary; instead a public minority interest is created. Because a subsidiary equity offering partly resembles both a seasoned equity offering (associated with a negative share price reaction) and a corporate spin-off (associated with a positive reaction), it was not obvious *ex ante* what the market's reaction to carve-outs would be

The Market Reaction to Equity Carve-outs

Our study examined the stock-market's response to 76 announcements of equity carve-outs by 63 NYSE and ASE firms over the period 1965 to 1983.[7] These announcements were clustered in the late 1960s through 1972 and in the early 1980s; there were no announcements in the five years 1973–7.[8] This pattern differs from the pattern of seasoned common stock offerings reported in three recent studies; in these samples about one-fourth to one-third of common stock offerings over the same 19-year period occurred in the five-year period 1973–7.[9] The pattern of equity carve-outs does, however, conform roughly to that of initial public offerings.[10]

In our sample of 76 carve-out announcements, 37 of the announcements state that the firm "has proposed" or "is considering" offering a portion of a subsidiary to the public. The remaining 39 report that an offering has been filed with the SEC. Some of these provide no details, while others describe what is being offered, when and why. Regardless of the nature of the announcement, our share price reaction tests are based on the date the earliest announcement about the subsidiary equity offering appears in the *Wall Street Journal*. To increase the likelihood that the test period captures the first public disclosure of information about the subsidiary equity offering, the test period is defined as the five trading days ending with the day of the *Wall Street Journal* announcement.

Seventy-three percent of the carve-out offerings were underwritten. The percentage of the subsidiary's equity offered ranged from 4 percent to 75 percent, with 81 percent of the sample with available data falling between 10 percent and 50 percent. The proceeds of the offerings ranged from $300,000 to $112,200,000. Carve-out proceeds as a percentage of the parent's common equity value ranged from 0.3 percent to 69 percent, with a median of about 8 percent.[11]

A subset of 26 sample firms also made a total of 39 public offerings of their own common stock or convertible debt (hereafter called "parent equity") within five years of their subsidiary equity offerings. Parent equity issues of sample firms were identified by searching the *Wall Street Journal* Index for each of the five years prior to, the year of, and, where possible, the five years following that firm's announcement of a subsidiary equity offering. The share price reactions to these 39 announcements are measured by the abnormal stock returns (percentage price changes adjusted for general market movements) over the five-day period ending with the date of the *Wall Street Journal* announcement.

The market reactions to the 76 equity carve-out announcements in our sample were estimated by calculating abnormal stock returns over the five-day period leading up to the *Wall Street Journal* announcement.[12] In addition to measuring five-day returns, we also measured cumulative average abnormal stock returns for the 76 carve-out announcements over an 85-day period beginning 44 days before the *Wall Street Journal* announcement and ending 40 days after. (These returns are shown in figure 14.1.) During the period starting 13 days before the announcement, the cumulative abnormal return drifts upward at an increasing rate from +0.8 percent to +4.95 percent at the announcement day. The cumulative abnormal return is nearly level in the subsequent eight weeks, ending with a value of +4.45 percent 40 trading days after the announcement.

In the case of the 39 sample firms which issued either seasoned equity or convertible debt within five years of the carve-outs, the cumulative return drops from +0.2 percent four days before the announcement of the offering of parent equity to −3.3 percent on the announcement day (see figure 14.1). In the eight weeks following the announcement of the parent equity offering, the return drifts downward to −4.7 percent by 40 trading days after the announcement.[13]

The variation in the market reaction to both the sample of carve-out announcements and the sample of parent equity offering announcements is considerable. Abnormal returns at carve-out announcements range from −12.1 percent to +19.5 percent, with a median of +1.6 percent. About two-thirds of these returns (50 of 76) are positive. In contrast, about 69 percent of abnormal returns (27 of 39) at the announcement of parent equity offerings are negative. The median abnormal return for this sample is −2 percent, and the range is from −16 percent to +17.5 percent.[14]

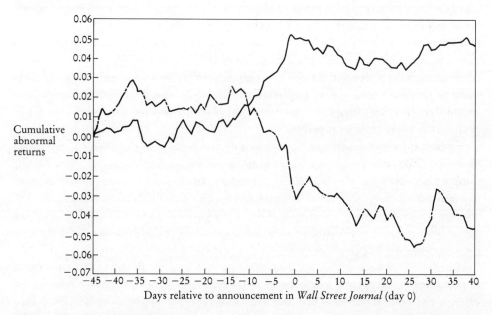

Figure 14.1 The stock-market response to announcements of equity carve-outs and parent equity offerings. Cumulative abnormal returns for 76 equity carve-out announcements made during the period 1965 to 1983 are shown by the solid line. Cumulative abnormal returns for 39 seasoned equity offering announcements made by the same firms are shown by the broken line. Market model parameters are estimated for each sample firm over trading days −280 to −161 relative to the announcement in the *Wall Street Journal*.

Why, Then, the Different Market Response to
Equity Carve-outs?

There are three differences between equity carve-outs and parent equity offerings which might account for the market's positive response to the former: (1) the separation of subsidiary investment projects from those of the parent firm for external financing; (2) the creation of a public market for subsidiary common stock; and (3) the restructuring of asset management and incentive contracts.

Separate financing for subsidiary investments

An offering of seasoned parent equity simply increases the number of outstanding equity claims on the consolidated assets. In contrast, an initial subsidiary equity offering "carves out" the assets of the subsidiary from the assets of the original entity. Thus, an equity carve-out allows a subsidiary to obtain separate funding for subsidiary growth opportunities.[15] The equity securities publicly offered represent claims on the cash flows of the subsidiary projects only.

If parent equity had instead been offered to finance the subsidiary's investment projects, the offered securities would represent a joint claim on both the parent and subsidiary projects. By separating the subsidiary projects from those of the parent, a carve-out may reduce the asymmetry of information between managers and investors about the asset base underlying the securities offered.[16]

The separate financing of subsidiary projects by an equity carve-out is expected to have a positive share price effect under either of two circumstances: (1) information is publicly revealed about the subsidiary's planned investment in a positive net present value project without negative implications about the value of the other assets of the consolidated firm; (2) separate financing implies that management will not forgo *future* positive net present value projects.

Support for viewing some carve-outs as a means of financing growth opportunities of the subsidiary apart from the parent company is found in the stated motives for our sample carve-outs. In the case of 59 of the 81 subsidiaries whose carve-outs were announced, we were able to find stated motives by reading annual reports, 10-Ks, registration statements, prospectuses and articles in the financial press. For 19 of these 59, at least part of the declared motivation was to enable the subsidiary to obtain its own financing for expected growth.

Additional support for viewing some carve-outs as a means of financing growth opportunities of the subsidiary is found in the nature of some of the carve-outs. In six cases, registration statements or prospectuses described a specific growth opportunity to be funded with the proceeds of the subsidiary equity offering. For example, Interferon Sciences was formed by National Patent Development in 1981 to develop its interferon program. The parent contributed basic technology and patents, which were reported as having a book value of about $600,000 or $0.20 per share. Shortly thereafter, 25 percent of Interferon Sciences was offered to the public at $10 a share; the proceeds were $10 million. The stated purpose of the offering was to finance the development of the interferon technology transferred by the parent to its subsidiary. Thus, Interferon Sciences represented primarily a growth opportunity, with virtually no assets-in-place. Other projects included investments in Atlantic City casinos, Hawaiian condominiums, oil drilling, and bioengineering products. In each case, the parent firm apparently rejected the option of funding the project by issuing parent equity and chose to offer separate equity claims on the growth opportunity by means of a carve-out.

Assuming that one purpose of a carve-out is to finance investment projects, a measure of the relative size of those projects is the proceeds of the carve-out offering as a percentage of the market value of parent equity. This size measure, it turns out, is positively correlated with the share price reactions of parent firms; that is, the larger the carve-out as a percentage of the total equity of the consolidated company, the larger in general was the positive market reaction.[17]

To provide evidence of the anticipated growth of carved-out subsidiaries, we computed the P/E ratios of 70 subsidiaries with available data at the time of or immediately after the carve-out. Relative to their parent firms, the carved-out subsidiaries had high P/E ratios. The median subsidiary P/E ratio was 21.7 (after excluding negative values caused by losses). In contrast, the median contemporaneous P/E ratio of the parent firms was 15. For the 58 parent-subsidiary pairs with available P/E ratios, the subsidiary had the higher P/E ratio in 43 cases (74 percent).[18]

Creation of a public market for subsidiary stock

An equity carve-out initiates public trading of the common stock of the previously wholly-owned subsidiary. The subsidiary is thus subject to all financial and other reporting requirements of public companies (for example, 10-Q and 10-K reports and proxy statements filed with the SEC, and annual reports issued to stockholders). These requirements can impose considerable costs on the parent company's stockholders. These costs consist of the direct costs of preparing audited financial statements and other required reports for the subsidiary, as well as any indirect costs of disclosing proprietary information to subsidiary competitors.

Such costs, however, may be more than offset by the benefits to parent stockholders of the increased supply of and demand for information about the subsidiary's growth opportunities. The carve-out of subsidiary stock *commits* the subsidiary to supply audited periodic financial reports prepared in accordance with prescribed measurement and disclosure rules, as well as other nonfinancial information about firm activities (such as the information in proxy statements). By making possible an equity investment in the subsidiary alone, the carve-out also increases the incentives of both individual investors and potential acquiring firms to gather and analyze information about subsidiary activities. The increase in both the supply of and demand for information about the subsidiary may increase the perceived value of subsidiary stock to individual and corporate investors.

Such an improvement in investor understanding is cited as a motive for 14 equity carve-outs in our sample. It is also cited in a recent announcement by Perkin-Elmer Corporation of its plan to carve out and sell to the public up to 19 percent of its minicomputer business, which was named Concurrent Computer Corporation. According to a *Wall Street Journal* report, the chairman of Perkin-Elmer said the carve-out plan "is intended to improve the visibility of Perkin-Elmer computers and thus improve sales and help attract investors."[19]

Perkin-Elmer completed the equity carve-out in January 1986 and described its advantages to parent company shareholders in a full-page *Wall Street Journal* advertisement with the following copy:

> Higher visibility and a sharp, singular focus will help Concurrent Computer Corporation attract and retain a strong, motivated management team. And lead to increased recognition in the financial community where shareholders will be able to benefit from its full potential.
>
> As the Perkin-Elmer Data Systems Group, our computer business was not accorded its true value. Yet, in just one week after its initial offering, the market has placed Concurrent Computer Corporation's worth at nearly a quarter of a billion dollars – enriching Perkin-Elmer's ownership as the major shareholder.[20]

The restructuring of asset management and incentive contracts

Many carve-outs are associated with a major restructuring of managerial responsibilities and incentives. Divisions are often regrouped into a new subsidiary for the public offering with a consequent realignment in the responsibilities of various managers. Furthermore, the incentive contracts of subsidiary managers are usually revised to incorporate subsidiary share prices and profits as measures of performance. Such internal structural shifts are seldom associated with seasoned equity offerings.

Stated motives for 11 of 59 sample subsidiaries mentioned a change in corporate focus through a restructuring program or a reduction by the parent of investment in the line of business of the carved-out subsidiary. Also worth noting is that 38 of the 73 carved-out subsidiaries (52 percent) had been formed as little as one year before the carve-out.[21] The formation of the new subsidiaries typically involved combining the operations of existing units, divisions or subsidiaries under a single management. Finally, management responsibilities in 12 cases were changed to the extent that one or more persons resigned a top management position with the parent to become president or CEO of the subsidiary.

Two pieces of qualitative evidence suggest that changes in the incentives of subsidiary managers are important considerations in carve-outs. The first is 10 statements of motive which focus on the improvements in managerial incentives associated with a public market for subsidiary shares. For example, in W. R. Grace's explanation of its decision to carve out a 27 percent interest in its El Torito restaurant chain, Charles Erhart, vice-chairman of Grace, said the environment at Grace inhibited the entrepreneurial style of El Torito's management. "These are people-sensitive businesses. They [El Torito management] are independent cats who need a piece of the action to motivate them."[22]

The second piece of evidence concerns the use of subsidiary share prices and profit figures in contracts with subsidiary managers. Of the 63 sample carve-out subsidiaries for which data are available, 59 (that is, 94 percent) adopted incentive compensation plans based on the subsidiary's stock – generally stock option plans. Most of these adoptions occurred within one year of the carve-out. In addition, at least 23 subsidiaries adopted incentive plans based on subsidiary net income.

This evidence suggests that restructuring of managerial responsibilities and incentives is frequently associated with equity carve-outs. To the extent that the market expects such restructuring to lead to improvements in management's efficiency in using corporate assets, we would expect a favorable share price reaction.[23]

After the Carve-out

Carved-out subsidiaries often experience some form of change in ownership following the carve-out. For our entire sample of 73 carve-outs, all but 14 of the subsidiaries as of February 1986 had undergone further changes since the initial public offering.[24]

One common fate of carved-out subsidiaries is complete separation from the parent by one of the following means: spin-off, purchase by the subsidiary of its stock held by the parent, leveraged buyout, sale to another firm, and bankruptcy/liquidation. Of the 73 carve-outs in our sample, 30 had separated from their parents by one of the above means as of February 1986 (see table 14.1). Fifteen of these 30 separations involved the outright sale of the subsidiary to another firm. Four were acquired by management in

Table 14.1 Ownership changes for 73 subsidiaries carved-out during 1965–83[1]

		Number of years between carve-out and event	
Reacquisition by parent	*Number*	*Average*	*Range*
Transaction complete	26	5.1	2–12
Proposal pending	2	5.5	5–6
Transaction proposed but failed	1	3	NA
Separation from parent			
Spin-off or purchase by subsidiary of its shares held by parent	7	5	1–12
Leverage buyout complete or pending	4	3.5	1–5
Sale to another firm	15	6.7	1–19
Bankruptcy or liquidation	4	3.75	1–7
	59[2]		

[1] These data cover the period from the carve-out announcement through February 1986.
[2] We found no information for five subsidiaries. Nine subsidiaries (of which eight were carved-out in 1993) have had no ownership changes.

leveraged buyouts (though all of these occurred after November 1984, reflecting the newness of the LBO phenomenon).

The length of the period between the carve-out and the separation varies considerably within our sample. Some separations occurred almost immediately (that is, within 1 or 2 years), while one divestiture occurred 19 years after the carve-out. The average period, however, is approximately 4 or 5 years for most of these changes.

The fact that so many carve-outs are followed by complete separation suggests that management may have originally intended the carve-out as a way of advertising the subsidiary – that is, as an intermediary stage in a process whose final goal was divestiture. The parent may have expected that the disclosure associated with a public market for subsidiary shares would eventually lead to a greater understanding (and thus willingness to pay a higher price) on the part of the potential acquirers.[25] For example, some insurance executives speculated that the 1985 carve-out of 49 percent of Fireman's Fund by American Express was "a way to attract higher bids for a sale of its entire interest in Fireman's Fund."[26]

Only slightly less common than complete separation, however, is the reacquisition of carved-out subsidiaries by the parent. In our sample, 26 subsidiaries were reacquired and another reacquisition is pending. Why do companies reacquire carved-out subsidiaries? One possible explanation is that the original carve-out decision was a mistake. An alternative explanation, however, is that reacquisition is attractive if the objectives of the carve-out can be accomplished with only a temporary public market for subsidiary shares. For example, the need for external equity financing of subsidiary growth will decline if the subsidiary's investment projects mature to the point where they generate sufficient profits for internal equity financing. The objective of informing individual investors and potential acquirers about a subsidiary's growth potential through audited subsidiary financial statements and other reports, as well as the increased incentives for private information collection, may be achieved by a temporary public market for subsidiary stock. Even the contracting gains associated with incorporating subsidiary stock price in the incentive contracts of subsidiary managers may be temporary.

One example of a carve-out followed quickly by a reacquisition proposal is the case of First Data Resources. American Express sold 25 percent of First Data for $14 a share in September 1983, and announced a plan to reacquire the shares for $36 a share (27 times earnings) in August 1985. The reacquisition was announced as part of a plan to narrow the corporate focus on consumer financial services. While some analysts speculated that the reacquisition might imply that the original carve-out was a mistake, the president of American Express, Louis Gerstner Jr., disputed this point by saying that the equity ownership taken by First Data management as part of the 1983 carve-out offering helped stimulate the subsidiary's rapid growth. (In the first six months of 1985, First Data's income was nearly 50 percent higher than in 1984.)[27]

The MGM/UA carve-out of its Home Entertainment Group mentioned earlier in this article was also followed by a reacquisition. Late in 1984 MGM/UA proposed a reacquisition at $28 in notes or MGM/UA stock; the carve-out offering price was $12.

It might be concluded from this proposal that the original purpose of the carve-out had been served and there was no longer a need for a public market for HEG stock.[28]

Subsequent ownership changes are easier to accomplish if the parent retains control of its carved-out subsidiary. In our sample, parent firms typically offered only a minority interest to the public, while retaining a majority or supermajority interest. Some of the parent companies in our sample also maintain control over the carved-out subsidiary by creating a special class of stock which increases the parent's voting power. For example, the parent might create and hold 100 percent of class B common stock carrying four votes while issuing common stock with one vote in a carve-out. These kinds of special stock arrangements were found in 15 of the 73 subsidiaries in our sample.

Besides facilitating ownership changes, there are two other advantages to the parent of maintaining a majority or supermajority voting interest in a carved-out subsidiary. First, effective control allows any existing operating and/or financial synergies to be maintained (although it is possible that the absence of operating synergies, in many cases, is an important motive for the carve-out in the first place). Second, 80 percent voting control of the subsidiary is required if the subsidiary is to be consolidated for tax purposes. Tax consolidation is beneficial if operating losses or tax credits which would otherwise go unused by either the parent or subsidiary can be used to offset taxable income of the more profitable firm, thereby reducing taxes to the consolidated entity.

The benefits of tax consolidation were cited in the case of Trans World Corporation's 1983 carve-out of its airline subsidiary. After the carve-out, public ownership was 19 percent of the common stock and 5 percent of the voting control (the parent retained preference shares with 10 votes apiece). Because the airline subsidiary generated both tax losses and investment tax credits that could be used to shield earnings of other units from taxation (as long as a consolidated tax return was filed), this arrangement was described as "having cake and eating it too."[29] Presumably, the "cake" came from the $78 million cash generated by the offering, which permitted the subsidiary to purchase new equipment, especially Boeing 767s.

Summary and Conclusions

We recently completed a study of 76 equity carve-out announcements by public companies traded on the New York and American Stock Exchanges. Our results indicate that in the five-day period culminating with the announcement of such carve-outs, the stock prices of parent companies announcing the carve-outs outperformed the market by almost 2 percent on average; the size of the average reaction is a positive 4 to 5 percent if an additional two weeks preceding the announcement are included.

In contrast, announcements of public offerings of parent common stock and convertible debt by a subset of the same companies have been associated with average shareholder losses of over 3 percent. Such a negative reaction to announcements of *parent* equity offerings is consistent, furthermore, with prior research on the stock price effects of changes in outstanding equity through public sale or repurchase of common stock and convertible debt, debt conversion, and exchange offers to current security holders.[30] Initial public offerings of subsidiary stock are thus the only means of raising outside equity capital (of which we are aware) which appear to communicate a positive signal to the stock market.

How do we account for this difference in the market's response to announcements of carve-outs and seasoned equity offerings?

An equity carve-out, first of all, allows public investment in subsidiary growth opportunities apart from an investment in the parent's assets. Such a security, by offering investors a "pure play," may have scarcity value if such opportunities are typically buried within a conglomerate structure.

A partial public offering also appears to offer an effective means of overcoming the financing problem caused by the potential information gap between insiders and public investors which appears to make conventional equity offerings quite expensive. Still another possibility is that the equity carve-out may improve public understanding of the subsidiary's growth opportunities. By making the subsidiary a public company, the carve-out may increase the supply of and demand for information about the subsidiary. Periodic, audited financial statements prepared by the subsidiary in accordance with regulations are issued to the public. Investors accordingly may have added incentives to analyze publicly available data and to search for private information about the subsidiary because of the new opportunity to trade subsidiary stock. Also, the readily observable market price of subsidiary stock may attract an acquiring firm and facilitate negotiations concerning the purchase price. If such an increased flow of information increases the perceived value of subsidiary stock to individual or corporate investors, it may partially explain the more favorable share price response to equity carve-outs than to parent equity offerings.

Alternatively, the market may be saying that the conglomerate is an inefficient organizational structure for capitalizing on such growth opportunities, and for providing the entrepreneurial climate necessary to do so. Equity carve-outs often are associated with a major restructuring of managers' responsibilities and incentive contracts, and the market may associate such restructuring with improvements in management's efficiency in putting corporate assets to their most valuable uses.

Notes

1 See Katherine Schipper and Abbie Smith, "A Comparison of Equity Carve-outs and Seasoned Equity Offerings: Share Price Effects and Corporate Restructuring," *Journal of Financial Economics* 15 (1986), pp. 153–86.

2 From "The Old Razzle-Dazzle," *Forbes*, February 14, 1985, pp. 43–4.

3 From "MGM/UA Movie-distributing Unit's Rise Has Other Studios Studying Its Strategy," *Wall Street Journal*, October 21, 1983.

4 The share price reaction of NYSE and ASE listed firms to an announcement of a public offering of seasoned common stock is the subject of the following published studies, all of which appeared in volume 15 (1986) of the *Journal of Financial Economics*: Ronald

Masulis and Ashok Korwar, "Seasoned Equity Offerings: An Empirical Investigation"; Paul Asquith and David Mullins, "Equity Issues and Offering Dilution"; and Wayne Mikkelson and Megan Partch, "Valuation Effects of Security Offerings and the Issuance Process." The share price reactions to public offerings of convertible debt claims on NYSE and ASE listed firms were examined by Larry Dann and Wayne Mikkelson in "Convertible Debt Issuance, Capital Structure Change and Financing-Related Information: Some New Evidence," *Journal of Financial Economics* 13 (1984). The results of these studies are as follows: For offerings by industrial firms, a statistically significant negative average abnormal stock return of 2 or 3 percent is documented in the two-day period ending with the *Wall Street Journal* announcement date. In the case of equity offerings by public utilities, the return is smaller (less than one percent), but still negative and statistically significant. Furthermore, a negative average share price effect of an increase in outstanding common equity through exchange offers and conversions of debt to common stock is documented by the following studies: Ron Masulis, "The Effects of Capital Structure Changes on Security Prices," Unpublished doctoral dissertation, University of Chicago, 1978; and Wayne Mikkelson, "Convertible Calls and Security Returns," *Journal of Financial Economics* 9 (1981).

Conversely, evidence exists that an increase in share price is associated with a *reduction* in outstanding common equity through repurchases of shares and exchange offers: Larry Dann, "Common Stock Repurchases: An Analysis of Returns to Bondholders and Stockholders," *Journal of Financial Economics* 9 (1981); Ron Masulis, "Stock Repurchase by Tender Offer: An Analysis of the Causes of Common Stock Price Changes, *Journal of Finance* 35 (1980), 305–19, (as well as the Ph.D. dissertation cited above); and Theo Vermaelen, "Common Stock Repurchases and Market Signalling: An Empirical Study," *Journal of Financial Economics* 9 (1981). Thus, the evidence suggests that an increase in outstanding equity is associated on average with a decrease in stock price, and a decrease in equity is associated with an increase in stock price.

5 A subsidiary equity offering also resembles a divestiture in that cash is received. However, a divestiture does not in general initiate the trading of subsidiary stock. Two studies (G. Alexander, P. Benson and J. Kampmeyer, "Investigating the Valuation Effects of Announcements of Voluntary Corporate Selloffs," *Journal of Finance* 29 (1984); and April Klein, "Voluntary Corporate Divestitures: Motives and Consequences," Unpublished doctoral dissertation, University of Chicago, 1983) both report positive abnormal returns of about 1 percent or less in a three-day period (Klein) and a two-day period (Alexander et al.) ending with the announcement of the divestiture in the *Wall Street Journal*.

6 See Katherine Schipper and Abbie Smith, "Effects of Recontracting on Shareholder Wealth: The Case of Voluntary Spin-offs," *Journal of Financial Economics* 12 (1983); Gailen Hite and James Owers, "Security Price Reactions around Corporate Spin-off Announcements," *Journal of Financial Economics* 12 (1983); and J. Miles and J. Rosenfeld, "An Empirical Analysis of the Effects of Spin-off Announcements on Shareholder Wealth," *Journal of Finance* 38 (1983).

7 Although there are 76 carve-out announcements, there are actually 81 subsidiaries in the sample because 4 announcement dates account for 9 subsidiaries. That is, 3 announcement dates involve 2 subsidiaries each and 1 date involves 3 subsidiaries. The number of parents (63) is also less than the number of announcements because of multiple carve-outs by the same firm. The largest number of carve-out announcements by a single firm is 3 (by W. R. Grace); 10 firms announced at least 2 carve-outs. Of the 81 subsidiaries in the announcement sample, 8 were not carved-out during the sample period, which ends in

December 1983. Thus, carve-outs of 8 subsidiaries were announced and later cancelled. Details of the sample selection procedures can be found in Schipper and Smith [1986], cited in note 1.

8   While it is possible that a number of carve-outs occurred during 1973–7 that we were not able to find, we do not think this is likely. Every initial public offering on the SEC's *Registrations and Offerings Statistics* tape for the years 1973–7 was checked and none was a carve-out by an NYSE or ASE listed firm.

9   See note 4 for full citations of the three studies of the market's response to announcements of seasoned equity offerings.

10   See Jay Ritter, "The 'Hot Issue' Market of 1980," *Journal of Business* 57 (1984).

11   The market value of parent common equity is measured by share price multiplied by the number of outstanding common shares at the end of the month preceding the carve-out announcement.

12   For details of the procedures used to compute abnormal returns and to perform statistical tests, see the appendix to Schipper and Smith [1986], cited in note 1.

13   t-tests for the significance of abnormal returns do not imply rejection at the 0.05 level (two-tailed) of the null hypothesis that the abnormal return is zero within the periods before or after the carve-out announcement. However, the t-statistic of +2.55 in the five-day announcement period leads to rejection of the null hypothesis of zero abnormal returns at better than the 0.02 level (two-tailed). Similarly, the abnormal returns before and after the announcement of the parent equity offerings are not significantly different from zero at the 0.05 level (two-tailed). However, the abnormal return of −3.5 percent in the five-day event period is significantly different from zero at better than the 0.01 level (two-tailed).

   The difference in the cumulative abnormal returns over the event period for the announcement of 76 subsidiary equity offerings versus 39 parent equity offerings is +5.3 percent, significant at better than the 0.005 level (one-tailed). The average difference in the cumulative abnormal returns in the five-day event period for 26 matched pairs of subsidiary and parent equity offerings by the same firm is +5.5 percent, also significant at better than the 0.005 level (one-tailed). For these pairwise comparisons, each subsidiary equity offering announcement is matched, if possible, with a parent equity offering announcement by the same company. If more than one parent equity offering was available for matching, priority was given to common stock over convertible debt offerings, and to proximity to the subsidiary equity offering announcement date.

14   Previous tests of share price reactions to announcements of offerings of seasoned equity have used a two-day event period (e.g., Asquith and Mullins [1986], Dann and Mikkelson [1984], Masulis and Korwar [1986], and Mikkelson and Partch [1986], all cited earlier in note 4. Because many of our announcements refer to SEC filings, we use a five-day event period. A two-day period, however, is reasonable for the 37 *Wall Street Journal* announcements of intentions to undertake an equity carve-out. For this subsample, the average two-day abnormal return is +1.2 percent (t = 1.91) and the median two-day abnormal return is +1.7 percent. A binomial test of the null hypotheses of an equal portion of positive versus negative two-day event period abnormal returns results in a z-statistic of +2.48, which is significant at the 0.007 level. In the entire sample, however, the two-day event period does not appear to capture the initial information release. For the entire sample of 37 intention announcements and 39 announcements that a registration statement has been filed, the two-day abnormal return is +0.7 percent (t = 1.59). These significance tests should be interpreted with caution, as they are not independent.

15   Other mechanisms for separate financing of investment projects include spin-offs and sales of limited partnership interests to finance research and development. In some cases, the tax code provides special incentives for the latter financing mechanism.

16   For a discussion of the information asymmetry financing problem, and why it may pay to fund growth opportunities separately from assets-in-place, see Stewart Myers and Nicholas Majluf, "Corporate Financing and Investment Decisions When Firms Have Information That Investors Do Not Have," *Journal of Financial Economics* 9 (1984).

17   The Spearman rank correlation between our size measure and the five-day abnormal returns associated with carve-out announcements is 0.27, which is significant at better than the 0.05 level (two-tailed).

18   A Wilcoxon test of the null hypothesis that the two samples are drawn from populations with the same median generates a t-statistic of 3.83, leading to rejection of the null hypothesis at better than 0.01 probability level. Hence, subsidiary P/E ratios tend to exceed the P/E ratios of the corresponding parent firms. Furthermore, these high subsidiary P/E ratios cannot be explained by low levels of risk. Of the 23 sample subsidiaries with returns on the CRSP Daily Excess Returns Tape within two years after the equity carve-out, 14 (61 percent) belong to the three highest of ten beta portfolios (6, 5, 3 respectively). It also is unlikely that the high P/E ratios can be attributed to the use of highly conservative accounting methods to measure subsidiary earnings. Through 1982, earnings figures reported in subsidiary registration statements were not required to include such corporate costs as interest, taxes, amortization of purchased goodwill, and certain administrative costs. It was not until 1983 that the SEC issued "carve-out accounting" rules that require proportionate allocation of these corporate costs to the subsidiary's earnings statement. Hence it is likely that the high subsidiary P/E ratios in our sample are indicative of high anticipated growth in subsidiary earnings. However, the high P/E ratios may also reflect the low earnings figures of young firms due to high research and development expenses and depreciation charges.

19   From "Perkin-Elmer Organizes New Computer Firm," *Wall Street Journal*, November 14, 1985.

20   *Wall Street Journal*, February 19, 1986.

21   Of the 32 subsidiaries in existence at least 1 year before the equity carve-out announcement, 17 had been previously acquired, 4 had been formed as part of a joint venture, and 11 were formed from existing divisions.

22   *Business Week*, December 19, 1983, contains additional information.

23   The principle of "informativeness," as developed by Shavell and by Holmstrom (See S. Shavell, "Risk Sharing and Incentives in the Principal and Agent Relationship" and B. Holmstrom, "Moral Hazard and Observability," both in the *Bell Journal of Economics* 10 (1979)), maintains that any (costless) variable which is marginally informative about an agent's actions can be used to increase the efficiency of the contract with the principal. Hence, if the subsidiary share price contains additional information about subsidiary managers' actions, agency theory suggests that the efficiency of managers' contracts can be improved by linking compensation to the subsidiary stock price performance.

     This requirement does not appear to be overly restrictive. The aggregation of the parent company with the subsidiary company for purposes of equity market valuation and financial reporting (i.e., presentation of consolidated financial statements) is likely to result in loss of information about the subsidiary's management's production, investment, and financing decisions. The contracting gains which may result from disaggregating agent performance measures for unrelated operations is discussed in the context of responsibility accounting in the following study: S. Baiman and J. Demski, "Economically Optimal Performance Evaluation and Control Systems," *Journal of Accounting Research* 18 (1980), Supplement, 184–220. Although the performance of the subsidiary and the parent company may be measured separately with internal (managerial) accounting procedures even before the equity carve-outs, in general such "divisional" accounting measures are unlikely to contain all the information contained in the subsidiary share price with respect to subsidiary management's actions. On this last point, see D. Diamond and R. Verrecchia, "Optimal Managerial Contracts and Equilibrium Security Prices," *Journal of Finance* 37 (1982), 275–87.

24   At the time of the original carve-out announcement, the market does not appear to respond differently to those carve-outs which later undergo some kind of restructuring. For carve-outs announced before 1983, a Mann–Whitney test for differences in abnormal returns at announcements of carve-outs that were later restructured versus those that remain unchanged results in a z-statistic of 0.82, which is not significant at conventional levels. Thus, there is not an *ex ante* perceived difference, in terms of impact on shareholder wealth, between carve-outs that were later reacquired, divested, spun-off or liquidated and those that have not undergone some further ownership or structural change.

  Parent firm share price reactions to announcements that subsidiaries are being divested or reacquired are small and positive. For a sample of eight divestiture announcements, the two-day average abnormal return is 2.8 percent (t = 1.88). For a sample of 13 reacquisition announcements, the two-day average abnormal return is 0.6 percent (t = 0.55). These results are consistent with little or no revision in market expectations associated with restructuring announcements.

25   As stated in note 24 earlier, parent firm share price reactions to announcements that subsidiaries are being divested are small and positive. For a sample of eight divestiture announcements, the two-day average abnormal return is 2.8 percent (t = 1.88).

26   See "Fireman's Fund Stock Offer Set by Parent Firm," *Wall Street Journal*, June 26, 1985. The carve-out offering was completed in October 1985 at $27.75 a share. By February 25, 1986, Fireman's Fund stock was selling at about $37.75 a share; to capitalize on this gain, American Express announced a plan to offer as many as 10 million shares plus warrants for another 10 million shares. (See "American Express Plans to Reduce Stake in Fireman's Fund by Second Offering," *Wall Street Journal*, February 26, 1986).

27   See "American Express Seeks Rest of Concern," *Wall Street Journal*, August 22, 1985.

28   These reacquisitions often involve premiums over the current market price of subsidiary shares or lawsuits by minority stockholders to increase the reacquisition price, or both. In the case of the Home Entertainment Group, settlement of a shareholder suit resulted in a reacquisition for $28 in cash (*Wall Street Journal*, April 24, 1985).

  As mentioned in note 24, parent firm share price reactions to announcements that subsidiaries are being reacquired are small and positive. For a sample of 13 reacquisition announcements, the two-day average abnormal return is 0.6 percent (t = 0.55).

29   See "Let Them Eat Stock," *Forbes*, April 25, 1983.

30   See note 4 earlier for a review of this research.

15

Divestitures: Mistakes or Learning?

J. Fred Weston

A divestiture is the sale of part of a company to a third party. Assets, product lines, subsidiaries, or divisions are sold for cash or securities or some combination thereof. The buyers are typically other corporations or, increasingly, investor groups together with the current managers of the divested operation.

Divestitures have represented a substantial fraction of M & A activity for decades. In the 1980s, some 35 to 40 percent of the mergers and acquisitions reported annually by W. T. Grimm were divestitures by other firms; and this is down from peak years of over 50 percent in 1975 and 1976, when M & A volume was considerably lower.[1] The stock market has responded favorably to these transactions. Companies announcing the sale of assets accounting for more than 10 percent of their total market value have experienced price increases of some 3 percent on average. And the larger the piece sold off, the more emphatic the market's sign of approval.

What are the causes and consequences of this high rate of divestiture activity? Some observers have argued that the high rates of divestitures are incontrovertible evidence of the failure of past acquisition programs. Others have been more cautious, suggesting that the pattern of acquisitions and divestitures reflects evolving corporate strategies that attempt to match perceived competitive advantages and internal capabilities to accelerating changes in the external market environment. Corporate combinations, they suggest, that may once have made sense can lose their justification over time; and thus even acquisitions and subsequent divestitures of the same businesses may, in many cases, be "rational" transactions both in coming and going.

The evidence that I present in this article provides some support for both of these positions; that is, it appears that both mistakes and learning are involved in divestiture activity. On balance, shareholder values have probably been increased in this overall process of buying and selling companies. And, even though acquisition and divestiture programs have not always made positive contributions to the values of individual companies, I would nevertheless argue that such transactions perform an important economic role in increasing the mobility of economic resources – one that is essential to the proper functioning of an enterprise system.

Reasons for Divestitures

Like M & A activity in general, corporate divestitures reflect continuing efforts by companies to adjust to changing economic and political environments. Much M & A activity has involved the movement by companies from industries with less favorable opportunities to those with better prospects. Many companies have also tried to take advantage of strengths in their existing product market areas to combine with capabilities in new product areas.[2] A related strategy was to establish at least a toehold in new product market areas. The hope was that initial entry could be a beachhead for further growth and development.

Other firms have felt less pressure to diversify outside their core businesses. For some this represented good prior strategic planning. For others it reflected shifts in the external economic and financial environment that turned out to be favorable for particular industries and firms.

The pressures for overcoming a firm's "strategic planning gap" or "aligning more effectively" with the changing environments have varied from industry to industry and during different time periods. And, like the circumstances besetting firms at different times in different industries, the motives for divestiture activity are many and diverse. Here is a short list of the ones I think most important.

1 *Dismantling Conglomerates.*   The 1960s marked the height of conglomerate merger activity. In part it stemmed from "defensive" diversification out of the aerospace and natural resource industries. In part it represented the philosophy that general managerial capabilities could be profitably transferred to diverse businesses. Many such conglomerates have proven to be inefficient combinations over time. Divestitures have been used to reduce the number and diversity of activities that had been assembled in firms such as Gulf & Western (Paramount) and ITT.

2 *Abandoning the Core Business.*   The sale by a company of its original business cannot be attributed to a diversification mistake, but to changing opportunities or circumstances. In 1987 Greyhound sold its bus business. In 1988 Du Pont divested its original commercial explosives business, Wurlitzer sold its basic piano and electric keyboard business (to Baldwin piano), and B. F. Goodrich Co. sold its remaining stake in the tire business.

3 *Changing Strategies or Restructuring.*   A change in strategic focus may reflect mistakes, learning, or realignment with the firm's changing environments. In 1983 Warner-Lambert sold its successful bakery unit, Entenmann's, to General Foods. In 1982, General Dynamics divested its telecommunications switching business to concentrate on defense business. In 1987 and 1988, Allegis Corp. sold its hotel and car rental units to become UAL Corp. and concentrate on operating United Air Lines, a reversal of a previous strategic plan. Alco Standard Corp. sold off distribution businesses and most manufacturing units after 1987 to focus on paper distribution,

office products, and food service equipment. Between 1985 and 1988, TRW divested about US$1 billion worth of lower-technology businesses in favor of the high-technology segments of aerospace and defense, automotive components, and information systems and services. Household International sold its manufacturing units to concentrate on financial services. IBM sold Rolm's manufacturing and development operations to Siemens AG, with whom a joint venture was formed for US sales and service operations for Rolm's switchboard business.

4 *Adding Value by Selling into a Better Fit.*   Dow Jones divested its texbook business to concentrate on business publishing and regional newspapers by selling its Richard D. Irwin unit to Times Mirror, a newspaper company which was seeking to expand in textbook and professional publishing. In 1986 IBM sold 81 IBM Products Centers, its US retailing operations, to Nynex, one of the regional telephone companies created in the AT&T court-directed divestiture. In 1988 IBM sold most of its US copier business to Eastman Kodak. Such sales may reflect different capabilities, different strategic philosophies, or different expectations.

5 *Large additional investment required.*   Sometimes remaining in a business requires additional investments that a firm is unable or unwilling to make. Thus in 1988 Eaton sold its defense electronics business, including the B-1B electronics system, to focus on two other major business areas. For similar reasons, Gould sold its antisubmarine warfare business to Westinghouse Electric.

6 *Harvesting Past Successes.*   Some divestitures represent the harvesting of successful investments, often stimulated by favorable market conditions. Here the purpose is to make financial and managerial resources available for developing other opportunities. Such divestitures represent successes rather than failures (or mistakes). Hanson PLC is said to make a business of this activity. Other examples are hotel sales by Hilton and Marriott.[3]

7 *Discarding Unwanted Businesses from Prior Acquisitions.*   Some divestitures of the type that involved selling to a value-increasing buyer were planned at the time of prior M & A activity. Such divestitures may have been pre-planned because they represented a poor fit with the acquiring firm. Sometimes such divestitures could be turned at a profit, sometimes they involved a loss that was offset by the good segments retained. Examples are Pullman's sales of Bruning Hydraulics and Waterman Hydraulics to Parker Hannifin in 1988 following its acquisition of Clevite Industries in 1987.

8 *Financing Prior Acquisitions.*   A number of divestitures also regularly follow major acquisitions or LBOs for financing reasons. Campeau Corp., which acquired Allied Stores in 1986, stated that it would sell 16 Allied divisions to pay down bank debt. Similarly, after its $6.5 billion acquisition of Federated Department Stores, Campeau engaged in a program of divestitures beginning in late 1988. Other similar patterns followed Beazer PLC's acquisition of Koppers Co. and Maxwell Communications' takeover of Macmillan Inc. Earlier Du Pont, which acquired Conoco in 1981, had sold off $2 billion of Conoco's assets by 1984.

9 *Warding Off Takeovers.*   Divestitures have functioned as a takeover defense by removing the "crown jewel" that attracted the takeover threat. A clear example was the sale by Brunswick Corp. of its medical division in 1982 to American Home Products

when facing a takeover threat from Whittaker. The proceeds to Brunswick from the sale of the division were $100 million more than Whittaker had offered for the entire company. Ironically, faced with a similar threat in 1989, Whittaker sold its chemical and technology operations.

10 *Meeting Government Requirements.* Divestments are a common requirement for obtaining government approval of a combination. Baker Hughes was required to divest its Reed Tool Co. subsidiary to comply with the Justice Department conditions for approval of its merger. Similarly, in 1988 Santa Fe Southern Pacific Corp. was required by the ICC to sell one of its railroads. In general, the government may require divestitures as a condition for approval when a combination includes segments with competing products. This holds for LBOs as well. KKR was required to sell off some RJR Nabisco product segments that overlapped with KKR's prior holdings.

11 *Selling Businesses to their Managers.* Corporate sales of divisions or business units to operating management are increasing both in number and size. W. T. Grimm reported in 1987 that LBOs and other going private transactions represented "a consistent 11% of total corporate divestitures.[4]

12 *Taking a Position in Another Firm.* Divestitures may be used to finance an investment in another firm. An example is the sale in 1989 by Emerson Electric of 5 units for $149 million to BSR International PLC for a 45% stake in the UK firm.

13 *Reversing Mistakes.* Exxon's acquisition of Reliance Electric and Mobil's purchase of Montgomery Ward are widely cited as failed attempts at diversification. Both sales were management buyouts.

14 *Learning.* Successful companies may divest businesses after learning more about them. Merck & Co., whose growth has been mainly internal, divested Baltimore Aircoil Co. and part of a Calgon Corp. acquisition after its experience and review process indicated that the businesses "no longer fit its basic long-range strategy."[5] ARA Services, which grew principally by acquisition, eventually divested a construction management business because of lack of fit. Also it divested a management consulting firm because it found that the business depended on key individuals while ARA was built on systems and controls.[6]

This list of motives for divestitures is not meant to be exhaustive, but only to illustrate the variety of factors that may be at work. Strategic planning, to be sure, is a difficult exercise in uncertainty; and corporate executives typically do not have a wealth of experience in getting into unfamiliar businesses that will serve them well in new situations. Consequently, given the many economic forces and corporate motives driving divestiture activity, it is very difficult to determine whether divestitures as a whole represent "successes" or "failures" for the divesting firms.

Analysis of Divestiture/Acquisition Percentages

As mentioned earlier, the high rates of divestitures have been judged by some as conclusive evidence of the failure of acquisition and diversification strategies. This view has been expressed most strongly by Michael Porter, as follows:

The track record of corporate strategies has been dismal. I studied the diversification records of 33 large, prestigious US companies over the 1950–86 period and found that most of them had divested many more acquisitions than they had kept. The corporate strategies of most companies have dissipated instead of created shareholder value.[7]

Porter's conclusion is based on a compilation of data on 33 companies over the period 1950–86. Each company entered, on average, 27 new "fields" (e.g., financial services) and 80 new "industries" (e.g., insurance) within those "fields." About 70 percent of these entries into new fields and industries were accomplished by means of acquisition.

In order to test the success of these forays into new areas, Porter calculated the ratios of divestitures to acquisitions for each company. On average, these 33 companies ended up divesting 53% of acquisitions in new industries and 60% of acquisitions in new fields. When the acquisitions were in fields unrelated to the companies' existing fields, the rate of divestitures was 74%.

Porter then went on to calculate divestiture ratios for each of the 33 companies over various time periods – for example, the percentage of a company's acquisitions in new industries made by 1980 and then divested by 1986 – as a means of ranking their performance. The range of this divestiture ratio among the 33 companies falls between 17% for the "best" corporate strategies and 87% for the "worst," with over 60% of the companies divesting more acquisitions than they kept.

Porter characterizes these results as "startling" and "sobering." But his results are not unexpected in view of the data on divestitures (regularly reported by W. T. Grimm and *Mergers and Acquisitions*) that show them ranging from 35 to 54 percent of acquisitions over the years 1975 to 1988. His data are for "entries" into new fields and industries, which are clearly more difficult than expansion programs. In fact, the Porter data could also be interpreted as evidence of strong and continuing restructuring activity by US corporations. His sample of 33 large, relatively mature corporations made an average of 115 new entries per company during the 1950–86 period, constituting somewhat over three new entries per year. They were thus far from passive in coping with the challenges of almost four decades of economic change. Hence, Porter's data, which he pronounces a "stark indication of failure," could with equal plausibility be attributed to a vigorous and profitable interaction between corporate strategists and shifting market forces.

Issues of method

Apart from this uncertainty about what divestiture ratios really tell us about past acquisition programs, there are also some fundamental weaknesses with the way such ratios have been calculated. First, all acquisitions and divestitures are given equal weight. A billion dollar transaction is given no more weight than the sale of a million dollar asset. What if most of the divestitures that enter into Porter's calculations were small and the acquisitions not divested were the larger ones? Or what if a large acquisition aimed at acquiring one particular segment was followed by the sell-offs of all the other segments judged in advance to be unattractive? The resulting divestiture-to-acquisition ratio would be well over 100 percent even though, by any reasonable financial or strategic tests, the acquisition and subsequent divestitures added to the value of the firm.[8]

Second, as Porter himself recognizes, divestitures may play a useful role in implementing successful strategies. For example, he cautions management against delaying divestitures after they have improved an acquired operation to the point where scarce financing and managerial resources could better be shifted to new activities with greater potential for improvements. Many other types of divestitures also represent successes rather than mistakes or failures. As suggested in my survey of divestiture motives, some divestitures occur after purchases of underperforming or undervalued firms, or after probing new product-market areas with controlled investments. Some divestitures were planned at the time of acquisition because of poor fit or because they could contribute to financing. Therefore, divestiture rates cannot be interpreted as unambiguous measures of failure.

Porter's divestiture ratios, in short, do not allow us to distinguish reliably between those firms that performed well and those that did not. Even if such measures were free of statistical infirmities, how would we know whether one firm's 200 percent divestiture ratio was worse than another firm's 20 percent ratio? Curiously, after laboriously ranking the companies in his sample, he declares the performance of all 33 companies "dismal" and sweepingly extends his conclusions to the "corporate strategies of most companies." "My data," he concludes, "give a stark indication of the failure of corporate strategies . . . Only the lawyers, investment bankers, and original sellers have prospered in most of these acquisitions, not the shareholders."[9]

Effects on Shareholder Value

The real test of corporate performance is in the returns to shareholders provided over time. Porter's conclusions presumably imply that most of the companies in his sample achieved below-average stockholder returns.

As I stated at the beginning of this article, tests of the immediate market reaction to announcements of divestiture typically show significant gains to the selling firm. Porter himself does not subject his assessments to the stock price test because, he argues, stock price movements – at least over the short run – are unreliable indicators. "The short-term market reaction," he says, "is a highly imperfect measure of the long-term success of diversification, and no self-respecting executive would judge a corporate strategy this way."[10] Porter's casual dismissal of the standard "event study" method ignores the findings of a vast body of research in financial economics supporting the methodology.[11]

Porter also argues that measuring the success of corporate diversification by its effects on shareholder value "works only if you compare the shareholder value that *is* with the shareholder value that *might have been* without diversification."[12] One could add the even stronger requirement that all other influences would have to be held constant as well. But many factors go into corporate strategic planning processes. Diversification is only one dimension and is interdependent with many others.[13] Given the many dimensions of corporate strategy, it is neither necessary nor informative to attempt to determine the impact on shareholder value of individual aspects of corporate strategy such as diversification alone. Hence analysis of shareholder returns over a long period is a meaningful exercise to which we shall return below.

Third, Porter also argues that the shareholder returns measure is defective because some companies start from a "strong base." Here he appears to confuse accounting and shareholder returns. Porter must have accounting returns in mind when he states that bad decisions can still produce good returns to shareholders because of a strong base. Stock prices, unlike accounting data, are forward looking; they already reflect the existence of a strong base. Thus, poor decisions coming after good performance will cause the stock price to decline in fairly short order – in some cases, upon the moment the bad decision is merely announced. If the company does not continue to meet the expectations of investors, stock returns will be lower than normal. To sustain above-normal market returns requires continuous improvement.

Therefore, it is useful to examine the event-study findings and then to look at the evidence on shareholder returns.

The market reaction to divestitures

There are three fairly similar "event studies" of divestitures that all reported similar results: namely, that companies announcing divestitures experienced (statistically significant) 1 to 2 percent average stock price increases (adjusted for general market movements) in the two-day period surrounding the announcement. The effects on the buying firms in these transactions were not significant.[14]

A later, more detailed study[15] found that when the selling firms do not disclose the transaction price when the sell-off is initially announced, there is no statistically significant effect on the seller's share price. But when companies do mention the price in the announcement, the size of stock price effect is a positive and increasing function of the percentage of the firm divested.[16] For example, when the percentage of the equity sold is less than 10%, there is no significant price effect. When the percentage of equity sold is between 10% and 50%, abnormal returns to the seller average a positive 2.5%. When the percentage of the equity sold is greater than 50%, the percentage abnormal return is over 8%.

When the abnormal gains to sellers from divestitures are aggregated, the totals represent substantial dollar amounts. A study by SEC economists published in this journal estimated that, over the period 1981–6, the stock price gains to sellers in corporate divestitures could be conservatively placed at $27.6 billion.[17]

These gains to sellers do not, of course, resolve our central question: Do divestitures represent the reversal of strategic "mistakes" or do they reflect a valuable on-going process of restructuring? The positive market response to divestiture announcements could reasonably be interpreted as the market's positive response to the correction of previous mistakes. The next issue, then, is how acquiring firms have performed when the earlier acquisitions were made.

The market reaction to acquisitions: some new evidence

In the case of acquisitions, there is little doubt that consistently large premiums are earned by selling firms. There is much less agreement, however, about the effects on acquiring firms. But the most recent large-scale study of acquisitions, published in 1988 by Michael Bradley, Anand Desai, and E. Han Kim, tells a plausible story.[18]

This study begins by dividing M & A transactions into three distinct time periods. The first period runs from 1963 to 1968, the year in which the Williams Amendment gave the SEC increased power over tender offers and which also saw the beginning of state takeover legislation. The third period begins with 1981, when antitrust restrictions were reduced, the financing of takeovers was expanded, and takeover defenses were strengthened. The findings of the study are summarized below:

- Average gains to targets increased sharply from about 18% prior to 1968 to approximately 36% thereafter.
- Acquiring firms earned positive average returns of about 4% during the first period (1963–7); positive, but insignificant returns during the second period (1968–80); and negative 3% returns, on average, during the third period (1981–4).
- When transactions involved only single bidders, the acquiring firms had significant gains in the first two periods and insignificant returns for the third period.
- When transactions involved more than one bidder the acquiring firms had insignificant returns for the first two periods and highly significant negative returns for the third period.
- Among multiple bidders, first-bidder acquirers had insignificant returns while late-bidder acquirers ("white knights") had significant negative returns, prompting Bradley et al. to conclude: "Clearly, the evidence is consistent with our contention that white knights, on average, pay 'too much' for the targets they acquire."[19]

This detailed evidence on acquisitions suggests that it was not so much that the strategies of acquiring firms were flawed, but that the victors in multiple bidding contests have increasingly been afflicted with what Richard Roll has called the "winner's curse."[20]

Some evidence on "long-term" shareholder returns

Porter reports that he measured shareholder returns to his 33 sample companies over the period of his study (1950–86) and compared them with divestment rates. He notes that "companies near the top of the list have above-average shareholder returns."[21] This statement is misleading because, in fact, most of the firms in his rankings outperformed the long-run market average. As shown in table 15.1, the shareholder returns (dividends plus capital gains) from 1950–86 for 21 of the 33 (64%) companies in his sample exceeded the market return. Another eight companies were within three percentage points of the market return; and only four firms substantially under-performed market averages. These findings, as well as others which break down the period 1950–87 into smaller segments, are clearly inconsistent with Porter's statement that "the corporate strategies of most companies have dissipated instead of created shareholder value."[22]

I also devised a simple test to examine Porter's claim that the most successful companies were those with the lowest percentage of acquisitions made by 1980 and then divested by 1986. In table 15.2, I ranked the 33 companies in Porter's sample according to their stock price performance over the period 1981–6, and then compared these shareholder return rankings against Porter's rankings to see if Porter's divestiture criterion had a strong correspondence with changes in shareholder value.

Using a form of analysis known as the Spearman rank correlation coefficient, I discovered that the relationship between Porter's acquisition/divestiture ratio and shareholder returns, far from being positive, was actually significantly negative! This negative relationship (which is statistically significant at the 5% level) suggests in fact

Table 15.1 Shareholder returns for Porter's sample, 1950–86*

Company	% Compound average annual return to shareholders 1950–86	Company	% Compound average annual return to shareholders 1950–86
Beatrice (1950–85)	28.91	General Mills	12.49
Gulf & Western (1965–86)	18.96	RCA (1950–85)	12.46
Rockwell	17.36	Procter & Gamble	12.26
Sara Lee	16.13	Borden	12.05
IBM	15.67	MARKET RETURN	11.96
Exxon	15.56	Westinghouse	11.61
Mobil	15.11	Continental Group (1950–83)	11.23
IC Industries (1964–86)	14.80	General Foods	11.21
CBS	14.79	Signal (1969–84)	10.62
Raytheon (1953–86)	14.79	Scovill (1951–84)	10.61
Johnson & Johnson	14.78	Xerox (1962–86)	10.11
United Technologies	14.38	Du Pont	9.59
TRW	14.22	Grace, W. R. (1954–86)	9.42
3M	14.20	Tenneco (1959–86)	7.99
ITT	13.87	Allied (1950–84)	6.86
Alco Standard (1970–86)	13.31	Cummins Engine (1965–86)	5.66
GE	13.01	Wickes**	—

* Based on CRSP monthly geometric returns converted to an annual basis. When data for the full period were not available from the CRSP tapes, the years provided are shown in parentheses following the company name.

** Wickes was not included because data were available on the CRSP tapes for only one year.

Table 15.2 Porter ranking relative to shareholder returns, 1981–6*

Company	Percent shareholder returns 1981–6*	Porter ranking	Company	Percent shareholder returns 1981–6*	Porter ranking
Sara Lee	39.92	18	Cummins Engine	18.65	30
Borden	39.21	10	Du Pont	18.59	8
Scovill	34.49	20	3M	17.14	5
Westinghouse	30.27	25	ITT	16.92	14
Gulf & Western	30.03	29	Rockwell	16.42	15
General Mills	29.33	28	Johnson & Johnson	14.94	1
Continental Group	27.12	27	IBM	14.47	7
Beatrice	26.62	13	United Technologies	11.51	4
IC Industries	26.38	11	TRW	9.94	6
General Electric	23.53	24	Mobil	7.52	9
General Foods	23.51	19	Xerox	6.90	26
CBS Inc.	22.67	32	Raytheon	6.71	3
Alco Standard	20.79	22	Signal	5.71	21
RCA	20.25	31	Allied	4.66	16
Procter & Gamble	19.51	2	Grace, W. R.	2.98	23
Exxon	18.95	17	Tenneco	2.68	12

The Spearman rank correlation coefficient is -0.3574 with a t-statistic of -2.10 which is significant at the 5% level.

*Based on CRSP monthly returns converted to an annual basis. The market return for 1981–6 was 15.03%.

that the lower the ranking by Porter (or the higher the divestiture rate), the higher the returns to shareholders.

I also used other time periods and other samples of companies in performing further tests of the relationship between divestiture rates and company performance. Sometimes the relationship was negative, as above; but in other cases, the relationship was positive or unreliably different from zero. In short, the evidence suggests no consistent relationship between rankings on divestiture/acquisition ratios and the success or failure of diversification programs or other aspects of strategic planning.

Conclusions

Divestiture/acquisition ratios do not provide unambiguous evidence on the success or failure of corporate strategies. Divestitures seem as likely to reflect past successes as mistaken attempts at diversification. Some are pre-planned for good business reasons. Some represent harvesting of sound investments. And some reflect organizational learning that contributes to improvements in future strategies.

Studies of the market reaction to divestitures report significant positive gains to sellers and normal returns to buyers. These results could, of course, be interpreted as the market's positive response to the correction of previous errors in strategy. But stock market studies of takeovers and mergers also consistently report net gains to shareholders. The returns to acquiring firms in single-bid takeovers were positive until 1980. In multiple bidder takeover contests, however, the winners may have paid too much, earning only normal returns before 1980 and experiencing negative announcement returns thereafter.

My own research demonstrates that the long-term (1950–87) returns to shareholders have been well above the average market-wide return for a large fraction of companies with high rates of divestitures. Although such evidence does not *prove* that acquisition/divestiture programs *per se* have increased shareholder value, it should give us pause before accepting sweeping indictments of past corporate strategies.

In short, the data on divestiture/acquisition rates portray a healthy and dynamic interplay between the strategic planning of US companies and continually shifting market forces. Divestitures are an important means of allowing firms to follow their perceived comparative advantages. Divestitures succeed in moving corporate resources to higher-valued uses or more efficient users; and, as a result, overall corporate efficiency increases. Although some sell-offs clearly represent efforts to correct previous acquisition mistakes, many others reflect modifications of initially good strategic decisions that required adjustments in response to changes in the external environment. Regardless of which version one accepts as the dominant explanation for divestitures – "mistakes" or "learning" – the persistently high numbers and values of such transactions constitute reliable evidence that the market system is working, ensuring the mobility of resources essential to the effective operation of an enterprise economy.

Notes

The suggestions of Kwang Chung, Stan Omstein and Richard Roll, and the research assistance of Dan Asquith and Susan Hoag are gratefully acknowledged.

1 W. T. Grimm *Mergerstat Review*, 1987, pp. 2, 9, 63. Purchase prices are available on only about half of the transactions, with divestitures in recent years running at about 35% of the dollar value of transactions.

2 The strategy literature urged them to attempt to do so. See the pioneering book by H. Igor Ansoff, *Corporate Strategy* (New York: McGraw-Hill, 1965).

3 This motive for divestiture is highlighted in the headline of the February 1989 issue of *Corporate Restructuring*: "A Seller's Market for Divestitures: Competitive Auctions, Multitude of Buyers Sustain High Prices for Corporate Sell-offs."

4 W. T. Grimm, 1987, p. 70.

5 See the presentation by its former chairman and CEO, John J. Horan, "Merck & Co.: Study in Internal Growth," *Mergers & Acquisitions Handbook*, M. L. Rock, ed. (New York: McGraw-Hill, 1987), p. 88.

6 As described by [an ARA executive,] William Fishman, the divested construction management business "was a good business, but not under our management. It continues to succeed under the original owner-management, which bought it back from us." The divested management consulting business was also described as "not a business we

belonged in, and it took us about four years to find that out." See William S. Fishman, "ARA Services: Seeking a Common Thread," *Mergers & Acquisitions Handbook*, p. 67.

7   Michael Porter, "From Competitive Advantage to Corporate Strategy," *Harvard Business Review*, (May–June 1987), p. 43.

8   A second area of ambiguity in Porter's procedures is that he does not give criteria for defining "fields" or "industries." To replicate the study as a scientific test or to understand what Porter actually did and what his data really mean, we would need to have more objective criteria. The US Government Standard Industrial Classification (SIC) Manual [1987] would be a helpful referent. Porter's illustration of "field" seems related to the SIC Code at the "division" level (e.g., D. Manufacturing); his designation of "industry" could be at the two-digit level (e.g., Major Group 20 – Food and Kindred Products); or at the three-digit level (e.g., 201 Meat Products); or at the four-digit level (e.g., 2015 Poultry Slaughtering and Processing). Without linking to a systematic classification system, Porter's groupings involve considerable subjectivity which could influence his results and make scientific retesting impossible.

9   Porter, 1987, p. 46.

10 Ibid., p. 45.

11 To characterize event studies as measuring "short-term market reactions" reflects a rather gross misunderstanding of the method and its underlying assumptions. The methodology measures stock price changes in relation to total market movements for samples of firms at different calendar time periods but centered with reference to the abnormal event measured. The measurement of the impact of an event in relation to total market movements is thus best viewed as an estimate of the market's assessment of the long-term effects of the "unusual" event being studied. Random influences are averaged out by the use of relatively large samples, and consistent results are obtained in a large number of studies.

12 Porter, 1987, pp. 45–6.

13 Porter's own writings convey the many dimensions of corporate strategies. In his earlier book, *Competitive Strategy* (New York: Free Press, 1980), Porter presented 134 checklists and checklist-like diagrams – one about every three pages. In his later book, *Competitive Advantage* (New York: Free Press, 1985), the number had expanded to 187 – one about every $2\frac{1}{2}$ pages.

14 The three studies are as follows: Gordon J. Alexander, P. George Benson, and Joan M. Kampmeyer, "Investigating the Valuation Effects of Announcements of Voluntary Corporate Selloffs," *Journal of Finance*, (June 1984), pp. 503–17; Prem C. Jain, "The Effect of Voluntary Sell-off Announcements on Shareholder Wealth," *Journal of Finance*, (March 1985), pp. 209–24; and Scott C. Linn and Michael S. Rozeff, "The Corporate Sell-off," *Midland Corporate Finance Journal*, (Summer 1984), pp. 17–26. For a good, non-technical summary of the evidence on divestitures, see especially the last of these three articles.

15 April Klein, "The Timing and Substance of Divestiture Announcements: Individual, Simultaneous and Cumulative Effects," *Journal of Finance*, (July 1986), pp. 685–97.

16 As measured by the price of the sell-off divided by the market value of the equity on the last day of the month prior to the announcement period.

17 Bernard S. Black and Joseph A. Grundfest, "Shareholder Gains from Takeovers and Restructurings Between 1981 and 1986: $162 Billion is a Lot of Money," *Journal of Applied Corporate Finance*, vol. 1, no. 1 (Spring 1988), pp. 5–15.

18   Michael Bradley, Anand Desai, and E. Han Kim, "Synergistic Gains from Corporate Acquisitions and their Division Between the Stockholders of Target and Acquiring Firms," *Journal of Financial Economics*, 21, (1988), pp. 3–40.

19   Ibid., p. 30.

20   See Richard Roll, "The Hubris Hypothesis of Corporate Takeovers," *Journal of Business*, (April 1986), pp. 197–216 (chapter 3 above).

21   Porter, 1987, p. 45.

22   Ibid., p. 43.

16

The Returns to Acquiring Firms in Tender Offers: Evidence from Three Decades

Gregg A. Jarrell and Annette B. Poulsen

Extensive empirical evidence supports the view that takeovers are beneficial to the shareholders of target firms.[1] Virtually every study has found that these shareholders receive large premiums, averaging about 30%, for their shares. The wealth effects on shareholders of acquiring firms, however, are much more puzzling. Researchers measuring these wealth effects have found them to average close to zero and to be negative for some categories of offers. The same logic that argues that large premiums paid in takeovers are evidence that takeovers benefit shareholders of target firms, also leads some to argue that the absence of stock price increases (and the existence of stock price declines in some cases) for bidding firms reflects neutral (or bad) investments by management of bidding firms.

In this study, shareholder wealth effects in tender offers are examined and, more specifically, characteristics of tender offer bids that may determine the returns earned by the shareholders of acquiring firms are explored. For more than 450 tender offers from 1963–86, acquiring firm shareholders experienced significant positive abnormal returns on average, though those returns did not nearly approach the abnormal returns to target firms. In the 1980s, however, abnormal returns to acquiring firms were negative on average (though not significantly so).

Several characteristics of tender offer bids that may affect the division of gains between target and acquiring firm shareholders are considered here. The evidence suggests that the relative size of the target to the acquiring firm plays a large role in determining returns to acquirers. In addition, increased competition for the target, measured by management opposition to the bid and the regulatory environment at the time of the bid, significantly lowers returns to the acquiring firm's shareholders.

While previous authors have studied similar determinants of shareholder returns, this work differs in several ways. Beginning in the 1960s and ending in the 1980s, this analysis covers three decades in which the takeover environment changed dramatically. The effect of the relative size of the target to the acquirer on acquirer returns is analyzed in a large sample of tender offers, where it has not been studied previously. In addition, through regression analysis, both the impact of relative size and the impact of competing bidders are incorporated into the cross-sectional analysis.

I   Determinants of Wealth Effects for Acquiring Firms

This section considers some of the rationale for negligible wealth effects to acquiring firm shareholders, and then discusses the variables used in the empirical estimates to explain acquiring firm returns.

A.   *Rationale for negligible wealth effects*

Finance theory predicts that firms undertake new capital investments when the investments have positive effects on firm value. McConnell and Muscarella [12] find support for this premise, reporting a significant, positive share price reaction on average when a sample of industrial firms announced increases in planned capital expenditures. Therefore, the evidence of negligible or negative wealth effects for acquiring firms at takeover announcements leads many observers to argue that acquisitions are poor investments. Others, however, have offered various rationales for why the observed wealth effects are consistent with value-maximizing behavior. Three explanations are considered in turn.

Wealth effects are disguised   Tender offer announcements may contain little information about the acquiring firm. If the investment in the target firm is small relative to the total value of the acquiring firm, the increase in value from the merger may not cause much change in the acquirer's share price. Asquith, Bruner, and Mullins [1, 2] note the importance of this consideration and find evidence that abnormal returns earned by acquirers increase as target size increases relative to acquirer size.

Additionally, relatively small wealth effects for acquiring firms may reflect market reaction to announcements about the financing of the bid, in addition to the reaction to the takeover itself. Recent empirical work has shown that, in general, announcements of additional equity issues by public corporations are accompanied by negative share price effects (Smith [19] summarizes this evidence.) If the acquirer finances the offer with an equity issue, positive announcement effects from the takeover can be offset by information released in the financing decision. Travlos [20] and Asquith, Bruner, and Mullins [2] show that in takeovers financed with new equity issues, the stock price returns to acquiring firms are significantly lower than in offers financed with cash.

In addition, the market may have already anticipated the acquisition strategy of the bidding firm, thus mitigating any valuation effect at the time of the formal announcement (see Schipper and Thompson [17]). For example, if the acquiring firm has announced that it is actively pursuing acquisitions, then any abnormal return at the announcement of a specific bid would reflect information about that specific bid relative to expected acquisitions, not about the desirability of the acquisition program in general.

The effect of competition on acquirers' returns   If there are no competing bidders for a target, the bidder should offer a price just high enough to obtain the number of shares the bidder desires. If alternative bidders, however, could also benefit from the merger gains, one would expect to see the offer price bid up and a larger share of the merger returns going to the target and a smaller share kept by the bidder.

Comment and Jarrell [4] and Bradley, Desai, and Kim [3] report that multiple bidders for a target are associated with significantly higher abnormal returns to target shareholders. Bradley, Desai, and Kim show that returns to acquiring firm shareholders are significantly positive in single-bidder contests and insignificantly different from zero in multiple-bidder contests.

The degree of competition among bidders is partially a function of government regulation. Jarrell and Bradley [7] argue that increased disclosure resulting from the adoption of the Williams Act in 1968 and amendments to the Williams Act in 1970 significantly affected the division of gains between target and acquiring firms in tender offers. Because competing bidders could use the information produced by the original bidder, Jarrell and Bradley hypothesize that returns to targets should have increased following the Williams Act and returns to acquirers should have decreased. Their evidence supports this hypothesis. They find that abnormal returns to bidders declined from an average of about 9% prior to the Williams Act to about 6% following the adoption of the Williams Act, and that returns to targets increased by about 20%.

More recently, Bradley, Desai, and Kim [3] consider the 1980s separately, arguing that the 1980s provided a more competitive atmosphere for takeovers. A more lenient antitrust attitude towards horizontal mergers and the rapid growth of innovative financing and defensive strategies encouraged competing bids. As expected, they find that returns to acquirers were significantly lower in the 1980s than in the 1960s or 1970s.

Small wealth effects correctly reflect neutral or bad investments by management   Evidence of relatively small or negative returns to acquiring firms in tender offers and mergers can be evidence that many takeovers are poor investments. Roll [16] suggests that managers undertake corporate combinations because of "hubris," and this "overbearing" confidence can result in overpayment for target shares. Wiedenbaum and Vogt [21] argue that managers prefer to increase the size of their corporation because the ability of shareholders to monitor management decreases in larger, more complex organizations.

Some empirical work supports this explanation of negative returns to acquiring firms. Mitchell and Lehn [13] find that firms which make "bad" acquisitions, as measured by negative returns at the announcement of a bid, are more likely to be the subject of later takeover bids themselves. Lewellen, Loderer, and Rosenfeld [11] find support for an additional implication of this explanation – that in those firms in which managers hold large equity positions, managers would be less likely to initiate takeovers resulting in the loss of shareholder wealth. They report a positive relation between the wealth effects from takeovers on acquiring firms and the percent of equity held by senior management.

B. Empirical tests

The role of several variables in explaining premiums earned by shareholders of acquiring firms are tested, including:

  i)   the relative size of the target to the bidding firm;
  ii) whether the bid is opposed at any time by the management of the target firm; and
  iii) the decade in which the transaction occurs, as a measure of the importance of regulatory and institutional changes.

The relative size variable allows us to address one aspect of the "disguised wealth effects" hypothesis.[2] One would expect that as the target increases in size relative to that of the acquirer, the impact of the acquisition would be more readily observed in the acquirer's return. Thus, if acquisitions are on average wealth-increasing projects for acquiring firms, the largest positive return should be observed when the target is large relative to the acquiring firm.

Asquith, Bruner, and Mullins [1, 2] and Travlos [20] have tested this variable in several takeover samples. In [1], Asquith, Bruner, and Mullins report a positive, significant relationship between relative size and the returns to acquirers in a sample of 211 mergers announced from 1963–79. The two later studies, however, find no significant relationship between relative size and returns to acquirers in cash offers. The two samples are drawn from a later period, 1973–83, and are dominated by merger transactions as opposed to tender offers.[3] The empirical tests here, in contrast, determine the relevancy of the relative size variable for a large sample of tender offers over an extended period of time.[4]

The effect of competition on acquiring firm returns is tested by classifying bids according to management opposition and the financial and regulatory environment. This examination of the relation between acquirer returns and management opposition to a bid is similar to the multiple-bidder test of Bradley, Desai, and Kim [3]. By including all contested bids, it can be determined if bidders receive lower returns when they must overcome not only competition from other bidders but also management opposition. When target management opposes a bid, the bidder usually has additional costs, including litigation and delay, and may be forced to pay higher premiums to target shareholders to encourage tendering.[5]

Jarrell and Bradley [7] and Bradley, Desai, and Kim [3] find that the financial and regulatory environment, as measured by the decade in which the bid occurs, is important in determining the wealth gains of shareholders of target and acquiring firms. The relevance of the regulatory environment is tested by measuring the impact of the decade in which the transaction takes place on the returns to the acquiring firm.[6]

II   Returns to Acquiring Firms in Tender Offers

A.   *Sample of tender offers*

The sample of tender offers from 1963–86 is derived from two sources. For those offers occurring from 1963–80, the Managerial Economics Research Center (at the University of Rochester) database (developed by Bradley, Dodd, Ruback, and Desai) is used. Tender offers from 1980–6 are identified from files at the Securities and Exchange Commission.[7] The offers are limited to those in which either the target or bidder firm, though not necessarily both, were listed on the New York or American Stock Exchange at the time of the offer. Only "successful" offers are included – offers in which at least some shares were purchased under the terms of the offer. The final sample includes 770 tender offers, including 526 exchange-listed targets and 462 acquiring exchange-listed firms.

The *Wall Street Journal* Index is used to determine event dates. The announcement date for the target is the trading day before the first mention of the tender offer. Similarly, the trading day before the first mention of the successful bidder in the transaction is used as the bidder's event date. In cases where the successful bidder is a second or third bidder, its event date is usually later than the target's event date.

It is also determined whether target management expressed public opposition to the offer by using the *Wall Street Journal* Index. A bid is treated as contested if the target management at any time publicly opposed the offer, even though most bids ultimately result in a negotiated agreement.[8]

To calculate the relative size of the target compared to the acquiring firm, divide target size by bidder size, and then transform the ratio to its logarithmic form. The size of the target and acquiring firms are measured as the value of outstanding equity of each firm three months prior to the target's event date. For those cases in which the value of outstanding equity could not be found for both the target and the acquirer, the value of equity was replaced with the level of sales in the preceding year for the firms, as obtained from *Dun & Bradstreets Million Dollar Directory*.[9]

Table 16.1 reports that 150 of the tender offers in the sample occur in the 1960s, 208 in the 1970s, and 412 in the 1980s. Note that the fraction of tender offers that were contested increased somewhat over the three decades for which there is data, supporting the perception that hostile tender offers have become relatively more important in recent years. In the 1960s, 32% of the offers were contested as compared to 35% in the 1970s and 39% in the 1980s.

Commentators have suggested that small firms were first able to acquire relatively much larger targets in the 1980s with the advent of innovative financing techniques such as junk bonds. The data in table 16.1 do not substantiate this impression. The largest average relative size is in the 1960s, when targets were on average 6.55 times larger than the acquirer. This average fell to 0.55 in the 1970s and then increased to 3.19 in the 1980s. The median relative size, perhaps the more relevant figure given the

Table 16.1   Descriptive statistics for successful tender offers from 1963–86

Years	Number of bids	Number contested (%)	Relative size target/ acquirer (number)	
			Mean	*Median*
1960s	150	48 (32%)	6.55	0.37
			(86)	(86)
1970s	208	73 (35%)	0.55	0.17
			(155)	(155)
1980s	412	161 (39%)	3.19	0.21
			(264)	(264)

Table 16.2   Cumulative abnormal returns (CARs) for all successful bidders and targets from 1963–86

Event window	CAR	t-Statistic	Number of firms
Bidding firms			
CAR(−2,+1)	0.70	2.67	461
CAR(−5,+5)	0.92	2.36	461
CAR(−10,+20)	1.96	3.47	462
CAR(−10,+30)	2.15	3.49	462
CAR(−20,+10)	1.29	2.35	462
Target firms			
CAR(−20,+10)	28.99	30.50	526

impact of a few large outliers on the average, also suggests this trend. At the median, the target was 37% the size of the acquirer in the 1960s, 17% the size of the acquirer in the 1970s and 21% the size of the acquirer in the 1980s.

B.   Price reactions to tender offer announcements

The stock return data used here is derived from the Daily Excess Stock Returns File provided by the Center for Research in Securities Prices (CRSP), estimated using the Scholes–Williams methodology [18]. For each firm, the time series of excess, or abnormal, returns around the announcement date is obtained. Abnormal returns reflect the extent to which a firm's stock over or under-performed the market relative to its previous relationship with the market. The abnormal returns (ARs) are summed for each firm over several time periods around the event date to find cumulative abnormal returns (CARs) by firm. The CARs are averaged across portfolios of interest, and t-statistics are computed using cross-sectional standard errors.

Overall, as reported in table 16.2, bidders on the average experience small, but statistically significant, wealth increases at the announcement of tender offers. For the smallest window of measurement, from two days before to one day after the bid, shareholders of 461 acquiring firms received a 0.70% appreciation in the value of their shares, significantly different from zero. In the longest window measured, the average CAR from 10 days before to 30 days after the bid is 2.15%, again statistically significant.

Consistent with the previous research in this area, it is shown that the cumulative abnormal returns of target firms are much larger than those of acquiring firms. In this sample, shareholders of targets in 526 bids received an average premium of 28.99%, measured from 20 days before to 10 days after the bid.

III   Determinants of Returns to Acquiring Firms

Ordinary least squares regression analysis is used to determine the impact of the explanatory variables on the acquiring firms' abnormal returns at the announcement of the tender offer. The regression results are reported in table 16.3. Panel A reports the regression results for 404 bidders and 356 targets for which sufficient data could be obtained.[10] The first two columns of panel A report regression results where the dependent variable in the regressions is the CAR earned by the acquirer over two event windows. The longer event window, from 10 days before to 20 days after the announcement, should more fully capture any information concerning the bid revealed in the period around the formal announcement. In the shorter window, measured from two days before to one day after the bid, the abnormal return measurement is narrowed to reduce the possibility of confounding events.

The intercept term represents the average CAR earned by acquirers when the other explanatory variables equal zero. Thus, the estimated intercept of 9.1% in the (−10, +20) regression represents the CAR earned by a bidder in an uncontested bid in the 1960s when the relative size variable, measured in logarithms, equals zero (i.e., the bidder and target are equal in size). The intercept equals 4.7% in the (−2,+1) regression, suggesting that the longer window more fully captures information about the bid.

The relative size of the target to the acquirer has a positive and significant effect on CARs earned by acquiring firm shareholders in both windows. The estimated coefficient of 1.9% (significantly different from zero) in the CAR(−10,+20) window indicates that if the target firm is twice as large as the bidder (log value of relative size = 0.693), the estimated CAR increases by 1.32%. As the target firm increases in size relative to the bidder, average CARs earned by acquirers increase significantly. This is consistent with the hypothesis that wealth gains accruing to acquirers are disguised when the target is relatively small.

The coefficient of the contested variable, equal to one if the bid is contested and zero otherwise, is negative and significantly different from zero in both windows − indicating that acquiring firms earn lower CARs if target management opposes the bid. This result illustrates the importance of competition in redistributing some of the gains in takeovers from acquirers to targets.

Table 16.3   Ordinary least squares regressions results explaining acquiring and target firms returns at announcement of tender offers from 1963–86 (*t*-statistics in parentheses)*

Panel A: Returns to Acquirers and Targets in All Tender Offers

	Acquirer		Target
	CAR(−10,+20)	CAR(−2,+1)	CAR(−20,+10)
Intercept	0.091	0.047	0.153
	(6.30)	(6.62)	(5.14)
Relative size in logs	0.019	0.007	−0.024
	(5.07)	(4.04)	(−3.43)
Contested	−0.031	−0.015	0.035
	(−2.63)	(−2.62)	(1.52)
1970s	−0.022	−0.020	0.143
	(−1.35)	(−2.49)	(4.18)
1980s	−0.044	−0.034	0.104
	(−2.88)	(−4.54)	(3.23)
R-squared	0.096	0.107	0.093
Number of firms	404	403	356

Panel B: Acquirer Returns by Decade

	1960s		1970s		1980s	
CAR =	(−10,+20)	(−2,1)	(−10,+20)	(−2,1)	(−10,+20)	(−2,1)
Intercept	0.110	0.047	0.054	0.024	0.040	0.012
	(4.68)	(4.22)	(3.06)	(2.75)	(2.63)	(1.63)
Relative size in logs	0.029	0.011	0.013	0.006	0.015	0.006
	(3.33)	(2.27)	(2.11)	(1.92)	(2.83)	(2.27)
Contested	−0.049	−0.004	−0.018	−0.014	−0.027	−0.018
	(−1.47)	(−0.28)	(−1.01)	(−1.57)	(−1.67)	(−2.25)
R-squared	0.146	0.091	0.036	0.036	0.042	0.038
Number of firms	74	74	127	127	203	202

* Dependent variable = Cumulative Abnormal Return over event window as indicated.

Dummy variables are used to determine the effect of the decade in which the bid occurs on acquirer returns. If the regulatory and financial environment has changed such that acquirers increasingly face additional competition for targets over time, one would expect acquirer returns to decline correspondingly. The time period is important; cumulative abnormal returns earned by bidders in the 1970s and 1980s are significantly lower than those in the 1960s, holding other determinants constant. In the (−10,+20) window, CARs are 2.2% lower in the 1970s and 4.4% lower in the 1980s than the 1960s. In the (−2,+1) window, CARs are 2.0% lower in the 1970s and 3.4% lower in the 1980s compared to the 1960s.

For comparison, similar regression results for 356 target firms are reported in the last column of panel A. Target CARs are measured from 20 days before to 10 days after the bid.[11] The results are consistent with the view that actual and potential competition affects the distribution of wealth gains in takeovers. If the bid is contested, target

CARs (measured from 20 days before to 10 days after the bid) increase (though not significantly) and target CARs increase significantly in the 1970s and the 1980s at the same time acquirer returns were declining.

Also, as the target increases in size relative to the acquirer, target CARs decrease significantly. While it is logical that acquirer returns should be a function of relative size, it is not clear why target returns should be. This result could support Roll's [16] suggestion that it is easier to acquire shares in a larger, more diffusely held firm and therefore the acquirer can offer a lower premium.

In panel B of table 16.3, results for similar regressions looking at the determinants of acquirer returns in each of the three decades are reported. The dependent variables are again the CARs of the acquirers measured from 10 days before to 20 days after and from 2 days before to 1 day after the bid. Overall, the results are substantially the same as the full sample (panel A). The intercept terms are significantly different from zero in each decade. For the longer window, the estimated intercept is 11.0% in the 1960s, 5.4% in the 1970s, and 4.0% in the 1980s. In the shorter window, the estimated intercept is 4.7% in the 1960s, 2.4% in the 1970s, and 1.2% (insignificantly different from zero) in the 1980s.

Relative size has a significant and positive effect in all three decades. Its estimated coefficient ranges from 2.9% in the CAR(−10,+20) window in the 1960s to 0.6% in the CAR(−2,+1) window in the 1970s and 1980s. It is not surprising that the largest impact for the relative size variable is observed in the 1960s given that the largest CARs are also observed in this period.

When the bid is contested, it has a negative effect on the CAR in every regression reported, but it is significantly different from zero only in the 1980s. This is similar to the results of Bradley, Desai, and Kim [3] – that "white knight"-type bidders explain most of the negative average returns to acquirers they find in the 1980s.

Overall, the reported regression results support the predicted relationships. The relative size of the target to the acquirer plays an important role in disguising the gains to acquiring firms from takeovers. When the target is relatively small, the acquiring firm earns significantly lower CARs. Competition for the target also significantly lowers acquiring firm CARs, as indicated by the contested variable and the secular decline in CARs over time.

IV   Conclusions

Researchers have suggested three general explanations of why returns to acquirers at the announcement of takeovers are close to zero and negative in some cases. First, the full wealth effects may not be observed in acquiring firm stock prices at the time of the bid because they are disguised in other information or are a relatively small component of acquirer wealth. Second, competition between alternative bidders ensures that any excess returns are earned by the targets. Third, the acquisitions are indeed poor investment projects for the acquirers and the wealth effects accurately reflect this.

The empirical work here supports the first two explanations. As the target increases in size relative to the acquirer, the acquirer experiences a significantly larger appreciation in its share price. Also, as competition for the target increases, returns to acquirers are affected – when target management opposes a bid, acquirer returns are lower. In addition, changes in the regulatory environment, innovations in financial markets, and defensive tactics have also increased competition for target firms over time. Returns to acquirers are significantly lower following the adoption of the Williams Act and its amendments. Also in the 1980s, returns to acquirers were lower than in the 1970s, though not significantly so.

Overall, these results help explain the low or negative returns to bidders in tender offers. While the gains to acquirers average close to zero, the cross-sectional evidence indicates that these returns follow systematic patterns with respect to the potential impact of the acquisition on the bidder and the amount of competition for the target. The results suggest that the pattern of acquirer returns in tender offers are explainable by factors consistent with value-maximization by bidders.

Notes

We thank Paula Moolhuyzen, Ken Lehn, Jeffry Netter, and our referees for many helpful comments and suggestions. The SEC, as a matter of policy, disclaims responsibility for any private publication or statement by any of its employees. The views expressed herein are those of the authors and do not necessarily reflect the views of the Commission or of the authors' colleagues on the staff of the Commission.

1   Jensen and Ruback [10] and Jarrell, Brickley, and Netter [8] summarize the evidence of the wealth effects of takeovers.

2   Other researchers have found that the financing decision is important in determining acquirer returns. Most tender offers are cash offers, however, and therefore we do not incorporate this consideration in our empirical work. *Mergers & Acquisitions* [14] reports that 117 acquirers in 120 tender offers in 1987 and 155 acquirers in 160 tender offers in 1986 offered all cash in return for target firm stock.

3   Asquith, Bruner, and Mullins [2] include only 34 tender offers in their sample of 197 takeovers while Travlos [20] considers 41 tender offers in 166 takeovers. Asquith, Bruner, and Mullins [1] do not report the composition of their takeover sample in terms of tender offers versus mergers.

4   This test could be interpreted alternatively. For example, Roll [16] suggests that findings for the relative size variable might reflect that acquirers more accurately value the target firm when it is larger or offer a lower premium because it is easier to acquire shares in a larger, less closely held firm. In either case, the larger the target the more positive the return the acquirers would experience.

5   See Jarrell [5] and Netter [15] for a discussion and empirical evidence concerning the impact of defensive litigation on the part of target management.

6   Though Jarrell and Bradley [7] compare tender offers before and after 1968, we compare offers before and after 1970. The 1970 amendments to the Williams Act extended the law to non-cash offers, significantly increasing the impact of the Williams Act.

7   Both datasets are drawn from tender offer documents filed with the Securities and Exchange Commission.

8   Jarrell [6] finds that of 412 bids in the 1980s, only 21 did not ultimately result in a friendly merger agreement.

9   Travlos [20] estimated a similar relative size measure as the value of shares sought divided by the value of the acquiring firm's shares as the measure of relative size. Though this variable might better estimate the impact of the acquisition on the acquirer, we cannot use Travlos' measure because we rely on the level of sales for non-traded targets and acquirers.

10 The decrease in the number of observations included in the regression analysis from the 462 acquirers and 526 targets for which we had CAR data results from missing data for relative size. Missing observations are distributed evenly throughout the full period of our sample.

11 We include the longer period before the bid because there is usually a significant run-up in target stock prices before formal bid announcements. See Jarrell and Poulsen [9] for evidence on the magnitude and determinants of run-up in target stock prices.

References

1   Asquith, P., R. Bruner, and D. Mullins, 1983, The Gains to Bidding Firms From Merger, *Journal of Financial Economics*, March, 121–40.

2   ——, 1987, Merger Returns and the Form of Financing, Working Paper, Harvard University.

3   Bradley, M., A. Desai, and E. H. Kim, 1988, Synergistic Gains From Corporate Acquisitions and Their Division Between the Stockholders of Target and Acquiring Firms, *Journal of Financial Economics*, May, 3–40.

4   Comment, R. and G. Jarrell, 1987, Two-Tier and Negotiated Tender Offers: The Imprisonment of the Free-Riding Shareholder, *Journal of Financial Economics*, December, 283–310.

5   Jarrell, G., 1985, The Wealth Effects of Litigation by Targets: Do Interests Diverge in a Merge, *Journal of Law and Economics*, April, 151–77.

6   ——, 1988, Affidavit in *RP Acquisition Corporation* v. *Staley Continental, Inc.*, US District Court for Delaware, Civil Action No. 88-190.

7   Jarrell, G. and M. Bradley, 1980, The Economic Effects of Federal and State Regulations of Cash Tender Offers, *Journal of Law and Economics*, October, 371–407.

8   Jarrell, G., J. Brickley, and J. Netter, 1988, The Market For Corporate Control: The Empirical Evidence Since 1980, *Journal of Economic Perspectives*, Winter, 49–68.

9   Jarrell, G. and A. Poulsen, 1989, Stock Trading Before the Announcement of Tender Offers: Insider Trading or Market Anticipation?, *Journal of Law, Economics and Organization*, Fall.

10 Jensen, M. and R. Ruback, 1983, The Market for Corporate Control: The Scientific Evidence, *Journal of Financial Economics*, March, 5–50.

11 Lewellen, W., C. Loderer, and A. Rosenfeld, 1985, Merger Decisions and Executive Stock Ownership in Acquiring Firms, *Journal of Accounting and Economics*, April, 209–32.

12 McConnell, J. and C. Muscarella, 1985, Corporate Capital Expenditure Decisions and the Market Value of the Firm, *Journal of Financial Economics*, September, 399–422.

13 Mitchell, M. and K. Lehn, Do Bad Bidders Become Good Targets. See chapter 4 above.

14 *Mergers & Acquisitions*, 1988, Tender Offer Update: 1988, May/June, 23–5.

15 Netter, J., 1989, Shareholder Wealth Effects of Litigation Based on Allegedly False Schedule 13D Disclosure, Working Paper, University of Georgia.

16 Roll, R., 1986, The Hubris Hypothesis of Corporate Takeovers, *Journal of Business*, April, 197–216.

17 Schipper, K. and Thompson, R., 1983, Evidence on the Capitalized Value of Merger Activity for Acquiring Firms, *Journal of Financial Economics*, March, 85–120.

18 Scholes, M. and J. Williams, 1977, Estimating Betas From Nonsynchronous Data, *Journal of Financial Economics*, December, 309–28.

19 Smith, C., 1986, Investment Banking and the Capital Acquisition Process, *Journal of Financial Economics*, January/February, 3–29.

20 Travlos, N., 1987, Corporate Takeover Bids, Methods of Payment and Bidding Firms' Stock Returns, *Journal of Finance*, September, 943–64.

21 Wiedenbaum, M. and S. Vogt, 1987, Takeovers and Stockholders: Winners and Losers, *California Management Review*, Summer, 157–68.

17

The Market for Corporate Control: The Empirical Evidence Since 1980

Gregg A. Jarrell, James A. Brickley, and Jeffry M. Netter

Corporate takeovers have been very big business in the 1980s. The Office of the Chief Economist (OCE) of the Securities and Exchange Commission estimates that shareholders of target firms in successful tender offers from 1981 through 1986 received payments in excess of US$54 billion over the value of their holdings before the tender offers. Almost $38 billion of the total was received after 1984. If we include the increased wealth of target firm shareholders resulting from leveraged buyouts, mergers, and corporate restructurings (prompted in large part by the threat of takeovers) these numbers are even larger. W. T. Grimm & Co. collects similar data for a larger sample of change-of-control transactions, including mergers and leveraged buyouts. They estimate that from 1981 to 1986 the total dollar value of the premiums over the pre-announcement price paid for securities involved in change-of-control transactions was $118.4 billion.[1] Corporate restructurings have created even more wealth. For example, Jensen (1986) estimated that the restructurings of Phillips, Unocal and Arco created total gains to shareholders of $6.6 billion by reducing investment in negative net present value projects.

There are numerous factors behind the high level of takeover activity in the 1980s. For example, antitrust regulators have come to understand that in the increasingly competitive international marketplace US interests are well-served by domestic mergers that could be objectionable in a more closed economy. Today's antitrust regulators almost never object to vertical combinations, and even horizontal mergers between industry leaders – completely taboo before the 1980s – are often allowed today.

Deregulation also has induced merger and acquisition activity by calling forth new skills and strategies, and new management teams to implement them. Many of the mergers, takeovers, and restructurings over the last ten years have occurred in industries that recently were deregulated, such as airlines and transportation, financial services, broadcasting, and oil and gas. For example, transportation and broadcasting together accounted for 20 percent of all mergers and acquisition activity from 1981 and 1984 while oil and gas accounted for another 26.3 percent (Jensen, 1986).

Other factors motivating the high level of takeover and restructuring activity in the 1980s include innovations in takeover financing, less potent state antitakeover regulations, the retreat by the Federal courts and regulatory agencies from protecting besieged target firms, and learning about the possible returns to this type of activity. These factors are critical to understanding why firms that were considered "untouchable" not long ago have been the targets of hostile takeovers with increasing frequency. This growing list includes USX, CBS, Phillips, and TWA, to name just a few.

The Council of Economic Advisors (CEA) in the 1985 *Economic Report of the President* provides data on the extent of the takeover activity in the 1980s and the importance of large transactions in explaining this activity. The CEA states that the increase in merger and acquisition activity in the 1980s is due to a large increase in the size of the largest transactions. Their evidence indicates that in the period 1981 to 1984 the average annual reported real value of mergers and acquisitions was 48 percent greater than in any four-year period from the late 1960s to the early 1970s. In addition, of the 100 largest acquisition transactions recorded through 1983, 65 occurred after 1982 and only 11 took place prior to 1979.

Returns to Bidders and Targets

Critics of takeovers question whether tender offers, mergers, and leveraged buyouts produce net gains to society. Critics argue any gains to a given party are simply redistributions resulting from losses to someone else (or more colorfully put, a pirating of assets by modern financial buccaneers). Also critics contend that battles for corporate control divert energy from more productive endeavors.[2] In this section, we find that such criticisms are ill founded, and thus conclude that battles for corporate control serve a beneficial function for the economy.

The market for corporate control is the market for the right to control the management of corporate resources. In a takeover, an outside party seeks to obtain control of a firm. There are several types of takeovers, including mergers, hostile and friendly tender offers, and proxy contests. In a merger the bidder negotiates an agreement with target management on the terms of the offer for the target and then submits the proposed agreement to a vote of the shareholders. In a tender offer, a bidder makes an offer directly to shareholders to buy some or all of the stock of the target firm. A "friendly" tender offer refers to offers that are supported by target management. The most controversial type of takeovers are "hostile" tender offers, which are tender offers that are opposed by target managements. In a proxy contest, a dissident group attempts through a vote of shareholders to obtain control of the board of directors. Finally, leveraged buyouts are buyouts of shareholder's equity, heavily financed with debt by a group that frequently includes incumbent management.

Many of the studies reviewed in this paper are event studies that measure the effects of certain unanticipated events (such as a takeover or other control contest) on stock prices, after correcting for overall market influence on security returns. Any finding of abnormal returns, therefore, shows how the stock market views the impact of the event on the firm's common stockholders. (See Brown and Warner, 1985, for a more thorough review of event study methods.)

Returns to shareholders of target companies

Shareholders of target companies clearly benefit from takeovers. Jarrell and Poulsen (1987a) estimate the premiums paid in 663 successful tender offers from 1962 to December 1985. They find that premiums averaged 19 percent in the 1960s, 35 percent in the 1970s, and from 1980 to 1985 the average premium was 30 percent. These figures are consistent with the 13 studies of pre-1980 data contained in Jensen and Ruback (1983) which agree that targets of successful tender offers and mergers before 1980 earned positive returns ranging from 16 percent to 30 percent for tender offers.[3]

Similar results are contained in studies of leveraged buyouts and going private transactions. Lehn and Poulsen (1987) find premiums of 21 percent to shareholders in 93 leveraged buyouts taking place from 1980 to 1984. DeAngelo, DeAngelo and Rice (1984) find an average 27 percent gain for leveraged buyouts between 1973 and 1980.

OCE (1985a) measures premiums paid by comparing the price per share offered by the bidder to the trading price of the stock one month before the offer, not adjusting for changes in the market index (also see Comment and Jarrell, 1987). Using a comprehensive sample of 225 successful tender offers from 1981 through 1984, including over-the-counter targets, OCE finds the average premium to shareholders to be 53.2 percent. OCE has updated these figures for 1985 and 1986 and finds a decrease over the last two years. OCE finds that the average premium is 37 percent in 1985 and 33.6 percent in 1986.[4]

While the evidence reported thus far indicates substantial gains to target shareholders, it probably understates the total gains to these shareholders. In many cases events occur before a formal takeover offer, so studies that concentrate on the stock price reactions to formal offers will understate the total gains to shareholders.

Several recent empirical studies examine the stock market reaction to events that often precede formal steps in the battle for corporate control. Mikkelson and Ruback (1985) provide information on the stock price reaction to Schedule 13D filings. Schedule 13D must be filed with the SEC by all purchasers of 5 percent of a corporation's common stock, requiring disclosure of, among other things, the investor's identity and intent. Mikkelson and Ruback find significant price reactions around the initial announcement of the filing, and that the returns depend on the intent stated in the 13D. The highest returns, an increase of 7.74 percent, occurred when the filer in the statement of intent indicated some possibility of a control change. However, the abnormal returns were only 3.24 percent if the investor reported the purchase was for investment purposes. Holderness and Sheehan (1985) find a differential stock-market effect to 13D filings depending on the identity of the filer. They show the filings of six "corporate raiders" increased target share prices by a significantly greater amount than a sample of other filers (5.9 percent to 3.4 percent).

More direct evidence that significant stock price increases occur prior to formal announcements of corporate events is contained in OCE (1987c) which finds a significant increase in the stock price of target firms in 172 successful tender offers in the period before any announcement of the offer. OCE finds a run-up in stock prices of 38.8 percent of the total control premium by the close of day *before* the offer announcement. The announcement date is, in the parlance of Wall Street, the date the target firm was put "in play" and represents some event having significant implications for corporate control. For example, the in-play date in some cases is the formal offer but in other cases is the eventual bidder's filing of a Schedule 13D with corporate control implications for the target.

While some commentators argue that price run-up before the formal announcements of tender offers indicates the presence of illegal insider trading, OCE's evidence demonstrates that the legal market for information can explain much of the run-up. OCE shows that a significant portion of the run-up can be explained by three readily identifiable influences on pre-bid trading: media speculation, the bidder's foothold acquisition in the target, and whether the bid is friendly or hostile. Systematic relations between these factors and run-up in target share prices indicate that there is an active market for information about impending takeover bids and a large portion of the run-up can be explained by factors other than illegal insider trading. OCE's results on pre-bid market activity are supported by Comment (1986).

Returns to shareholders of acquiring companies

The 1980s evidence on bidders comes from Jarrell and Poulsen (1987a), with data on 663 successful tender offers covering 1962 to 1985. Table 17.1 summarizes the excess returns to 440 NYSE and AMEX bidders. For the entire sample period bidders on average realized small, but statistically significant, gains of about 1 to 2 percent in the immediate period around the public announcement. Most interesting is the apparent secular decline in the gains to successful bidders in tender offers. Consistent with the

Table 17.1 Cumulative excess returns to successful bidders for tender offers during 1960 to 1985, by decade

	Cumulative excess returns in percent			
Trading-day interval	*All*	*1960s*	*1970s*	*1980s*
−10 to +5 (*t*-stat.)	1.14	4.40	1.22	−1.10
	(2.49)	(4.02)	(2.12)	(−1.54)
−10 to +20 (*t*-stat.)	2.04	4.95	2.21	−0.04
	(3.31)	(3.52)	(2.87)	(−0.04)
Number of observations	405	106	140	159

Source: Jarrell and Poulsen (1987a)

previous studies reviewed by Jensen and Ruback (1983), table 17.1 shows positive excess returns of 5 percent during the 1960s, and a lower, but still significantly significant, positive average of 2.2 percent over the 1970s. However, the 159 cases from the 1980s show statistically insignificant losses to bidders.

How the distribution of takeover gains is determined

Companies that are targets of takeovers receive the bulk of the value created by corporate combinations and these gains are not offset by losses to acquirers. As one might predict, an important factor in determining how these takeover gains are split seems to be how many bidders are trying to acquire the target company. In fact, the secular decline in the stock returns to bidders probably reflects the increased competition among bidders and the rise of auction-style contests during the 1980s.[5]

Conditions which foster an increase in multiple bidding tend to increase target premiums and reduce bidder returns. For example, Jarrell and Bradley (1980) demonstrate that Federal (Williams Act) and state regulations of tender offers have this effect because they impose disclosure and delay rules that foster multiple-bidder, auction contests and preemptive bidding.[6] In addition to greater regulation, other factors contributing to this increased competition include court rulings protecting defensive tactics, the inventions of several defenses against takeovers, and the increase in sophisticated takeover advisers to implement them.

Interesting support for this theory in the banking industry is provided by James and Weir (1987). Federal and state banking regulations effectively limit the number of eligible acquisition partners, thus affecting the number of potential substitutes for bidders or targets in particular transactions. For 39 proposed banking acquisitions, James and Weir measure a positive relation between the bidder's share of the takeover gains and the number of alternative targets, and a negative relation between the bidder's share and the number of alternative bidders.[7]

The source of takeover gains

Shareholders of target companies definitely gain from mergers and tender offers. But much uneasiness has been expressed at who might be paying for those gains. In their summary several years ago, Jensen and Ruback (1983, p. 47) were forced to conclude that "knowledge of the sources of takeover gains still eludes us."[8] The studies they reviewed did not allow them to judge the many redistributive theories, which suggest that shareholder gains are offset by economic losses to others. Since then, many popular "redistributive theories" have been examined. The evidence has led many financial economists like Jensen (1986, p. 6) to attribute takeovers, leveraged buyouts, and restructurings to "productive entrepreneurial activity that improves the control and management of assets and helps move assets to more productive uses." We now turn to a review of the most important of these redistributive theories.

Short-term myopia and inefficient takeovers   This theory is based on an allegation that market participants, and particularly institutional investors, are concerned almost exclusively with short-term earnings performance and tend to undervalue corporations engaged in long-term activity. From this viewpoint, any corporation planning for long-term development will become undervalued by the market as its resource commitments to the long-term depress its short-term earnings, and thus will become a prime takeover candidate.

Critics of this theory point out that it is blatantly inconsistent with an efficient capital market. Indeed, if the market systematically undervalues long-run planning and investment, it implies harmful economic consequences that go far beyond the costs of inefficient takeovers. Fortunately, no empirical evidence has been found to support this theory. In fact, a study of 324 high research and development firms and of all 177 takeover targets during 1981–4 by the SEC's Office of the Chief Economist (OCE, 1985b) shows evidence that (1) increased institutional stock holdings are not associated with increased takeovers of firms; (2) increased institutional holdings are not associated with decreases in research and development; (3) firms with high research and development expenditures are not more vulnerable to takeovers; and (4) stock prices respond positively to announcements of increases in research and development expenditures.

Further evidence opposing the myopia theory is provided by Hall (1987) in an NBER study and by McConnell and Muscarella (1985). Hall studies data on acquisition activity among manufacturing firms from 1977 to 1986. She presents evidence that much acquisition activity has been directed towards firms and industries which are less intensive in R&D activity. She also finds that firms involved in mergers show little difference in their pre- and postmerger R&D performance compared with industry peers. McConnell and Muscarella, in a study of 658 capital expenditure announcements, show that stock prices respond positively to announcements of increased capital expenditures, on average, except for exploration and development announcements in the oil industry.

Undervalued target theory Recalcitrant target management and other opponents of takeovers often contend that because targets are "undervalued" by the market, a savvy bidder can offer substantial premiums for target firms while still paying far below the intrinsic value of the corporation. By this theory, it becomes the duty of target managements to defend vigorously against even high premium offers since remaining independent, it is argued, can offer shareholders greater rewards over the long term than are offered by opportunistic bidders seeking short-term gains.

However, the evidence shows the promised long-term gains from remaining independent do not usually materialize. When a target defeats a hostile bid, its post-defeat value reverts to approximately the (market adjusted) level obtaining before the instigation of the hostile bid (Bradley, Desai and Kim, 1983; Easterbrook and Jarrell 1984; Jarrell 1985; Ruback, 1986). Bhagat, Brickley and Lowenstein (1987) used option pricing theory to show that the announcement period returns around cash tender offers are too large to be explained by revaluations due to information about undervaluation.

This evidence indicates that the market does not, on average, learn much of anything that is new or different about target firms' intrinsic values through the tender offer process, despite the tremendous attention lavished on targets, and the huge amounts of information traded among market participants during takeover contests. If undervaluation had indeed been present, then the deluge of new information on the intrinsic value of targets should have caused fundamental price corrections even in the event of takeover defeats. But in the overwhelming majority of cases studied, prices dropped rather than increased for target firms that fought off takeovers.

Do tax effects motivate mergers and takeovers?   Tax motives have long been suspected as an important cause of merger and acquisition activity. Indeed, the Tax Reform Act of 1986 contains several provisions aimed at reducing the tax benefits available through mergers.[9] Most recent studies, however, assign tax benefits a minor role in explaining merger and takeover activity. Auerbach and Reishus (1987a) study 318 mergers and acquisitions during 1968–83 to estimate the tax benefits available in these transactions from increased use of tax losses and credits. They found that these tax benefits in general were not a significant factor in the majority of large acquisitions. In a fair number of transactions, however (potentially 20 percent of the mergers), tax factors did appear to be significant enough to affect the decision to merge.[10] Lehn and Poulsen (1987) find, in their study of leveraged buyouts from 1980–4, that the premiums paid are directly related to potential tax benefits associated with these transactions, suggesting that in part these leveraged buyouts are motivated by tax considerations.

In summary, acquiring firms' tax losses and credits, and the option to step-up the basis of targets' assets without paying corporate level capital gains, are two tax benefits that appear to have had some impact on merger activity. However, the evidence suggests that much of the takeover activity in the last 20 years was not tax motivated.

Do bondholders lose from takeovers?   Some critics of takeovers suggest that the premiums paid by bidders are not a result of any wealth enhancing changes, but instead represent a redistribution from the holders of the target's bonds and preferred equity. For example, the bonds of an acquiring firm can drop in value if the acquiring firm pays cash for a riskier target firm. Given that the combined value of the two firms remains unchanged, the decline in the bond value will be captured as a gain by some other class of security holder (such as common stockholders).[11] However, the empirical evidence does not support this argument.

Denis and McConnell (1986) examine the returns on various classes of the securities of a sample of 132 mergers in the period 1962 to 1980. Denis and McConnell's results are consistent with earlier studies in that they find gains to mergers and no losses to bondholders. Their results indicate that on average holders of common stock, convertible and nonconvertible preferred stock, and convertible bonds in the acquired firm gain from a merger. Those who hold nonconvertible bonds in the acquired firm and convertible bonds, nonconvertible bonds, and nonconvertible preferred stock in the acquiring firm neither gain nor lose in a merger. Denis and McConnell also find some evidence that the acquiring firms' common shareholders do not lose and may gain from mergers, especially in the days immediately following the announcement. Lehn and Poulsen's (1987) study of 108 leveraged buyouts from 1980 to 1984 finds no support for the redistribution theory. They find no evidence that the shareholder value created by the leveraged buyouts comes at the expense of preferred shareholders or bondholders. In sum, the evidence provides no support for the hypothesis that the supposed gains from acquisitions are actually transfers from the holders of senior securities to the holders of common stock.

Do labor's losses finance takeovers? Recent takeovers in the airline industry have involved conflict between acquiring-firm management and the (usually) unionized labor of the target firm. These conflicts have contributed to the popular generalization that shareholder premiums from takeovers come largely at the expense of labor. Shleifer and Summers (1987) articulate this view more rigorously, focusing on implicit long-term contracts between labor and incumbent (target) management. They argue raiders can sometimes exploit these contracts by buying a controlling share of the equity and financing the premium by using pressure tactics to force significant wage concessions. In theory, this activity can be socially inefficient by ruining the market for these implicit long-run labor contracts and forcing labor and management to use less efficient contracting devices.

This redistributive theory from labor to shareholders has not been tested widely, but a recent NBER study by Brown and Medoff (1987) presents statistical evidence based on Michigan's employment and wages that fails to support it. Although this close look at Michigan is not necessarily indicative of the US experience (for example, it contains few large mergers or hostile tender offers), the results are that wages and employment rise on average for firms that are involved in acquisitions.

Summary of source of gains

The various redistribution theories of takeover gains have been the subject of considerable empirical work since the Jensen and Ruback (1983) review. Most convincing is the empirical rejection of the undervaluation theory: target firms cannot be depicted generally as being "undervalued" by the stock market. Also soundly rejected by the data is the short-term myopia theory. The evidence gives tax-benefits theories at least a minor role in explaining merger and tender offer activity. Finally, evidence is inconsistent with the theories that the stock-price gains to shareholders come from bondholders and labor.

Although some individuals (incumbent management, for example) obviously lose in at least some takeovers, the literature, while not conclusive, offers little or no support for the notion that the redistribution theories explain a major portion of the apparent gains from takeovers. It has been impossible so far to find systematic losses which could offset the enormous gains to target and bidding firm shareholders from mergers, tender offers, and other corporate-control activities. We therefore conclude that evidence is consistent with the notion that these corporate transactions reflect economically beneficial reshufflings of productive assets.

The Effects of Defending Against Hostile Takeovers

Defensive strategies against hostile takeovers have always been controversial since they pose a conflict of interest for target management. After all, takeovers can impose significant welfare losses on managers, who may be displaced and lose their organization-specific human capital. These conflicts may tempt some managers to erect barriers to hostile takeovers, thus insulating themselves from the discipline of the outside market for control at the expense of their shareholders and the efficiency of the economy.

However, providing target management with the power to defend against hostile takeover bids might also help target shareholders during a control contest. Target management can in certain cases defeat bids that are "inadequate." Although this rationale is popular, the evidence discussed earlier shows that in very few cases do these alleged long-term gains of independence actually materialize. The other benefit of resistance comes when resistance by target management helps promote a takeover auction. Litigation and other blocking actions can provide the necessary time for the management of the target firm to "shop" the target and generate competing bids. This auction rationale for resistance is harder to reject statistically. Evidence on occasional shareholder losses after the defeat of a takeover attempt does not in itself disprove the auction theory. This negotiating leverage can be expected to fail in some cases, with the sole bidder becoming discouraged and withdrawing. It is a gamble. The hypothesis is rejected only if the harmful outcome of defeating all bids is sufficiently frequent and costly to offset the benefits of inducing higher takeover prices. One must also consider the social cost of tender offers that never occur because of the presence of defensive devices. Unfortunately, this deterrence effect is very difficult to measure and we present no direct evidence of the extent of these costs.

Evidence on the effects of defensive measures by target management is obtained mainly from two approaches, the event-type study and the outcomes-type study. The event-type study recognizes that an efficient market must judge this cost-benefit tradeoff when it adjusts the market value of a firm in response to the adoption of a charter amendment or some other kind of resistance. Alternatively, the outcomes-type study examines the actual outcomes of control contests over a significant time horizon among firms using a common kind of resistance – say all firms adopting poison pills. That is, an event study measures the stock price reaction to the introduction of defensive devices while outcomes studies follow the use of defensive devices in control contests to determine their effects on the outcomes of the contests.

Many defensive measures must be approved by a vote of the shareholders. Hence, voting has the potential to block management-sponsored proposals that harm shareholders, depending on the costs and benefits to individual shareholders from collecting relevant information and voting. In general, a shareholder with a small amount of shares will not invest heavily in the voting process since a small number of shares will not generally affect the outcome regardless of how they are voted. However, if individual voting and information costs are near zero even the shareholder with few shares can be expected to vote against management on value-decreasing proposals. Alternatively, large outside block holders (like institutional investors) internalize more of the benefits from participation in the voting process and can be expected to take an active interest in voting on antitakeover proposals even when the information gathering and voting costs are positive. Since voting rights can block harmful measures, we distinguish between two broad categories of defensive measures, those receiving approval by voting shareholders and those adopted unilaterally by management.

Defensive measures approved by shareholders

Antitakeover amendments generally operate by imposing new conditions that must be satisfied before changing managerial control of the corporation. They are almost always proposed by management and they usually require majority voting approval by shareholders. Proposed antitakeover amendments are very rarely rejected by voting shareholders; Brickley, Lease, and Smith (forthcoming) find for a sample of 288 management-sponsored antitakeover proposals in 1984 that about 96 percent passed.

Supermajority amendments   Most state corporation laws set the minimum approval required for mergers and other important control transactions at either one-half or two-thirds of the voting shares. Supermajority amendments require the approval by holders of at least two-thirds and sometimes as much as nine-tenths of the voting power of the outstanding common stock. These provisions can apply either to mergers and other business combinations or to changing the firm's board of directors or to both. Pure supermajority provisions are very rare today, having been replaced by similar provisions that are triggered at the discretion of the board of directors. This allows the board to waive the supermajority provisions allowing friendly mergers to proceed unimpeded.

Five years ago, Jensen and Ruback (1983) found mixed evidence on the effect of supermajority amendments passed before 1980. However, a more recent study by Jarrell and Poulsen (1987b), derived from OCE (1985c), covers 104 supermajority amendments passed since 1980 and reports significant negative stock-price effects of over 3 percent around the introduction of the proposals. They also show that firms passing supermajority amendments have relatively low institutional stockholdings (averaging 19 percent) and high insider holdings (averaging 18 percent), which they interpret as helping to explain how these amendments received voting approval despite their harmful wealth effect. That is, firms proposing these amendments have fewer blockholders with incentives to invest in the voting process. Jarrell and Poulsen further conjecture that the increased shareholder resistance to harmful supermajority amendments helps explain their declining popularity in contrast to the success of the fair price amendment which appears less likely to harm shareholders (as discussed below).

Fair price amendments   The fair price amendment is a supermajority provision that applies only to nonuniform, two-tier takeover bids that are opposed by the target's board of directors. Uniform offers that are considered "fair" circumvent the supermajority requirement, even if target management opposes them. Fairness of the offer is determined in several ways. The most common fair price is defined as the highest price paid by the bidder for any of the shares it has acquired in the target firm during a specified period of time. Jarrell and Poulsen (1987b) report that 487 firms adopted fair price charter provisions between 1979 and May 1985, with over 90 percent of these coming in the very recent period of 1983 to May 1985.

The stock price effects reflect the low deterrence value of the fair price amendment. Jarrell and Poulsen (1987b) report an average loss of 0.73 percent around the introduction of these amendments, which is not statistically significant. They also show that firms adopting fair price amendments have roughly normal levels of insider holdings (12 percent) and of institutional holdings (30 percent). They interpret this evidence as supporting the view that shareholder voting retards adoption of harmful amendments, especially when insider holdings are low and institutional holdings are high. Further support for this view is provided by Brickley, Lease, and Smith (forthcoming) who document that "no" votes on antitakeover amendments (especially ones that harm shareholders) increase with institutional and other outside blockholdings, while "no" votes decrease with increases in managerial holdings.

Dual-class recapitalizations   These plans restructure the equity of a firm into two classes with different voting rights. Although several methods are used, the common goal is to provide management or family owners with voting power disproportionately greater than that provided by their equity holdings under a "one share-one-vote" rule.[12]

Evidence before and after 1980 has confirmed that the market generally values shares with voting power more than those without. Lease, McConnell, and Mikkelson (1983) examine 30 firms having dual-class common stock and show that voting stock on average trades at a significant premium, ranging from one to seven percent. A recent paper by OCE (1987a) examines the monthly stock prices of 26 OTC and AMEX firms having dual-class common and shows an average discount of 4 to 5 percent for low-vote common, though the discount is reduced when the low-vote stock has rights to preferential dividends.

Of course, the fact that the market values voting power does not demonstrate that dual-class recapitalizations reduce the overall price of stock. DeAngelo and DeAngelo (1985) examine in detail 45 firms that had dual-voting common stock as of 1980. They find that, after restructuring, management and family insiders control a median of 57 percent of the votes and 24 percent of the common stock cash flows. This confirms that dual-class structures often confer substantial voting powers on incumbent management. However, DeAngelo and DeAngelo also suggest that the shareholders of the firms in this sample found it beneficial to contract with incumbent management to limit the competition for management of their firms. They argue that shareholders rationally accept a reduced potential for hostile takeovers in return for other benefits, such as greater incentives for incumbents to make specific long-term investments in human capital.

Two recent studies have addressed the empirical question of whether dual-voting structures are beneficial, as DeAngelo and DeAngelo suggest, or harmful to outside shareholders. Partch (1987) examines the stock-price reaction around the announcement of the proposed dual-class recapitalizations for 44 firms. She reports non-negative share-price effects. However, for more recent recapitalizations, Jarrell and Poulsen (forthcoming, extending OCE 1987a, 1987d) find negative effects at the announcement of dual-class recapitalizations. For a sample of 89 firms delisting from 1976 through 1987, they report an average abnormal stock price effect of −0.93 percent.

If dual-class recapitalization proposals are viewed primarily as takeover defenses, their announcement should cause negative stock price reactions, similar to those observed at the announcement of supermajority amendments. However, firms announcing dual-class recapitalizations have some unusual characteristics. Jarrell and Poulsen (1988) find that the average net-of-market return to their 94 dual-class firms over the year preceding the recapitalization is over 37 percent. Jarrell and Poulsen and Partch both find that insider holdings average 44 percent before the recapitalization, and that recapitalization significantly increases insider voting control. These two characteristics suggest that the typical dual-class firm is already controlled by insiders and the recapitalization provides a means to raise needed capital for positive net present value projects without the dilution of control.

Changes in the state of incorporation   Changing the state of incorporation can affect the contractual arrangements between management and shareholders. For example, some states such as Ohio, Indiana, and New York have elements in their corporate codes that make takeovers more difficult than in other states. Dodd and Leftwich (1980) find that firms change their state of incorporation after a period of superior performance and that the change itself is associated with small positive excess returns. More recently, Romano (1985) finds a statistically significant price increase around the reincorporation announcement in a sample of firms that reincorporate for various reasons. However, in the subsample of 43 firms who reincorporated as an antitakeover device she found a small, statistically insignificant price increase at the announcement of a reincorporation. The evidence is not conclusive but it does indicate that reincorporating in a new state does not on average harm shareholders.

Reduction in cumulative voting rights   Cumulative voting makes it possible for a group of minority shareholders to elect directors even if the majority of shareholders oppose their election. Dissidents in hostile takeovers and proxy contests will often attempt to elect some board members through the use of cumulative voting. Bhagat and Brickley (1984) examine the stock price reaction to 84 management sponsored charter amendments that either eliminate or reduce the effect of cumulative voting. Since these amendments decrease the power of dissident shareholders to elect directors, they increase management's ability to resist a tender offer. Bhagat and Brickley find statistically significant negative abnormal returns of about one percent at the introduction of these charter amendments.

Defensive measures that do not require shareholder approval

Four general kinds of defensive measures do not require voting approval by shareholders: general litigation, greenmail, poison pills, and the use of state antitakeover laws. With the exception of general litigation, these defensive actions are associated on average with negative stock-price reactions indicating that in most cases they are economically harmful to stockholders of companies whose management enacted them.

Litigation by target management   As described earlier, litigation can be expected to hurt shareholders of some target companies by eliminating takeovers and to help shareholders of other companies by giving their management time and weapons to cut a better deal. Jarrell (1985) examines 89 cases involving litigation against a hostile suitor based on charges of securities fraud, antitrust violations, and violations of state or Federal tender offer regulations. His results show that litigation usually delays the control contest significantly and that litigating targets are frequently the beneficiaries of auctions. The 59 auction-style takeovers produced an additional 17 percent excess return to shareholders over the original bid, while the 21 targets that remained independent lost nearly all of the original average premium of 30 percent. Overall, Jarrell concludes that this evidence cannot reject the theory that on average target litigation is consistent with shareholder wealth maximization.[13]

However, harm can result from certain types of defensive litigation. Netter (1987) finds that litigation based in part on a claim alleging the filing of a false Schedule 13D Item 4 can be detrimental to target shareholders. In an exhaustive sample of all cases where target management filed a suit alleging (among other things) that a bidder filed a false 13D Item 4, he finds that target shareholders are better off if their management loses the case than if they win. If the target firm wins the case its share price declines by a significant amount (an abnormal return of negative 3.37 percent in the two-day window around the decision) while if the bidder wins, the stock price of the target firm increases by a significant amount (positive 3.15 percent abnormal return in the two-day window.

Targeted block stock repurchases (greenmail)   Greenmail occurs when target management ends a hostile takeover threat by repurchasing at a premium the hostile suitor's block of target stock. This controversial practice has been challenged in federal courts, in congressional testimony, and in SEC hearings, and it has brought negative publicity both to payers and to receivers of greenmail. In reviewing earlier studies, Jensen and Ruback (1983) conclude that greenmail repurchases are associated with significantly negative abnormal stock returns for the shareholders of the repurchasing firms (probably because they eliminate potential takeover bids) and significantly positive abnormal stock returns for shareholders of the selling firms. These negative effects of greenmail repurchases contrast sharply with the normally positive stock-price effects associated with nontargeted offers to repurchase a company's own stock.

Since then, three new empirical studies have contributed to a more complex and less conclusive discussion of greenmail transactions. These studies indicate that it is not necessarily in the interests of shareholders to ban greenmail payments. Such a ban has the potential to discourage outside investment in the potential target's stock by investors anticipating greenmail payments and hence reduces the incentives of outsiders to monitor managers.

Mikkelson and Ruback (1985) examine 39 cases of greenmail (based on 13Ds filed during 1978–80). They find a significant stock-price loss of 2.3 percent upon the announcement of the repurchases. However, they also report an average gain of 1.7 percent over the entire period including the original stock purchase by the hostile suitors. Holderness and Sheehan's (1985) outcome-type study includes 12 cases of greenmail, and they report a pattern of returns consistent with the evidence of Mikkelson and Ruback. Although the greenmail transaction itself harms target shareholders, the net returns to stockholders resulting from the initial purchase and related events is positive. A more comprehensive sample of targeted block stock repurchases is covered by OCE (1984). This study includes 89 cases of large repurchases (blocks greater than 3 percent of the outstanding common stock) from 1979 to 1983. The initial announcement of investor interest induces a positive return averaging 9.7 percent, while the greenmail transaction is associated with a stock price loss of 5.2 percent.

Poison pills   Since its introduction in late 1982, the "poison pill" has become the most popular and controversial device used to defend against hostile takeover attempts. Poison pill describes a family of shareholder rights agreements that, when triggered by an event such as a tender offer for control or the accumulation of a specified percentage of target shares by an acquirer, provide target shareholders with rights to purchase additional shares or to sell shares to the target at very attractive prices. These rights, when triggered, impose significant economic penalties on a hostile acquirer.

Poison pills are considered very effective deterrents against hostile takeover attempts because of two striking features. First, pills can be cheaply and quickly altered by target management if a hostile acquirer has not pulled the trigger. This feature pressures potential acquirers to negotiate directly with the target's board. Second, if not redeemed, the pill makes hostile acquisitions exorbitantly expensive in most cases. As an obstacle to hostile takeover attempts, the poison pill is unmatched except by dual-voting recapitalizations or direct majority share ownership by incumbent management. The concern over poison pills was heightened by the Delaware Supreme Court's 1985 ruling in *Moran* v. *Household International*[14] that poison pills do not require majority voting approval by shareholders.

The most comprehensive study of poison pills is Ryngaert (forthcoming), which is an outgrowth of OCE (1986). The Ryngaert study features an exhaustive collection of 380 poison pills adopted from 1982 to December 25, 1986. Over 80 percent of these were adopted after the *Household* decision. Ryngaert divides his sample into discriminatory pills (the most restrictive) and flip-over pills (the least restrictive). He also accounts for whether firms are subject to takeover speculation and whether confounding events that contaminate the data occur close to the announcement of the pill. The stock-price effect over the 283 cases with no confounding events is a statistically significant −0.34 percent. Focusing on 57 cases subject to takeover speculation, the average loss is 1.51 percent, also statistically significant. These results are supported by the findings of Malatesta and Walkling (1988).

Discriminatory pills have more harmful effects on shareholder wealth than do flip-over pills. Also, the discriminatory pills that threaten the hostile suitor with severe dilution have become increasingly popular. Ryngaert reports that pill-adopting managements own a surprisingly low average of around 3.0 percent of their firms' outstanding stock. This fact, together with high institutional holdings, suggest that many of these firms would have difficulty obtaining shareholder voting approval if it were required.

Ryngaert also examines the stock-price effects of important court decisions emanating from legal battles involving pill defenses during 1983–6. He shows that 15 of 18 pro-target, pro-poison-pill decisions have negative effects on the target's stock price, and 6 of 11 pro-acquirer decisions have positive effects on the target stock price. This evidence is inconsistent with the theory that pill defenses improve shareholder wealth by strengthening management's bargaining position in control contests.

Although these losses are not large in percentage terms, these empirical tests suggest that poison pills are harmful to target shareholders.

State antitakeover amendments   In addition to the Williams Act at the Federal level, tender offers are regulated by many states. So-called first-generation state antitakeover regulations are antitakeover laws that were passed by the states before the 1982 Supreme Court decision in *Edgar* v. *Mite*.[15] The Jarrell and Bradley (1980) study of state and Federal regulation of tender offers finds that first generation state regulations significantly increase the premiums paid in tender offers. Smiley (1981) illustrates the deterrent effects of these early state takeover regulations.

However, first generation antitakeover laws were generally extinguished in *Edgar* v. *Mite* when the Supreme Court ruled the Illinois antitakeover law unconstitutional. Justice White's opinion held the Illinois takeover statute was preempted by the Williams Act and constituted an undue and direct burden on interstate commerce. As a result over 20 states passed second generation antitakeover laws to attempt to pass constitutional muster under the Supreme Court's reasoning. While some of them have also been ruled unconstitutional, the Supreme Court in 1987 (*CTS* v. *Dynamics Corp. of America*) ruled the Indiana antitakeover law constitutional.[16] This decision already is leading states to pass third generation antitakeover laws that would be constitutional under the CTS reasoning.

Two recent studies, Ryngaert and Netter (1987, based on OCE, 1987c) and Schumann (1987) provide more direct evidence on the wealth effects of state antitakeover regulations. Ryngaert and Netter examine the stock price effects of the passage of the Ohio antitakeover law on shareholders of firms chartered in Ohio. This act was passed during (and apparently motivated by) Sir James Goldsmith's attempted hostile takeover of Goodyear. They find that the passage of the law was accompanied by a significant stock-price loss of up to 3.24 percent to the shareholders of firms incorporated in Ohio with less than 30 percent inside ownership. This evidence on the impact of state takeover laws is supported by Schumann (1987) who finds a decline of approximately one percent to shareholders of New York firms on the announcement and passage of a New York antitakeover law. While these laws potentially could be beneficial to the individual states (if jobs are kept in the state by preventing takeovers), shareholders are harmed by state antitakeover regulations.

Summing up defensive tactics

Four years ago Jensen and Ruback (1983) reviewed empirical studies of antitakeover charter amendments, shark repellents, changes of incorporation, and greenmail. They conclude (p. 47): "It is difficult to find managerial actions related to corporate control that harm stockholders; the exception are those actions that eliminate an actual or potential bidder, for example, through the use of targeted large block repurchases or standstill agreements."

Since their review, the defensive arsenal available to target management has been strengthened. These defensive tactics have been developed through a fascinating process of sequential innovations, as specific defenses arise to counter improved bidder finances and other tactics. In 1983, the now common fair-price amendment was a novel idea and the poison pill was not yet invented. Financial economists in academia and government have kept close pace with these developments, providing timely analyses of new charter amendments, poison pill defenses, greenmail transactions, and so on. While Jensen and Ruback were correct in predicting this area would be a "growth industry," we cannot reiterate their then-accurate conclusion that harmful defensive tactics are rare.

Conclusion

In the 1980s, the market for corporate control has been increasingly active, and the quantity of output of academic researchers studying corporate control questions has mirrored the market activity. This review has confirmed the basic conclusions of Jensen and Ruback's (1983) review article and has shed light on some questions Jensen and Ruback were forced to leave unanswered. Financial researchers continue to find larger premiums being paid to target shareholders for later tender offers than for earlier tender offers. Acquirers, however, receive at best modest increases in their stock price, and the winners of bidding contests suffer stock-price declines as often as they do gains. This pro-target division of takeover gains appears to be partially a result of improved defensive tactics that can effectively delay execution of the bid and allow the target to receive improved bids from others or fashion a defensive restructuring and stock buyback. The evidence further suggests that the premiums in takeovers represent real wealth gains and are not simply wealth redistributions.

Prominent in the 1980s are new studies of defensive measures, such as antitakeover charter amendments, targeted block stock repurchases (greenmail), dual-voting re-capitalizations, state antitakeover laws, and poison pills. The general finding, although it is far from conclusive, is that defensive measures that require shareholder voting approval are less likely to be harmful to shareholder wealth than are defensive measures not subject to shareholder approval. Fair-price charter amendments and dual-class recapitalizations that require shareholder approval are not shown to be harmful to stock value, while poison pills and greenmail-type repurchases that do not need shareholder approval appear on average to reduce shareholder value. However, some proposals that require a favorable vote from shareholders to implement (e.g., super-majority provisions and the elimination of cumulative voting) on average appear to reduce shareholder wealth. These findings raise serious questions about whether the business judgment rule is operating too broadly as a shield for defensive actions by target managements.

Notes

We are especially grateful to Joseph Stiglitz, Timothy Taylor, and Annette Poulsen for their many helpful comments and suggestions. The Securities and Exchange Commission as a matter of policy disclaims responsibility for any private publication or statement by any of its employees. The views expressed here are those of the authors and do not necessarily reflect the views of the Commission or the authors' colleagues on the Staff of the Commission.

1   These estimates understate the total premiums (dollar value of the percentage increase in the target's stock price caused by the takeover) paid in change-of-control transactions. OCE's sample is limited to the first successful tender offer for a firm. Thus, if an "auction" for the firm develops, resulting in an even higher offer price, they do not capture that additional premium. In addition, no account is made for tender offers that do not ultimately succeed. Shareholders may sell their shares in the market at the premium induced by the offer before it is known that the offer fails. The W. T. Grimm data also understates the total profits earned by stockholders because they calculate the premium based on the market price only five days before the initial public announcement and do not capture the premium attributable to increases in share prices that occur more than five days in advance of a public announcement.

2   Many critics of acquisition activity (such as the Business Roundtable) are primarily concerned with alleged abuses arising from hostile takeovers. The other types of acquisition activity are approved by target firms' management who allegedly are the individuals most concerned with the welfare of the target firm and its shareholders.

3   Jensen and Ruback (1983) review 13 studies published between 1977 and 1983 – six on mergers and seven on tender offers. Their survey provides a concise summary of the pre-1980 data. But because of the lengthy review process for academic journals, the most up-to-date sample used in these studies ends in 1981, and most do not go beyond the late 1970s. This paper can be considered an update of Jensen and Ruback with a focus on recent empirical studies that cover takeovers made in the 1980s.

4   The OCE (1985a) study also explicitly tests and rejects the popular theory that two-tier tender offers disadvantage target shareholders. Some observers argue that two-tier offers – in which the bidder first makes an offer for control of the firm and then makes a "clean-up" offer for remaining shares at a lower price – coerces shareholders to tender to avoid the clean-up price. OCE finds that two-tier offers have overall premiums that are nearly identical to the average for any-or-all offers and that there is no evidence that two-tier offers "stampede" shareholders into unwise trading decisions.

5   Bradley, Desai, and Kim (1984) show that targets gain more in multiple bidder than single bidder contests.

6   The Williams Act contains the Federal regulations of tender offers and was enacted in July 1968. Its main components are disclosure requirements, a regulated minimum offer period, and antifraud provisions that give target management standing to sue for injunctive relief.

7   Other evidence supporting this point includes a recent paper by Guerin-Calvert, McGuckin, and Warren-Boulton (1986) that re-examines the effects of state and Federal regulations of tender offers. They also find the regulations increase the incidence of multiple-bidder auction takeovers among all control contests. Also consistent with this result is the evidence on the French experience presented by Eckbo and Langohr (1986). They show that the imposition of disclosure-only (not delay) rules governing tender offers in France significantly shifted the gains in French takeovers from acquirers to targets.

8   Jensen and Ruback review the empirical work testing the market power theory of takeovers by Eckbo (1985) and Stillman (1983). This theory is that increased monopoly power in product markets explains takeover gains. Jensen and Ruback conclude the evidence rejects this theory as the source of gains from takeovers. Recent papers by Eckbo and Weir (1985) and by Eckbo (1985) provide empirical support for the conclusion that except in isolated cases, increased market power cannot explain the gains from takeovers.

9   A review of the effects on the takeover market of the change of the 1986 Tax Reform Act is contained in Steindel (1986). The 1986 Tax Reform Act repeals the General Utilities doctrine, which states that corporations liquidating their businesses are not subject to capital gains tax on the value of their assets. A firm using General Utilities in a liquidation (the purchaser of at least 80 percent of the stock of a corporation may treat the transaction for tax purposes as a liquidation) avoids the tax liability that comes with appreciated assets. Steindel argues that the repeal of the General Utilities doctrine combined with the changes in corporate tax rates reduces the attractiveness of many mergers and acquisitions. Other tax changes with effects on takeover activity include the increase in the personal capital gains tax and new rules on the transfer of net operating loss carryforwards.

10 However, Auerbach and Reishus (1987b) compare actual mergers over 1968–83 with a control group of nonmerging firms and conclude that the potential increase in interest deductions and unused tax losses and tax credits of the acquired firms have not driven acquisitions.

11 The senior security holders of the target firm can also lose depending on the takeover's effect on the riskiness of their claims.

12 For over 60 years, the New York Stock Exchange did not allow any member firm to have a dual-class capitalization structure, but it has recently proposed a liberalization to allow dual-class listings in response to competitive pressures from Amex and OTC markets. Amex currently allows dual-class listings with some restrictions, and the OTC market has no restrictions beyond usual state-law requirements.

13 Jarrell also notes that while defensive litigation redistributes premiums it also, by reducing incentives to engage in takeovers and through the cost of the litigation itself, can reduce social welfare.

14 *Moran* v. *Household International*, 490 A.2d 1059 (1985).

15 *Edgar* v. *Mite*, 457, US 624, 102 S. Ct. 2629 (1982).

16 *CTS* v. *Dynamics Corp. of America*, 107 S. Ct. 1637 (1987).

References

Auerbach, Alan J. and David Reishus, 1987a, Taxes and the Merger Decision. In Coffee, J. and Louis Lowenstein, eds, *Takeovers and Contests for Corporate Control*, Oxford: Oxford University Press.

Auerbach, Alan J. and David Reishus, 1987b, The Effects of Taxation on the Merger Decision, NBER Working Paper.

Bhagat, Sanjai, and James Brickley, 1984, The Value of Minority Shareholder Voting Rights, *Journal of Law and Economics* 27, 339–65.

Bhagat, Sanjai, James Brickley, and Uri Lowenstein, 1987, The Pricing Effects of Inter-Firm Cash Tender Offers, *Journal of Finance* 42, 965–86.

Bradley, Michael, Amand Desai, and E. Han Kim, 1984, Determinants of the Wealth Effects of Corporate Acquisitions, working paper, The University of Michigan.

Bradley, Michael, Amand Desai, and E. Han Kim, 1983, The Rationale Behind Interfirm Tender Offers: Information or Synergy? *Journal of Financial Economics* 11, 183–206.

Brickley, James, Ronald Lease, and Clifford Smith, 1988, Ownership Structure and the Voting on Antitakeover Amendments, *Journal of Financial Economics* 20, 377–417.

Brown, Charles and James L. Medoff, 1987, The Impact of Firm Acquisitions on Labor, NBER Working Paper.

Brown, Stephen J. and Jerold B. Warner, 1985, Using Daily Stock Returns: The Case of Event Studies, *Journal of Financial Economics* 14, 3–31.

Comment, Robert, 1986, Price and Volume Before Tender Offers: Market Anticipation Activity or Inside Trading, working paper, New York University.

Comment, Robert and Gregg A. Jarrell, 1987, Two-Tier Tender Offers: The Imprisonment of the Free Riding Shareholder, *Journal of Financial Economics* 19, 283–310.

Council of Economic Advisors, 1985, The Market for Corporate Control, *Economic Report of the President*, 187–216.

DeAngelo, Harry and Linda DeAngelo, 1985, Managerial Ownership of Voting Rights: A Study of Public Corporations With Dual Classes of Common Stock, *Journal of Financial Economics* 14, 33–69.

DeAngelo, Harry, Linda DeAngelo, and Edward M. Rice, 1984, Going Private: Minority Freezeouts and Stockholder Wealth, *Journal of Law and Economics* 27, 367–402.

Denis, Debra K. and John J. McConnell, 1986, Corporate Mergers and Security Returns, *Journal of Financial Economics* 16, 143–87.

Dodd, Peter and Richard Leftwich, 1980, The Market for Corporate Charters: "Unhealthy Competition" Versus Federal Regulation, *Journal of Business* 53, 259–83.

Easterbrook, Frank H. and Gregg A. Jarrell, 1984, Do Targets Gain From Defeating Tender Offers? *New York University Law Review* 59, 277–99.

Eckbo, B. Espen, 1985, Merger and the Market Concentration Doctrine: Evidence from the Capital Market, *Journal of Business* 58, 325–49.

Eckbo, B. Espen and Herwig Langohr, 1986, The Effect of Disclosure Regulations and the Medium of Exchange on Takeover Bids, working paper.

Guerin-Calvert, Margaret, Robert H. McGuckin, and Frederick R. Warren-Boulton, 1986, State and Federal Regulation in the Market for Corporate Control, US Department of Justice, Economic Analysis Group Discussion Paper, 86–4.

Hall, Bronwyn H., 1987, The Effect of Takeover Activity on Corporate Research and Development, NBER Working Paper.

Holderness, Clifford G. and Dennis P. Sheehan, 1985, Raiders or Saviors? The Evidence on Six Controversial Investors, *Journal of Financial Economics* 14, 555–79.

James, Christopher M. and Peggy Weir, 1987, Determinants of the Division of Gains in Corporate Acquisitions: Evidence from the Banking Industry, working paper, University of Oregon.

Jarrell, Gregg A., 1985, The Wealth Effects of Litigation by Targets: Do Interests Diverge in a Merger? *Journal of Law and Economics* 28, 151–77.

Jarrell, Gregg A. and Michael Bradley, 1980, The Economic Effects of Federal and State Regulations of Cash Tender Offers, *Journal of Law and Economics* 23, 371–407.

Jarrell, Gregg A. and Annette B. Poulsen, 1987a, Bidder Returns, working paper.

Jarrell, Gregg A. and Annette B. Poulsen, 1988, The Effects of Recapitalization with Dual Classes of Common Stock on the Wealth of Shareholders, *Journal of Financial Economics* 20, 129–52.

Jarrell, Gregg A. and Annette B. Poulsen, 1987b, Shark Repellents and Stock Prices: The Effects of Antitakeover Amendments Since 1980, *Journal of Financial Economics* 19, 127–68.

Jensen, Michael C., 1986, The Takeover Controversy: Analysis and Evidence, *Midland Corporate Finance Journal*, 6–32.

Jensen, Michael C. and Richard S. Ruback, 1983, The Market for Corporate Control: The Scientific Evidence, *Journal of Financial Economics* 11, 5–50.

Lease, Ronald C., John J. McConnell, and Wayne H. Mikkelson, 1983, The Market Value of Control in Publicly Traded Corporations, *Journal of Financial Economics* 11, 439–72.

Lehn, Kenneth and Annette B. Poulsen, 1987, Sources of Value in Leveraged Buyouts. In *Public Policy Towards Corporate Takeovers*. New Brunswick, NJ: Transaction Publishers.

Malatesta, Paul H. and Ralph A. Walkling, 1988, Poison Pill Securities: Stockholder Wealth, Profitability, and Ownership Structure, *Journal of Financial Economics* 20, 347–76.

McConnell, John J. and Chris J. Muscarella, 1985, Capital Expenditure Decisions and Market Value of the Firm, *Journal of Financial Economics* 14, 399–422.

Mikkelson, Wayne H. and Richard S. Ruback, 1985, An Empirical Analysis of the Interfirm Equity Investment Process, *Journal of Financial Economics* 14, 523–53.

Netter, Jeffry M., 1987, Shareholder Wealth Effects of Litigation Based on Allegedly False Schedule 13D Item 4 Disclosure, working paper.

Office of the Chief Economist, Securities and Exchange Commission, 1985a, The Economics of Any-or-All, Partial, and Two-Tier Tender Offers.

Office of the Chief Economist, Securities and Exchange Commission, 1987d, Update – The Effects of Dual-Class Recapitalizations on Shareholder Wealth: Including Evidence from 1986 and 1987.

Office of the Chief Economist, Securities and Exchange Commission, 1986, The Effects of Poison Pills on the Wealth of Target Shareholders.

Office of the Chief Economist, Securities and Exchange Commission, 1984, The Impact of Targetted Share Repurchases (Greenmail) on Stock Prices.

Office of the Chief Economist, Securities and Exchange Commission, 1985b, Institutional Ownership, Tender Offers and Long Term Investment.

Office of the Chief Economist, Securities and Exchange Commission, 1987b, Shareholder Wealth Effects of Ohio Legislation Affecting Takeovers.

Office of the Chief Economist, Securities and Exchange Commission, 1985c, Shark Repellents and Stock Prices: The Effects of Antitakeover Amendments Since 1980.

Office of the Chief Economist, Securities and Exchange Commission, 1987c, Stock Trading Before the Announcement of Tender Offers: Insider Trading or Market Anticipation?

Office of the Chief Economist, Securities and Exchange Commission, 1987a, The Effects of Dual-Class Recapitalizations on the Wealth Of Shareholders.

Partch, Megan., 1987, The Creation of A Class of Limited Voting Common Stock and Shareholders' Wealth, *Journal of Financial Economics* 18, 313–39.

Romano, Roberta, 1985, Law as a Product: Some Pieces of the Incorporation Puzzle, *Journal of Law Economics and Organization* 1, 225–67.

Ruback, Richard S., 1986, An Overview of Takeover Defenses, Working Paper #1836-86, Massachusetts Institute of Technology.

Ryngaert, Michael, 1988, The Effect of Poison Pill Securities on Shareholder Wealth, *Journal of Financial Economics* 20, 377–417.

Ryngaert, Michael and Jeffry Netter, 1987, Shareholder Wealth Effects of the Ohio Antitakeover Law, working paper.

Schumann, Laurence, 1987, State Regulation of Takeovers and Shareholder Wealth: The Effects of New York's 1985 Takeover Statutes, Bureau of Economics Staff Report to the Federal Trade Commission, March.

Shleifer, Andrei and Lawrence Summers, 1987, Hostile Takeovers as Breaches of Trust, NBER Working Paper.

Smiley, Robert, 1981, The Effect of State Securities Statutes on Tender Offer Activity, *Economic Inquiry* 19, 426–35.

Steindel, Charles, 1986, Tax Reform and the Merger and Acquisition Market: The Repeal of General Utilities, *Federal Reserve Bulletin of New York*, Autumn, 31–5.

18

The Effects of Antitakeover Amendments on Takeover Activity: Some Direct Evidence

John Pound

I Introduction

Antitakeover amendments change the structure of the corporate charter and ostensibly increase the bargaining power of management when confronted with a hostile outside contest for control of the corporation. Recent evidence shows that, as of December 1986, over 40 percent of the Fortune 500 had adopted some form of "shark repellent" amendment,[1] that over 700 New York Stock Exchange (NYSE) corporations have adopted one or more such amendments since the NYSE began keeping an informal log in the late 1960s,[2] and that over 650 nationally listed corporations have adopted antitakeover amendments since 1980.[3]

Three types of antitakeover amendments are most prevalent among major corporations. The most common, in terms of the number of recent adoptions, is the so-called fair price amendment, which requires that an equal price be paid for each share in a merger.[4] A second type of amendment is the simple supermajority requirement, which generally sets the number of shares required to approve a merger at between 66 and 80 percent. The third common type of amendment is the so-called classified board provision, which staggers terms of directors so that only a small minority (usually one-third) can be removed by vote at any one time. The staggered board amendment is clearly efficiency enhancing only if the board acts, on average, as an efficient bargaining agent for shareholders. During the late 1970s and early 1980s, it was common for supermajority and classified board amendments to be proposed and adopted together as a package of takeover defenses.

The amendments focus attention on the nature of the principal-agent relationship between management and shareholders[5] and on the efficiency of shareholder oversight. Proponents argue that the amendments can correct a serious collective choice problem affecting target shareholders' tendering decisions in the event of a control offer.[6] The problem occurs because less than all shares – in some cases, a bare 50 percent majority

– are needed to transfer control of the corporation.[7] Given this, any individual shareholder attempting to hold out and bargain with target management for the economically competitive takeover premium faces the possibility of being undercut by a majority and thus ending up in the back end of the takeover transaction, which may carry a significantly lower premium. Each of the three types of amendments described above arguably gives target management or target shareholders greater bargaining power, either by making it less likely that control will be transferred without the assent of all shareholders or by making it more expensive for the bidder to replace the board without the complicity of target management.

The case against antitakeover amendments is based on the fact that the amendments serve to increase managerial bargaining power – and hence managerial discretion for self-interested behavior – in the single situation in which such self-interested behavior is most likely to occur if there exists any imperfection at all in the managerial labor market. In addition, recent evidence suggests that the aforementioned bargaining imperfection may not be a significant distortion in tendering decisions.[8] It has thus been argued that the additional bargaining power conferred by the amendments is actually used by managements to pursue their own interests rather than those of shareholders.

Each of these effects – pro- and anti-shareholder – implies that antitakeover amendments systematically affect shareholders' gains from takeover activity. If the amendments are pro-shareholder, this must be because they increase the expected blended premium accruing in a takeover bid while not significantly diminishing the probability of such a bid occurring. Conversely, if the amendments are anti-shareholder, the most likely reason is that management uses them to increase bidder costs and hence to decrease the probability of bids. Costs may be increased either through more trenchant resistance, which increases bidders' transactions costs, or through the necessity of increased compensation to target management. It is also possible, though not likely, that, in bids that do occur, shareholders' gains are decreased in order to increase managerial compensation.

To date, evidence on the effects of antitakeover amendments has not centered on estimating their direct effects on takeover activity, but rather has consisted of analyses of the average effects of amendment adoptions on stock prices. At least three such studies exist, which use somewhat conflicting methodologies and end up with inconsistent results. However, the most recent study provides quite strong evidence.[9] By using a large sample, by controlling for confounding events, and by separating amendments by type, the authors show that non-fair price amendments, which are primarily supermajority and classified board amendments, cause significant negative excess returns in the neighborhood of 3 percent.[10] By contrast, the more prevalent fair price amendments appear to have no significant effect on shareholder wealth. In addition, the authors find that the incidence of fair price amendments is growing while the incidence of harmful amendments appear to be declining. Furthermore, they find that fair price amendments are associated with higher institutional ownership and lower insider ownership than are other types of amendments. They argue, on the basis of these trends, that informed shareholder-voters weed out malodorous amendments, albeit imperfectly and with considerable delay.

Even with careful methodology and strong results, however, it cannot be reliably concluded from the stock price evidence that the amendments themselves significantly alter the management–shareholder contract as it pertains to the market for corporate control. It is possible, indeed probable, that the decision to adopt an antitakeover amendment itself conveys information to the market and that it is this information and not the structural effects of the amendment that drive the adoption-period market reaction. With such signaling effects, the announcement- and adoption-period behavior of security returns will reflect not only the amendments' direct effects but also the additional information conveyed by the firm's decision to pursue the adoption of an amendment. This sort of problem is a growing difficulty throughout the corporate control literature, rendering precise valuations of certain corporate policies extremely difficult.

The most important confounding information potentially conveyed by amendment announcements is management's assessment of the probability that the firm in question is likely to become a takeover target. Because the commitment to an amendment is costly and, measured in terms of expected takeover-related gains, less costly the more a takeover attempt is likely, amendment adoption might be expected to signal an increased firm-specific probability of takeover, relative both to other firms in the market and to the preceding, pre-amendment regime.[11] This effect, if present, would militate toward setting some (unknown) positive average excess return as the null hypothesis for event studies of amendment adoptions.[12]

A second possible signaling effect militates in the opposite direction. If managements invoke antitakeover amendments as an attempt to protect themselves from unwanted bids, the mere adoption of an amendment may send a negative signal about managerial quality. If this is the case, an observed negative excess return in response to amendment adoption may be caused not solely by a change in expected shareholder gains from takeovers but also by a change in expected returns in the absence of takeover activity.

To address these problems, this paper offers empirical evidence on the direct effect of antitakeover amendments on takeover activity. The evidence determines the structural effects of the amendments, exploring how they affect management, target shareholders, and potential and actual bidding firms. This evidence is used to generate a direct test of the power of the event-study evidence, asking whether the expected value change greeting amendment adoptions appears, *ex post*, to constitute a correct prediction. The results thus provide perspective on the magnitude of the potential signaling problems discussed above (which cloud the results of a number of important studies of the market for corporate control) as well as providing a more complete picture of the actual effects of antitakeover amendments on takeover bids.

II Antitakeover Amendments and Shareholder Gains from Takeover Activity

This section presents tests of the effects of antitakeover amendments on shareholders' expected gains from takeover activity. The tests focus on firms adopting supermajority and classified board amendments in combination, which, recent evidence suggests, has a negative effect on shareholder wealth. The tests examine the amendments' effect on the frequency of, and gains accruing from, takeover activity. These two factors together determine expected gains to shareholders from takeover bids.

To test whether supermajority and classified board amendments decrease the probability of takeover bids, I collected an experimental sample of 100 NYSE-listed firms that adopted as a package both a supermajority and a classified board amendment in the period 1973–9 and that showed no confounding events around the adoption period. I selected these firms using the informal log kept by the NYSE of changes in voting rights for listed firms.[13] For each firm, sufficient information had to be available in relevant news sources and in the NYSE log to determine the exact type of amendment, the date of adoption, and the relevant control-related events occurring in the period surrounding adoption and in the subsequent test period.

I then assembled a complementary control group, consisting of 100 NYSE firms that, for the period examined, could reliably be determined to have adopted neither supermajority nor classified board amendments. Again, the NYSE log confirmed that candidate firms were free from amendment adoption during the period in question, and relevant news sources had to be sufficient to ensure full reporting of control-oriented activity involving the firm. These firms were stratified over the 1973–9 period in the same distribution as the experimental group. That is, the two samples contain temporarily matched pairs of adopting and nonadopting firms.

To determine the effects of the amendments on takeover frequency, I followed each firm in these two groups from the adoption date forward to December 1984 and utilized the *Wall Street Journal* Index, the *Business Index*, *Predicasts/Findex*, the *Business Periodicals Index*, and the *News Bulletin of the Securities and Exchange Commission* (SEC) (the latter lists tender offer filings with the agency). For each firm, these sources were scanned for evidence of control-oriented activity against the firm; activity defined as, at a minimum, a formal offer to purchase by an outside entity. For each sample this protocol resulted in 817 firm years of market exposure.

Given the potential informational effects of the amendments, described in the previous section, and the documented unpredictability of takeover activity, the use of a control group that is equivalent only in rough size and exchange listing (as opposed, for example, to industry matching) suggests a one-tailed test for the deterrent effects of amendments. If the amendments do not serve as a takeover barrier, the experimental group of firms should be expected to show at least as high a frequency of takeover offers as the control group because, by incurring the costs of amendment adoption, they have signaled a higher-than-average takeover susceptibility.[14] Thus, the hypothesis tested was that

$$P_a^t \geq P_c^t \tag{1}$$

where P_a^t is the frequency of takeover for firms with antitakeover amendments, and P_c^t is the frequency of takeover for firms in the control group.

Table 18.1 The effect of antitakeover amendments on the frequency of takeover bids

Sample	Offer frequency
With antitakeover amendments	0.28
Control sample (no amendments)	0.38

Note: Table measures the frequency of takeover attempts against 100 NYSE firms with and 100 NYSE firms without supermajority and classified board amendments, measured from 1974–84. Frequency is percentage of firms in each sample receiving at least one formal acquisition offer over the period. z-statistic for null hypothesis of no differences between the samples $= 2.54$. $p < 0.25$.

The results of this frequency test are displayed in table 18.1. They are quite striking, confirming a significant deterrent effect for antitakeover amendments at the 0.01 level. Firms with antitakeover amendments show a 26 percent lower frequency of takeover attempts over the period examined. In economic terms, this represents a substantial divergence.

To examine differences in takeover-bid-induced target firms returns, I adopted a portfolio comparison approach. I measured premiums across contests with and without target antitakeover amendments and inferred that differences stem from the amendments' presence. Power problems obtain with this test if it is found that the amendments cause a change in the expected takeover premium because, without a fully specified model of takeover premiums, antitakeover amendments may proxy for other variables. However, because of the bias introduced by omitted variables, it is also true that rejection of any relation between antitakeover amendments and premiums is of high power.

Utilizing several large tender offer data bases,[15] I developed a sample containing 65 takeover contests in which the target firm had both a supermajority amendment and a classified board amendment in place at the time of the initial takeover bid. These contests were stratified over the period 1974–84. I developed a control sample of 98 bids, in which the target firm did not have supermajority or classified board amendments in place. The sample was stratified over time in the same proportion as the experimental group of bids. Each of these firms had to have been the subject of a tender offer for control; the relevant bid announcement dates had to be available in the *Wall Street Journal* or other equivalent news sources; and stock returns data had to be contained on the CRSP tapes.[16]

For each of the two samples of firms, I created an excess returns portfolio, defined as the cumulative average of the excess returns from the market model. I estimated a market model on the basis of daily returns for each target firm for the period from 190 days to forty days prior to the announcement date for the first acquisition offer, deriving

$$R_{it} = \hat{\alpha}_i + \hat{\beta}_i(R_{mt}) + \varepsilon_{it}, \tag{2}$$

where R_{it} is the observed return on firm i in month t, and R_{mt} is the observed return on the market portfolio for month t.

These equations were then forecast forward from day -40 to the announcement day for the highest offer made for the target,[17] deriving

$$\hat{E}R_{it} = R_{it} - \hat{\beta}R_{mt} - \hat{\alpha}_i, \tag{3}$$

where ER_{it} is the estimated excess return for firm i on day t, and $\hat{\ }$ denotes an estimated value.

For each firm, I then summed excess returns from day -40 to the day of the highest offer to yield cumulative excess returns, by

$$\hat{C}ER_i = \sum_{t=-40}^{N} \hat{E}R_{it} \tag{4}$$

By incorporating not just the first but also the highest bid made for the target firm, the window used captures any significant additional returns facilitated by the presence of antitakeover amendments. The CERs were then averaged across firms in each portfolio to derive portfolio excess returns.

The appropriate test for a difference in premium between these two samples is two-tailed, as it is possible that the amendments serve to decrease shareholder gains from takeovers (if some portion of a fixed level of gains is transferred from target shareholders to management) as well as to increase gains if the shareholder interests hypothesis holds. Table 18.2 presents the mean return and the standard error of the mean return for each portfolio, along with a test of the null hypothesis that mean returns are equal across the two portfolios. As can be seen, the null of equal portfolio CERs cannot be rejected. Indeed, returns across the two portfolios are very close in economic terms, differing by less than 10 percent, despite the considerable variance of firm-specific returns within each portfolio. Returns in both portfolios, moreover, are in line with other broad evidence on average takeover premiums already contained in the literature.[18]

Table 18.2 The effect of antitakeover amendments on takeover premiums

Sample	Average bid premium (SE)
With antitakeover amendments ($N = 65$)	0.514
	(0.039)
Control sample (no amendments) ($N = 98$)	0.488
	(0.029)

Note: Table measures takeover bid premiums for sample of 65 targets with supermajority and classified board amendments and 98 targets with no antitakeover amendments, measured as excess returns from the market model over a period from 40 days before the first bid announcement to the date of the highest bid announcement. t-statistic for no difference between sample means $= 1.35$. p (two-tailed test) > 0.25.

It thus appears that supermajority and classified board amendments do not serve to increase takeover-related gains to shareholders in takeover contests that do occur while concurrently acting as a significant deterrent to the instigation of control contests. These results stand in support of the managerial interests hypothesis and confirm the recent stock returns-based findings specific to these two types of amendments.[19]

A more quantitative, if stylized, comparison is possible between the recent stock price evidence on the amendments and the data contained in Table 18.1 and 18.2. The stock price data show a net decrease in expected wealth of between 3 and 5 percent as a consequence of amendment adoption. The results in tables 18.1 and 18.2 show that, on average, a firm taken at random from the market has approximately a 4.9 percent chance of becoming a takeover target in a given year[20] and that, if such a bid should occur, the expected premium is approximately 45 percent over previous market value. This means that, for a random NYSE firm, the possibility of takeover bids generates a component of expected annual returns with a value of about 2.2 percent. By contrast, for a firm with antitakeover amendments, the annual probability of takeover drops to 3.6 percent, and the expected takeover premium is 48 percent. This implies that the annual expected takeover premium drops to approximately 1.7 percent.

Given a total expected annual return in the 7–10 percent range, and, for simplicity, ignoring changes in risk, the amendment-caused loss in expected returns as measured by tables 18.1 and 18.2 thus constitutes about 5–7 percent of annual expected returns. Assuming stability in the returns-generating process over time, this evidence implies that the amendments' adoption should be associated with a 5–7 percent capitalized loss in the adoption period, in the absence of significant signaling effects stemming from the adoption decision. This obviously squares very closely with the returns behavior that is shown to exist around adoption. The evidence thus lends support to the conjecture that the market is rational in assessing the amendments' effect on future returns. However, the slightly lower value of the actual stock price reaction to amendment adoption may suggest that something about the firm caused the possibility of the antitakeover amendment adoption to be partially anticipated by the market.

A final question about antitakeover amendments' effects on expected shareholder gains is whether they tilt bidders' incentives away from partial and two-tier offers and toward any-or-all offers. Such an effect, protecting the rights of shareholders in the back ends of deals, is the benefit alleged to derive from the amendments by those suggesting that in their absence there is a collective choice problem in shareholders' tendering decisions. Such an effect may exist even given the results shown in table 18.2, which indicates no difference in average premiums in the presence of the amendments, because these premiums constitute blended measures that average front-end offers with the market's estimate of back-end pay-offs. If the takeover market is competitive, the presence of supermajority amendments might encourage more equal treatment while leaving total blended premiums unchanged, although this would involve reductions of the front-end offer to offset increases in back-end compensation.

Table 18.3 The effect of antitakeover amendments on minority shareholder wealth

Type of Bid	Frequency antitakeover sample	Frequency SEC master sample
Any or all	0.65	0.80
Two tier	0.15	0.17
Partial	0.20	0.13

Note: Table measures the frequency of any-or-all, partial, and two-tier takeover bids in sample of 65 bids in which target had supermajority and classified board amendments, compared to equivalent frequencies in SEC master sample of all bids from 1980 to 1984.

This question can be examined by comparing the relative frequency of different types of offers occurring in the antitakeover amendment sample with existing data on the relative frequency of different types of offers across all recent takeover bids.[21] Antitakeover amendments can be inferred to have some positive effect on minority shareholders if they result in a higher proportion of any-or-all offers than obtains across the market in their absence.

Table 18.3 presents this comparison. It shows that the proportion of any-or-all offers is in fact lower in the antitakeover amendment sample than across the market as a whole. This is a surprising result and argues that the amendments do not have a significant positive effect on minority shareholder wealth. A possible reason is that, if antitakeover amendments make takeover bids more costly – as they must if they are to have significant deterrent effects – and if the takeover market is competitive in their absence, then the amendments may make some any-or-all bids too costly to carry out. In this case, the bidder's alternatives will be to abandon a control attempt altogether or to attempt to gain control through the use of a more coercive, partial bid. The latter alternative is obviously the very strategy that antitakeover amendments militate against, according to their proponents.

III   Managerial Gains and the Nature of the Takeover Deterrent

Define the total cost to a bidder of a takeover transaction as consisting of three components: direct compensation to target shareholders (C_s), direct compensation to target management (C_m), and transactions costs associated with the bid (C_t). The total cost of a bid (TC) is expressed as

$$TC = C_s + C_m + C_t \tag{5}$$

Table 18.2 demonstrates that C_s is unchanged in the presence of supermajority and classified board amendments. Therefore, the deterrent effect of the amendments must spring from the ability of an empowered target management to impose higher costs on potential bidders than would occur in the amendments' absence – in the form of an increase in C_m, an increase in C_t, or both. Either by elevating transactions costs or by increasing direct compensation, antitakeover amendments shift the expected gains from some takeover bids from positive to negative.

It is difficult to measure either changes in direct managerial compensation or transactions costs directly, but several inferential measures are again possible using the two samples of takeover targets developed for measuring takeover premiums. The first, simpler task is to test for a higher average level of transactions costs in the sample of contests in which targets had antitakeover amendments in place. One proxy for transactions costs is the frequency of trenchant managerial resistance across bids with and without antitakeover amendments, which is likely to engender higher fees for investment banking and legal services, higher SEC filing fees, and the like. If trenchant resistance is higher in those contests with the amendments in place, an inference can be drawn that this resistance is indicative of a higher average level of bidder transactions costs in these cases.

To measure trenchant resistance, I examined the two samples of takeover contests for several managerial activities that have generally been concluded to constitute significant, costly tender offer resistance. These included lawsuits by targets; appeals to regulatory agencies – such as antitrust – for blocking action; and various market-based actions designed to introduce delay and inflate bidder costs.[22] The frequency of significant takeover resistance across the two samples was then tabulated and compared.

The results are contained in table 18.4 and once again are surprisingly strong. Significant takeover resistance appears to be approximately twice as likely among targets containing supermajority and classified board amendments as it is for targets without antitakeover provisions. The frequency of resistance in the control sample, moreover, is in line with other authors' findings for larger samples of takeover activity. This evidence suggests that the amendments' deterrent effects come in part from a significant increase in the expected level of transactions costs that bidders estimate to be associated with a takeover bid.

It is more difficult to determine whether the direct takeover-related compensation paid to managers is also increased by the presence of the amendments. Data on target

Table 18.4 Antitakeover amendments and the frequency of takeover resistance

Sample	Resistance frequency
With antitakeover amendments ($N = 65$)	0.68
Control sample (no amendments) ($N = 98$)	0.38

Note: Table measures the frequency of managerial resistance to initial takeover bids for 65 targets with supermajority and classified board amendments and 98 targets with no antitakeover amendments. Resistance was coded only if target management undertook costly action, such as litigation, in opposition to the initial bid. z-statistic for hypothesis of no difference between sample frequencies = 2.89. $p < 0.01$.

managements' compensation in takeover contests are difficult to assemble. The approach used here is inferential, using the success of managerial resistance as a proxy for relative managerial gains. Unsuccessful resistance is defined as occurring when a control transfer takes place over the continued objections of target management. Successful resistance takes place when the final transaction (which involves target acquisition in all but two cases, in each subsample) takes place on terms that target management has specifically endorsed. Given table 18.2's evidence that expected shareholder compensation is unchanged in the presence of the amendments, and given the higher frequency of managerial resistance in the presence of antitakeover amendments, if it is found that the amendments render managerial resistance more successful, it can be inferred that the total cost of takeover bids has been increased by increasing managerial compensation.

Table 18.5 shows the proportion of all initially resisting target managements who continued to express opposition through the transfer of control. When combined with the data in table 18.4, these results once again are suggestive. Although a considerably higher proportion of managements in the antitakeover amendment sample expressed initial opposition to takeover bids, in none of these cases was control ultimately transferred over managements' continued objections. By contrast, in the control sample, although a lower proportion of all managements expressed initial opposition to the takeover bid, over one-third of those that did ultimately lost control of their firm while still opposed to the acquisition. These results suggest that the amendments confer sufficient additional bargaining power to target managements to ensure that bidders will be forced to secure managements' approval of the deal. Given that average premiums are no higher in the antitakeover amendment sample, the implication is that part of the increased costs imposed by antitakeover amendments comes in the form of higher direct compensation paid to target managements to purchase their support for control transfer.[23]

This conclusion is supported by comparing the ultimate premium paid to target shareholders, across the two takeover samples, in the cases involving successful acquisitions that were characterized by initial managerial resistance. Table 18.6 presents

Table 18.5 Antitakeover amendments and the success of managerial resistance

Sample	Frequency of control transfer
With antitakeover amendments ($N = 32$)	0.00
Control sample (no amendments) ($N = 36$)	0.39

Note: Table measures the frequency of control transfer over continued opposition by target management for 65 targets with classified board and supermajority amendments and 98 targets with no antitakeover amendments. z-statistic for hypothesis of no difference between the frequencies = 4.02. $p < 0.01$.

Table 18.6 Antitakeover amendments and takeover premiums for resisting targets

Sample	Average bid premium (SE)
With antitakeover amendments ($N = 32$)	0.589
	(0.057)
Control sample (no amendments) ($N = 36$)	0.594
	(0.047)

Note: Table measures takeover bid premiums for 32 initially resisting firms with classified board and supermajority amendments and 36 resisting firms without antitakeover amendments. Premiums are measured as excess returns from the market model from 40 days prior to the initial bid announcement to the date of the highest offer. *t*-statistic for hypothesis of no difference between sample means $= 0.11$. $p > 0.25$.

these results.[24] As can be seen, there is no change in premiums in the antitakeover amendment sample, despite the fact that almost twice as many of these acquisitions ultimately occurred with managerial approval. Once again, this result implies that bidder costs may be elevated in the presence of antitakeover amendments by the need to pay a higher level of managerial compensation rather than by increases in direct shareholder compensation.

IV Conclusions

This paper presents new tests of the effects of antitakeover amendments by examining the amendments' direct effects on takeover activity. The focus is on supermajority and classified board amendments whose adoption appears to have significant deleterious effects on stock prices. Taken in sum, the evidence tends to support the view that these amendments increase the bargaining power of management in the event of a control bid, to the detriment of shareholder wealth. The amendments appear to reduce the frequency of takeover bids significantly while not improving the expected value of shareholder gains in those takeover contests that do occur.

It remains for further research to determine whether, as some have argued, the shareholder oversight process works to militate against abusive managerial initiatives over time. It is true that the frequency of both supermajority and classified board amendments has declined in recent years and that the frequency of so-called fair price amendments, which do not appear to carry adverse stock price consequences, has increased. Yet the former types of amendments continue to be proposed and passed. Furthermore, on close inspection it appears that not all recent fair price amendments are alike; some contain strictures that are very unlikely to be met in the event of a hostile bid. Thus it may be that some proportion of these apparently harmless amendments are abusive as well. Overall, these considerations suggest that the shareholders' ability to police management through the enforcement of contracts is imperfect, although far from nonexistent.

Notes

I am indebted to Philip Dybvig, James Heard, Roger Ibbotson, Gregg Jarrell, Robert Shiller, and an anonymous referee for comments and suggestions. I am also grateful to the Investor Responsibility Research Center for providing research support.

1   *Antitakeover Charter Amendments: A Directory of Major American Corporations* (Investor Responsibility Research Center, Washington, D.C., 1985).

2   Internal log of corporate charter revisions (New York Stock Exchange, ongoing).

3   Gregg Jarrell and Annette Poulsen, Shark Repellents and Stock Prices: The Impact of Antitakeover Charter Amendments Since 1980, 19 *J. Fin. Econ.* (1987).

4   Generally, fair price amendments are structured so that violation of the fair price provision invokes a restrictive supermajority condition, which in some cases may be effectively impossible to satisfy. Some fair price amendments also carry extremely restrictive "procedural" requirements that also serve to impose heavy costs on a potential bidder. While the amendments have a general similarity, it is a mistake to assume that all fair price amendments create identical incentives.

5   The question of managerial accountability arises throughout the literature on tender offer resistance. For example, Frank Easterbrook and Daniel Fishel, The Proper Role of a Target's Management in Responding to a Tender Offer, 94 *Harv. L. Rev.* 1161 (1981), have questioned whether lawsuits by target managements are consistent with fiduciary duties.

6   See Lucian Bebchuck, A Model of the Outcome of Takeover Bids (Discussion Paper, Harvard University Law School Program in Law and Economics, November 1985); Harry DeAngelo and Edward Rice, Antitakeover Amendments and Stockholder Wealth, 11 *J. Fin. Econ.* 329 (1983).

7   The majority vote needed to gain control is a function both of existing corporate charter provisions and of the relevant state statutes governing corporate structure, which generally set a default on the necessary majority. State provisions have vacillated over the past decade, as a number of state statutes setting high majority requirements (for example, two-thirds) have been struck down in the federal courts.

8   For evidence that back ends – even in explicit two-tier tender offers – carry a relatively small penalty compared to front-end premiums, see Robert Comment and Gregg Jarrell, Two-Tier Tender Offers: The Imprisonment of the Free-riding Shareholder, *J. Fin. Econ.* (1988). Back-end shareholders are compensated at well above pre-offer market prices. For evidence that tender offers are rationally rejected – that is, are rejected only when the expected compensation from rejection is nonnegative – see Michael Bradley, Interfirm Tender Offers and the Market for Corporate Control, 53 *J. Bus.* 345 (1980). For evidence that the takeover market is competitive in the sense that bidders' expected gains from a higher offer than the successful offer are nonpositive, see Richard Ruback, Competition in the Market for Corporate Control, 11 *J. Fin. Econ.* 141 (1983).

9   See Jarrell and Poulsen, note 3.

10 The evidence on straight supermajority amendments is surprising, as these amendments appear to carry no adverse implications for management's ability to impose arbitrary costs

on the takeover process. Rather, they seem to be a relatively pure approach to vesting more power with target shareholders.

11 This case is less clear when the amendment is undertaken in reaction to an alteration of the state laws setting default merger guidelines. However, it is still relevant if the control is defined properly – which, in this case, would mean comparing adopting firms to nonadopting firms from the same state and in the same time period.

12 Such results are reported in Scott Linn and John McConnell, An Empirical Investigation of the Effects of "Antitakeover" Amendments on Common Stock Prices, 11 *J. Fin. Econ.* 383 (1983).

13 Many thanks to the exchange for providing this log for the sampling exercise.

14 The argument is only strengthened if takeover activity is somewhat predictable on an industry-specific basis. In this case, amendment adoptions (because of their cost) should come in industries experiencing significant takeover activity. Thus, a comparison of takeover frequency between adopting firms and random nonadopting firms (the latter presumably in less takeover prone industries) should show at least as high a takeover frequency for adopting firms. By contrast, the effect would be less strong if the control group were industry matched.

15 Included were the tender offer data bases maintained by the Managerial Economics Research Center at the University of Rochester and an internal SEC list of all tender offer registrations filed with the agency since 1976.

16 The CRSP tapes are compiled by the Center for Research in Securities Prices, University of Chicago.

17 One methodological problem occurs in measuring returns on the basis of the highest offer date. Firms exhibiting trenchant takeover resistance may show little share price reaction to increased offers because the market may by then heavily discount the probability of the offer's success. This was corrected for in both samples simply by calculating the blended per-share value of final offers directly for those targets ultimately defeating all outstanding offers to remain separate.

18 See, for example, Comment and Jarrell, note 8.

19 Jarrell and Poulsen, note 3.

20 This is calculated by taking the number of bids (38) occurring in the sample and dividing by the total number of firm years of exposure (817).

21 The latter, aggregate data have been compiled by Comment and Jarrell, note 8.

22 Further examples are the creation of new preferred stock, asset purchase or sale over bidder objections, and the placing of a block of stock with a friendly third-party corporation.

23 Note that the increased managerial satisfaction in the antitakeover amendment sample does not come from a higher frequency of success in retaining independence. In each sample, two firms were successful in preserving autonomy by defeating all outstanding bids.

24 Premiums were again measured using the market model. The measurement window was from 40 days prior to the initial takeover bid announcement to the announcement day for the highest offer for the target.

19

The Information Effects of Takeover Bids and Resistance

John Pound

1 Introduction

This paper offers new evidence on whether takeover bids and resistance convey information to the market about the stand-alone value of target firms. I test whether analysts' earnings forecasts shift systematically in reaction to bids and resistance. Evidence shows that during takeover bids analysts face incentives to continue forecasting for the target firm as an independent entity. For this reason changes in earnings forecasts for these firms provide information about whether the market systematically revises its view of targets' stand-alone performance, and hence their stand-alone value, in response to takeover bids and subsequent resistance.

A schematic for the tests is provided in figure 19.1. To test whether takeover bids convey information about stand-alone value, I compare consensus per-share earnings forecasts issued in the month that the first takeover bid is announced with those issued in the preceding month. To examine the effects of resistance on stand-alone value, I compare bid-month forecasts with forecasts issued in the month that the takeover contest is resolved. In each two-way comparison, the forecasts are for earnings in the fiscal year after the one in which the takeover contest occurs. This prevents bias from

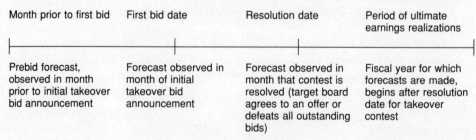

Month prior to first bid	First bid date	Resolution date	Period of ultimate earnings realizations
Prebid forecast, observed in month prior to initial takeover bid announcement	Forecast observed in month of initial takeover bid announcement	Forecast observed in month that contest is resolved (target board agrees to an offer or defeats all outstanding bids)	Fiscal year for which forecasts are made, begins after resolution date for takeover contest

Figure 19.1 Schematic representation of the timing of earnings forecast observations, takeover bids, and takeover contests.

one-time unanticipated expenditures on the takeover transaction itself. The tests use a sample of 94 firms that were targeted for takeover between 1979 and 1984.

The use of this direct measure of expected future performance yields some new evidence on the information content of takeover bids and resistance. First, initial takeover bids do not cause a significant, systematic change in earnings forecasts for target firms. This is additional evidence in favor of the synergy view of merger motives, and against the hypothesis that an economically significant proportion of takeover bids is based on prior undervaluation of targets. The evidence is consistent with the results of other studies that have examined takeovers' information effects using stock returns [Bhagat, Brickley, and Lowenstein (1987), Bradley, Desai, and Kim (1983)]. It extends the results of these studies by showing that the market's estimate of an important direct measure of future performance does not change in response to the announcement of either successful or unsuccessful takeover bids.

The data also show that takeover resistance by target management causes a significant negative shift in earnings forecasts. During resisted takeover, earnings forecasts decline by approximately 7 to 10 percent. This result extends previous evidence showing neutral or negative share-price effects from various types of takeover defenses [Dann and DeAngelo (1988), Ryngaert (1987), and Jarrell (1985)]. The data are consistent with the theory that managerial resistance directly decreases the value of target firms, either because of entrenchment [Easterbrook and Fischel (1981)] or because resistance conveys information to the market about weakness in the target firm [Shleifer and Vishny (1986)]. The results reject the hypothesis that resistance affects only the probability that the target will be successfully acquired, while leaving its expected stand-alone value unchanged. This suggests the need for further research into the motivations for takeover defenses.

In section 2, I describe the properties of the earnings forecast data, the tests, and the sample of firms used. Section 3 presents results. Section 4 discusses the results in light of the inherent limitations of earnings forecast data. Section 5 presents conclusions.

2   Test Methodology, Sample, Data, and Data Alignment

2.1   Test methodology

2.1.1   Earnings forecasts during takeover bids

My tests are based on the assumption that during takeover bids analysts continue to issue forecasts for target firms as stand-alone entities. A priori, other possibilities clearly exist. Analysts could stop forecasting during takeover contests or attempt to forecast the performance of the target as an acquired entity. Both theoretical considerations and empirical evidence, however, support the idea that they continue to forecast stand-alone values.

Analysts do not refrain from forecasting when confronted with takeover bids because doing so would damage their reputations. Takeover bids typically have large per-share value implications and thus create high demand among investors for analysts' evaluations. Available evidence, including reports from brokerage houses and sources such as *Value Line*, indicates that analysts attempt to meet this demand by evaluating the fairness of offers and making recommendations about tendering decisions. Earnings forecasts, which are a central component of analysts' reports, are typically critical to these evaluations. The forecasts are used to estimate the value of the target should current bids fail and the firm remain independent.[1] Earnings forecasts for future fiscal years are usually compared with the target's prebid price and with the bid price, to evaluate the size of the offered premium. For example, in evaluating the fairness of Nestlé's 1984 bid for Carnation, *Value Line* stated: "The offer is a fair one, in our opinion. It is 14.4 times 1984's estimated earnings and 12.6 times 1985's – a healthy price for a food company, even one as cash rich and profitable as Carnation."

Available evidence suggests that analysts do not attempt to evaluate the value of the target to the bidding firm by forecasting the earnings performance of the target should it be acquired. When targets are acquired, they are restructured into the new parent, making forecasts based on their pretakeover configuration irrelevant in evaluating their value to the acquirer. Analysts report that the fit between the acquirer and the target, the target's net cash flow, and its balance sheet positions are typically the principal factors in their evaluation of potential acquisition value.

Evidence from analysts' retail reports and a survey of 24 analysts conducted for this paper both support the hypothesis that analysts continue to update their earnings forecasts during takeover contests and continue to forecast for the target as an independent firm.

2.1.2   Test method

The tests in this paper use the most broad-based and widely-analyzed earnings-forecast data base, the IBES data base maintained by Lynch, Jones, and Ryan of New York. The historical IBES tape, which covers approximately 5,000 corporations and 2,500 analysts, contains monthly observations of mean and median earnings forecasts for the current fiscal year (FY1) and the next fiscal year (FY2), and measures of dispersion. Several studies have analyzed the behavior of the consensus forecasts in this data base and their relationship to security prices. Brown, Foster, and Noreen (1985) provide an extensive analysis as well as a summary of other research. Among their more important findings are the following:

i)   Monthly firm-specific FY2 IBES forecast revisions contain insignificant positive autocorrelation (pp. 21–5).

ii)   IBES FY2 forecasts appear to contain little average positive or negative bias (pp. 47–51).

iii) There is significant positive covariance between IBES forecast revisions and firm-specific excess security returns (pp. 102–9).

These findings provide an important statistical basis for tests using the IBES data. Finding (i) implies that consensus IBES forecasts move fairly efficiently in response to new information. Finding (ii) implies that forecast levels (as opposed to forecast revisions) are typically fairly efficient reflections of current information. Finding (iii) implies that analysts revise their forecasts in response to information that causes a change in market values. The results thus suggest that the forecasts should move in response to takeover bids if these bids do in fact convey important new information about targets' stand-alone values.

On the basis of this evidence, I use a straightforward event-based approach to test whether takeover bids and resistance release information to the market about targets' future earnings performance and hence their stand-alone values. If takeover bids convey no information, then on average, for a random sample of target firms, FY2 forecast revisions occurring in the month that takeover bids are announced should equal zero. Similarly, if takeover resistance conveys no new information about future earnings, then for a random sample of targets resisting takeover bids, the average forecast revision during the takeover contest should equal zero. Rejection of either of these hypotheses would indicate that takeover activity conveys systematic positive or negative information about the stand-alone value of target firms.

To pose these tests, I first calculate forecast revisions for each firm in the sample over the relevant event period. Using the average of these firm-specific revisions, I then use a standard t-test to test the hypothesis that the average revision equals zero across the sample. The test uses a cross-sectional standard error, formed from the observed variance of forecast revisions across firms during the measurement period. The cross-sectional standard error is used rather than a standard error based on the historical variance of the sample firms' forecast revisions, because of the likelihood that major takeover-related news increases the variance of revisions in the event period.

The power of these tests will be reduced if there is cross-sectional dependence across the forecasts in the sample: that is, if

$$E_t(FY2^f_{it+1} - FY2^f_{it} | FY2^f_{jt+1} - FY2^f_{jt}) \neq 0, \tag{1}$$

where $FY2^f_{it}$ is an IBES FY2 consensus forecast for firm i, issued in month t, and $FY2^f_{jt}$ is an IBES FY2 consensus forecast for firm j, issued in month t. This problem should not compromise the tests in this study because the sample of 94 takeover targets received bids across the six-year period 1979–84. There is little clumping of event dates. It should also be of little concern because tests have shown that, even for perfectly aligned forecasts, dependence across revisions is negligible.[2]

For those firms that ultimately defeat takeover bids and remain independent, it is also possible to compare analysts' forecasts made at the conclusion of the takeover contest with actual realized FY2 earnings. This test provides inferential evidence on the accuracy of analysts' bid-period and resistance-period forecast revisions, for both defeating targets and others. Targets that remain independent are usually characterized by long takeover contests and often complex resistance and bidding strategies. If analysts are efficient in incorporating information about these contests into their forecasts, then it is more likely that their forecast revisions are reliable indications of how bids and resistance affect future earnings performance for the entire sample.

I present two tests of the efficiency of analysts' earnings estimates for defeating targets made at the conclusion of the takeover contest. The first examines overall forecast accuracy by comparing the dispersion of forecast errors for defeating target firms with the average accuracy of the forecasts in the IBES universe. Given the uncertainties created by the takeover contest, it would not be surprising for defeating targets' forecasts to be more dispersed in relation to ultimate earnings realizations than IBES forecasts on average. I calculate the mean-squared forecast error (MSFE) for these forecasts and compare this with available summary data on the MSFE for all IBES FY2 forecasts. MSFE is calculated by averaging squared forecast errors and multiplying the result by 100, i.e.,

$$\text{MSFE} = \frac{1}{n}\left[\sum_{i=1}^{n}\frac{[\text{Realized earnings}_i - \text{Forecast earnings}_i]^2}{\text{Market price}_i \text{ at forecast date}} *100\right] \qquad (2)$$

A second set of tests examines the *ex post* bias of the defeat-date consensus target forecasts. Systematic positive or negative bias might suggest that analysts consistently under- or overreact to the process of takeover bid, resistance, and defeat. To test for *ex post* forecast bias, I run a cross-sectional regression of the following form:

$$FY2^a_i/P_{it-1} = \alpha + \beta(FY2^f_i/P_{it-1}) + \varepsilon_i, \qquad (3)$$

where $FY2^a_i$ is actual FY2 per-share earnings for firm i, $FY2^f_i$ is the consensus defeat-date FY2 earnings forecast for firm i, and P_{it-1} is the per-share market value of firm i at the beginning of the month before the first takeover bid announcement.[3] This regression requires a heteroskedasticity correction because the interval from defeat date to earnings realization is different for different firms in the sample. The White (1980) heteroskedasticity-consistent covariance matrix is used to correct for heteroskedasticity of unspecified form. The correction uses the square of the ith observed error term from the regression as an unbiased estimate of the true variance of the ith residual. In these regressions the relevant test statistics are calculated using the chi-squared distribution.[4]

2.2   Data and data alignment

In the tests, I use consensus FY2 IBES forecasts for each firm as a proxy for the market consensus forecast. It is an open question in the expectations literature whether the mean or the median better represents the consensus forecast. I report results for the mean forecast because the mean is more sensitive than the median to shifts in individual analysts' forecasts. This is a desirable characteristic because, as I discuss in section 4, earnings-forecast revisions may not be sufficient to reflect the full-information effects of takeovers. Using the median would make the tests even less sensitive, since changes in individual analysts' forecasts will not always alter the median. They will always alter the mean unless they are perfectly offsetting.[5]

To standardize forecast revisions across the sample, I divide each per-share forecast revision by the per-share price of the firm at the beginning of the month of the first forecast. This procedure makes the economic importance of the revisions comparable across firms, expressing it as a percentage of each firm's total market value. It also improves the distribution of revisions, in comparison with normalizing on past forecasts or past earnings, because of the instability of earnings series. For example, for a firm with a current market price of US$30 per share, a forecast revision from $0.01 to $0.03 per share is 200% if expressed in terms of the initial forecast, and a change from $-0.01 to $0.03 is -400%. The relative importance of these changes is better expressed as 0.02/30 and 0.04/30 respectively.[6]

To align IBES forecasts with event dates, I combine information from IBES on survey methodology with existing evidence on the timelines of analysts' forecast updating conventions. The literature suggests that, in response to new earnings announcements, approximately 85% of all forecasters update and reanalyze their forecasts within five business days.[7] IBES reports surveying contributing forecasters at the end of each monthly reporting period, requiring analysts to certify whether the forecast on the IBES record is the current forecast. Forecasters are also expected to call in significant revisions to IBES on their own initiative. IBES rechecks the currency of forecasts that lie "well outside" the distribution of most forecasts for each firm at the end of each reporting month.[8]

These factors suggest the following data-alignment convention. A minimum of six business days was allowed between the event day – the initial announcement of a takeover bid or takeover resolution – and the close of the IBES reporting period for the event month. If the event fell within the six-day window – for example, two days prior to the IBES reporting close – the following month was considered the announcement month. This updating convention makes it likely that the event-period consensus forecast will incorporate all event-inspired forecast revisions, while shifting a minimum number of revisions ahead into a new forecasting month.[9]

2.3 Sample

The sample of takeover targets used for the test is developed from an SEC list of all tender offers filed with the agency from 1976 to 1984. Targets must satisfy the following criteria: each is the subject of a tender offer for control; each is followed by securities analysts whose earnings forecasts are listed on the IBES data tape; and each has sufficient news coverage in the *Wall Street Journal* and the *New York Times* to determine the nature of the control contest (hostile or friendly), the outcome, and the relevant event dates. A tender offer for control is defined as a tender offer to purchase shares in a target corporation in which the bidder previously owned less than a 25% interest and that, if successful, would result in the bidder owning at least 51% of the target. In addition, the stated purpose of the bid must be outright acquisition of the target. A friendly takeover bid is defined as one for which the first news is of a pending acquisition agreement between a bidder and the target rather than an unanticipated offer. A hostile takeover bid ending in acquisition is defined as one in which the target's board at a minimum recommends that shareholders reject the first publicly identifiable offer, but in which the target is ultimately acquired as a consequence of some bid that temporally overlaps the initial bid. A hostile bid in which the target retains autonomy is defined as one in which the target defeats all outstanding takeover offers that overlap the initial offer. This definition does not ensure that the target is never taken over, but rather provides that a particular auction process ends with the target firm remaining independent. It is thus an *ex ante* criterion.[10]

One further sampling criterion is that the entire takeover contest, measured from the month of first bid to the month of resolution, must take place within a given fiscal year. This criterion is necessary to ensure that year-ahead earnings forecasts used for the tests do not become current-year forecasts by the end of the takeover bid. If this were to occur, forecasts could change significantly as a result of the inclusion of one-time-only charges associated with the takeover contest itself, such as expenditures on legal and investment banking fees. The purpose of the tests is to capture permanent changes in performance expectations, not one-time expenditures.[11]

I begin sampling using all targets from the most recent period covered by the data base, 1981–4. I use this period because substantial changes appear to have occurred in takeover regulation and dynamics since 1980.[12] Of the approximately 200 firms receiving tender offers for control during the 1981–4 period, 80 have the necessary IBES earnings forecast data for the period from pretakeover bid to postcontest resolution. Of these, 30 are targets of friendly bids, 31 are targets of hostile bids and are ultimately acquired, and 19 are targets of hostile bids and retain their independence. To make statistical tests on the latter sample possible, its size is expanded to 33 firms by sampling back in the data base through 1979. The total sample thus contains 94 target firms.

The samples of friendly, hostile/successful, and hostile/unsuccessful takeover attempts are of approximately equal size, which does not reflect the relative frequency of these types of targets in the universe. The bias toward resisting targets is probably due to the larger average size of these firms during the sampling period. Larger firms are more widely followed by analysts and hence more likely to be covered by IBES. In the tests, I also include a "composite" estimate for all targets, constructed by weighting the results for each of the three samples by their relative frequency in the universe of targets from 1979–84.[13]

3   Results

3.1   *The information content of initial takeover-bid announcements*

Table 19.1 presents results of tests for systematic earnings-forecast changes around takeover-bid announcements. The tests compare firms' consensus FY2 forecasts for the month before the first news of a takeover bid with the forecast made in the month the bid is announced. Panel A presents data on the average forecast revision in the announcement month for each of the three samples of takeover targets described in section 2. Panel B presents the nonparametric frequency distributions of the announcement-month revisions. As described above, in all the tests the forecast data have been price-normalized by the per-share price of each firm at the beginning of the month preceding the first takeover announcement. In thinking about the results,

Table 19.1 Behavior of year-ahead (FY2) consensus earnings forecasts in the month of initial bid announcements, for three samples of takeover targets, conditioned on *ex post* information about managerial resistance and contest outcome. Total sample size is 94 targets; the sample period is 1979–84

Panel A

Average revision in consensus (mean) FY2 per-share earnings forecasts in the month of initial takeover-bid announcements, compared with mean FY2 forecast in the month immediately preceding first news of takeover bid.

Sample	Average revision[a,b]	t-statistic
No resistance from target[c] ($n = 30$)	−0.00076	−0.75
Resistance/target acquired[d] ($n = 31$)	−0.00323	−1.67
Resistance/target remains independent[e] ($n = 33$)	0.00310	1.93
Weighted sample average[f]	−0.00091	−0.67

Panel B

Nonparametric distributions of year-ahead (FY2) earnings-forecast revisions[a] in the month of takeover-bid announcements for three samples of takeover targets, conditioned on *ex post* information about managerial resistance and contest outcome.

Sample	% positive	% negative	% unchanged
No resistance from target[c] ($n = 30$)	23	29	48
Resistance/target acquired[d] ($n = 31$)	23	40	37
Resistance/target remains independent[e] ($n = 33$)	35	28	37
Weighted sample average[f]	25	32	43
IBES universe[g]	42	39	19

[a] Revisions are calculated as $([FY2_{it}^f - FY2_{it-1}^f]/P_i)$, where $FY2_{it}^f$ is the consensus forecast for firm i in the month of the takeover-bid anouncement, $FY2_{it-1}^f$ is the equivalent forecast in the month immediately before the takeover-bid announcement, and P_i is the per-share market price of firm i at the beginning of the month immediately preceding the initial takeover-bid announcement.

[b] To put revisions in terms of the previously forecast level of earnings, rather than price-normalized terms, multiply by a prebid P/E ratio of approximately 15. To put revisions in percentage terms multiply by 100. Thus, for example, as a percent change over previously forecast earnings, multiply $(-0.00076)*(1.5*10^3) = 1.14\%$.

[c] An unresisted takeover bid is defined as one for which first news is of a pending acquisition agreement between a bidder and the target rather than an unanticipated offer.

[d] A hostile takeover bid ending in acquisition is defined as one in which the target's board at a minimum recommends that shareholders reject the first publicly identifiable offer, but the target is ultimately acquired as a consequence of some bid that temporally overlaps the initial bid.

[e] A hostile bid in which the target retains autonomy is defined as one in which the target defeats all outstanding takeover offers that overlap with the initial offer.

[f] Weighted sample average is calculated by weighting mean revisions for the three subsamples by their approximate frequency in the population of all takeover targets in the sample period. Weights are: friendly targets 0.55, resisting/acquired 0.30, resisting/independent 0.15.

[g] IBES universe is reported in Brown, Foster, and Noreen (1985).

however, particularly for average forecast revisions, it is helpful to convert the data back into a change over the preannouncement earnings forecast. This can be done by multiplying any of the average forecast revisions shown in the tables by 15, to reflect the approximate pretakeover average price/earnings ratio in the sample of firms, and then multiplying by 100 to express the result in percentage terms. Thus, for example, a price-normalized average revision of 0.001 can be restated as an earnings-forecast-normalized revision of about 0.015 or as an earnings forecast increase of about 1.5%.

The data in table 19.1 all show negligible information effects, on average, from the announcement of takeover bids. Panel A shows that the average FY2 earnings-forecast revision in the takeover-bid announcement month is less than 5% of previously forecast earnings for all three samples of targets. Its sign varies across the samples, and for each group it is not possible to reject the null hypothesis of no average information effect at conventional 5% or 1% levels.[14]

Panel B's nonparametric data further support the hypothesis of no significant bid-period forecast revisions. For all three groups, there is a high proportion of unchanged forecasts in the announcement month.

A strict interpretation of these data is that, on average, takeover bids yield little new information, positive or negative, about the probable future performance of target firms as stand-alone entities. This suggests that bids themselves are not expected to increase target performance significantly. The negligible shift in earnings expectations also implies that the market assesses a very low probability that any given bid is motivated by undervaluation of the target. A high proportion of undervaluation-motivated bids would cause a large probabilistic shift in the performance expectations for all targets, because bids would then be signals of prior undervaluation [Grossman and Hart (1981)].

For a variety of reasons, these tests could understate the true signaling effect of takeover bids. Lags in forecast revisions could be introduced by the mechanics of the IBES data base. Analysts may not react as quickly and consistently to initial takeover-bid announcements as was suggested by the discussion in section 2. This latter possibility must be given some weight in light of the high frequency of unchanged event-period forecasts shown in table 19.2, panel B. It may be that immediately following a takeover bid, analysts adopt a "wait and see" attitude.

Caution in viewing the data is also a matter of degree, however. The data certainly allow rejection of the hypothesis that bids change market participants' average view of the target firm in any radical way. This is a refinement of existing knowledge. The evidence shows that changes in future performance expectations cannot explain much of the 40% average premium associated with takeover transactions.[15]

3.2   *The information content of takeover resistance*

Table 19.2 presents the results of tests examining how targets' FY2 earnings forecasts change during resisted takeover attempts. The tests compare the forecast for each firm made in the month of the initial takeover bid with the forecast made in the month the contest is resolved. Resolution, for targets that are ultimately acquired, is deemed to

Table 19.2 Behavior of year-ahead (FY2) consensus earnings forecasts during takeover contests, for 64 resisting takeover targets split into two samples based on *ex post* information about contest outcome. Sample drawn from the period 1979–84

Panel A
Average revision in consensus (mean) FY2 per-share earnings forecasts, measured from the month of initial takeover-bid announcement to the month of takeover-contest resolution.

Sample	*Average revision*[a,b]	*t-statistic*
Resistance/target acquired[c] ($n = 31$)	−0.00876	−2.54
Resistance/target remains independent[d] ($n = 33$)	−0.00525	−2.02

Panel B
Nonparametric distributions of forecast revisions during takeover contests for two samples of resisting takeover targets conditioned on *ex post* information about contest outcome.

Sample	*% positive*	*% negative*	*% unchanged*
Resistance/target acquired[c] ($n = 31$)	12	56	32
Resistance/target remains independent[d] ($n = 33$)	18	57	25

---

[a] Revisions are calculated as $([FY2_{it}^f - FY2_{it-1}^f]/P_i)$, where $FY2_{it}^f$ is the consensus forecast for firm i in the month of the takeover-contest resolution, $FY2_{it-1}^f$ is the equivalent forecast in the month of the initial takeover-bid announcement, and P_i is the per-share market price of firm i at the beginning of the month immediately preceding the initial takeover-bid announcement.

[b] To put revisions in terms, of the previously forecast level of earnings, rather than price-normalized terms, multiply by a prebid *P/E* ratio of approximately 15. To put revisions in percentage terms multiply by 100. Thus, for example, as a percent change over previously forecast earnings, multiply $(-0.00525)*(1.5*10^3)$ = 7.88%.

[c] A hostile takeover bid ending in acquisition is defined as one in which the target's board at a minimum recommends that shareholders reject the first publicly identifiable offer, but the target is ultimately acquired as a consequence of some bid that temporally overlaps the initial bid.

[d] A hostile bid in which the target retains autonomy is defined as one in which the target defeats all outstanding takeover offers that overlap with the initial offer.

---

have occurred when the bidder has been tendered a controlling interest in the target. For targets remaining independent, the resolution month is the one in which the last outstanding bid in the overlapping-bid auction process, beginning with the first bid, is withdrawn.[16] Panel A presents data on average price-normalized forecast revisions; panel B presents data on the nonparametric distribution of positive, negative, and unchanged forecast revisions over the event period.

The results all indicate that during takeover contests, targets' FY2 earnings forecasts are systematically revised downward. The nonparametric data in panel B show that the distribution of revisions is shifted significantly for both samples. Almost 60% of all revisions are negative in each sample and only about 15% positive. This confirms that the negative average revisions are not the result of a few large negative outliers.

The average downward revision is large in economic terms, compared with the documented effects of takeover resistance on stock returns. Dann and DeAngelo (1988) report that defensive asset and ownership changes cause a 2% to 3% negative stock price effect. Jarrell (1985) reports that litigation by target management causes an insignificant target stock-price reaction. Ruback (1988) reports that defeats by targets of outstanding bids cause a 7% to 10% negative price response. Bradley (1980) shows rejection of any given tender offer to be a fair game with zero expected value consequences. The earnings-forecast reactions in table 19.2 thus show that resistance conveys more negative information about targets' stand-alone value than is revealed in stock returns.[17]

Although these results show that, on average, the market lowers its expectations about future performance in response to managerial actions that impede takeover bids, it is not possible to say why. Perhaps resistance strategies directly harm the productivity of corporate assets. Or resistance may signal managerial self-interest and thus the likelihood of worse future performance. It may also, however, signal that the firm is economically weaker than previously supposed. In this case, resistance is not necessarily against shareholder interests. Further research is necessary to determine which of these hypotheses is correct. But the evidence here, although not conclusive about the management motives, does confirm that resistance changes the market's perception of targets' fundamental stand-alone values.

The results in table 19.2 also show that the negative effects of resistance are roughly the same whether targets remain independent or are ultimately acquired. This result is relevant to the debate over whether managerial motivations differ across contests with these two outcomes. Some observers have suggested that "trenchant" resistance, designed to keep targets independent, is more perverse in its economic consequences than resistance undertaken purely to bargain with bidding firms over premiums. The data do not support this conjecture.

As with the bid-announcement data, there are several possible sources of bias in table 19.2's results. First, and perhaps most obvious, the negative forecast revisions may reflect the possibility that the takeover contests will continue into the next fiscal year. In this event, analysts might revise their FY2 forecasts downward to reflect the probability that the one-time expenses associated with the contest would affect FY2 rather than current earnings. To test this possibility, I also examined current-year (FY1) earnings forecasts from the beginning to the end of these contests. During contests, analysts lower FY1 earnings estimates across the firms in the sample by an average of approximately $12 million more than they lower FY2 estimates. This amount is roughly consistent with reported average expenditures on investment banking and legal fees. This suggests that the FY2 revision represents the permanent component of expected earnings changes, related not to one-time changes in income and expenditure but to changed expectations about long-term managerial performance.

A second potential bias in the tests, which is harder to quantify, stems from the possibility that analysts wait before incorporating in their forecasts the information effects of initial takeover bids. If they do, the forecast revisions in table 19.2 represent the combined information effects of initial takeover bids and subsequent takeover resistance. Current theories suggest only the possibility of positive information effects from initial takeover bids. Thus, if analysts do wait and this effect is significant, the expected forecast revision over contests would be positive without an economic effect from takeover resistance. It is impossible to test this possible bias with the earnings-forecast data base; but if this updating lag is present, the negative consequences of resistance are probably greater than implied by the forecast revisions in panel A.

3.3 The ex post *earnings performance of targets remaining independent*

The most fundamental concern about both the takeover-bid and takeover-resistance tests presented above is the assumption that analysts quickly and efficiently change their predictions for target firms in response to information conveyed by takeover contests. Analysts' forecasts may in fact be wrong or useless in the event of takeover activity. The revision-based tests above, which are not tied to actual observed earnings performance, leave this possibility unaddressed.

This section presents data on the accuracy of analysts' defeat-date earnings forecasts for the 33 targets ultimately remaining independent. Defeating targets are probably the biggest challenge to analysts, because these contests are generally the longest and most complex. Moreover, the evidence presented in section 3.2 above shows that, on average, forecasts for these targets are revised substantially during contests. Thus, if analysts' predictions about these targets are on average correct, it augurs well for the data on other, less complex, takeover bids in tables 19.1 and 19.2.

Table 19.3 presents the price-normalized mean-squared forecast error (MSFE) for the sample of defeating targets and FY2 MSFEs for the IBES universe, as reported by

Table 19.3 Mean-squared forecast error (MSFE) for consensus (mean) earnings forecasts; for earnings in the fiscal year following the defeat of the takeover bid, for 33 targets that defeat takeover bids and remain independent. Sample drawn from the period 1979–84. Compared with MSFE for IBES universe, as calculated by Brown, Foster, and Noreen (1985), for forecasts made for time horizons from 22 months prior to 10 months prior to earnings realizations. MSFE is calculated as

$$\text{MSFE} = \frac{1}{n}\left[\sum_{i=1}^{n} \frac{[\text{Realized earnings}_i - \text{Forecast earnings}_i]^2}{\text{Market price}_i \text{ at forecast date}} * 100 \right]$$

Sample	Mean-squared forecast error
Targets resisting and remaining independent ($n = 33$); average forecast made 16 months prior to realization	0.5157
IBES Universe, forecasts made 22 months prior to earnings announcement	1.041
" 21 "	0.928
" 20 "	0.883
" 19 "	0.828
" 18 "	0.777
" 17 "	0.742
" 16 "	0.725
" 15 "	0.658
" 14 "	0.549
" 13 "	0.520
" 12 "	0.498
" 11 "	0.431
" 10 "	0.371

Brown, Foster, and Noreen (1985). The comparison between MSFE for the defeating target sample and the universe of IBES firms suggests that takeover contests do not create additional uncertainty, as measured by the dispersion of average *ex post* forecast errors. Because of the uneven timing of bids across fiscal years and their differing durations, the FY2 forecast horizon for the target sample runs from 20 to 11 months, with an average of 16 months. Yet the MSFE for the 33 defeating targets is smaller than that for the 16-month horizon for the IBES universe. Its size is between those of the 12- and the 13-month horizons.

Table 19.4 presents tests for *ex post* bias in the defeat-date forecasts for the 33 defeating targets, in relation to realized FY2 earnings. Panel A presents the heteroskedasticity-corrected results for the cross-sectional bias test specified by eq. (3), along with the chi-square statistic for the unbiasedness hypothesis that $\alpha = 0$ and $\beta = 1$.[18] Also presented in table 19.4, panel B is a simple nonparametric summary of the proportion of the forecasts that ultimately proved too high, too low, and exactly accurate. As can be seen, the evidence does not suggest significant bias in the defeat-date forecasts. The regression shows earnings to be somewhat lower across the sample

Table 19.4   Tests for *ex post* bias in the defeat-date forecasts for defeating targets

---

Panel A

Test of rationality (bias) of defeat-date consensus earnings forecasts, for fiscal year after takeover defeat, for 33 targets that resisted bids and remained independent drawn from the period 1979–1984. The regression is specified as

$$FY2_i^a/P_{it-1} = \alpha + \beta \, [FY2_i^f/P_{it-1}] + \varepsilon_i,$$

where $FY2_i^a$ is realized earnings for firm i for the second fiscal year after the takeover defeat date, $FY2_i^f$ is forecast earnings for the second fiscal year out, measured in the IBES reporting month of the takeover defeat date, and P_{it-1} is firm i's per-share market value 30 days before the first takeover bid anouncement. Standard errors are corrected for heteroskedasticity of unknown form with White's (1980) heteroskedasticity-consistent covariance matrix.

α (t-stat.)	β (t-stat.)	R^2
−0.0054 (−0.29)	0.7917 (3.56)	0.247

Chi-square statistic for the unbiasedness hypothesis that $\alpha = 0$ and $\beta = 1$: 4.96; significance level = 0.087.

Panel B

Frequency of optimistic, pessimistic, and accurate forecasts in the sample, as measured by the value of $FY2_i^a - FY2_i^f$, where $FY2_i^a$ is realized earnings for firm i for the second fiscal year after the takeover defeat date, $FY2_i^f$ is forecast earnings for the second fiscal year out, measured in the IBES reporting month of the takeover defeat date.

Sample	% optimistic[a]	% pessimistic[b]	% accurate[c]
Defeating targets (*n* = 33)	45	45	10

---

[a] Optimistic forecasts: $FY2_i^a - FY2_i^f < 0$.
[b] Pessimistic forecasts: $FY2_i^a - FY2_i^f > 0$.
[c] Accurate forecasts: $FY2_i^a - FY2_i^f = 0$.

than was forecast when the takeover contest was resolved. However, the hypothesis of unbiasedness is not rejected at conventional levels. Moreover, the nonparametric test, which might be judged more powerful in this sample size, shows an exactly symmetric distribution of optimistic and pessimistic forecasts.

Overall, these results do not suggest that analysts are substantially wrong in their views of the defeating targets' future performance. The results thus provide some confirmation that the bid- and event-period revisions reported in sections 3.1 and 3.2 are efficient estimates of the effects of these events on target firms' future earnings performance. The results also strengthen the specific conclusion that, for these targets at least, bids are not motivated primarily by undervaluation. There are no short-term performance breakthroughs apparent for defeating targets, on average, in the one- to two-year interval after the takeover contest is resolved. This evidence works against the often-heard allegation that hostile bids are launched when the market fails to recognize that new, higher target performance is "just around the corner".

4 Earnings-forecast Data and the Limits of the Tests

The year-ahead earnings-forecast data used here are clearly an imperfect measure of the expected future performance of takeover targets. Forecast revisions may be smaller or larger than the true shifts in the market's expectations about targets' stand-alone values. This section reviews possible reasons for spurious movements in the data and assesses their potential impact on the results reported above.

Forecasts might move too little primarily because of their short time horizon. Forecasts for the fiscal year after the current one might miss important revaluations based on information about targets' longer-term performance. For example, a revaluation might occur because a takeover bid informs the market that higher profits will ultimately accrue from a five-year research and development program. Or revaluation might occur because the market believes the bid will induce the target firm to restructure; major restructuring programs may take years to execute and even longer to be fully reflected in earnings performance.

Forecasts might also move too little because of their limited relationship to corporate performance and hence appropriate market value. Major performance changes can occur, yet have little impact on short-term accounting earnings. Indeed some corporate strategies, such as a commitment to research and development expenditures, usually decrease short-term earnings, while increasing long-term value. Takeover-induced revaluations could be due to revaluations of cash flows, tax profile, expected dividend payout rates, or other aspects of performance that have no direct impact on accounting earnings.

Finally, consensus forecasts might move too little in response to takeover-bid announcements because of either analyst behavior or purely mechanical problems with the IBES survey. Some analysts may wait for a period before forecasting in response to takeover bids, although the survey undertaken for this paper did not uncover any evidence of such behavior. IBES may not be perfectly efficient in gathering its month-end forecasts, thus causing some revisions to drop out of the event period. These problems could lead to underestimation of any information effect from takeover bids and resistance.

Earnings forecasts could also move too much in response to information conveyed by takeover contests. This possibility is less likely, given the structure of the tests and my sample design. One possible cause of excessive forecast reaction would be direct one-time expenditures on takeover defenses, such as legal fees, that deplete earnings. This possibility is mitigated by examining earnings forecasts for the fiscal year after the takeover bid; one-time expenditures tend to accrue in the year of takeover contests. A second possible cause of forecast oversensitivity would be restructuring activity causing temporary revenue increases, such as asset sales. This possibility is mitigated by two factors. First, the sample of firms used in the tests is primarily pre-1985, when defensive restructuring was relatively rare. Most defenses in the sample consist of legal and tactical blocking strategies. Second, the earnings forecasts and realizations used are calculated before extraordinary items and thus exclude the effects of such one-time restructuring-based changes as asset write-downs. Thus, oversensitivity of forecasts to takeovers is likely to be a less compelling concern than undersensitivity.

The stronger possibility is thus that forecasts will move too little to reflect true changes in targets' stand-alone value. If this is the case, takeover bids may contain significant information about stand-alone value, despite the failure of this paper's tests to reject the null hypothesis of no systematic forecast revisions at takeover-bid announcements. Concurrently, the negative consequences of takeover resistance may actually be substantially larger than implied by the evidence in table 19.2. The seriousness of the problem depends on the correlation between true (unobservable) information effects of takeover bids and their effects on earnings forecasts.

To analyze the potential impact of this problem, it is useful to weigh the evidence on earnings-forecast revisions contained in table 19.1 against the average effect of takeover bids on stock returns. Table 19.1's data show that earnings forecasts move by less than 5% in response to takeover-bid announcements. In contrast, takeover bids cause market-adjusted values to increase by about 35% to 40% on average. This suggests that even if the correlation between earnings-forecast changes and true information effects is imperfect, true information effects are probably still small in relation to takeover premiums. Moreover, given that the average weighted earnings forecast for all takeover targets, as reported in table 19.1, is negative, the correlation between forecast revisions and true information effects would have to be negative for takeover bids actually to contain significant positive information about target firms. Thus, while the potential problem of forecast insensitivity must be kept in mind, it is unlikely that the problem reverses or invalidates the result shown in tables 19.1 and 19.2.

5   Conclusions

This paper has used consensus earnings forecasts as a proxy for the expected value of takeover targets as stand-alone entities to test the information effects of takeover bids and resistance. The use of earnings forecasts allows a direct test for systematic information effects across all types of takeover contests, yielding data on the evolution of the market's estimate of targets' future performance if they are not taken over. Tests were conducted for three samples of target firms: targets of friendly bids, targets of hostile bids that were ultimately acquired, and targets of hostile bids that defeated auction contests to remain independent.

On average, across all three groups, initial takeover bids do not seem to convey significant information. Target firms' earnings forecasts for future years are not revised in a statistically or economically significant way in response to bid announcements. This implies that bids themselves are not expected to increase targets' economic performance. It also suggests that the market perceives an insignificant proportion of bids to be predicted on prior undervaluation of target firms.

When takeover bids are resisted, average earnings forecasts are revised downward. These revisions are economically and statistically significant. This implies that the market interprets typical resistance strategies as negative signals about future performance. Moreover, the data show that takeover resistance conveys negative information whether the target firm is ultimately acquired or remains independent.

For those firms defeating all bids to remain independent, an additional test shows the defeat-date earnings forecasts to be close to actual earnings. The forecasts are also as accurate as forecasts made for similar horizons across the universe of companies that analysts follow. These findings suggest that analysts react efficiently in incorporating information from takeover bids in their forecasts. Hence the average forecast revisions associated with takeover bids and resistance are likely to be unbiased measures of actual revisions in the market's earnings expectations conditional on these events.

Notes

I am indebted to P. Asquith, P. Dybvig, R. Ibbotson, P. O'Brien, R. Romano, S. Ross, and particularly to G. Jarrell, R. Shiller, and M. Jensen (the editor) for comments on earlier drafts. I am also indebted to seminar participants at Harvard Business School, the Kennedy School of Government at Harvard University, the Simon School of Business at the University of Rochester, the Sloan School at MIT, UCLA Business School, UCLA Economics Department, the University of Chicago Business School, the University of Southern California Business School, and Yale University.

1   This does not imply that forecasts incorporate the potential effects of future takeover resistance. The forecasts are designed to help investors make a tendering decision. Should investors not tender, and thus the current offer fail, no resistance is necessary. Thus current forecasts, at any point in the takeover-bid process, should incorporate only the effects of resistance observed to that time.

2   An additional test was performed to control for the possibility that the results are in fact entirely due to systematic, market-wide forecast revisions. Each firm's forecast revision in the event period was subtracted from the average "market" forecast revision for that month, for the universe of firms followed by IBES. The no-signaling hypothesis is then that this "net-of-market" forecast is equal to zero. This is an *ad hoc* test as there is no well-specified model suggesting the relationship between firm-specific forecast revisions and

systematic, market-wide factors. None of the results of these "market-adjusted" tests differ from those for the unadjusted tests. The market-adjusted results are therefore excluded from the tables in interests of clarity and economy.

3   Defeat-date market values were not used because they are likely to contain some residual expected takeover premium, and thus may not accurately reflect the expected stand-alone value of the firm.

4   To check for cross-sectional dependence over the forecast horizon used in these tests, the regressions were also run with forecasts that netted out market-wide earnings movements. No significant difference in the results emerged.

5   Tests were also conducted with the median to test whether results are sensitive to the specification of the consensus forecast. No significant differences were found. In the interest of economy, the tests using the median measure are not reported here.

6   Because the latter point is open to debate, the tests were replicated normalizing by the previously forecast level of earnings. No material differences were found from the price-normalized results, so these additional figures are not reported here. The relationship between the price-normalized results and earnings-normalized results is discussed in detail in the next section.

7   For a survey of the literature on analysts' updating behavior, see Brown, Foster, and Noreen (1985).

8   This criterion is based on the judgment of those tabulating the data rather than on any absolute statistical rule.

9   When initial takeover-bid announcements fall either very early or very late (within the six-day month-end window) in the IBES reporting period, it is possible that information about subsequent managerial reaction to the bid may also fall within the announcement-period revision. To test whether this problem was affecting results, the tests were replicated with very early and very late announcements deleted. The announcement-month information effects were not statistically or substantively changed.

10   The criterion for defeating targets has strengths and weaknesses. The strengths derive from its *ex ante* specification. Presumably, management may not want to preserve autonomy forever; often resistance appears to be aimed at a particular auction process. An *ex post* criterion mandating some arbitrary period of preserved independence (such as five years) may bias the sample in a different way. The weakness is that by the sampling criteria employed here a defeating target may be acquired literally weeks after the end of an existing auction contest. In practice, however, this did not occur. All defeating targets preserved autonomy for at least one year after defeating the auction process.

11   The one-year criterion exempts some long contests, characterized by particularly trenchant resistance, from the sample. Five contests from the sampling universe were excluded because they ran longer than one fiscal year. This may create a bias in the tests for the effects of resistance, but it is not possible a priori to define the direction of the bias.

12   For example, Bradley, Desai, and Kim (1988) report a significant change in the gains to both bidding and target firms since 1980.

13   Weights were calculated directly from the master list of all takeover targets. They are: friendly targets 0.55, resisting/acquired 0.30, resisting/independent 0.15.

14   I also tested the significance of the results using a measure of the historical variance of the 94 target firms' one-month forecast revisions. A higher event-period variance might indicate that more information about targets was released in the event period, but that its effects were not systematic in sign across the targets. Historical forecast revision variance

was estimated by drawing one forecast revision for each target firm at random from those forecast revisions occurring not earlier than two years nor later than six months prior to the announcement of the initial takeover bid. The price-normalized average forecast revision in this sample was 0.0015, or approximately 1.5% of the level of previously forecast earnings. The standard error of the mean revision was 0.0012, or 1.7% of the level of prior earnings. These data imply that takeover bids cause very little change in the pattern of forecast revisions during the takeover bid event period, relative to the historical behavior of revisions. *t*-statistics in table 19.1 would be only marginally changed by using the historical as opposed to the sample-period forecast variance, and the significance of the results would be unchanged.

15 Some cross-sectional analysis was undertaken using the bid-period forecast revisions and bid-period, firm-specific excess returns. Regressions were run of firm-specific excess returns on firm-specific forecast revisions to see whether some component of the observed takeover premium could be explained by the relative size of the forecast revision. The results were not significant. This is probably due to the well-known problems inherent in measuring firm-specific excess returns around takeover bid announcements. They are thus not reported here.

16 Revisions during friendly acquisition processes were not examined because for most firms, the interval between announcement and consummation was too short, creating a biased (and very small) subsample available for analysis. Further, it seems very likely that analysts perceive little postbid incentive to update forecasts when an undisturbed merger agreement is being executed.

17 An additional test was conducted to examine the relationship between firm-specific excess returns over takeover contests and firm-specific forecast revisions. The firm-specific excess return from bid to resolution date was regressed on the firm-specific forecast revision for the same period. This regression showed no relationship. This is further support for the hypothesis that firms' stock returns are dominated during takeover contests by the changing probability of takeover bids and do not reflect changes in the market's view of firms' stand-alone values.

18 Heteroskedasticity correction was necessary because of the uneven forecast horizons across different firms, obtaining because takeover defeats came at varying stages in firms' fiscal year. The White (1980) correction was used.

References

Bhagat, S., J. Brickley, and U. Lowenstein, 1987, The pricing effects of interfirm cash tender offers, *Journal of Finance*.

Bradley, M., 1980, Interfirm tender offers and the market for corporate control, *Journal of Business*, 345–76.

Bradley, M., A. Desai, and E. Kim, 1983, The rationale behind interfirm tender offers: information or synergy? *Journal of Financial Economics* 11, 183–206.

Bradley, M., A. Desai, and E. Kim, 1988, Synergistic gains from corporate acquisitions and their division between the shareholders of bidding and target firms, Working paper (University of Michigan, Ann Arbor, MI).

Brown, P., G. Foster, and E. Noreen, 1985, Security analyst multi-year earnings forecasts and the capital market, Studies in accounting research 21 (American Accounting Association, Sarasota, FL).

Dann, L. and H. DeAngelo, 1988, Corporate financial policy and corporate control: a study of defensive changes in asset and ownership structure, *Journal of Financial Economics* 20, 87–127.

DeAngelo, H. and E. Rice, 1983, Antitakeover amendments and stockholder wealth, *Journal of Financial Economics* 11, 329–59.

Dodd, P. and R. Ruback, 1980, Tender offers and stockholder returns, *Journal of Financial Economics* 5, 105–38.

Easterbrook, F. and D. Fischel, 1981, The proper role of a target's management in responding to a tender offer, *Harvard Law Review* 94, 1161–96.

Grossman, S. and O. Hart, 1981, The allocational role of takeover bids in situations of asymmetric information, *Journal of Finance* 36, 253–70.

Grossman, S. and O. Hart, 1980, Takeover bids, the free-rider problem, and the theory of the corporation, *Bell Journal of Economics* 11, 151–77.

Jarrell, G., 1985, The wealth effects of litigation by targets: do interests diverge in a merge?, *Journal of Law and Economics* 28, 151–77.

Jensen, M., 1986, The takeover controversy: Analysis and evidence, Working paper (University of Rochester, Rochester, NY).

Ruback, R., 1988, Do target shareholders lose in unsuccessful control contests? In: Alan Auerbach, ed., *Corporate Takeovers: Causes and Consequences* (University of Chicago Press, Chicago, IL).

Ryngaert, M., 1987, The effect of poison-pill securities on shareholder wealth, *Journal of Financial Economics* 20, 377–417.

Shleifer, A. and R. Vishny, 1986, Greenmail, white knights, and shareholders' interests, *Rand Journal of Economics* 17, 293–309.

The Value Line investment survey (Value Line Inc., New York, NY).

White, H., 1980, A heteroskedasticity-consistent covariance matrix estimator and a direct test for heteroskedasticity, *Econometrica* 48, 817–38.

Index

Note: underlined page references indicate tabular information only; *italic* page references diagrammatic information only; those prefaced with the letters fn are footnotes.